One of Us

One of Us

The Story of Anders Breivik
and the Massacre in Norway

Åsne Seierstad

Translated by
Sarah Death

virago

VIRAGO

First published in 2013 by Kagge
First published in Great Britain in 2015 by Virago Press

1 3 5 7 9 10 8 6 4 2

Copyright © Åsne Seierstad, 2015
Translation © Sarah Death, 2015

A CIP catalogue record for this book
is available from the British Library.

Hardback ISBN 978-1-84408-919-2
C-Format ISBN 978-1-84408-920-8

Typeset in Perpetua by M Rules
Printed and bound in Great Britain by
Clays Ltd, St Ives plc

Papers used by Virago are from well-managed forests
and other responsible sources.

MIX
Paper from
responsible sources
FSC® C104740

Virago Press
An imprint of
Little, Brown Book Group
100 Victoria Embankment
London EC4Y 0DY

An Hachette UK Company
www.hachette.co.uk

www.virago.co.uk

Contents

Part Two

Part Three

Author's Note

Everything in this book is based on testimony. All the scenes are constructed according to witnesses' accounts.

Anders Behring Breivik's childhood and adolescence is told through a number of sources, including his mother and father, friends, family and his own accounts to the police and in court. I have also had access to all reports about his childhood from the Oslo social services.

When it comes to the planning of his act of terror, I have, in addition to other sources, used his diary and log from the manifesto. When I refer to what he thinks in certain situations, and how he feels about them, it is always based on what he has himself said. Often I have quoted him directly and used his exact words; at other times more indirectly, just referring to what he has recounted.

The other sources from Utøya are the surviving victims. They have shared their stories and observations with me, their thoughts and feelings. Together with the perpetrator's accounts, this made it possible to reconstruct the terror attack minute by minute.

There is a longer review of my working methods at the end of the book.

Åsne Seierstad
Oslo, 12 November 2014

She ran.

Up the hill, through the moss. Her wellingtons sank into the wet earth. The forest floor squelched beneath her feet.

She had seen it.

She had seen him fire and a boy fall.

'We won't die today, girls,' she had said to her companions. 'We won't die today.'

More shots rang out. Rapid reports, a pause. Then another series.

She had reached Lovers' Path. All around her there were people running, trying to find places to hide.

Behind her, a rusty wire fence ran alongside the path. On the other side of the netting, steep cliffs dropped down into the Tyrifjord. The roots of a few lilies of the valley clung to the mountainside, looking as though they had grown out of solid rock. They had finished flowering, and the bases of their leaves were filled with rainwater that had trickled over the rocky edge.

From the air, the island was green. The tops of the tall pines spread into each other. The slender branches of thin, broadleaved trees stretched into the sky.

Down here, seen from the ground, the forest was sparse.

But in a few places, the grass was tall enough to cover you. Flat rocks hung over one part of the sloping path, like shields you could creep under.

There were more shots, louder.

Who was shooting?

She crept along Lovers' Path. Back and forth. Lots of kids were there.

'Let's lie down and pretend we're dead,' one boy said. 'Lie down in strange positions, so they think we're dead!'

She lay down, one cheek facing the ground. A boy lay down beside her and put his arm round her waist.

There were eleven of them.

They all did what the one boy said.

If he had said 'Run!' perhaps they would have run. But he said 'Lie down!' They lay close together, their heads turned towards the forest and the dark trunks of the trees, legs against the fence. Some of them huddled up against each other, a couple were lying in a heap. Two girls, best friends, were holding hands.

'It'll be fine,' one of the eleven said.

The heavy rain had eased off, but some last drops were still trickling down their necks and sweaty cheeks.

They took in as little air as possible, trying to breathe without a sound.

A raspberry bush had strayed out onto the cliff. Wild roses, pale pink, almost white, were clinging to the fence.

Then they heard footsteps approaching.

He advanced steadily through the heather. His boots stamped deeply into the ground as he walked over harebells, clover and trefoil. Some decaying branches snapped underfoot. His skin was pale and damp, and his thin hair was swept back. His eyes were light blue. Caffeine, ephedrine and aspirin ran in his bloodstream.

By this point he had killed twenty-two people on the island.

After the first shot, it had all been easy. The first shot had cost him. It had been almost impossible. But now, pistol in hand, he was relaxed.

He stopped on the little rise that provided cover for the eleven. From there, he looked calmly down at them and asked: 'Where the hell is he?'

His voice came loud and clear.

Nobody answered, nobody moved.

The boy's arm lay heavily on her. She was wearing a red water-proof jacket and wellingtons, he was in checked shorts and a T-shirt. She was tanned, he was pale.

The man on the rise started from the right.

The first shot entered the head of the boy lying at the end.

Then he aimed at the back of her head. Her wavy, chestnut brown hair was wet and shiny in the rain. The shot went right through her head and into her brain. He fired again.

The boy with his arm around her was hit. The bullet went through the back of his head.

A mobile phone rang in a pocket. Another bleeped as a text came in.

A girl whispered: 'No . . . ' in a low, scarcely audible voice as she was shot in the head. Her drawn-out 'No-o-o' faded into silence.

The shots came every few seconds.

His weapons had laser sights. The pistol sent out a green trace, the rifle a red one. The bullets hit where the trace pointed.

A girl near the end of the row caught sight of his muddy black boots. At the back of his heels, down at path level, metal spurs protruded. On his trousers a chequered reflective strip lit up.

She was holding hands with her best friend. Their faces were turned to each other.

A bullet seared through the crown, the skull and the frontal lobe of her childhood friend's head. The girl's body jerked, the twitchings ran into her hand. Her grip slackened.

Seventeen years is not a long life, thought the one still alive.

Another shot rang out.

It whined past her ear and sliced her scalp. Blood ran over her face and covered the hands her head was resting on. One more shot.

The boy beside her whispered: 'I'm dying.'

'Help, I'm dying, help me,' he begged.

His breathing grew quieter and quieter, until there was no more sound.

From somewhere in the middle of the group came a weak moaning.

There were faint groans and a few gurgling sounds. Then only a little squeak or two. Before long there was silence.

There had been eleven pounding hearts on the path. Now only one was still beating.

A bit further along a log was wedged at an angle, covering a hole in the fence. Several people had crawled through the little opening and down a steep slope.

'Girls first!'

A boy was trying to help people down. When the shots rang out from the path, he took off to make the leap himself. He jumped down from Lovers' Path over wet sand, pebbles and shale.

A girl with long curly hair was sitting furthest out on a rocky ledge. She saw him as he jumped and called his name.

He paused as his foot made contact with the ground, stopped and looked round.

'Sit here with me!' she called.

There were young people all along the ledge. They squeezed together to make room. He sat down beside her.

They had met the night before. He came from up north, she was from the west.

He had lifted her up onto the stage during the concert. They'd taken a walk along Lovers' Path and a rest on the promontory. It had been a dark and cold night for July. She had borrowed his jersey. On the final climb back up to the tents he had asked her to give him a piggyback, he was so worn out. She had laughed. But she had carried him. Just so he would be near her.

The killer kicked the eleven bodies on the path to check they were dead. Shooting them had taken two minutes.

He was finished here and so he went on along Lovers' Path.

Inside his uniform he wore a medallion on a silver chain, a red cross on white enamel. The cross was encircled by silver decorations, a knight's helmet and a skull. Now, it knocked against the hollow of his neck as he strode steadily on, looking about him. The sparse trees were on one side, the steep drop beyond the fence on the other.

He paused by the log. He looked over it, down the steep drop.

A foot was protruding from a rock ledge. He saw something coloured in a bush.

The boy and girl on the ledge clutched each other's hands. When they heard the heavy footsteps come to a halt, the girl closed her eyes.

The man in the uniform raised his rifle and took aim at the foot.

He pressed the trigger.

The boy gave a cry and his hand slipped out of hers. Sand and grit sprayed into the girl's face.

She opened her eyes.

He tumbled down. Did he fall, did he jump, she did not know. His body was thrown further as he was hit again; in the back. He floated in the air.

He landed at the water's edge, slumped over a rock. The bullet had passed through his jacket, through the jersey he had lent her the day before, through his lung and through his chest cavity before ripping open the artery in his neck.

The man on the path was jubilant.

'You will all die today, Marxists!'

He raised his weapon again.

Part One

A New Life (1979)

We want to be loved; failing that, admired; failing that, feared; failing that, hated and despised. At all costs we want to stir up some sort of feeling in others. Our soul abhors a vacuum. At all costs it longs for contact.

Hjalmar Söderberg, *Doktor Glas*, 1905

It was one of those clear, cold winter days when Oslo glistens. The sun, which people had almost forgotten, made the snow sparkle. Keen skiers cast long looks out of their office windows, up to the white hilltop, the ski jump and the blue sky.

Homebodies cursed the temperature of minus twelve, and if obliged to venture out they went with a shiver, in thick fur coats and lined boots. Children were bundled up in several layers of wool under their quilted snowsuits. There were shrieks and squeals from the toboggan slopes in the playgrounds of the kindergartens that had opened everywhere as more and more women started working full time.

Piled along the fences round the hospital grounds there were towering heaps of snow, ploughed from roads and pavements. The cold made the snow creak beneath the feet of those passing the old hospital building in the north of the city.

It was Tuesday the thirteenth, in the second month of the year.

Cars drove up to the main entrance, stopped and waited while

doors opened and prospective mothers eased themselves out, leaning on men who were to become fathers. All were engrossed in their
own big drama, a new life on its way.

Since the early seventies, fathers had been allowed to attend births
at public hospitals. Once banished to the corridor, they could
now be there for the birth, see the head pushing its way out, smell
the blood, hear the baby give its first cry. Some were handed a pair
of scissors by the midwife so they could cut the umbilical cord.

'Sexual equality' and 'new family policy' were key slogans through
the decade. Children and home were no longer purely a women's
sphere. Fathers were to be involved in caring for their children from
birth. They were to push prams, prepare baby food and join fully in
raising the child.

A woman was lying in a room in great pain. The contractions were
violent, but the baby was holding back. It was already nine days past
its due date.

'Hold my hand!'

She moaned the words to the man at the head of the bed. He took
her hand and held it hard. It was his first time at a birth. He had three
children from a previous marriage, but back then he would wait in
the corridor until it was time to see the babies nicely parcelled up,
two in pale blue blankets and one in pink.

The woman panted. The man held on.

They had met just a year earlier, in the basement laundry room of
a block of flats in the Frogner area of town. She was renting a shoe-
box on the ground floor, while he owned a larger flat on the floor
above. He – a newly divorced diplomat in the Norwegian Foreign
Office, with a home posting after spells in London and Teheran. She –
an auxiliary nurse and the single mother of a four-year-old daughter.
He was forty-three, a gaunt man with thinning hair, she eleven years
younger, slim, pretty and blonde.

Soon after they met in the laundry she found herself pregnant.
They got married at the Norwegian Embassy in Bonn, where he
was attending a conference. He stayed for a week, she for barely

two days, while a friend looked after her daughter in Oslo.

She was initially pleased to be pregnant, but within a month or two she was racked with doubts and no longer wanted the baby. Life seemed uncertain, sinister. Whenever the three children from his previous marriage came to visit he appeared cold and remote. It felt like madness, having another baby with someone who seemed to take so little pleasure in children.

The month she became pregnant, legislation permitting abortion on demand was introduced in the Norwegian parliament and passed by a single vote. It only came into force the following year. The law gave women an unlimited right to abortion up to the twelfth week of pregnancy, with no requirement to appear before a medical board. After twelve weeks, abortion was only available on specific grounds. She had taken so long to make up her mind that it was in any case too late to scrape the foetus out. It took root in her womb.

She soon started to suffer from sickness and felt distaste for the tiny life that was acquiring new senses and abilities week by week as it absorbed nutrition and continued to grow. Its heart beat steadily and strongly, its head, brain and nerves were all developing at a normal rate. There was no detectable abnormality, no club foot, no indicators of extra chromosomes, no hydrocephalus. On the contrary, it was a lively baby, in good health according to the doctors. Annoying, its mother felt. 'It's as if he kicks me almost on purpose, to torment me,' she told a friend.

The baby was blueish when he came out.

Abnormal, thought his mother.

A fine boy, said his father.

It was ten to two, in the middle of the day. The boy immediately exercised his lungs. A normal birth, according to the hospital.

There was an announcement in *Aftenposten*:

Aker Hospital. A boy.
13th February. Wenche and Jens Breivik.

Later, they would each tell their own story of the birth. She would say it was dreadful, and that it had been disgusting to have her husband there. He would say that it all went well.

The child had probably been harmed by all the pain-relief drugs she had received, his mother said. The boy was fit and healthy, said his father.

Later still, they had differing versions of most things.

The Norwegian Foreign Office had introduced flexible working arrangements for young parents, and allowed newly fledged fathers to stay at home with the mother and baby for the initial period after the birth.

But when Wenche came home from the hospital to the flat in the patrician apartment block in Frogner, there was something missing.

A father who had not made sure there was a changing table in place when the newborn came home was one who did not welcome the baby, so Wenche had heard, and she brooded over this as she changed the baby on the bathroom floor. Times might have moved on, but Jens belonged to the old school, and she was the one who fed the baby, sang to him and lulled him to sleep. She suffered her way through breastfeeding, growing sore and tender. A darkness had descended on her, a depression that carried all her earlier life within it.

Finally she shouted at her husband, telling him to go and buy a changing table. Jens did so. But a wedge had been driven between them.

The boy was given the name Anders.

When the baby was six months old, Jens Breivik was appointed a counsellor at the Norwegian Embassy in London. He went over first and Wenche followed with the children, towards Christmas.

She was very much alone in their flat in Prince's Gate. It was enormous and most of the rooms were not in use. When her daughter started at an English school, Wenche stayed at home with Anders and the au pair. The great metropolis made her feel stressed and uneasy.

There in Prince's Gate she shut herself increasingly into her own world, as she had learnt to do when she was little.

Not so long ago, they had been in love. Back home in Oslo she had a box of notes and love letters he had written.

Now she walked round the grand flat, filled with regrets. She reproached herself for marrying Jens and letting the baby bind her to him still further. Early on, she had noticed traits in her husband that she did not like. He was sulky, wanted everything his own way and was incapable of taking other people's feelings into account; things like that played on her mind. I mustn't tie myself to him, she had told herself at an early stage. Yet she had done exactly that.

When they got married, she had been several months pregnant. She had entered into the marriage with her eyes closed, hoping that when she opened them again everything would be all right. After all, her husband had a good side; he could be kind and generous, and was a very tidy person. He seemed good at his job; he was out at a lot of receptions and official functions. She had hoped their life together would improve when they became a proper family.

In London she grew increasingly unhappy. It seemed to her that he only wanted an immaculately groomed wife and a dust-free home. Those were the things that interested him. Not her. Nor their son.

She felt he was forcing himself on her. He felt she was distant and not there for him. He said she was using him, and had been thinking only of her own interests when she married him.

By the spring, Wenche had fallen into a deep depression. She would not acknowledge it, however, thinking it was her surroundings that were making her unhappy. She could not bear her husband, nor her existence. Her head was a mess, her life meaningless.

One day she started packing.

When she had been packing for three days, she told her husband she wanted to take the children home. Jens was dismayed and asked her to stay. But it seemed simpler to go.

So she went. Left Jens, left Hyde Park, the Thames, the grey weather, the au pair, the domestic help, the life of privilege. She had lasted six months as an embassy wife.

Back in Oslo, she filed for divorce. Now she was alone again, this time with two children.

Wenche had nobody else. She had no relationship with her own family, which consisted of her mother and two older brothers. She had no contact with the father of her daughter. He was Swedish and had only seen his daughter once, when she was a few months old; he had left as quickly as he arrived.

'How could you give up your posh life and beautiful home in London?' one of her few girlfriends asked.

Well, it wasn't London that was the problem, she now said. It had all been pretty perfect, in fact, just with the wrong man. Stubborn, temperamental and demanding were words she used to refer to her ex-husband. Cold, unaffectionate – that was how he described her.

The marriage was past salvaging. Through a lawyer they came to an agreement. She would have Anders and he would pay child support. Under the agreement, she could live in his flat in Fritzners gate for two years.

Three years would pass before Anders saw his father again.

Wenche's life had been all about loss.

It had been all about being alone.

The coastal town of Kragerø, 1945. As peace came, the builder's wife got pregnant. As the birth approached, she started getting flu-like symptoms and was confined to bed by paralysis in her arms and legs. Anne Marie Behring was diagnosed with polio, a much-feared illness with no known cure. Wenche was cut out of her belly in 1946. By then, the mother was almost completely immobile from the waist down and one of her arms partially paralysed. Wenche was sent to an orphanage as soon as she was born and spent the first five years of her life there. Then one day the fair-haired girl was brought home. The orphanage was closing down.

She was left to her own devices. Her father, Ole Kristian Behring, was often out at work and her mother locked herself away and scarcely went out among people. No one was to laugh at her deformity.

When Wenche was eight her father died. Home grew darker still, and her mother ever more demanding. It had been 'wicked' of Wenche to give her mother 'this illness'.

The little girl had two elder brothers. One left home when their father died, the other was aggressive and quick-tempered. He took out his feelings on his sister. He cuffed her so often that the skin behind her ears was raw and he thrashed her legs with stinging nettles. Skinny little Wenche would often squeeze behind the stove when her brother was after her. His hands could not reach her there.

Conceal and keep silent. Everything at home was tainted with shame.

When her brother was in a bad mood she would stay out all evening, only going home when it got dark. She wandered round Kragerø alone, she wet herself, she smelled, she knew she would be in for a hiding when she got home.

When she was twelve, she considered jumping off the cliffs. The cliffs, so steep and tempting.

But she did not jump. She always went home.

The house was dilapidated and had no running water. She was the one who kept things in order, washed and tidied, emptied and cleaned the chamber pot kept under the bed that she shared with her mother. Even so, 'You're fit for nothing!' shouted her mother. 'This is all your fault!'

She would rather have functioning legs than a daughter.

Wenche did not measure up, did not fit in, wasn't good enough. She was never allowed to invite anyone home and did not make friends with any of the other girls, who were quick to taunt and exclude her. The family lived such an isolated life that its members were seen as gloomy, even creepy. People kept their distance, though many of the neighbours felt sorry for the little girl who worked so hard.

Wenche would lie in bed at night twisting her head from side to side to shut out the sounds of the house. The worst of these were the thuds as her mother moved about. She used two stools to drag herself across the floor. She raised them one by one, leaning her body on them in turn as she went, bringing each of them down on the floorboards with a thump.

Wenche lay there hoping her mother would one day come to love her.

But her mother merely became ever more demanding and dependent. Her brother ever more brutal. When Wenche was well into her teens, she happened to hear from a neighbour that he was actually a half-brother – born outside wedlock, his father unknown – a great disgrace in Kragerø at the time. This secret had been kept from her, as had the fact that her other brother was her father's son from an earlier marriage.

Her mother began to complain of hearing voices in her head. And when a man moved in, Wenche's mother accused her daughter of trying to steal him. But she still expected Wenche to stay at home and look after her for the rest of her life.

When Wenche was seventeen she packed a case and left for Oslo. It was 1963. She had no qualifications and did not know anybody, but she eventually got a position as a cleaner at a hospital, and later at Tuborg brewery in Copenhagen and then as an au pair in Strasbourg. After five years on the run, from her mother and brother, and from Kragerø, she trained as an auxiliary nurse in Porsgrunn, an hour's travel from her hometown, and got a job at the hospital in neighbouring Skien. Once there, she discovered to her surprise that people liked her. She found herself respected and valued at work.

She was quick, clever and considerate, her colleagues thought, even quite funny.

When she was twenty-six she got pregnant. The baby's Swedish father asked her to have an abortion. She insisted on keeping the child and gave birth to a daughter, Elisabeth, in 1973.

Many years were to pass before Wenche made a short visit to her home town. By then, her mother was seriously ill. According to her case notes, she increasingly suffered paranoid delusions attended by persecution mania and hallucinations. Wenche's mother did not leave her sickbed again and died alone in a nursing home in Kragerø. Her daughter did not attend the funeral.

*

The art of concealing anything painful or ugly had become second nature to Wenche, and would stay with her for the rest of her life. Dulling the ache beneath a polished surface.

Every time she moved, Wenche chose to live in one of the nicer districts of Oslo, even if she could not afford it, even if as an auxiliary nurse she did not 'fit in'. Her attractive appearance was her own glossy façade. She was always smartly dressed and freshly coiffed when she was out and about, favouring high-heeled shoes and fitted dresses and suits from the capital's more exclusive clothes shops.

When she got home from London her life started to unravel. She was now in her mid-thirties and living in Jens's flat in Fritzners gate, but did not know many people. She had no one to help her and was initially tired, then exhausted, and before long completely shattered. She felt powerless and isolated.

There must be something wrong with Anders, she decided. From being a calm baby and a fairly placid one-year-old, he turned into a clingy, whining child. Moody and violent. She felt like peeling him off her, she complained.

At night, she often left the children alone. A neighbour with a daughter the same age as Elisabeth remarked to her that this was not the done thing. 'They're asleep when I leave and asleep when I get back,' Wenche replied. She added that she had to take whatever night shifts she could get.

'At Elisabeth's they never have dinner,' the neighbour's daughter said to her mother. Economies were made on everything that could be hidden behind the front door.

As soon as they had returned from London in August 1980, Wenche applied for, and was granted, financial assistance from the social services office in Oslo's Vika district. The following year, in May 1981, she rang the office and asked if it would be possible to have a support worker or some respite care for the children. In July she applied for weekend respite care for both children. She told social services that she thought a male support worker would be a good idea for her daughter, perhaps a youngish student, according to the office log. But it was from Anders that she felt the most pressing need for relief, she told the office on that occasion. She could no longer cope with him, she said.

At that point, Anders had passed his second birthday and Elisabeth was eight. Elisabeth was following in Wenche's footsteps, turning into a 'spare mother' for Anders and for her mother.

In October 1981, weekend respite care was approved for Anders twice a month. Anders was allocated to a newly married couple in their twenties. When Wenche brought the boy to them for the first time, they found her rather odd. The second time, they thought she was nuts. She asked if Anders could occasionally touch his weekend dad's penis. It was important for the boy's sexuality. He had no father figure in his life and Wenche wanted the young man to assume that role. Anders had no one to identify with in terms of his appearance, Wenche stressed, because 'he only saw girls' crotches' and did not know how the male body worked.

The young couple were speechless. But they were too embarrassed to report what she had said. They took Anders out on trips to the forest and countryside, and to parks and playgrounds around the city. He liked being with them and they thought he was a nice little boy.

One weekend, Wenche did not turn up with Anders. She had decided it was not a suitable weekend home for her son. 'Mother difficult to please, keeps demanding more,' the social services office recorded in May 1982. She applied for a different weekend home for her son. 'The daughter, aged nine, has started wetting herself,' wrote the social services.

The month before, Wenche had gone to the foster-home section at the child welfare office. She was looking into the possibility of having both children fostered. She wanted them to 'go to the devil', she told the child welfare office.

Autumn arrived and life got even darker. In October, Wenche called in to the Frogner Medical Centre. 'Mother seemed severely depressed,' they noted. 'Thinking of just walking out on the children and leaving them to society, to live her own life.'

Wenche and the children had now been living in Fritzners gate for just over two years. The period she and Jens had agreed to was over and Jens wanted his apartment back. But Wenche put off the move. She did not feel up to it.

A nervous wreck, was how she described herself. As Christmas approached, she hit rock bottom. It was simply beyond her to create any kind of festive mood.

She was going to pieces.

She had to keep a permanent eye on Anders to avoid what she called minor disasters. He would hit her and Elisabeth. If she told him off, he would merely smirk. If she shook him, he would just shout 'It doesn't hurt, it doesn't hurt.'

He never gave her any peace. At night he would lie in her bed, clinging to her, pressed up against her. She said it felt as if he was forcing himself on her.

Swirls of Light

But the greatest of these is love.

First letter of Paul to the Corinthians

Darkness had descended on the north of the country, above the Arctic Circle.

It was pitch black when you woke up, dark when you went out, barely light at midday and black again when you went to bed. The cold bit into your cheeks. People had cut loads of logs, and were quick to shut the door to keep snowstorms and winter out.

In the mountains the bear had retired to her lair. Even the cod in the sea were more sluggish. It was a matter of conserving energy for the spring and the light. Humans and nature had begun their annual hibernation. Everyone slept more and moved less. The lucky ones warmed each other.

People were less happy than in the summer. The pain of winter had arrived.

But then there were the moments when the dark sky burst into flames.

'She wants to dance,' people said, staring out of their windows.

For Aurora Borealis – the northern lights – are never still. They swirl across the sky in ribbons and flashes, in arcs and loops, they curl up and meander, recede, fade almost to nothing, and then flare into life again, trembling.

You never can tell with the Aurora Borealis, the flaring lights that have taken their name from the Roman goddess of dawn – Aurora – and the Greek word for the north wind – Borealis. When the sun goes into hiding in winter, it sometimes flings particles toward the earth that collide with gases, creating flickers that can be observed near the pole. The flickers can shine quietly and scarcely move, and then suddenly there is a lightning flash, and once again they explode into chains and spirals.

You never can tell with people, either. They can lie there under their duvets, weighed down by melancholy, and suddenly flare into glimmering life.

They dress up and go out. And sparkle like any other natural phenomenon.

It was one of those nights, the evening of St Lucia's day, in Lavangen in 1980.

The young people were wiggling and twisting on the dance floor. They wore tight trousers, some with flares. The girls were in tight tops with puffed sleeves. The boys wore shirts. The dance band on stage was playing cover versions of Smokie, Elton John and Boney M. They were from the villages scattered round the arms of the fjord that extended into the interior of the northern county of Troms. It was the annual pre-Christmas party, it was hope and expectation, it was getting drunk and messing about.

Tone came in. She was a rosy-cheeked beauty of fifteen. Right after her came Gunnar. He was a tearaway of eighteen.

Out of my league, they both thought when they saw each other in the dim lighting that night.

Tone had flicked her fringe out and over with curling tongs, just like the blonde one in *Charlie's Angels*. Gunnar had a mullet hairstyle: short at the sides, long and slightly wavy at the back. She still had a bit of puppy fat, he was thin and wiry.

They lived on the shores of different fjords, she in Lavangen, he in Salangen. Tone had seen him once before. She had to go to Salangen for her dental check-ups, because there was no dentist in her village.

After her appointment she generally popped into the baker's, another amenity they did not have where she lived. There she was, standing in the window in the low, white wooden building on the sloping street down to the fjord, buying pastries. Three boys were walking past the shop. The one in the middle shone so brightly between the other two.

That's the best-looking boy I've seen in my whole life, she thought.

And here he was now. The boy from the baker's. Standing in front of her. And the band on stage was playing the Bellamy Brothers.

> If I said you had a beautiful body, would you hold it against
> me?
> If I swore you were an angel, would you treat me like the
> devil tonight?

Of course she said yes.

A girl approached Tone on the dance floor.

'You friend's in the queue outside, but she hasn't got enough money to get in.' Tone gave a start. 'She asked me to come and get you, so she could borrow some money.'

'Hmm,' mumbled Tone, but she did not go out, then or later. Just imagine if her friend were to steal the boy who was holding her round the waist right this minute.

No, now she wanted to dance.

They met as often as they could. They went to and fro by bus, or got friends to drive them. An hour each way. Once Gunnar passed his test it was easier, he would borrow his father's car and race over to see Tone, floating home later. They celebrated the return of the sun as winter drew to a close. In April, Gunnar was sent to do his military service much further south, in Jørstadsmoen outside Lillehammer. Tone wrote long love letters. Gunnar tried his hand at poetry. He usually crumpled his attempts into a ball and threw them away, but every now and then he would send one.

A place, one night in December, two lovers stand close together, and they will always remember, they want each other for ever, ran the words on the pale blue sheet of paper.

The love of their life was what they found, in each other's arms that day, and they wanted it always to be around, never change or fade away.

We're the boy and girl in my poem you see, and I'm so sad when you're not near, it's the emptiest time of all for me, so comfort me and write to me.

Tone started at a boarding high school in Harstad, a couple of hours' drive from Lavangen.

Yesterday I just stayed in my room crying all day. A friend from my class came in and asked what was the matter. I couldn't talk, just showed her your picture. Then she understood, Tone wrote, and went on: *You bet I was relieved to get my period on Sunday.*

At the appointed time she would sit ready on the steps by the telephone box, guarding it, afraid someone would come along and want to use it just then, just as he picked up the phone at the camp two thousand kilometres away and dialled the number. The rings came once a week, at the exact same time.

Once Gunnar had completed his military service he started at the teacher training college in Tromsø. Gunnar, nineteen, almost twenty, was specialising in the new subject of Computing and Information Technology. He also took some PE teaching options, in case computers did not turn out to be the future.

Tone, now seventeen and in her last year of secondary school, moved in with him. They rented a tiny place of their own. Finally they could be together all the time.

'Like winning the pools,' was how Gunnar described meeting Tone. 'Sheer luck.'

There was nothing better than her.

The happiness almost hurt.

In the dark season they hid under the duvet. They only glanced up to look when the northern lights were dancing.

As teenagers they were already dreaming of the children they would have.

Changes in the Country

The old Prime Minister was worn down by recurring migraines. The doctor had ordered him to take sick leave, to rest and get his strength back, but the modest man did not feel he could. The son of a working-class family with a strong work ethic, he was not comfortable taking time off. But he did drop hints to those closest to him about the illness that sometimes paralysed him.

Beginning in the mid-1970s, Norway's oil income had grown vigorously, and the ailing man born in the woods by the railway lines was the first Prime Minister to make serious use of the new money. Over a long career in politics, Odvar Nordli had helped expand Norway's generous welfare provisions and public health system. During his time as Prime Minister, from 1976 to 1981, the trade union movement consolidated its power, and people gained more time off and more money to spend during it. Under Nordli, all workers were given the right to full pay from the first day they went off sick.

The global economy, meanwhile, experienced a sharp downturn. Norway tackled the recession of the mid-1970s with a policy of its own, freezing wages and prices to keep unemployment down. Nordli was to be the last Norwegian Prime Minister with an unshakeable faith in strong state control of the economy and in the political regulation of interest rates, the property market and the financial sector.

But the wind from the right in the USA and Britain was now reaching Norway. The railway worker's son was to be one of its first victims.

Norway's Labour Party — Arbeiderpartiet — had been running the country virtually without a break since 1935. The political mood swing in the country coincided with escalating intrigues in the party leadership. The whispering in corners became a buzz, and dissatisfaction within the party refused to be quelled.

At the end of January 1981, the party press office issued a statement declaring that Odvar Nordli wished to resign. The old Prime Minister had not taken part in the decision and tried to deny it. But things were moving too fast, it was an ambush, a coup, and Nordli, known as a kind man, was too loyal to the party to denounce it in the media. He gritted his teeth and silently conceded defeat.

The country waited. The Prime Minister had announced his departure, but who would take over?

The tension finally broke after a meeting at the home of Nordli's predecessor, Trygve Bratteli. The party's co-ordinating committee, five powerful men and one woman, had gathered.

Odvar Nordli insisted at least on a say in who was to take over. His nominee was the party veteran Rolf Hansen. But the sixty-year-old Hansen was adamant that he did not want to be Prime Minister; his answer was to point to the only woman in the room, Gro Harlem Brundtland, a young doctor and campaigner for free abortion. The choice aligned with the mood in the party: a grass-roots campaign to make her leader had just begun.

Three days later, on 4 February 1981, Gro Harlem Brundtland was standing outside the Royal Palace, smiling for the press after presenting her new administration to the King. The government was predominantly male, the woman in the red and blue silk outfit having inherited most of its ministers from her predecessor.

That February day nonetheless marked the start of a new age. Gro, as she was soon called, was Norway's first female Prime Minister, and the first Prime Minister from the Labour Party to have a university degree. She'd been born into the political elite, the daughter of a prominent Cabinet minister, Gudmund Harlem.

Throughout the post-war period, the Labour Party's Prime Ministers were drawn from the working class. Einar Gerhardsen, a former communist and the main architect behind Norway's welfare state, had worked as an errand boy from the age of ten. Oscar Torp, who replaced Gerhardsen as Prime Minister for a brief period in the 1950s, was in paid employment when he was eight. Trygve Bratteli, who became Prime Minister in 1971, was the son of a cobbler and worked as an errand boy and builder before becoming a whale hunter.

With its roots in the working classes, the Labour Party fought to remove the barriers to advancement in a class society and make sure employees and their bosses had the same opportunities.

But in one area the idea of equality was less pervasive. It was men who wielded the power. They were the ones who became party leaders, trade union bosses, Prime Ministers, and – above all – they were the ones who were listened to in the inner circles of power.

The women's movement of the 1970s paved the way for Gro Harlem Brundtland. Having grown up in a family where it was natural for men and women to share the domestic tasks, she slipped into Norwegian politics with exceptional self-confidence.

The campaign against her was equally potent, and a variety of techniques were used to suppress her in the run-up to the general election in the autumn of 1981. Her opponents in debates often countered her statements by referring to what 'others in the party' had said. Epithets like 'shrew' and 'virago' were bandied about and stickers started appearing in windows and cars bearing the simple slogan 'Kick Her Out'.

She received hate mail and insults were hurled at her in the street; a woman could not lead a *country*. When told to get back to the kitchen sink, Brundtland's style was to brush such comments aside. An authoritative figure, she rarely let herself be knocked off course.

The 'Kick Her Out' stickers were in particular evidence on the BMWs and Mercedes-Benzes in the areas of detached houses and elegant apartment blocks in Oslo West, where people were tired of Labour being almost continually in power.

It was the area where Wenche and her children lived.

Labour and Gro failed to win the voters' confidence in the September 1981 election. When the right won its first general election in post-war Norway, glasses were raised in the homes of Frogner.

Finally taxes would come down, and the focus would be on individual freedoms.

But the Breivik family needed the help of the welfare state. By then, Anders's mother had already been in touch with social services several times, asking for help. As a single mother she was defined as vulnerable and the state would therefore step in to provide financial support.

The new conservative regime removed interest-rate caps, gave banks more room for manoeuvre, deregulated property prices and made plans to privatise a variety of services.

As Gro began her determined struggle to get back into power, Wenche and the children were struggling to find a foothold in a day-to-day existence that seemed like quicksand. 'Hell' was Wenche's word for life at that time. The divorce papers were taking an age to come through and she felt caught in limbo, left alone with sole responsibility for the children and no home of her own. The wrangling over how their shared assets were to be divided intensified. Anders just wanted somewhere he could feel safe.

Later, it was Gro, the powerful woman of his childhood, who would be the target of his hate. The woman who symbolised the new, self-confident Norway. The new Norway in which young women would soon be storming the bastions of male power and boldly taking top positions as if it were the most natural thing in the world.

Silkestrå

All happy families are alike; each unhappy family is unhappy in its own way.

Leo Tolstoy, *Anna Karenina*

Five rooms for the family of three. Plenty of space, bright, modern and brand-new. A room each, with doors they could close, a living room where they could have guests, a kitchen and a balcony looking out over the play area in the 'blue garden' between the flats. The new housing cooperative behind the Frogner Park had been designed with families in mind. The three-storey apartment blocks extended across the green parkland in a maze-like layout, with sheltered spaces, footpaths and little garden areas, where the benches, slides and swings were painted bright colours.

The cooperative went by the appealing name of Silkestrå – Silken Straw – and Wenche was one of the first buyers.

It was thanks to Jens's membership of the Oslo Housing and Savings Society that they got the opportunity to buy a stake there. He also paid the deposit on the flat.

Moving out of Fritzners gate seemed to take for ever. Wenche did all the packing herself. First in newspaper, then in boxes. She threw out her old life, the letters and papers she had accumulated in drawers and cupboards.

Once they were finally installed in the light flat on the top floor in

Silkestrå, Wenche was able to breathe a sigh of relief. She could go out for a smoke on the balcony and she could see trees and sky, a real middle-class idyll. Just behind the block of flats there was a patch of woodland with rare oak trees, streams and little paths.

She could relax here and they could be happy.

But her energy drained away. The move from Frogner to neighbouring Skøyen had exhausted her, as had the division of assets that had finally taken place. From now on she was on her own. Many of the flats around hers were still standing empty. Her children were always arguing and fighting. Anders was an angry boy and his punches were hard.

At the start of the new year in 1983, Wenche contacted the family counselling service at the Oslo Health Board and asked for a new respite care placement for her son. Daily demands of a purely practical kind, like dropping him off at the Vigeland Park nursery that was within walking distance from their flat, or fetching him in the afternoons, seemed insurmountable. He might disappear from her on the way: he was often simply running off. The nursery had also expressed concern about the boy. He found it hard to make friends, he never invented games of his own and he didn't cry if he hurt himself.

'Clingy and difficult, demands a lot of attention,' Wenche told the officer dealing with her case at the Oslo Health Board. 'Aggressive, and nasty with it,' said the case notes.

She was very keen to have a diagnosis for Anders. Perhaps there was some kind of medicine he could take? She told the counsellor she wondered whether Anders might have diabetes, referring to the baby's bottle of cordial he clung to at home. But he coped without the bottle at nursery, and he had shown no interest in it when he was with his weekend family. It was at home that he needed it. And there was nothing wrong with his blood-sugar levels.

Wenche had two faces to show to the world. Mostly she showed the smiling, chattering, carefree one. But sometimes she was distant, and would walk straight past without saying hello, or looked away. If she did say anything it was in a drawling voice, her words almost slurred.

Neighbours talked about it. She wasn't drunk, it wasn't that; could it be drugs?

The neighbours on Wenche's staircase soon started to get the feeling things were not as they should be behind the family's front door. Anders was rarely at the play area; both children were sort of invisible, silent, scared. The neighbours called him 'Meccano Boy' because he was like something made out of a construction set, stiff and angular. But it was his big sister the neighbours were most worried about. She acted like a mother to both Wenche and her little brother. She was the one who kept things in order at home, and looked after Anders.

'Wenche doesn't pick up signals,' said one neighbour to another. The woman in the flat opposite would wait inside her own front door whenever she heard Wenche on the stairs. 'You could never get away. She went on and on, talking a load of rubbish and jumping from one subject to another, especially sex – she always had lots to say about sex. She twisted words and phrases and laughed a lot at her own stories,' she said later. It surprised the neighbours that Wenche had no inhibitions, even when the children were there and listening to her innuendo. It was usually Elisabeth who finally managed to get her mother through the front door by saying something like, 'We'll have to go now Mum, or our frozen stuff will start to melt. We'd better put it in the freezer or it might get spoilt.'

The rumours were going round. There were lots of male visitors, the neighbours gossiped. It was embarrassing to encounter them on the stairs and avoid their glance or pass them when they rang the doorbell of Wenche's flat. And Wenche was always out and about, they muttered to each other. Even at night. No one ever saw 'a babysitter or grandma' going in. When Wenche once asked a neighbour to come and take a look at something that was not working in the flat, the neighbour was struck by the fact that there was no sign of any children living there; it was as if they did not exist.

One day Jens Breivik received a call from one of the neighbours, complaining that there was a lot of noise in the flat, and that Wenche was often out, day and night. The neighbour hinted at the numerous male visitors and said the children were left to their own devices.

Jens did nothing. He had a new life in Paris, a new wife and new worries.

One morning, a young, female neighbour heard loud noise coming from the flat again and decided the time had come to investigate. She rang the doorbell. Elisabeth opened the door just a crack. 'Oh no, there's nothing wrong here. Mum's asleep at the moment,' she said, holding the door in place. Beneath her thin arm a boy stood staring straight ahead, his face impassive.

The neighbours' respect for the right to privacy outweighed their concerns for the children. And anyway, the family was already on the radar of the child welfare authorities, Wenche having asked for help herself. The adviser at the Vika social services office had been seriously troubled by Wenche's last visit and judged the family to be in need of psychiatric help rather than child welfare support. She referred them to the Centre for Child and Adolescent Psychiatry. Two weeks before Anders's fourth birthday, at the end of January 1983, the family was called in for evaluation.

The staff found the woman who came along to the meeting confused and on edge. She had great difficulty even locating the place, despite the careful instructions she had been given. It proved beyond her to find her way there with the children, and she was granted free transport by taxi.

The family was registered with the day section for families, where the children were to be evaluated by a child psychiatrist and their mother by a psychologist. There were therapists, nurses and child welfare officers on hand at the centre. These specialists would observe the family's interaction in the course of everyday activities like mealtimes and play and carry out psychological tests on all three of them. Behavioural problems in children could be the result of relations within the family, and if 'things were sorted out in the family' the symptoms could subside.

Anders was placed in the nursery at the centre. He was also free to go to the playroom where there were cars, dolls, teddy bears, a puppet theatre, cowboys and Indians, paints and crayons, scissors and paper and games.

The specialists observed a boy who took no joy in life. Completely unlike the demanding boy his mother had described.

'Marked inability to enter into the spirit of games. Takes no pleasure in the toys. When the other children are playing, he operates alongside them. He is wholly unfamiliar with "Let's pretend" games. He is always wary during play. Anders lacks spontaneity, appetite for activity, imagination or ability to empathise. Nor does he have the mood swings seen in most children of his age. He has no language for expressing emotions,' wrote Per Olav Næss, the child psychiatrist responsible for evaluating him. When playing shops, he was interested in how the cash register worked rather than in the game as a whole.

'Anders demands surprisingly little attention. He is cautious, controlled, rarely pesters anyone, is extremely clean and tidy and becomes very insecure if this is not possible. He does not take the initiative in making contact with other children. He participates mechanically in activities without showing any pleasure or enthusiasm. Often looks sad. He finds it difficult to express himself emotionally but when a reaction eventually comes, it is a remarkably powerful one,' the report continued.

Restless activity took over whenever he became aware that someone, an adult or another child, was trying to make contact. It was as if he instantly activated a defence mechanism that sent out the message 'don't bother me, I'm busy' when anyone wanted anything of him. The child psychiatrist also noted a feigned, defensive smile.

Anders, however, quickly proved capable of adapting to his new surroundings. After just a few days he decided he liked coming to the nursery at the centre and thought it was 'stupid to go' at the end of his session. He showed pleasure in mastering new skills and was able to accept praise. The staff at the centre concluded that it was not a question of individual psychological damage in Anders; that is, damage that could not be undone by putting him in a new and positive care setting. He had considerable resources to draw on. It was the situation at home that was undermining him. The general conclusion was that Anders had been made a scapegoat for his mother's frustrations.

The psychologist at the centre talked to his mother and carried out some tests, and found a woman who lived in her own private, internal world and had an underdeveloped sense of how to relate to people around her. Her relationships with those close to her were characterised by anxiety and she was emotionally marked by depression and by being in denial of it, said the case summary at the end of her time at the centre.

'She is threatened by chaotic conflicts and shows signs of illogical thought when under pressure. Mentally she has a borderline personality disorder and functions very unevenly. Given a structured situation for living she can function well, but she is vulnerable in a crisis.'

Wenche's behaviour towards Anders could change rapidly. One minute she would be pleasant and kind, only to start shouting aggressively at him the next. Her rejections could be brutal. The staff at the centre heard her yell at her son: 'I wish you were dead!'

Anders's mother was soon a topic of conversation among the staff.

'Even in a clinical setting, she spoke uncritically about her aggressively sexual fantasies and fears, and her attitude to the male staff was very ambivalent,' wrote the psychologist Arild Gjertsen. At times she was very flirtatious. But he also noted that she became more composed as her time at the centre went on.

The families being evaluated were usually discharged after the four-week observation period, and were then supported by the child welfare and child psychiatry services in their own locality. The Breivik family's sessions at the centre led the specialists to conclude that family life was harming the children, particularly Anders, so it was recommended that social services look into the possibility of fostering.

'The whole family is affected by the mother's poor psychological functioning. The greatest impact is on her relationship with Anders. There is a duality to this relationship, in that on the one hand she ties him to her symbiotically, while on the other she rejects him aggressively. Anders is the victim of his mother's projections of paranoid aggressive and sexual fear of men generally. Elisabeth escapes some of this, not least because she is a girl. For her part, Elisabeth goes too far in the precocious maternal role she adopts towards Anders.'

The conclusion was that 'Anders needs to be taken out of the family and into a better care setting because his mother is continually provoked by the boy and is locked in an ambivalent position, making it impossible for him to develop on his own terms.'

Mother and daughter were probably better able to live together, the centre thought. But Elisabeth's progress, too, should be carefully monitored, as there were some danger signals, such as the fact that she had few friends and tended to get very wrapped up in her own fantasies.

The Centre for Child and Adolescent Psychiatry reported in a letter to the local child welfare office: 'The profoundly pathological relationship between Anders and his mother means early intervention is vital to prevent seriously abnormality in the boy's development. Ideally he should be transferred to a stable foster home. The mother is however strongly opposed to this, and it is hard to predict the consequences of enforced intervention.'

As Anders's mother had requested respite care in the form of a weekend home, the centre suggested an initial effort to build on this, with foster parents who understood that the arrangement might become permanent.

The Centre for Child and Adolescent Psychiatry emphasised to the local child welfare office that this was a matter of importance, and that work should start at once on finding a suitable weekend home. The centre offered its assistance in evaluating foster homes, mediating between the family and the respite home and remaining involved to ensure things were moving in the right direction.

Then something happened that botched the plan. Jens Breivik, who was now stationed in Paris, received the report from the Centre for Child and Adolescent Psychiatry. Through his lawyer, he demanded immediate transfer of Anders's care to him. The diplomat wanted an interim injunction that would give him emergency custody of the boy straight away, while he explored permanent custody through the courts. Wenche, who had welcomed the prospect of weekend respite care, now refused point-blank to accept any help at all. It might give her ex-husband an advantage in court. Wenche again hired the lawyer who had helped her with the divorce and dividing the assets. He wrote that 'respite in the form of a foster home for Anders is a solution that my client finds utterly objectionable. Furthermore, the need for respite ceased to apply a long time ago.'

At that point the Centre for Child and Adolescent Psychiatry and the child welfare office stood back and awaited the outcome of the case at Oslo City Court. In October 1983 the court ruled that Anders's situation did not require urgent action and that the boy could live with his mother until the main court case started.

As Jens Breivik understood it, the court had concluded there was no serious negligence on Wenche's part and he therefore had little prospect of winning custody of his son. In the early 1980s it was in any case unusual for a court to find in a father's favour in child custody cases. The mother generally took priority.

Jens Breivik had not seen his son for three years. Now he gave up his demand to take charge of Anders's care and the case was never brought before the court. His lawyer wrote to the Centre for Child and Adolescent Psychiatry that Jens Breivik and his current wife had begun to have their doubts after they learned about the preliminary meeting at Oslo City Court. Initially, 'their impression had been that Anders was in a critical state, and they had not hesitated to open their home to him. Now, however, they feel they will have to fight to get Anders. This is a new development and they feel they have been thrust into a situation in which they had no intention of becoming embroiled.'

But the young psychologist at the Centre for Child and Adolescent Psychiatry did not want to give up on Anders. Just a month after the City Court ruling, Arild Gjertsen asked the child welfare authorities in Oslo to instigate standard proceedings to have Anders taken into care, that is, to separate him from his mother by force. Gjertsen emphasised that 'We stand by our original conclusion that Anders's care situation is so precarious that he is at risk of developing more

serious psychopathology and we hereby restate our assessment that
an alternative care situation is necessary for Anders, which we consider to be our duty under The Children's Act § 12, cf. § 16a. Since
the father has withdrawn his civil action, child welfare authority
should take up the case on its own grounds.'

In November of the same year, Wenche's lawyer accused the
psychologist of 'monomanic victimisation'.

'Admittedly I am not a psychologist, but in my thirty years of
practice I have acquired something young Gjertsen may be presumed
to lack, namely a wide-ranging and detailed knowledge of human
behaviour. On this basis I can express my firm conviction that if
Wenche Behring is not qualified to look after Anders without the
intervention of child protection agencies, then there are in fact very
few, if any, mothers in this country qualified to raise their children
independently,' he wrote to the child welfare authorities.

There was no more the specialists at the centre could do. They
were not authorised to take any formal steps; only the child welfare
department could take such action.

The serious concerns of the Centre for Child and Adolescent
Psychiatry now had to be weighed against a new assessment from the
Vigeland Park nursery, which referred to Anders as a 'cheerful, happy
boy'. Jens Breivik complained that the assessment had come from the
pen of a nursery employee who was a friend of Wenche's.

When the Child Welfare Board held its hearing to consider
whether Anders should be taken into care, Wenche arrived well prepared at the Vika social services office, along with her lawyer. He
stressed that Anders's mother had now recovered from the short-
lived crisis that had resulted from her difficult divorce. The officer
originally handling the case had left, and the young replacement had
scarcely any experience of child welfare issues and had never been
called before the board before. When she attended the meeting she
had not worked on the case beyond reading the papers. It proved an
uncomfortable experience for the young welfare officer, who felt she
had been thrown to the wolves.

It was only on specific and very serious grounds such as battery, abuse or obvious neglect that legal authority could be granted under the Child Welfare Act for the enforced placement of a child in a foster home. Social services suggested a compromise. The family would be monitored for the time being.

Three checks were carried out, one with notice and two unannounced, in the winter of 1984. The social welfare office report of these visits to Silkestrå ran as follows: 'The mother appeared organised, tidy and in control, easy to talk to, calm and unruffled regardless of the subject under discussion. The girl was calm, well behaved and watchful. Anders was a pleasant, relaxed boy with a warm smile that immediately makes one like him. During conversations in the home he sat up at the table, busy with games, plasticine or Playmobil toys.' The report also said that not a single cross word was exchanged between the family members. Anders was never whiny or obstructive. 'The mother never changes her expression and does not get upset if difficult situations arise with Anders. She speaks calmly and Anders accepts her instructions and does as she says.' The only reservation expressed by the home visitor from social services was that the children's mother had sent them out for pizza, although they were 'possibly a bit young to run that sort of errand, and one might add that pizza can scarcely be called a nutritious meal'.

At the very end, the home visitor did say there could be grounds for concern about how the mother might cope with potential crises in the future, but this in itself was not considered sufficient to warrant removing the boy from his mother's care.

Around midsummer 1984, when Anders was five, the child welfare board in Oslo reached its unanimous verdict:

'The necessary conditions for taking the child into care have not been met. Case dismissed.'

Peeing on the Stairs

What a little brat, thought a young mother from one of the neighbouring staircases, who had tried yet again to get a hello out of Anders. He never responded, just looked away or turned aside.

Oh well, she thought, and went on her way.

Anyone watching the children at play would notice the boy who was nearly always by himself. He would observe from the sidelines, never get involved in anything. But the busy parents had enough to do keeping track of their own kids. The gardens and pathways round the blocks of flats at Silkestrå were teeming with children.

Then, something new happened on the estate. A number of the unsold flats were bought up by Oslo City Council and allocated to refugee families. Asylum seekers from Iran, Eritrea, Chile and Somalia moved into the flats round the blue, green and red gardens, and gradually the scent of garlic, turmeric, allspice and saffron drifted out through open balcony doors.

Until the early 1980s, Oslo's Skøyen was a district of dazzling whiteness. Few foreigners found their way to Norway. At the start of the preceding decade, Norway had fewer than a thousand non-Western immigrants: 1971 saw the first influx of foreign workers as the Norwegian state tackled a labour shortage by issuing an invitation to Pakistan. Six hundred single men came over to work that year, taking jobs that most Norwegians did not want. But the foreign workers did not move into Skøyen. They lived in cramped and miserable conditions in run-down parts of the city.

In 1980, the first asylum seekers arrived. Refugees presented themselves at Norway's borders, asking for protection. This had never happened before. In 1983, the first year the Breivik family lived at Silkestrå, 150 asylum seekers came to Norway. The year after that, three hundred. Three years later, the number was almost nine thousand.

A Chilean family moved in on the floor below the Breiviks. They had fled Augusto Pinochet's persecution, and after almost a year at the asylum seeker reception centre in Oslo they were given a flat at Silkestrå. Wenche was the first person to turn up on their doorstep, with a warm 'Welcome' and a child in each hand.

Anders took a liking to the youngest daughter of the family, a little tot with curly hair, two years younger than he was.

Eva gradually started to tag along with the boy from the second floor wherever he went. For his part, he thawed out with the new girl, grew more talkative and taught her new Norwegian words every day. With the Latin American family, he felt secure.

Eva got a place at his nursery in Vigeland Park, and when Anders moved on while she still had two years left at nursery he waited for her every afternoon after school.

Smestad was a school for conditioned children who had fathers with freshly ironed shirts, posh middle names and villas with big gardens. King Harald went to school there after the war, and was later followed by his own children, Prince Haakon Magnus and Princess Märtha Louise. The Prince was six years older than Anders and finished his last year at primary just as Anders was starting.

This school district is a dark blue belt in Oslo and it helped deliver the right wing's election victory in 1981. A wave of privatisations and deregulation of property prices followed. The value of housing-cooperative flats soon soared.

In the spring of 1986, the year Anders Breivik started school, the Labour Party returned to power. The Conservative Prime Minister Kåre Willoch had faced a vote of confidence after proposing to raise petrol prices and failed to win the support of the right-wing Progress Party.

Suddenly, Gro Harlem Brundtland was Prime Minister again. This time she was better prepared. She became the first head of government in the world to form a Cabinet with as many female ministers as male ones: eight out of seventeen Cabinet posts, plus herself at the top.

This was a new Labour Party, which tapped into the spirit of the age and carried forward many of the economic changes brought in by Kåre Willoch's Conservative government.

At the same time, Brundtland's policies gave women a set of rights that no other country could match. Pragmatic as she was, Gro set out to make life more practical for women, and for men. Her government extended maternity leave, built nurseries and gave more rights to single parents, and there was a focus on improving children's and women's health. In the wake of these reforms came a stream of new, confident women who wanted to play their part in society.

Not everyone was happy. State feminism was the insult hurled by some. A matriarchy, complained others. The term 'vagina state' was later coined. But it was still Gro Harlem Brundtland who put her stamp on Norway more than any other politician in Anders's school years.

Anders himself was growing up in a female world consisting of his mother, his sister and Eva. It was fun playing with Anders, Eva thought, at least for a while. Because Anders was always the one who decided on the game. It was only when they were at her flat that she had a say. They built a den in the living room, played with her dolls or just hung around in the kitchen with her parents. When they were upstairs at Anders's place they never played where his mother was. Round there, they were never allowed to stay in the living room, which was always kept pristine, nor in the kitchen. They were only allowed to be in his room and they had to keep the door closed. That was where Anders had his toys and games, all arranged in neat rows on the shelves. Wenche really preferred them to play outside. Because Anders's mother liked peace and quiet.

Whenever Eva tried to play with other children Anders pulled her away; he wanted to keep her to himself. He liked it best when there were just the two of them.

But sometimes the group took over. There were so many young-sters at Silkestrå it was difficult to keep the others at bay. In the basement there was a room where some parent had installed a table-tennis table. The children would take their cassette players down there and dance to Michael Jackson, Prince and Madonna, and later to rap music. Anders found his own spot. He always sat on the ven tilation pipes in the corner and did not join in the dancing or the table tennis. From there he could see everything, and was left in peace. There was a smell of urine in that corner. Whenever the smell spread through the basement, Anders got the blame. 'It stinks of pee, it must be Anders!' the others laughed.

The ants in the wall had a permanent path from the grass, across the tarmac, along the edge of the footpath, across a grating and up the steps. Anders would sit there waiting.

'You're going to die!'

'Got you!'

He picked them up one by one and squashed them. Sometimes with his thumb, sometimes his index finger. 'You and you and you and you!' he decided, there on the steps, master of life and death.

The little girls found him disgusting. He was so intense, and he was cruel to animals. For a while he had some rats in a cage and would poke them with pens and pencils. Eva said she thought he was hurt-ing them, but he took no notice. Anders caught bumblebees, dropped them in water and then brought them up to the surface in a sieve so he could watch them drown. Pet owners at Silkestrå made it clear to their children that Anders was not to come anywhere near their cats or dogs. Anders was often the only one not invited to come and stroke other children's new puppies or kittens.

Little by little, Eva started to get a feeling that something was wrong. But she dared not tell her parents that she did not want to play with Anders any more, because her mother and Wenche were by now good friends. Wenche was teaching them how to adapt to life in

Norway, and she passed on clothes that no longer fitted Anders and Elisabeth.

Eva never told her parents that it was Anders who broke the heads off the neighbours' roses, leaving just the stalks; who threw stones through open windows and ran away; or that he teased and bullied kids who were smaller than him, ideally the new arrivals who had not acquired the language to defend themselves.

One of his victims was a skinny little boy from Eritrea. On one occasion, Anders found an old rug, rolled him up in it and jumped up and down on him. 'Don't do that, you're hurting him!' cried Eva. But she stood on the sidelines, watching.

There was only one thing Anders could not abide. Being told off. Then, he would melt away while the other kids were left there to take a scolding for scrumping apples or ringing on doorbells and running away. Anders would creep out again when things had calmed down.

Once, he could not get away in time and was caught by Mrs Broch. To get his revenge after her rebuke, he peed on her doormat. He peed on her newspaper. He peed in her letterbox. Later, he went and peed in her storeroom. It was from then on that he got the blame for the stale urine smell in the basement.

One of the victims of his bullying was a girl with a mental disability. One day, Anders squashed a rotten apple into the face of the girl's favourite doll just as her father was going by. 'You bother my daughter one more time and I'll hang you on the clothesline in the cellar,' her father, a university professor, roared.

Anders took notice. A father's threats were something he had respect for. He never went near the girl again.

He was by now seeing his own father in the school holidays. The first time, he was four and a half and his father took him for a week's summer holiday at a cabin by the sea. Jens would occasionally ring Wenche and say he wanted to see his son. The boy sometimes ran and hid, and the other children were sent out to look for him.

Jens usually spent his summers at a country cottage in Normandy.

Then Wenche would deliver Anders to the Scandinavian Airlines staff at Oslo airport, and after a two-hour flight he would be picked up by his father in Paris. Sometimes his older half-siblings would be there. They went on family outings or to the beach. At the summer cottage it was mainly Jens's third wife who took care of the little boy. She had no children of her own and grew fond of Anders, who also became attached to her. He was overjoyed whenever she offered to read him a story. 'Do you really want to?' he would ask her. 'Are you sure you've got time?' He would sit curled up on her lap for hours while he was being read to. He calmed down there. And seemed to forget everything around him.

When Eva started school, Anders was in Year 3. He would not acknowledge her any longer. Not at school, that is.

The blue garden, the park and the forest were separate from school – like different continents. Their friendship only belonged in one of them.

This gave the little girl the space she needed to find her own friends. One of them was the girl who lived on the ground floor of their block of flats. She was scared of Anders too. Every time she went out of the door, she was afraid he was going to spit on her from the second floor. It had only happened once, but that was enough to make a horror of gobs of spit dog her entire childhood.

Eva finally got her own group of friends. She was now tough enough to say no to Anders when he wanted her to come out and play.

Anders was on his own again.

But one day he latched onto some classmates. It proved not to be so hard, after all. He just said hello, and they said hello back.

In his primary-school years, there was nothing very remarkable about Anders. He was there, but did not draw attention to himself. He joined the Scouts, he played football and rode round on his bike with his friends.

What marked him out from the others was that his parents were never there for him. The football team relied on parents to take turns driving the players to matches and tournaments. He always had to get a lift with others, mostly with Kristian, who lived close by. Team sports were never really Anders's thing. He had poor ball control and often misjudged passes, but he was there.

Anders was average at most things: average height, average at school, an average sort of bully. He was far from the worst, and also capable of showing a kind of concern, like helping a bullied child who'd been hit in the face with a snowball look for his glasses. If the glasses were covered in snow he would brush them clean before handing them back.

One boy in the class was a particular target. Ahmed was nicely dressed, tall and dark – the only Pakistani in the school. He would generally sit and read in the library at break time so he would not have to face the school playground alone.

They called him Brownie.

Then one day Ahmed retaliated for the first time, and knocked Anders over. When Anders struggled to his feet, battered and bruised, everything had changed.

It was the start of a friendship.

They ran around the forest together, played basketball, went to each other's flats to watch films. Even at primary school, the two of them were keen to earn money. Every day they waited for the news-papers to arrive. Once the copies of *Aftenposten* had been delivered they transferred them to their trolleys and lugged them round to the front doormats in the neighbourhood.

Anders had found a friend.

Al-Anfal

Remember when God revealed to the angels: 'I am
with you, so grant believers resolve. I shall cast terror
into the hearts of the unbelievers. So strike above the
necks, and strike their every finger!' For they defied
God and His Messenger, and who so defies God and
His Messenger, God is severe in retribution. Here it is:
so taste it! For the unbelievers the torment of the Fire!

The Qur'an, 8:12–14

It was no coincidence that Saddam Hussein chose a chapter from the
Qur'an to name the assault he was planning on the Kurds. *Al-Anfal*
means spoils of war and is a reference to God's order to Muhammad
to do battle against the infidels with all his might.

And the unbelievers shall be herded into hell, said God to Muhammad
after the first great battle for Islam in Badr in 624, *in order that God
may distinguish the depraved from the pure. He shall heap the depraved one
upon the other, piling them all up, and deliver that pile to hell. These are truly
the losers.*

The officers of the Iraqi army in 1988 similarly ordered their soldiers to tie the Kurds together head to toe, blindfold them and dump
them from trucks into ready-dug mass graves in the desert. The victims landed on top of the still-warm bodies of dead neighbours,
brothers and other relatives, and lay there waiting to be shot.

Al-Anfal is the Kurds' holocaust – a genocide committed with the ultimate aim of Arabising Kurdistan. Arabisation had already been going on for decades. The Kurds and other minorities had been forcibly moved from border areas, while Arab tribespeople were brought in from the south under the supervision of the Iraqi army. It was important for the government to take control of the oil-rich areas around Kirkuk and Khanaqin.

The Iraqi army command calculated how to kill the maximum number of people quickly and efficiently. The villages to be cleansed were first surrounded by soldiers, then the people were forced from their houses and driven away. On reaching the place of execution they were handed over to firing squads from the elite security forces. Bulldozers covered the bodies with sand and earth, and the Kurdish problem was on the way to a solution.

By naming the campaign of extermination after a sura of the Qur'an, the Iraqi government sought to legitimise its executions as a war against unbelievers. The Kurdish mosques in areas selected by the Prohibited Villages Committee of Central Security were razed to the ground by the army's corps of engineers. First with dynamite, then with bulldozers. A decree from the highest level ordained that no settlement was to be spared. After the raids, the destruction was inspected by helicopter, and if as much as a single building remained standing the area commander was held to account.

One lovely spring morning, the scent of flowers and sweet apples came wafting across the rooftops in a village high up in the Kurdish mountains. Then people's eyes began to water and their skin to burn. The babies died first, then the toddlers, then the old people, and finally even the strong. Those who survived were left blind or with other serious after-effects.

In the next phase, village after village was bombed with mustard gas, sarin and other nerve agents. This culminated in the attack on Halabja in March 1988, which killed five thousand people, and left thousands more scarred for life.

*

In the midst of all this there lived a young Kurdish man by the name of Mustafa. He was a trained engineer and had served in the Iraqi army, repairing tanks and military equipment in the south of the country. Mustafa felt himself to be a slave of the system, trapped and under surveillance. The Iraqi intelligence services, trained by the East German Stasi, had ears and eyes everywhere.

After his military service, Mustafa found work as an engineer at the water and sewage works in the Kurdish city of Erbil, and was there when *al-Anfal* started. Frightened voices whispered stories about the mass graves, the blue-black faces, the desiccated eyes. Stories that were dangerous to repeat.

Working in the accounts office of the waterworks was a beautiful, elegant woman with black curls, six years younger than Mustafa. She had a laugh that came floating out of the door and along the corridor as he passed. Her family had fled from Kirkuk, and she was obliged to abandon her university course when *al-Anfal* began.

Mustafa's first ploy was to make sure the girl got to know his sister. Then, when the entire workforce was sent by a state committee to make an inventory of a warehouse, he saw to it that he and she were standing beside each other, sorting goods.

She was called Bayan. And she was everything he wanted.

A few days after that, he got his sister to ask her: 'Do you want to marry my brother?'

Bayan did.

It was snowing when they got married in February 1992. That meant good fortune!

But after the Iraqi army moved out of the town, conflicts erupted between the various Kurdish factions. There was shooting on the streets, prices went through the roof and the Iraqi dinar plummeted. Buying a simple meal took plastic bags full of banknotes.

It also snowed on one of the last days of December that year, as Mustafa drove his pregnant wife through the potholed streets of Erbil at top speed. Bayan groaned with pain every time they hit a bump, her contractions coming thick and fast. An icy wind blew in with them as Mustafa opened the main door of the hospital. Even inside, the temperature was only just above freezing; there was no electricity and all the paraffin was gone. Once Bayan was safely in bed, Mustafa sent word to their friends and relations, who collected enough fuel to get the hospital generator going.

The steady drone of the motor was soon providing an accompaniment to the cries of the women in labour.

Snow for their wedding in February and on the day of the birth. Doubly good fortune, thought Mustafa as he waited in a corridor reeking of paraffin. This must be a child born under a lucky star.

Three women each gave birth to a daughter in the labour ward at Erbil that night.

Two of them were given the name Befrin, which means Snow White, after the beautiful snow flurries that were filling the air.

Bayan put her daughter to her breast. No, not Snow White, she thought. You're not a Snow White.

'Let's call her Maria,' suggested Mustafa.

'No, I know a sick old lady called that. She can't be named after a dying woman,' said Bayan.

'You choose then,' smiled Mustafa.

The brand-new mother looked down at her firstborn child. The baby had big, brown eyes and her head was wreathed in thick, dark hair. You look like a princess, thought Bayan.

A name that meant princess came into her mind.

'Bano,' she said. 'We'll call her Bano.'

Our Children

I am a father of two
You are a mother of two
Let hurrahs ring round the Earth
For they are our masterpiece!

Einar Skjæraasen, 'Onga våre'

The month the Soviet Union collapsed, there were blue stripes in the pregnancy test.

At last!

It had been quite a wait. Tone and Gunnar had both qualified as teachers. They had moved north, as far north as they could get, to Kirkenes, right up by the Norwegian–Soviet border. When they went camping and fishing round the Pasvik valley, they could see over to the formerly mighty neighbour, which was now on the verge of collapse. The same forest on both sides, but a steady and advanced welfare state on one side, and social and industrial decline in a ticking environmental nightmare on the other.

They had moved up north because special rates on paying down student loans were available if you took a job in Finnmark, Norway's northernmost county. Tone got a job at the upper secondary school in the former mining town and Gunnar taught at the secondary school, where he soon became the teachers' union representative.

As the pregnancy test showed its blue stripes in December 1991, Gorbachev's empire was being broken up into fifteen republics. Tone and Gunnar decided to celebrate the pregnancy with a trip to the other side, to the nearby city of Murmansk, where people were still living in some sort of equality of poverty.

The people of northern Norway had a lot to thank the Soviets for. Hitler's army torched every building in Kirkenes and other towns and villages in Finnmark before it was sent south by Stalin's troops in 1944. People up here had not forgotten it was the Red Army that liberated them. But since the war there had been precious little contact between the two peoples.

Now, the parents-to-be stood on deck in the cold on their way into the huge city and saw the vast collection of nuclear submarines in the ships' graveyard stretching halfway along the fjord.

Tone shivered. What if the radiation damaged the baby? A new life, vulnerable and longed for. She would have to be more careful now.

The snow melted, spring came, and spring turned into summer. A summer of sorts, at any rate, with average temperatures at midsummer of six to seven degrees centigrade, which suited a mother-to-be who was growing larger and feeling hotter all the time.

It was the end of July when the contractions started.

The birth at Kirkenes hospital was long and hard. It took all the long, light night. Towards morning the baby finally arrived, big and bonny. They would call him Simon, Tone decided.

When a little brother put in an appearance eighteen months later, Simon treated him like a teddy bear. He would lie beside the baby tickling him, especially his earlobes. If Simon was going out, he would throw his toys into the playpen so his brother wouldn't feel lonely.

It was little Håvard who turned out to be the showman of the family. He was especially keen on singing. He often put on concerts at home, with the rest of the family as his audience.

Two teachers with two children, an average Norwegian family.

Every weekend they were out and about around Pasvik with the boys in child carriers, fishing for wild salmon in the rivers, lighting bonfires under the midnight sun, before they all slept in the tent they carried with them. In July they picked bilberries, in August it was cloudberries, and in winter they wrapped the children up in sheepskin and pulled them out into open country on a little sledge.

If Simon and Håvard's feet got cold, their parents would have them run barefoot on the crusted surface of the snow. An old American Indian trick, their father told them. The first time, he had to dance in the snow with bare feet himself before the two chilly boys were convinced. It worked: the blood was soon coursing round their veins.

Gunnar taught his boys to distinguish between the tracks of wild creatures and tame ones. Wild animals walked in a straight line, tame ones tended to wander more aimlessly. The lynx, with its big, round pawprints, always chose its course and stuck to it. So did the wolverine with its long, narrow prints.

He impressed on the boys that they had to be alert to the dangers of nature. Wolves could attack something as big as an elk, and scarcely an anthill was left undisturbed if bears were on the prowl.

One summer's day, when the family was taking a break, on the hill behind them a wolf stood staring. Thin and grey, it almost blended into the rocky mountainside. Gunnar froze.

'Keep still. Don't move,' he said to the two boys. Tone picked up Håvard and Gunnar led Simon away, walking backwards. Very calmly, without any sudden movements, they withdrew up the slope to the road. The wolf slipped between the trees and was gone.

'It is time for the kids to get to know their kin,' Tone said one day. Distances in northern Norway are vast, and trips are expensive. It was time to go home. In Kirkenes they had a council flat, it was a nice one, but it wasn't theirs.

'We need to find something of our own,' Gunnar agreed.

They were lucky: the house next door to Gunnar's grandparents fell vacant. So they moved one county south, to the place where Tone saw Gunnar for the first time: Salangen, in Troms.

'What a romantic place,' exclaimed Gunnar when he returned to

Upper Salangen, a short distance up from the fjord on the way to the high fells, an untamed bit of the natural world.

'We've got to make sure we meet people,' Tone soon concluded. So she and the woman next door started a revue group. Then they needed writers and performers. Gunnar had once penned love poems, hadn't he, so perhaps he could write some scripts? As for Tone, she was eager to try her hand as a stage diva.

The car was a great place for practising revue numbers. The whole family bellowing out. Håvard always the loudest.

A girl lives in Havana, makes her living how she can, sitting by her window, beckons to a man!

Every year, after the New Year's Eve fireworks, the children of Upper Salangen put on a show. Astrid, the eldest of the neighbours' children, was the director. The children devised comedy routines and practised their gymnastic displays. As the new year started, *Reserved* signs on cushions and chairs around the house showed the grown-ups where to sit.

Håvard usually opened proceedings with a show tune. Simon was too shy to stand on stage, so he was the lighting technician. Throughout the show he carefully kept the family flashlight trained on the performers on the stage. He was never prouder of his younger sibling than on New Year's Eve, when Håvard stood up there alone on stage, expertly illuminated by his big brother.

Gunnar's scripts and lyrics soon earned quite a reputation in the district, and schools and children's clubs started to ring up and ask him to write something for them. The PE and IT teacher spent whole evenings writing and composing. He learnt to read and write music, and once the children were in bed he would sit, polishing up dialogues and scales.

The two boys learnt to trust in themselves early on. From Year 1 at school they went off on their own across the garden, up the lane to the main road, then along to the crossroads where the school bus stopped. In winter, when the polar night descended on northern Norway, it was mostly pitch dark, as neither the lane nor the main road had street lights. One morning Tone was standing at the window with her coffee when she saw a shadow in the early-morning gloom. A huge bull elk was bearing down at top speed on Simon, who was ploughing along, head down, through the squally wind and snow. The elk and the seven-year-old were on course to blunder straight into each other. Tone cried out as she lost them both from sight in the snowy storm. She rushed out in her slippers and yelled.

When she caught up with Simon, down by the road, he looked up at her and asked, 'Why are you shouting?'

The boy hadn't even noticed the elk. With his back to the wind Simon looked at his mother.

'Don't worry about me, Mum,' he said calmly. 'I'm a man of nature.'

Young Dreams

Journey with me
Into the mind of a maniac
Doomed to be a killer
Since I came out of the nutsac

Dr Dre & Ice Cube, 'Natural Born Killaz', 1994

Anders had to find a name. Before he could write on walls, he needed to find a really good *writer* name. It mustn't have too many letters, preferably between three and five. Some letters were cooler than others, and it was important that they looked good together, leaning on each other. He experimented in his room with felt pens and paper, producing several rough sketches.

The more you wrote your name, the more the name became yours. He had admired the big boys' signatures around the city. Bye-bye, dull, ordinary Anders, hello tagger. The name was supposed to express something of who you wanted to be, mark you out from the crowd.

He chose a character from Marvel Comics. The Marvel universe was ruled over by the all-powerful Galactus. One of his henchmen had betrayed his race by executing his own people. This executioner was fearless and unscrupulous, filled with defiance and greed – qualities that appealed to the mighty Galactus after several of his henchmen had fallen prey to pangs of conscience on being obliged to

kill their own. Galactus entrusted him with the job of head executioner and gave him a double-edged axe to carry out the death raid.
The executioner's name was Morg.

M and O flowed nicely across the sheet of paper, the R was hyper-
cool but the G was tricky.

Anders left the narrow footpath between the apartment blocks in
Silkestrå, looking for flat surfaces. In place of a double-edged axe,
the thirteen-year-old had equipped himself with marker pens and
aerosol cans. He had bought them with the money he'd earned deliv-
ering papers in the neighbourhood. The world beyond the blue
garden and the copse lay before him, waiting. He discarded his childhood like an old rag. Suddenly there were lots of identities he could
choose from.

He was a tagger,
a writer,
an artist,
a hooligan,
an executioner.

*

It was 1992. He changed schools when he went up to secondary
level. In his new form at Ris, the pupils came from a variety of different primary schools and only a few of them already knew him, so
he could create himself all over again. The insecurity and hesitation
of his childhood years were less evident. He was still quiet and cautious during lesson time, not one to put up his hand or try to speak,
but outside the classroom he knew what he wanted.

Four boys in the form found each other. One called himself
Wick, another *Spok*, and then there were *Morg* and Ahmed. Spok
was new in town and didn't know anybody at the start of the
school year. He had a round, childish face with freckles and his hair
parted in the middle, and he thought Anders seemed nice, a bit
shy. Wick was tall and lanky with a distinctly square chin and forehead. Both lived near by. Ahmed was Anders's Pakistani friend
from primary. At secondary school, he was still the only immigrant
in the class.

The four classmates found each other through a shared obsession.

They entered their teens in the golden age of hip hop, and lapped it up. They listened to rap at home, on their Walkmans on the way to school, and they went to concerts at the punk club Blitz. Anders practised his breakdance spins in the blue garden. He overcame his previous reluctance to join in the dancing competitions in the basement, throwing shyness to the wind.

The music originally created in the Bronx in the late 1970s took Oslo by storm. The breakbeat loops of funk, disco and electronica were scratched over and over again, with rhythms marked by drums, bass and guitar. 'Hip hop, don't stop'. DJs were the new heroes, and with the needle in the groove they moved the vinyl records back and forth; there was cutting and phasing, crossfading and sampling. The turntable had become an instrument in its own right, and local Oslo rappers gradually emerged, singing about their own reality of teen life in the city.

The music was raw and fast, and frequently aggressive. The first rappers in the Bronx had an anti-violence, anti-drugs, anti-racism message, and hoped that hip hop would replace street violence. People would meet to party, not to fight. Later on, the music often came to validate and glorify street violence and gangsta rap was often sexist and racist in nature, its words riddled with references to drugs. Hip hop was a lifestyle with seemingly simple rules, as explained by KRS-One and Marley Marl, among the first rappers from the South Bronx: 'Hip is the knowledge. Hop is the movement. Hip and Hop is an intelligent movement.'

Anders strove to be both the *hip* and the *hop*. *Hip* meant being up-to-date and relevant. Keeping up, getting it, being shown respect. As for the *hop* part, he practised hard on the paved path that crossed the grass outside his block of flats. He tried breaks and spins but never pulled off a headspin or backspin. He hadn't enough rhythm or body control to be a good dancer.

Perhaps he could be a rapper? After all, he kept a diary, writing down his thoughts and experiences like the rappers did. But he hadn't got the right sort of voice for rap; it was high and soft, like a girl's.

So he opted for hip hop's third form of expression: graffiti.

If breaking was visual rap in three dimensions, then graffiti was frozen breaking. The letters twisted, just as the dancing body did. To produce fine lines you had to let your body sway, readying yourself so the rhythm travelled from your body to your hand as it directed the aerosol paint can at the wall.

Graffiti tapped into the pulse of growing bodies. The lines on the wall were like them: angular, hard, insistent. The motifs had to involve speed and movement, be tough yet playful. But it was also a culture of performance and achievement. Everything was judged and then approved or rejected. If you had a good style and some original designs, you could mark yourself out from all the anonymous urban youths and shine a little.

In the area where Anders grew up, the young people's aspirations were strictly divided between tagging and tennis. It wasn't here, in the land of nice villas set among old apple trees and peonies, that Morg's role models hung out. .

Ris was a secondary school on the well-to-do west side of Oslo, with pupils from an area stretching from the ski jump at Holmenkollen to the lower ground at Skøyen. Most of them grew up with the self-confidence that goes with a big garden, and they spent their time outside school on the ski tracks, the football pitches and the tennis courts. At weekends they got together at home-alone parties or watched films in each other's basement TV rooms. It was important to have the right logos on your shirt or padded jacket, like Polo, Phoenix or Peak Performance. Anders's classmates were aiming for careers in law or finance. In the 8A class photo of 1993, most of them were wearing white polo shirts with the necks rolled down, under shirts or woollen sweaters.

One boy in the middle of the back row stands out from the rest. In an outsized check shirt and a hoodie, Anders stands there smiling with earphones in his ears. The pose and the plugged ears marks his distance from the others.

The class could broadly be divided into four groups. There was the

contingent with the polo-necked shirts, the straights. They were the
majority. Anders was never with them. Then there were a few with
shaved heads who went round in flying jackets, turned-up camouflage
trousers and black boots. They flirted with neo-Nazism and liked
heavy metal. Anders was on nodding terms with them. They didn't
bother anybody, and nobody bothered them. They were against immigration, and since Anders had some foreign friends he didn't hang out
with them. Anyway, he couldn't stand heavy metal. Then there were
the hip-hoppers. They did a bit of tagging and were on the rebellious
side, would-be gangsters. If the hip-hop movement once had a political message, it had got lost on the way to Ris. Ideologically, tagging
had no particular aim other than to serve as a marker of freedom; it
was essentially anarchic. That left the losers. There were a couple of
them. They kept a low profile.

Anders belonged to the third group. He had gained a kind of
respect at the school, where he came to be seen as a troublemaking tagger, a bit of a bully. If you said anything wrong you were in
for it.

Anders now carried himself with confidence and was not afraid to
speak up and say what he thought. He had acquired the right look at
the hip-hop store Jean TV in Arkaden, Oslo's first indoor shopping
centre. He had Nike on his feet, outsize trousers and a Champion
hoodie. Every morning he styled his hair in front of the mirror, parting his fringe in the middle and making several applications of hair gel
so it would stay in place. The tough image was supposed to look acci-
dental, but the troublemaking tagger was very vain and fretted about
his big nose.

The gang of four started on a small scale, spending hours sketching
on paper before they graduated to neighbourhood walls and fences,
or crept into the school grounds in the evening. Later on they took
to sneaking into the local bus station after the buses had stopped running for the night. They carried rucksacks full of spray cans and wrote
their names in hard, angular letters.

Once they had conquered the locality, Morg wanted to go further afield. He bought a map of Oslo and one day Spok came into his room, which was always in immaculate order, to find him sitting like a general about to go into battle. He pointed and outlined, indicating districts of the city, streets and buildings. He knew who the leading taggers were in the areas he wanted to dominate; he knew where they lived and relished the thought of his own signature adorning a wall in their territory. He had reconnoitred to identify the best times for a quick escape. It was as if he were planning a raid or robbery, with detailed routes that included exit strategies if the police turned up. Spok sat there with his innocent baby face, so often his passport out of trouble, quietly taking it all in. When Anders had presented the whole plan, Spok said he thought it was a great idea.

The boys were still 'toys', novices. Though it seemed free and anarchic from the outside, the graffiti community was strictly hierarchical. You had to find which rung of the ladder you were on. Being a toy was fine, most of them were, but it was seen as uncool to be a wannabe, somebody trying to be more than he was.

For the ambitious, the goal was to be a king. That was the title bestowed on the top writers, the ones who were both good and daring. To become a king you had to pull off a memorable stunt, like bombing a whole wall, writing over a whole underground train or tagging somewhere that was under strict surveillance. Your name should be visible in the city centre, the most closely watched place, in the main thoroughfare of Karl Johans gate or along the underground line that runs from the central station via the Parliament to the Royal Palace. There was no point being King of Skøyen.

'How can I get to the top?' Anders asked a classmate, one of the straights, when they were hanging about on the steps by Majorstua metro station after school one day. 'What are *they* doing that I'm not?'

'Well, I suppose you just need to tag in all sorts of places where people can see,' said his classmate. 'Like on that wall there.' He pointed over to the jeweller's shop on the other side of the road.

Anders said nothing, simply crossed straight over to the exclusive jeweller's with its white marble walls, whipped out a felt pen and wrote 'MORG' right across the wall. Then he turned on his heel and walked calmly away with his head held high, across the busy shopping street and out of sight. His classmate was dead impressed. There were heavy fines for tagging. Anders isn't scared of anything, thought his classmate, who had been poised to run.

To climb the ladder you also needed to keep in with the right people. One afternoon the four Year 8 students went over to the taggers' hangout at Egertorget in the middle of Karl Johans gate. The steps down to the Parliament underground station served as their 'Writers' Bench'. They sat round in groups, almost all boys and anything from a handful of kids to around fifty, showing each other sketches, sharing ideas and talking about bombing raids. Here you could find everyone from ultra-reds of the Blitz community to young guys from broken homes, the odd petty criminal and plenty of wild cards. There was a larger proportion of immigrants than in most other gatherings of young Norwegians in the 1990s.

All newcomers were treated with scepticism. You couldn't just turn up at the Writers' Bench. Someone had to vouch for you, someone had to know you. Otherwise you were told to get lost, and if you didn't take the hint you would be forcibly ejected.

If you wanted to stay, you had to prove yourself. You had to bomb your way up. To really earn some cred you had to pass the ultimate test: get arrested and show you wouldn't squeal.

It all started so well. In the mid-1980s, when the graffiti trend crossed the Atlantic, it was seen as a new and interesting youth phenomenon. Norway's first newspaper article on the subject, in the tabloid *Verdens Gang*, used words like 'tremendous professionalism' to describe a 'work' in the underground. The public transport company Oslo Sporveier referred to the writers as 'graffiti artists'. The boys, their names given in full, proudly acknowledged their deed. The only thing the company asked of the youths was that they get permission before letting loose with their aerosol cans along the line.

Over the years that followed, the language changed. It was no longer art but vandalism. Oslo Sporveier claimed the graffiti made its passengers feel less safe. Millions of kroner were spent on cleaning.

'Increasing numbers find their property defaced by this scrawl. We need a swift and forceful response,' said a Progress Party spokesman in Parliament, demanding action from Labour's Minister of Transport.

By the time Anders came on the street scene, words like 'war' and 'hooligans' kept recurring. 'We're fighting a mafia,' a section leader from Oslo Sporveier told the media in the summer of 1993. 'This mafia is well organised, with communication equipment, its own radio station and a magazine. I would call it a war, what's going on between Oslo Sporveier and the graffiti mafia.'

The Oslo Sporveier security guards went out of their way to make life difficult for the repeat offenders. The security guards employed by the Consept company were the ones the taggers found roughest. A few of them were former hired thugs, and occasionally meted out their own kind of justice.

As the 1990s wore on, more and more young people were arrested by the police, and some of them were given prison sentences and astronomical fines amounting to hundreds of thousands of kroner, a debt to the state that would hang over the teenagers into adult life. Those with convictions could no longer go on tagging because the police knew their tags. The prison sentence was often suspended but would be reimposed if there were any further breaches of the law.

When questioning their teen suspects, the police tried to get them to inform on each other. The interviewers tricked many into giving away their mates by saying they had already confessed. It wasn't easy for a fourteen-year-old to stand up to experienced detectives.

The police hunt changed the character of the graffiti scene. Guts started to matter more than talent. There was more daubing, less art. To produce what was called a 'piece', a picture of reasonable size with a number of different motifs and colours, took time, concentration and no disturbance. A successful piece was not something you could just spray up while looking over your shoulder. It became a case of 'hit and run'. 'A society gets the graffiti it deserves,' commented one criminologist on the street galleries that grew ever scruffier.

With the penalties now so severe, the taggers had to make extra sure to eject any potential squealers at an early stage, and it grew even harder for newcomers to join their circle. But luckily for the posh boys from Skøyen, Ahmed knew one of the older taggers, *Minor*. He provided Morg and friends with an entrée to that desirable set of steps.

In the winter of 1994, when Anders was in Year 8 at school, the camera lenses of the world were for once trained on Norway. The government wanted to highlight healthy living, and Members of Parliament appeared on television jumping up and down and slapping their arms to keep warm, under the slogan 'A Fit Nation for the Winter Olympics'.

The Oslo city authorities had a major push to make the city spotlessly clean and shiny, and ran aggressive campaigns to mobilise public opinion against 'vandalism, violence and defacement of the city' in the run-up to the Olympic Games. The Labour city council launched an anti-graffiti campaign that became known as 'Taggerhead'. Posters on the underground showed a boy with an empty expression. The space where his brain should have been was filled with a ball bearing like those inside aerosol paint cans.

The Lillehammer Games of 1994 generated a mood of national excitement, the Norwegian athletes won a string of gold medals and the whole country let itself be intoxicated by Gro Harlem Brundtland's slogan: 'It's typically Norwegian to be good at things.'

Anders, who had just turned fifteen, couldn't have cared less about being good at skiing. He had nothing in common with the aristocracy in knee breeches, up on the hill. Since his last, truncated stay with his weekend parents as a two-year-old, no one had taken him on any Sunday trips to the forest. The city was his jungle.

These were quiet weeks in the capital. It was bitterly cold all over Oslo. The days were an icy blue, the nights clear and starry. Morg did not let temperatures of minus twenty deter him from the only competition that mattered – winning the title of King. Several nights a week he climbed down from the balcony of his apartment to leave his signature on the city.

One night, he and Ahmed traipsed down to the bus station in Skøyen. One of them would keep watch while the other tagged. They swapped places, got freezing cold and swapped again, keeping their arms moving to stay warm. In the middle of the Winter Olympics, at around two in the morning while Morg was on guard, they got caught.

The boys were arrested and taken to the police station. Their parents were called. Their misconduct was reported and registered, but since neither of them had been arrested before, and in view of their age, their punishment was to wash buses for a couple of weeks in the summer holidays. But they were warned to stop tagging and told they would not be let off so lightly next time.

At last they had something to brag about at Egertorget. They had kept their mouths shut.

Anders peppered his story with gestures and phrases he had picked up from the immigrant gangs. Sometimes he substituted Arabic words for Norwegian ones, like the toughs in the hard gangs did.

Fucking hell, it's him again, thought *Net*, a tagger from the East End, in slight irritation. Unaware of each other, Morg and Net had both spent periods at the Centre for Child and Adolescent Psychiatry. Net was a rebellious boy who bristled at the slightest thing. He went to the school at the centre and was under observation at the same time as Anders was attending the nursery there. Having grown up in Grünerløkka, which in the 1980s was a working-class district that Ris parents instructed their offspring to avoid, he had the credibility that Anders lacked. He started tagging when he was twelve and was among the most skilful, a graffiti artist with a style all of his own. In adult life, Net was to become part of the established art world.

'Consept was after us and the law took us,' Anders went on in his immigrant speak, his 'Kebab Norwegian'. 'It was, like, well sick!'

There was furtive laughter from the steps.

Not many West Enders came to Egertorget, so Net had noticed Anders, the nobody with a craving to be let in. But Net could also see that Anders wanted more than simply to hang out there. He was ambitious and determined, not just vaguely interested like so many of the others. Should they accept him?

It was a feeling that ran deep. You just couldn't trust that lot from the other side of town. The West End might have the capital, but the East End boys owned the street: the walls were free.

And anyway, Morg was so ordinary, in Net's opinion. Mediocre. Average. No particular asset to a crew.

Becoming part of a crew was the next step for Anders. Before he could be King. Put his name alongside the greats. But to be part of all that, you had to be invited to join. And the invitation was slow in coming.

As the hard layer of trampled snow turned to slush in March, Morg found himself arrested again. Again he kept his mouth shut. And again he walked free.

In the fifteen years of Anders's lifetime, the number of non-Western immigrants in Norway had risen almost fivefold. In Oslo, the change was even more marked. By about the mid-1990s, a third of those living in the eastern areas of Oslo city centre were from immigrant backgrounds. The largest group was the Pakistani community, who had come to Norway for work in the 1970s. Their children had one foot in each culture; the girls were closely supervised and generally not allowed out after school, the boys had a freer rein.

In Anders's eyes, the foreigners were the heroes. Their gangs were rougher round the edges and tougher than those of the Norwegian kids. The Labour-run city council had bought flats for refugees on the western side of town to counteract the ghetto effect in the east. The flats were in the blocks and terraces round where Anders lived, and were referred to as 'the slum' by the snobs who lived further up the hill in the same school catchment area.

There were sharp contrasts between the socially sheltered Norwegian middle class and the immigrants. Inherited codes of honour that were alien to Norwegians explained some of the conflicts that arose, but often it was just that people found it hard to get along. Wenche grew more and more vocal in her annoyance with the Somali children running round the blocks of flats and making a noise at all hours of day and night, while the foreign arrivals could be bitter about Norwegians who welcomed them by throwing firecrackers onto their balconies. One Somali father on an adjoining staircase armed himself with a bat so he could administer a good hiding to the boys who had sprayed water at his son. 'Don't water my son!' he yelled out over Silkestrå.

It wasn't worth picking fights with the gangs. One of Anders's friends was beaten up by a foreign gang as a payback for something. A few days later, the gang leader was clubbed down by two Norwegians outside the Rimi supermarket and left bleeding in the street. Revenge had to be countered with yet more revenge. One evening, some of the gang members climbed over the wall of the Bygdøy mansion belonging to the shipping billionaire John Fredriksen, the richest man in Norway. His fourteen-year-old twin daughters had friends round at the time, and the boy who had carried out the revenge attack – the boyfriend of one of the daughters – was there. The gang got in through an open window. Their intended target hid in Mrs Fredriksen's wardrobe. They found him, dragged him out, beat him until he was covered in blood, broke his fingers and threw him down a flight of stairs. Leaving the boy lying unconscious on the floor, the gang calmly left.

The gangs had their territories and defended them like young wolves. Where Anders lived, the boundary ran along the tram line. It was wisest to stay on the right side of it. Skøyen, Hoff, Majorstua, Marienlyst and Tåsen were all controlled by different gangs, most of them based on ethnicity, and if any of them needed help they would call in their relations from the East End.

A new term entered the Norwegian vocabulary in the 1990s: child robbery. Gangs would board the underground in the east, cross the city centre and emerge in the west. It was boys against boys, kids against kids. And the kids of Ris had lots of things the kids from the satellite towns wanted. The worst thing was when the gangs decided you were 'indebted'. There was nothing for it but to pay up. A debt often arose out of thin air, or on spurious grounds like 'You looked at me. Now you owe me.' One of the gang might give you a shove and say you were in the way, and as a punishment you would have to pay.

Nobody squealed to the police. You didn't dare.

It was best to cross to the other side of the street when you saw certain Pakistanis or Somalis in a bunch, or get off the underground at the next stop if they were patrolling through the carriages.

The Norwegians got called potatoes.

Fucking darkies, they shouted back.

Yogurtface!

Bloody Pakis!

Anders felt most at home with the brownies.

One day, Morg tagged the windows of the headmaster's office at Ris with spaghetti stripes. Knut Egeland, who demanded almost military discipline of his pupils and often came to school in uniform, was determined to reprimand him. The headmaster came into the classroom where Anders was sitting at his desk before a lesson and punched him in the chest. It was a blow with some force to it. Anders got to his feet and asked if he shouldn't return the punch.

'Hit me if you dare,' replied Egeland. It took a little while, as if Anders were thinking it over, and then he punched the headmaster in the chest, right on his pacemaker. Egeland rocked backwards while the teacher and the other pupils looked on in shock. The old man recovered and hissed, 'An eye for an eye, a tooth for a tooth,' before walking out of the room.

Respect, that was what that punch gave Anders.

The little kids in Skøyen looked up to Morg; they knew that 'last night Morg was here, and here, and there'. He had style, he had attitude. His letters were pointed at the top, rounded at the bottom and had forward-sloping shadows. Great shapes, the younger boys thought. Morg used loads of colour, often lots of different ones, at least three or four, and he favoured soft, pastel shades.

The colours varied, depending on the spray cans available. Among the taggers, the rule was that the paint had to be stolen. They stole it from petrol stations and building suppliers, especially from the big chains, not from the little shops – that was seen as uncool. The boys crept into the stores like thin, hooded shadows, prowled along the shelves and made sure a can or two fell into their rucksacks before coolly going to the counter to buy a cola, or they might simply grab a couple of aerosols and run. The spray cans were expensive, about a hundred kroner each. You needed at least three to four to create a decent piece, not even a particularly big one. Some walls took more paint than others: old stone walls soaked up the spray paint like mad, but for smoother surfaces like buses and trams you didn't need as much.

Anders didn't want to steal. He wanted to buy. Go to the checkout and pay.

In Denmark the spray cans were a quarter of the price. Morg, Spok and Wick made a plan to catch the ferry over to Copenhagen; they would only need to be away for two nights and they told their parents they were staying over at each other's. Altogether they bought almost three hundred cans, lugging heavy bags home with them on the ferry. As the ship pulled out of the harbour, the fourteen-year-olds' names were called over the loudspeaker system. There was nothing for it but to report to the captain. They spent the rest of the night sitting on the bridge, under arrest.

It was Spok's parents who had suspected something was up, and it did not take many phone calls before they worked out what was going on. They rang the ferry company, which immediately found the boys on the passenger list.

What's all the fuss about, Morg's mother said when Spok's father told her they had found the boys on the ferry from Denmark. He thought her irresponsible; she thought he was overreacting. Spok and Wick found their parents waiting on the quayside in Oslo the next morning. Nobody had come for Anders.

Spok's parents did all they could to get their son out of what they saw as a negative environment. Spok started playing football as a cover, but continued to juggle the two worlds, the straight and the crooked, and went on tagging.

Anders was the one driving him on. He was running his own race and had systems for everything. His mother had now moved into a terrace of flats in Konventveien, where he stacked all the dearly acquired aerosol cans along by the wall under the veranda. He arranged them by number and colour codes in long, shining rows. He hoarded more of some colours and those cans protruded further out from the wall than the rest. Green. Orange. Yellow. Silver.

Inside the flat, beyond the spray cans, there was another war, sometimes cold and sometimes hot. The neighbours could hear the exchanges through the thin walls. Elisabeth's teen rebellion had arrived with a vengeance. Doors slammed, glasses and saucepans went flying and hit the walls. The girl had years of anger to vent.

As a rule, Anders vanished into his room whenever his mother and sister were arguing, and only appeared in the kitchen for meals. Then it was Elisabeth's turn to leave the room. She refused to eat with her mother and half-brother, and usually sat in her room on her own with a plate on her lap.

But outside the home, Elisabeth blossomed. She was attractive and popular, witty and amusing. And she wanted to get away. Away from her mother, away from Silkestrå, away from Norway. When she was eighteen, she went to America as an au pair. California was the place for her. Now she was saving up to go back; for good, she hoped.

While Anders was at secondary school, Wenche started going out with an army officer. Tore and Anders got on well with each other. He was a warm person and easy to be with. For a few years he was a sort of father figure for Anders, though he didn't hide the fact that he thought Anders was a bit of a weakling, clumsy and awkward at men's jobs like hammering in nails and mending bikes.

Once Anders was in his teens, he was able to go by himself on his bike to his father's place in Fritzners gate when he was invited to dinner. They sometimes played Monopoly or Trivial Pursuit, and his father helped him with his homework. On one occasion his father invited him on a trip to Copenhagen. But theirs was never a close relationship. Jens was basically dissatisfied with his son and annoyed by his habits. He stayed in bed late and when he finally got up, he prepared himself about ten slices of bread to eat in front of the television, his father complained. He found him lazy and unenthusiastic, apathetic and taciturn. He wasn't very curious or eager to learn, his father remarked. No, the boy liked the easy life and being waited on, Jens thought.

Anders's father did notice, however, that he sometimes seemed vulnerable and sad, as if there were something troubling him. But Anders never shared any problems with him or said what the matter was.

The boy was craving love and attention, and it was as if he longed for something that was missing in his life, his father later admitted. But he was incapable of meeting the boy's needs. He remained aloof and never made Anders feel loved.

The first time Anders was caught tagging, the police rang both his parents. His father was outraged that Anders had committed a criminal act. He threatened to cut off all contact with him.

The second time it happened he reacted coldly.

Anders promised not to do any more tagging. His father contented himself with that.

Anders was developing a steady hand. He didn't mess anything up, the paint didn't bubble, the lines came out even, without wobbling. He applied the silver spray paint without letting it drip onto or dust the black, while still keeping the colour even and filling in the whole picture.

But one day somebody openly mocked Morg on Egertorget. Mocked his inflated ambition. His boastfulness, his exaggerated hip-hop walk and the way he wore his trousers back to front to be cool. Trousers that were to be as outsized as those worn in music videos.

The taunts continued the next time he came along. And the next. Morg seemingly took no notice. Ahmed wasn't there any more. He had been expelled from Ris for making trouble and now hung out with friends and relations in the East End. Spok and Wick found themselves caught in the middle. They didn't play an active part in the bullying, but took an imperceptible step back whenever it started. They didn't want to risk being dragged into anything. On the way home, Anders tried to make a joke of the whole thing.

It didn't take long for the big taggers to show Morg that he was no longer welcome. They didn't say it outright, just went from openly ridiculing him to totally ignoring him.

'I didn't have the balls to do anything,' admitted Spok many years later. 'I just stood there like a moron and hoped they wouldn't start on me.'

Anders had committed a cardinal sin. He hadn't known his place. He was a toy but had behaved like a king. In other words, like a wannabe.

Anders fought tooth and nail to keep his place in the community. But the bullying spread to his own little clique and his friends deserted him.

A pitiless panel composed of Wick and Spok delivered the *coup de grâce*.

Morg was thrown out of the gang.

At a much later date, when Wick was called in to be interviewed by the police about the friend with whom he had broken sixteen years before, he reverted to the value judgements of a teenage tagger: 'He belonged to the cool gang for a while, even though he wasn't cool. He was basically a fifth wheel. In the end we wouldn't put up with him any longer.'

The logic was clear. 'We soon realised we wouldn't get anywhere with Anders in tow, so we had to make a choice. Either stand up for him or join one of the top taggers.'

With Anders gone from the Writers' Bench, both Spok and Wick were recruited by good crews and went on tagging.

Cool or not cool, that was the question.

But Anders didn't give up tagging. If he just carried on, if he just got better and better, they would have to acknowledge him and he could be a king after all.

He started tagging with boys younger than himself. Boys who hadn't picked up on the fact that Anders wasn't hip any more.

One of them was a skinny little kid from one of the biggest houses in the neighbourhood, whose parents were away a lot. He was in the year below Anders at Ris, did a bit of tagging and was dumbfounded by the sight of the arsenal of aerosol cans neatly stowed under the veranda. Anders used to spend a lot of time considering the colours he would use, weighing the cans in his hand before he covered up his palette along the wall so it couldn't be seen from the path.

The top taggers were obsessive about having all their equipment in order, while the small fry went round aimlessly, without a plan.

One evening Anders pointed out a place he wanted to tag. He had his eye on a piece done by one of the big names. The younger tagger protested.

'No way. You can't write over that!'

'I tag where I like,' said Anders as he took the first paint can out of his bag.

In addition to the countless understandings about what was cool, the graffiti community had two absolute rules that should not be broken: don't tell on anyone, and don't tag over other writers' pieces.

There were subtle, fluid exceptions. A king could write over the tag of a toy, but not the other way round. Someone good could write over someone bad. A big, coloured piece was permitted to cover a simple tag. A piece that was starting to fade could be written over, if you asked the permission of the person who had put it up. You could make the judgement yourself, but it had better be a good one.

'Let's find a bare wall instead.'

'No, I want to tag here,' insisted Anders in the darkness of the bus station.

'You gotta ask first!'

Anders turned to the wall. He flicked the cap off the spray can and raised his hand.

He pressed the button.

The spray hit the wall, spreading over the other tagger's name.

MORG it said, for the passengers to read the next morning.

MORG, it informed the tagger whose signature had been obliterated.

A king could do what he wanted.

Not a toy.

He had thrown down the gauntlet.

Just before Christmas when he was in Year 9, Anders went by himself to Copenhagen to replenish his stock of spray cans. He bought all the colours he needed, put them in his bag and caught the train home. On 23 December, when he got to Oslo Central, he was stopped by the police. They confiscated the contents of his bag – forty-three cans of spray paint – and sent him to the child welfare duty officer, who informed his home. The officer wrote the following report: 'Mother not aware he had been in Denmark. He went to Denmark once before without telling his mother. The records show the boy received two previous warnings for tagging and vandalism in February and March 1994.'

The child welfare office conducted interviews with Anders and his mother in the new year and logged that the latter was concerned her son might be turning to crime. There was 'genuine concern about his involvement in the tagging community,' wrote the child welfare officer. 'Such communities are known for activities and behaviour bordering on the criminal. The boy himself claims he no longer spends his time with any tagging community.'

Anders was certainly right about that. He no longer had a community.

The child welfare log ended as follows:

02.02.95: Letter from Anders that he no longer wishes to co-operate with the child welfare authorities, as a result of 'disclosures' at school.

07.02.95: Meeting scheduled with the boy at the office. Did not attend.

13.02.95: Meeting scheduled with mother and son at the office. Neither attended.

Not turning up to a pre-arranged meeting was an effective tactic for avoiding the spotlight of the child welfare office. The case was not pursued because it was 'not judged serious enough to warrant intervention and support on the part of child welfare officers'.

'Morg's squealed.'

At Egertorget, the boys sat talking. Net wasn't surprised when word spread. Nobody knew what he had said, who he had informed on, or whether anyone had been arrested as a result. It didn't help. Once the rumour was out, you were marked.

Backs were all that Anders saw now. No one wanted anything to do with him.

School became an extension of the nightmare. As soon as Anders appeared, whether it was before lessons or in the evening, kids ganged up on him. And these were people not remotely connected to the tagging community. He had turned into someone everybody could trample on. His favourite phrases were circulated and mocked, and his big nose was caricatured.

Anders started lifting weights, ideally twice a day. He developed quickly, from thin and weak to broad and strong. His classmates wondered if he was on steroids. At Ris, weight training was seen as far from cool; it was only years later that it became trendy.

Anders was left sitting alone now. Well, not invariably. Sometimes he sat with a couple of others from the fourth group: the losers.

'Outcasts stick together,' laughed the cool kids.

The class yearbook had a damning verdict:

'Anders used to be part of the "gang" but then he made enemies of everybody,' was the book's summary for the leavers of spring 1995. 'Anders has staked it all on getting a perfect body, but we have to say he's still got quite a way to go. Apart from that, Anders spends a lot of time in Denmark getting materials for his "art". In Year 7, Anders had something going with X, but now he's got an admirer in Tåsen (with red hair and freckles). Anders often does stupid, unprovoked things, such as hitting the headteacher.'

The piece finished by saying he now hung out with the losers in the class, who were mentioned by name. Nobody got off lightly.

Anders was desperate to find out who had written it, so he could beat him up.

The girl in the class with whom Anders was said to have had 'something going' was also furious with whoever had composed the entry. It amounted to bullying, because being together with Anders was the last thing anybody would think of. They would be outcasts themselves, then.

It all came back, crystal clear, to Morg's former friend Wick when the police put the yearbook in front of him sixteen years later.

'Yes, that's how it was,' said Wick, the tall, dark one in the gang. Then he suggested a slight rewording: 'Not enemies, it was just that he was pushed out. Not wanted in the gang any more.'

As he sat in the sterile interview room trying to define why Anders was rejected, Wick recalled everything in minute detail. He remembered a pair of outsized hip-hop jeans, a make called Psycho Cowboy. The jeans were very popular, but disappeared overnight, after a few months of fashion hype.

Then they were 'one of the worst things to be seen in', recalled Wick. 'And Anders went on wearing his just a bit too long.'

Is there anything worse than being rejected by your friends?

Yes, perhaps there is.

Being disowned by your father.

After his third arrest, Jens Breivik made it clear to Anders that he wanted nothing more to do with him. His son had broken his promise to give up tagging.

The decision was final.

Anders was fifteen.

He would never see his father again.

To Damascus

There is fighting in the streets of Erbil. Blood wets the sand that covers the cracked asphalt. Rubbish is mixed with desert dust and the stench of war fills the alleyways and squares. Life has gone underground, and flickers over a low flame.

It is 1996.

The Iraqi army has withdrawn, and the war being fought is no longer for freedom, but between the Kurds themselves, for power and money. Erbil is a city where old rivalries are never forgotten, only intensified and mythologised by fresh killings leading to further years of blood feud and enmity. Kurdistan is ripping and hacking itself to pieces. The fighters occupying the city are choking it to death.

Every night families are torn apart. Children are killed by other children's fathers, or by young men who might become fathers one day.

In the cellars, people sit in darkness for days, weeks, months, while the militias battle it out above their heads. Children try to invent a game down there, in the cellars, because children will always want to play. Fathers are nervous and restless; should they be taking up arms as well? Should they be choosing sides? Should they?

Mustafa chooses life.

He is holding a four-year-old in his arms. Bano, his firstborn. With bullets whizzing through the streets above them and rockets landing God knows where, he wonders how to cope with everyday existence, how to find food for his family, how to get water, fuel and all the rest of it.

'Why must we stay in here?' whines the little girl. 'I want to go up!'

Not a single glimmer of light finds its way into the cold room. It's a relief that their neighbour built a proper cellar.

'Let's go up and play,' begs Bano.

This little girl, conceived and born when snow was in the air, who wants to be part of everything, to have answers to everything – she is the apple of his eye. She learnt to walk at nine months, to put together long sentences when she was two; now she talks like a schoolgirl.

Bayan is sitting with Bano's little sister on her lap. Lara was born eighteen months after Bano. Bayan had wanted a boy. She comes from a traditional family, where a woman gains worth and status only once she has borne a son. Now she is pregnant for the third time, and the oppressive cellar atmosphere is making her queasiness worse. She groans. This isn't how life was meant to be.

Suddenly there is a huge bang. The house shakes, its framework creaks. Something shatters and makes a tinkling noise as it falls to the ground. The windows? The crockery?

The children wail, and terrified shouts can be heard. The parents sit there numbly, ready to evacuate the cellar if they have to. Two girls who share the darkness with them start to cry. The elders recite from the Qur'an, a stream of mumbling verse coming from their barely open mouths. Sirens pierce the night.

But the house stays standing, the cellar does not collapse or get filled with falling earth or plaster, no beams come crashing down. Is it over?

Not for the children. Lara is too upset to settle. Bano is crying hysterically. She turns her head to her father in the darkness.

'Why did you want children when you knew there was a war?'

Mustafa sits in silence, rocking his daughter to comfort her. Then he hands her abruptly to her mother. He goes up the narrow flight of steps and opens the door onto the night. Something's on fire, just down the street. Black smoke is rising into the air. A rocket has hit his neighbour's house. One daughter is dead.

Before the next day is over, the neighbour's twelve-year-old has been buried.

That evening, once they had put the children to bed and mumbled an assurance that tonight they would be safe, Mustafa and Bayan sat up talking. Mustafa had made his mind up. Bayan hesitated. They took the decision before morning came. They wanted to leave Iraq.

If only they could just have left, taken flight. But Iraq was one big prison. Without an exit permit they would get nowhere; the borders were closely guarded. Iraq was a land that was difficult to go to, hard to live in and almost impossible to leave. Mustafa, who was still a mechanical engineer at the water and sewage works in the city, tried to make contacts who might be able to help them. He offered bribes, he saved up and started currency dealing, looking desperately for a way out. His children should not grow up in fear of their lives.

A son was born, and Bayan could finally call herself *Umm Ali*, mother of Ali. They celebrated; civil war or not, a child is still a source of joy.

A year passed, then two, and in the third, Bano started school. Mustafa got her a decent pair of shoes; he bought a rucksack and a water bottle. Everything of quality, that was important now she was entering a new phase of her life, he told himself.

School life suited Bano well; she was mature for her age and had spent a lot of time indoors, where she loved to read. Lara was less well behaved, and more daring, always getting dirty, clambering around the bombsites to discover things, playing at war in the ruins with her cousins Ahmed and Abdullah. Lara was always the boss. She was the best of friends with the two boys and played them off against each other whenever it suited her. As the middle child, she was left more to her own devices, and was more independent than her sister;

Bano had grown accustomed to attention and admiration, and thrived when people noticed her.

To survive the rampant inflation and be able to save up for their escape, Mustafa and Bayan both worked full time. The grandmothers looked after all the cousins while their parents were at work.

To get passports, Mustafa invented a story involving a pilgrimage to Zeinab's shrine in Damascus. Zeinab was the granddaughter of the prophet Muhammad. According to the Shia Muslims she was buried in Damascus, while the Sunnis claimed she was laid to rest in Cairo. Three summers after the fatal rocket hit their neighbours' house and burnt the eldest daughter to death, the local authorities approved their application to make the pilgrimage.

The parents didn't tell the girls they would not be coming back. Their daughters could give the game away, as zealous intelligence officers at the border could be expected to question the children. They would only take a small amount of luggage with them, so as not to give away their plan to escape.

On the Thursday before their departure, Bano was chosen as *pupil of the week* at school. She received a little plaque, which she put up on the wall above her bed, and couldn't make out why her grandmother was in such floods of tears. She was delighted with the award and hung her school uniform neatly in the wardrobe, ready for when they got back from the pilgrimage.

The morning they were due to leave, there was a total solar eclipse. They had heard you could go blind if you looked at the sun before it disappeared, so the family stayed inside all day.

The following night, Mustafa could not sleep. For decades, the nights had been the worst. Nights were the time when the Ba'ath party militias came for people, consigning them to torture and never-ending darkness in the dungeons of Saddam Hussein. The soldiers would turn the house upside down in their search for weapons or banned manifestos and writings. They would smash down doors or sneak in over the flat roofs where families dried clothes, stored junk or kept hens. No windows were secure, no doors, reinforcements or locks could keep out the forces of the state. The neighbourhood was sometimes awoken by the sound of men howling. They knew it was all over when the Ba'ath Party arrived.

During the worst spells of political terror – the bomb attacks and street fighting – Mustafa would toss and turn, waiting for dawn. The days were safer than the nights. He lay there listening in the darkness. You didn't need to open your eyes to know daylight was on its way. Daylight, even before the sun had risen, meant the sound of Primus stoves being lit, the smell of fresh bread, the first shuffle of footsteps down below, the click of the door handle as someone went out to get some flatbread before it ran out. Daylight meant the first call to prayer, while it was still dark. Only when the muezzin's holy words had died away, when the real morning arrived with farmers offering freshly strained yogurt, white cheese with salt, tea and bread, only then could he relax and sleep.

If you didn't hear the lighting of the stoves or smell the fresh bread it was a signal that the city was under attack, or that there had been warning of an attack, and there was a state of *Maneh al-Tajawel* – a curfew.

That August morning they got up before daylight, before the heat arrived. They all squashed into a car, so tightly packed that none of them could turn and look back at the house with the flat roof where the line of clothes would soon dry in the sun.

They drove out into the desert. Out here on the sandy plains, Abbasid, Moguls, Turkmens, Mongols, Persians and Ottomans had built their civilisations. They had all fought fiercely for Erbil – *the four gods* – as the city's name means. Here Alexander did battle with the Persian king Darius, here the first soldiers of Islam fought for their faith, and this land was the original home of the Kurdish warrior hero Saladin, who captured Jerusalem from the Crusaders.

Over the centuries, the city had become increasingly difficult to seize, situated as it was behind high walls on a flat-topped mountain reaching ever closer to the sky. It was a man-made mountain, created by people rebuilding on the ruins of those they had conquered. Now only the old town still lay behind the walls; the settlement had over-flowed onto the plain, where it lay unprotected from desert storms and militia feuds alike.

Bayan was already regretting it all. There was no way it could end well. This was where they belonged. This was where they ought to live and die.

Mustafa gave her hand a squeeze. 'Everything will be all right in the end,' he said.

Though they had an exit permit from Iraq, they took a smuggling route as they approached the border because they had no Syrian entry permit. Half the money had already been handed over and a relation would pay the rest once Mustafa rang to say they were there. They had no idea where 'there' was. Nor did the smugglers, yet.

The family of five was crammed into a little boat with many other refugees. The boat set off to cross the Khabur River, a tributary of the Tigris. The banks were patrolled by Iraqi and Syrian troops on their respective sides.

Bayan cried throughout the crossing. 'Imagine, I'm leaving my country! How can I leave my country?'

Lara, now five, regarded her parents in bafflement. It was strange to see them unhappy. They were the ones who looked after her, Bano and Ali. Now she had her turn to comfort *them*. Why did they have to go on this journey if it made everyone so sad?

Bano was uneasy too. Mustafa tried to hold her attention with a story about a girl who fell out of a boat into the water. That little girl fell over the side because she couldn't sit still, and was eaten up by a big fish, a huge fish. Mustafa was groping for words, an enormous fish, and then she lived there, in the belly of the fish, with all the other children the fish gradually gobbled up. Mustafa was just talking away because he was afraid the soldiers on the bank would notice the boat and start firing. 'And then the fish spat out all the children onto the shore,' he improvised.

Bano suddenly interrupted his story. 'Daddy, we're going to die now,' she said.

Her mother flinched.

'I feel so close to God,' Bano said to no one in particular. 'It's as if I'm in the clouds, looking down on you. The clouds are under me. I can see you in the boat, down below. I can see you all together.'

Mustafa started to pray.

God, There is no god but He, Living and Everlasting. Neither slumber over-takes Him nor sleep. To Him belongs what is in the heavens and what is on earth.

The others sat motionless in the boat while Mustafa quoted from the prayer *Ayat al-Kursi*. This was the prayer he always turned to when he was lying awake at nights feeling frightened.

He knows their present affairs and their past. And they do not grasp of His knowledge except what He wills. His throne encompasses the heavens and the earth; Preserving them is no burden to him. He is the Exalted, the Majestic.

After this prayer he asked God to protect Bayan and the children, and, as is the Muslim way, he put his hands in front of his face, then held them out and blew, as if to blow the prayer up to God. Finally he turned his face out to the waves and blew for as long as his breath would allow him.

The engine stopped. They slid in towards a sandbank and the boat made gentle contact with the Syrian shore. A waiting car took them to the Kurdish town of Qamishli, where they spent the night before travelling on to Damascus. In the Syrian capital, with its carved façades, beautiful palaces and spies on every corner, they stayed in a small room.

Nobody bothered them, and they bothered nobody. Bayan felt as if the heat and dust were settling on her in a layer. She missed her kitchen, her cool living room, her sisters.

After a month in Damascus, they were issued with Iraqi passports and plane tickets to Moscow.

In the Russian capital, they were accommodated in an Aeroflot hotel at Sheremetyevo airport. A man came up to their hotel room and gave them an envelope with some new tickets in it.

The destination was written in Cyrillic script – it had four letters.

Asking for Protection

'They've all got fair hair,' exclaimed Bano. Dressed in a bright green top and orange skirt, she was running across the pale wooden floor of the airport. Bayan had bought colourful clothes for the children at a market in Damascus. Lara was in a sunshine-yellow dress and Ali was in red. That way it would be easier to keep track of the children on the journey, Bayan had decided.

They walked along a corridor in the brand-new arrivals hall and Mustafa spelled his way through the notice *Welcome to Oslo Airport*. The soaring ceiling was clad in light wood and the dividing walls were of clear glass and concrete, while the floor was laminated wood or slate flagstones. Going along the corridor, they could see out on one side to the spruce forest over which they had just flown, and on the other they were looking down on the people who were about to board flights. They came to a kind of conveyor belt and the little girls stood wide-eyed as the floor carried them forward.

But most of their attention was focused on the people.

'Princess hair, real princess hair,' Lara whispered to Bano.

Their passports and visas were in order, so they slid through passport control. The luggage arrived and they walked out of the terminal building.

Outside, people were lightly dressed for the unusually warm September day. To the Iraqi arrivals it felt cool.

They had never seen so much greenery all in one go. Even the roadsides were a mass of green. Areas of green heath and fields sped by on the other side of the car window. The forest seemed to go on for ever.

Then they saw a few scattered tower blocks, then more, and soon they were down in the hollow where Oslo lies and they could see out over the fjord and all the little islands. Now they were driving along streets with pavements, there was a tunnel, and they were in the city. They went straight to the police station.

'My name is Mustafa Abobakar Rashid. I am a Kurd from Iraq and I want to seek asylum for myself and all my family.'

They had their details taken and were sent to the Tanum transit and reception centre, where they were registered again and had interviews and health checks.

'What an awful place,' complained Bayan. The room they had been given was cramped and there were people everywhere, people crying and shouting and quarrelling in every language under the sun, all of them gesticulating wildly.

'It's going to be fine,' said Mustafa. 'Here we won't have to worry about how to get fuel and food. Look, there's water in the taps, clean drinking water, and heat in the stoves. And the most important thing is that there's no war, and nobody who wishes us ill. We can sleep soundly here.'

A few days later they were moved to a centre for asylum seekers. Mustafa was optimistic. 'You see, we'll soon have a house of our own,' he told Bayan. His wife was sceptical, and asked him to see if he could press their case and get things moving.

Bano started at the centre's school and learnt to sing Norwegian children's songs. She was given books and coloured pencils, while Lara was sent to the centre's kindergarten with Ali. Mustafa dipped deep into their travel budget to buy a big dictionary at a cost of five hundred kroner. He pored over it every evening. 'We've got to know the language if we're going to get jobs,' he said, learning lists of words by rote.

The months passed. They were getting nowhere. Perhaps they wouldn't even be allowed to stay. They could be sent back. The atmosphere at Nesbyen asylum centre was one of gloom and despondency. Some of the people suffered mental health problems. Young men fired up with adrenalin and hope felt their lives were falling apart. Inevitably there was trouble.

How much Bayan regretted that they'd come! This is wrong, she thought. She felt worn to the bone. By their flight, by her fear, by all the things she had to cope with. In Erbil she had had a big house and her own place to cook. Here there were five of them in one room, and she had to queue up to cook their meals on the dirty electric rings.

Bayan clashed with the Somali women; she felt they did just as they liked and ignored the kitchen rules. Bano and Lara argued with everybody. Alinda hit Ali, so Lara hit Alinda, and that was how the children spent their days. Swearwords were among the first items of Norwegian vocabulary Bano and Lara picked up; some of the children had been in Norway longer than they had. Ali had his toys stolen, some of Bano and Lara's things went missing. The dream of all people from every corner of the globe living in harmony with each other was severely tested in this place where everybody blamed and gossiped about each other. Who would be allowed to stay? Who would have to go? And why do they get to stay when we have to go? Grudges and jealousy, not unity and solidarity, were the hallmark of the Nesbyen asylum centre.

Of course things had been difficult back home but in this barren land, where all the leaves had abruptly fallen from the trees and all the colours had gone, Kurdistan appeared in a beautiful and rosy light. The ground froze solid and darkness descended. Winter depression set in long before the season truly arrived.

Bayan lied about it whenever she wrote or rang home. 'Yes, it's really nice here,' she said. 'We've got a good house, lovely and quiet.' She felt guilty about lying, but she couldn't face telling her family, relatively prosperous by Erbil standards, how far they had sunk.

'Remember your dad's an engineer,' she impressed on Bano, liking to see herself as better than the others at the centre.

In one of his asylum interviews, Mustafa asked for somewhere else to live, saying how cramped it was for three children and two adults in one room.

'So you thought you could come to Norway and get a house, eh?' asked the interviewer, while Mustafa bowed his head.

In October 2000, just over a year after they arrived in Norway, the family was allocated to a local-council district – Nesodden, a peninsula in the Oslo fjord. They moved into a flat with three bedrooms, a green kitchen and a little living room.

They would have preferred to live with most of the other Kurds in the centre of Oslo, but the ferry over to the heart of the capital took barely half an hour, they consoled themselves.

Nesodden is a peaceful spot. In summer, the peninsula is crisscrossed by footpaths and tracks. Bathing places lie like pearls along the water's edge. In winter, the cross-country skiing trails take over from the paths, and people can easily do without cars. This is the chosen home of those who want to escape the bustle of the city but still like to get quickly to the latest production at the Oslo Opera House if the fancy strikes them, the choice of those who want the best of both worlds and it is here, on Nesodden, that the Rashid family ended up.

In the middle of the school year, Lara was put in Year 1 and Bano in Year 2 at Nesoddtangen School.

Lara soon felt left out. Nobody wanted to play with her. 'We can't understand what you're saying!' laughed the other girls in the class.

Bano coped better. Suddenly the roles were reversed. Pampered Bano proved tough while her sister Lara, always the strong, independent one, seemed to lose all her confidence.

'Don't play with her, she's really stupid,' the girls said to their classmates whenever Lara came up. 'This is a game for those who speak Norwegian.'

'But I can speak Norwegian!' objected Lara.

'We mean speak it *properly*,' they retorted.

The Rashid girls were different from the others in so many ways. For their school lunches their mother often gave them leftover portions of yesterday's dinner. 'Eugh, your lunches stink!' someone said. 'Don't sit near us!'

The other girls had pink rucksacks with hearts or Barbies on, the Rashid sisters had cheap brown ones. They were endlessly picked on for those rucksacks, for their clothes from the second-hand shop, for their weird parents, their weird accents; they were even teased for having extra Norwegian lessons. 'What do you two actually do in your extra lessons? You never seem to learn anything!'

So much for diversity.

Nesodden is known as an open-minded sort of place, one where advocates of alternative teaching methods and vegetarianism have more supporters than other parts of the country, and where the concentration of artists, both established and unrecognised, supplies the idyll with local colour. But for the two Kurdish girls, it was narrow-mindedness that dogged them at the start.

Bullying behaviour was not always picked up on at the after-school club, and every day Lara's school bag would be hidden somewhere different.

'Tell me where it is!' begged Lara.

'Eh? What did you say? We don't understand what you're saying!'

One day they poured milk into her shoes. She never said anything about the bullying at home. Her mother and father still hadn't found jobs, and they were out of sorts and missing their former home.

But when a new gang of boys started hassling Lara, she finally told her mother. Bayan went round to see the parents of each of the boys and demanded they be made to stop.

'Crybaby!', 'Telltale!' were the names hurled at Lara the next day at school.

'My mum took no notice of yours anyway,' said one of the worst offenders. 'She couldn't tell what she was saying! Ha ha!'

And this was supposed to be some sort of paradise?

They had ended up in the wrong place.

*

At the after-school club, the sisters would often sit drawing. Lara always drew princesses with wavy, light yellow hair, blue eyes and pastel-coloured dresses. She could have wallpapered her room with all her versions of yellow hair and pink tulle.

Bano's lines were rougher. If she drew princesses, hers always had dark skin and black hair.

'That's the wrong colour,' a girl said to Bano.

Bano gave her a hard stare. 'It's my picture,' she replied. 'I'll draw what I like.'

'But it looks ugly.'

Bano just went on with her colouring. She made the face on the sheet of paper darker and darker. She added thicker strokes of black to the hair.

Then she held the picture up in front of her.

'There,' she said. 'Now she's exactly the way I want her.'

Bano found a drawing pin and put the dark girl up on the wall.

Lara kept her eyes fixed on her big sister.

That was how she wanted to be. Almost imperceptibly she raised her head, putting down the light yellow crayon.

A Place on the List

Get rich or die trying.

Progress Party Youth debate forum,
Anders Behring, 11 August 2003

He's walking with the West End at his back, towards Youngstorget square.

Right after New Year he had received the invitation to the inaugural meeting. He had marked the date on the calendar and put on a suit to mark the occasion. He often dressed that way these days, in a perfectly ordinary suit, nothing fancy, but it had to look expensive. He was good at wearing things with flair so they seemed expensive; he'd got that from his mother. She often found cheap clothes in sales that could be made to look exclusive in combination with her cool, blonde appearance. From her he had also learned to treat his clothes with care. He always hung them up on hangers after he'd worn them, or put them back in the cupboard, neatly folded. He always changed when he got home to make his nicer, brand-name garments last longer.

He held himself upright as he made his way along the slushy street. His steps were a little cautious. He called himself metrosexual; he dressed up, wore make-up and used vitamin-enriched hair products. He had ordered Regaine from America, which promised to stop hair loss and trigger the follicles into new growth. He could still conceal his incipient bald patch with a good cut but his hairline was definitely receding. There was a great deal about his appearance that grieved him and he spent a long time in front of the mirror. Too long, thought his friends, who would laugh whenever he overdid the make-up. When he started wearing foundation, they teased him even more. It's concealer, he objected. In summer he applied bronzing powder, and he kept a whole row of aftershaves in the bathroom.

His nose was new. An experienced surgeon had made a small incision, removed some bone and cartilage from below the bridge and sewn the skin tautly back in place. When the bandage was removed, his nose was just as he wanted it, as it ought to be: a straight profile, quite simply, an Aryan nose.

At secondary school they had made fun of his bumpy nose. The kink in the bone had annoyed him since his early teenage years. Later he complained to friends that the shape of his nose made him look like an Arab. As soon as he could afford it he booked himself in for surgery at Bunæs, one of Norway's leading plastic surgery clinics. He also asked about a hair transplant, but was told the results were unpredictable and the transplant process could leave disfiguring scars, so he had not made up his mind yet.

He crossed the government quarter, where you could walk straight through the main building, past the reception area under the Prime Minister's office. That was the quickest route; it saved some metres and several minutes not having to go round what was known as the Tower Block.

The government quarter was a fusion of functionalism and brutalism dating from the 1950s. The architect commissioned to design it, modernist Erling Viksjø, made so bold as to ask Pablo Picasso if he would design murals for the complex. Enthused by the Norwegian architect's raw concrete, the artist agreed to produce some sketches. If he liked them, the Norwegians could use them. The project was kept strictly secret, under the code name Operation Pedersen. Picasso's lines were marked into the concrete before the wall was pebble-dashed with rounded river stones and the lines were then sandblasted. It was Picasso's first monumental work. The reliefs of his *The Fishermen* took up the entire end wall of one of the buildings, and if lucky enough to be invited to the higher floors you could admire several more of Picasso's works adorning the staircase in the Tower Block.

The Prime Minister's office was at the top of the building, on the seventeenth floor. On this unusually mild January evening in 2002, the incumbent was Kjell Magne Bondevik of the Christian Democratic Party. For now, the office was empty because the Prime Minister was in Shanghai, where he had just enjoyed a fine array of fish dishes prepared by Chinese and Norwegian chefs using raw ingredients from the fish farms along the Norwegian coast. In his speech, the Prime Minister spoke enthusiastically about aquaculture and generously offered Norwegian fishery expertise to a billion Chinese.

One government building from the turn of the previous century was preserved when the old neoclassical quarter was demolished; its decoration was inspired by medieval motifs and incorporated dragon-style ornamentation derived from Snorri Sturluson's history of the Norse kings. On the pediments flanking the main entrance were the opening words of the national anthem, 'Yes, we love this country,' with the line of music engraved alongside. These buildings which the young man was just passing housed Norway's centre of power. The High Court was here, the Prime Minister's office and the major government departments.

To get to the next seat of power – Youngstorget – you crossed Einar Gerhardsen's Square, where the low, circular base of a fountain was empty for the winter. From there, a narrow footpath ran down to Møllergata. Just to the left was number 19 – the police station that the Nazis had used as a torture chamber during the Second World War. The collaborator Vidkun Quisling was arrested and held in the building after the Nazi's defeat, until he was executed by firing squad one October night in 1945.

On the other side of the square stood an imposing red-brick building. High on the wall were a rose and a sign saying *Labour Party*. With its monumental air, the building was reminiscent of one of Stalin's

Moscow skyscrapers – though on a more modest scale – a nod to the functionalism of the 1930s.

All the labour-movement organisations were based in this part of town. The House of the People, where the Confederation of Trade Unions had its headquarters, dominated one whole side of the square. In the corner between the two buildings stood a tall bronze statue – a worker with a sledgehammer over his shoulder, on his way to his factory shift. Every May Day a wreath was laid at his feet. It was here at Youngstorget that thousands of socialists, communists and Labour Party supporters rallied before setting out on their march through Oslo to mark International Workers' Day.

As the man in the suit crossed the square, the area looked rather run down, with a number of shops standing empty. The district had acquired a reputation as the seediest in Oslo, a neighbourhood of strip clubs and little kebab shops. But things were about to change. The rockers would soon take over. Music nerds would open bars and cafés and hipsters would start heading down here to hear new bands and drink beer.

As for him, he preferred the established bars and nightclubs for the young West Enders with plenty of money to spend. He lived right by Frogner Park, in what he called the most prestigious district in Oslo. No matter that the flat he shared with some fellow students from the Commerce School was dark and uninviting, the address was exclusive.

Down here, on the other hand, was where the alternative, leftie types, the immigrants and the people on benefits lived. A quarter of the pupils at the school in Møllergata were from Somalia, and only a small minority were ethnic Norwegians.

Side by side with the Labour Party stronghold was a much lower building, painted in the pale pink of a marzipan rose. It had an unobtrusive entrance beside a fish shop. On its façade, shining letters announced *Fremskrittspartiet* – the Progress Party.

He opened the door and went up to the first floor. On the stairs he passed posters with slogans like 'You are Unique!' and 'Born Free, Taxed to Death'. In the offices hung a large flag with the logo of the

Progress Party Youth. The toilet walls were adorned with press cuttings of stupid things said by the Socialist Left.

In his pocket he had a pack of Lucky Strikes, a lighter and a pen. He was the type who took notes.

'Anders Behring.'

He said his name clearly, emphasising every syllable.

'Do you come from the Bering Strait?' laughed Thomas Wist-Kirkemo, one of the early arrivals.

'My name does indeed,' Anders replied. 'I'm possibly related to Bering, the Dane who discovered the sea passage.' He preferred his mother's name now, it sounded posher and more select than his father's rural last name.

The offices were full of ashtrays. The room reeked of old cigarette ends. There were piles of beer cans on the floor. The place was used for meetings and for parties, one sometimes leading to the other.

Someone from county level had come to lead the meeting. He was in no hurry to start: only a few had turned up. But in the end he rapped his gavel to open proceedings and everybody introduced themselves. There were five of them. They were briefly told about the policies of the Progress Party before the new Oslo West branch was formally constituted.

'Which of you wants to stand for election?' asked the leader.

They all put up their hands.

'Okay then, who's the oldest here?'

It was Thomas Wist-Kirkemo. He was four years older than Anders, and was unanimously voted in as chair. Then they had to elect his deputy. Anders quickly raised his hand and said 'I'd like to do that.' No one else laid claim to the position, so he got it. The other three were made committee members. There was a round of applause for the elections and then they decided to go for a beer at Politikern, a bar for ambitious young politicos in the arcade on Youngstorget.

Anders was in a good mood. He had been a member of the Progress Party since he was eighteen – he had even been a committee member in the Uranienborg-Majorstuen branch – but it was only when he got the invitation from the party, eager to build up its youth wing, to join one of the three new local youth branches it was setting up in Oslo that he decided to make the commitment.

He supported what the others said and was generous with compliments. He listened more than he spoke and was more restrained than he usually was in discussions with his friends. He could often be quite provocative and would never concede a point. Out on the town, it was not unusual for him to end up in quarrels with a certain amount of pushing and shoving, though seldom in actual fights.

So these five – they were now a group, a gang – would have to stand together to change Norway.

'We need to make our mark on the city council,' said Anders. 'Get more young people in.' The others nodded. This evening they agreed about everything. 'The trouble with the Labour Party,' he went on, 'is that there's no way of getting rich with them in power!'

After the meeting, Anders strolled westwards with his new title. The streets grew wider, the clothes in the shop-window displays more expensive, the pavements began to be lined with poplars, pollarded for the winter, and there were large detached houses with gardens.

Here he was, the deputy chairman of the Progress Party Youth, Oslo West branch, walking home.

The ideals of his tagging phase had long since been abandoned. He had turned in the opposite direction. Tagging circles were more red than blue, and the hippest concerts were held at Blitz, where anti-racism was high on the agenda. Anders was now involved with the party that had most actively opposed the taggers. It was several years since he had last been arrested, with spray cans and a stolen emergency hammer in his rucksack, bombing a bridge at Storo in the north of Oslo. He was fined three thousand kroner and called it a day. By then he had already started at Hartvig Nissen, an upper secondary school specialising in drama, where many of the students had artistic aspirations. The saggy Psycho Cowboy jeans and Kebab Norwegian were out of place among the cultural snobs and would-be actors, and though he was pleased to be elected class rep, he felt uncomfortable there. He didn't understand the codes, was seen as a social misfit, and left after a year.

He started in the second year at Oslo Commerce School. Even in that conservative milieu he clung on to his tagger style for a while. He still favoured a cool, rolling walk like in the music videos from the Bronx. Some people sniggered openly when he used Pakistani expressions or gang-talk. But word had come with him that he was not somebody to be messed with. 'He's nuts, steer well clear of him,' his new classmates were warned.

So he reinvented himself once again. Slimmer-fit Levi's and polo shirts were the order of the day now, preferably with the little crocodile on the chest. He adopted an educated, well-articulated way of speaking, replacing the East End elements with more refined expressions. He donned a smile and an accommodating air. At the Commerce School he found himself in the company of aspiring financial whizz-kids with inheritances to look forward to, along with yuppies keen to make money fast. Outside school he had a part-time job as a telephone salesman for Telia, in which he pushed everything from hunting, fishing and music magazines to scratch cards, wine calendars and crime fiction. He proved to have a flair for selling, but was soon working mainly on the customer-service side because he handled complaints so well. The boss saw him as responsible and entrusted him with tasks beyond what was normally expected.

At high school he began speculating in shares, and one day made two hundred thousand kroner in a single transaction. It inspired him to carry on trading in shares, and he took an increasing number of days off. As time went by he hardly had time to attend classes, and just before Christmas in his final year he sent a letter to the school.

I hereby give notice that after serious consideration I have decided to leave the third year. Thank you for an instructive time at the school. In brackets underneath he wrote: *P.S. (Just a joke) If I had not had to do French I would be staying on.*

His mother was upset when he told her what he had done. He'd grown so headstrong lately, she said, and she was worried about his future. He'd always had good grades, often top marks, so why leave just six months before his final exams? But her eighteen-year-old had urgent things to attend to, and school was slowing him down.

He told his mates he didn't want a boss above him, creaming off the profits. He told his own boss he wanted to leave his job in telephone sales and set up his own business. That was where the money was. And while his fellow students were choosing their universities or colleges, he put all his energy into becoming a millionaire.

Thanks to his little jobs and some hard saving, he had a starting capital of a hundred thousand kroner for the company, Behring & Kerner Marketing, that he was going to run with a friend. They had an office in the basement of the terrace in Konventveien into which Wenche and Anders had moved after Elisabeth emigrated to California. Anders's business idea was inspired. He had told his former boss why he was leaving, to be sure, but he had pulled the wool over his eyes as well, because before leaving Telia he had got access to a database of foreigners in Norway, people he called 'priority-A customers, the heavyweights', and he had surreptitiously copied the database. Now he could ring round these customers and offer them cheaper call charges.

But it turned out not to be that easy to get rich overnight. Most customers were sceptical about being contacted by the two teenagers and stayed with Telia. Then Anders fell out with Kerner, later referring to him as incompetent. He vowed never again to start a business with a friend without sales experience. After a year he wound up the business, all his capital gone.

Anders went back to telephone sales. Before long he was promoted to team leader. By scrimping and saving, he slowly built up fresh starting capital. He had got a new idea. He wanted to set up databases of rich people, potential investors in industry and commerce, and then sell those databases to interested parties. But he was unable to find out how to locate the information he needed and had to shelve the idea.

Then he decided advertising was the thing: he was a seller, after all.

He set up a firm selling outdoor advertising space, aiming to undercut one of the big players. Clear Channel had contracts with landlords to display advertising round the city, but while the cost of hiring advertising space had risen significantly, payment to the property owners had remained static. His plan was to ring round to the owners and offer them slightly more than they were getting. But first he needed to get hold of the property and company numbers, and they were far from readily available. It cost money and they had to be retrieved from public offices.

One day when he was brooding on the matter he ran into Kristian, the neighbour whose parents had always given him a lift to football matches. After a brief chat in the street, Anders offered him a job in his one-man business and Kristian, bored with his own job, accepted.

They found affordable premises on Øvre Slottsgate in the offices of a law firm. The rent included use of the communal lunch room, where they shared a fridge with Geir Lippestad, the lawyer who owned the firm. Sometimes the boys ate their lunches with Lippestad, at the time representing the neo-Nazi Ole Nicolai Kvisler, who stood accused of murdering fifteen-year-old Norwegian-Ghanaian Benjamin Hermansen in an Oslo suburb. Anders in particular was interested in talking to the lean, balding lawyer about the case.

Anders was busy making contacts and building networks. He dreamt of joining the Masonic lodge and was trying to find someone who would propose him as a member, someone to suck up to, as his friends put it. Once in the lodge he would be among the elite, the way Anders saw it.

'You've really got the knack of manipulating people!' his new partner said admiringly. Kristian was impressed by his associate's talent for getting what he wanted. Anders had been given access to the computers at the municipal Agency for Planning and Building Services and had copied everything he needed, entirely free of charge. That was a good start. Even so, the project ran out of money after a year, and it wasn't long before the rent and telephone bills were going unpaid. Anders sold the business to a company that dealt in billboards on a large scale, and emerged with the same sum of money he had started out with. Breaking even. Kristian, for his part, decided to work for the company that had bought them out, and the two boys parted.

Anders had come up with a new way of getting rich. Advertising placards could also be mobile. Then you didn't have to pay anything for the site, because the street was free. He planned to take on an unemployed academic to cycle round the city with placards fixed to a trailer. He made a prototype in the basement at home and negotiated a contract with Platekompaniet, a chain of music and DVD stores. The contraption was sent out on its rounds but the construction was not solid enough and the placard blew over on the first day, injuring a woman. The business folded, having generated no income.

Anders's friends made a joke of the fact that he had insisted on an unemployed academic to ride the bike. As if to make the point that education was good for nothing. Anders, who had not taken his final exams at upper secondary, boasted that he had studied enough to use the title *Bachelor of Small Business and Management*, and that he had completed the entire syllabus of the MBA course.

At this time he was also taking part in the Progress Party's course in preparation for political office. The first evening focused on ideology and, according to the programme, 'the big names in what today we call liberalism, such as John Locke, Adam Smith and Ayn Rand'. The next session covered the history of the Progress Party, and on the third evening the aspiring politicians had to give lectures on topical party issues. In addition, they were taught how to spread the message, which felt like home ground to Anders. Selling was his forte, after all. He had just had a bit of bad luck.

Oh, it was that irresistible urge to get rich . . .

He conscientiously attended all the meetings of the Oslo West branch. They laid plans for various activities leading up to the Oslo City Council elections in 2003. But turnout at the meetings was poor, and not much came of it all. He and Thomas Wist-Kirkemo did not get on particularly well. Thomas felt he wasn't really getting through to his deputy and invited him out for a couple of beers to get to know him.

Anders was bubbling over with ideas for getting rich. When Thomas steered the conversation to more personal matters, Anders went quiet and turned evasive, or changed the subject back to his business ideas.

Thomas was also juggling plans for a company and wondered if they should work together.

'No thanks, I'd never dream of mixing business and friendship,' Anders replied.

What friendship, thought Thomas.

Anders went on talking about his entrepreneurial schemes. He was considering fixing billboards to a car trailer rather than a bicycle; a car was more solid.

They stayed chatting until late, before parting to go home. When Thomas got back to his student accommodation at Kringsjå, his girl-friend was already asleep. She woke up when he got into bed.

'Have a nice evening?'

'Well, a bit boring. I went out with Behring and it's so hard to get anywhere near him,' he sighed. 'I don't know what to make of him. He's so ambitious, but sort of hollow at the same time.'

Anders was increasingly drawn into the Progress Party Youth's social scene. They were all around the same age, most of them were single, and it was an open, liberal circle. The youth leaders saw it as part of their recruitment strategy to attract the members to social events.

In the Oslo West gang he got to know a girl who was the same age as him, but who was already making a career for herself in the party. Lene Langemyr was as thin as a rake with a playful expression and short, untidy hair. Smart and always ready with an answer, she sailed effortlessly into Anders's life. They went to pre-parties, parties and afterparties together, visited each other, watched films and talked, went on outings and attended meetings with the other would-be politicians.

They fell for each other. She thought he seemed intellectual and rather exciting. She wasn't the studious type herself, she laughed, as he lectured her on Adam Smith and Ayn Rand.

She was from the town of Grimstad in the south of Norway, not far from where Anders's mother grew up. But really she was from New Delhi. There, she had been left on the doorstep of one of the city's many orphanages one April day in 1979. Six weeks later she was brought to Norway. On Whit Sunday, a couple stood waiting at Oslo airport for the tiny girl. The information pack from the adoption agency had advised them, 'If you cannot see a dark-skinned child fitting into your home then do not take the risk of adopting a baby from another country' as the children could 'turn out to be quite dark-complexioned'. In addition, the skin could darken with age.

Dolly, as she had been called at the children's home, found herself growing up in a ready-made family of three older brothers. She tried to emulate them, her body grew strong and swift, she wanted to prove herself their equal and never cried when she hurt herself. Lene was eight when she first learned to fire an airgun; she loved the shooting range and being taken along on hunting and fishing expeditions.

Lene showed no interest in researching her roots. What would be the point? She was Norwegian and had a family who loved her. But sometimes the feeling of having been unwanted overwhelmed her.

'I wasn't loved by my mother,' she told Anders. 'I wouldn't have been left there otherwise.' She struggled with her sense of guilt at not having come up to scratch, she skipped school, wanted to get away, broke any rule she could, left upper secondary in the second year and rang the local recruitment office of the National Service Centre. The summer she turned eighteen she passed the physical tests and was called in for evaluation at Camp Madla, Norway's largest recruit-training college, just outside Stavanger.

'Hah, you'll be home after a week,' predicted her mother.

After two weeks she was elected to represent the other recruits. She was the first girl, and the first dark-skinned recruit to fill the position.

Lene was absorbed in being Norwegian and saw red on man-oeuvres when Muslim recruits would not eat because they were served pork in their field rations. She was not sympathetic to those who asked for the kitchen to use special pots and pans to prepare halal food.

'What if there's a war? Is the field kitchen going to take special pans on operations for you? No, everybody has to adapt to conditions,' she informed them.

Adapt, as she had done herself. She felt it in her bones. These guys had been born in Norway; they were Norwegian and couldn't expect special treatment.

'It brings out the hatred. I find it so dispiriting,' she told Anders later. 'My mother always said that wherever you go, you ought to adapt to the local way of life. Out of respect. They've got to do that too.' The armed forces should stand for integration, not segregation.

It was her experiences in the military that prompted her to get involved in politics. She had moved to Tromsø, where she got in touch with two right-wing parties and asked them to send their material. The Progress Party Youth got in first. Within a few months, Lene was its leader in Tromsø and the regional chair in the Troms county organisation. In October 2000, Norway's largest paper, *Verdens Gang*, published a big feature: 'Dark-skinned and leader of Progress Party Youth'. A barrier had been broken, the paper said. Lene was quoted as saying that 'tougher immigration policies and strengthening the armed forces are the things I care about most'.

Then restlessness set in again and she moved to Oslo, where she became the manager of a clothes shop in the Oslo City shopping centre. Once the shop closed for the day she made her way on high heels over to Youngstorget. There she would hang out at Progress Party HQ or prepare meetings and speeches. It was there she and Anders met.

A critical attitude toward Islam was common ground for Lene and Anders at the time. Because Lene's appearance meant she was often mistaken for a Pakistani girl, she was frequently on the receiving end of comments in the street. 'Get dressed!' Muslim men would shout at her if she were wearing a strappy summer dress. She complained to Anders that men sometimes harassed her when she was lightly clothed, rubbing up against her in queues or groping her in the street. She was annoyed that it was immigrants, not Norwegians, who called her Norwegianness into question. She felt she was more exposed than her blonde sisters, and if she tried to buy a smoky-bacon sausage at a kiosk, she would often be asked if she realised it had pork in it. 'I know that, and I love them,' Lene would answer, in her sing-song Grimstad dialect.

'"We do what we like with our women, so keep out of this or you'll be sorry",' she had been warned when being critical of Islam, she had told Anders. 'It must be awful to be a woman in that culture,' she said to him one evening when they were on their own.

The Progress Party was a young party. Its forerunner had been set up in 1973 by Anders Lange, a forestry technician and anti-communist, under the name *Anders Lange's Party for a Major Reduction in Taxes, Duties and Public Intervention*. The role of the state was to be minimal, in direct contrast to Labour's welfare state. The party received support from the apartheid regime in South Africa for their 1973 election campaign. Lange said of Idi Amin's regime in Uganda that 'blacks needed white people to be in charge'.

He was critical of the fight for women's liberation and of welfare provision such as maternity leave. 'No one who has a good time with her husband in bed deserves financial help as a result,' he said in one of his speeches.

But the year after founding his party, the colourful racist died and the young, ambitious Carl Ivar Hagen succeeded him as party chairman. In 1977 the name was changed to the Progress Party, and in the early years the party hovered at around 3 or 4 per cent in the polls. What had started out in the 1970s as a movement among individual members of the public against taxes and other duties developed a wider populist appeal in the yuppie era of the 1980s, when the country was caught up in the liberal spirit of the age. Even so, the People's Party was not exactly mainstream and failed to attract the mass of voters.

Then the letter from Mustafa arrived:

You are fighting in vain Mr Hagen! Islam, the one true faith, will be victorious here in Norway, too.

It was 1987. The number of asylum seekers and refugees coming to Norway had shot up. From around a hundred per annum, the figure had risen: almost nine thousand had sought refuge in the last year. The Labour government planned a campaign to explain to people why Norway would have to take more refugees.

At an open election meeting in Trøndelag Hagen started reading out parts of the letter. "'Allah is Allah and Muhammed is his prophet,'" he read. "'One day mosques will be as common in Norway as churches are today. My great-grandchildren will see this. I know, all Muslims in Norway know, that the Norwegian population will find its way to the faith one day, and this land will become Muslim! We are having more children than you, and a considerable number of true Muslim believers come to Norway every year, men of a fertile age. One day the infidel cross will be wiped from your flag!'"

This threat shocked the audience. The letter from Mustafa proved to be a turning point in the immigration debate, which came to dominate the election campaign that year. It later turned out that the letter was bogus. It was clearly a gaffe, but Hagen protested his innocence. He had done nothing but read from a letter he had received.

In any case, the party's support tripled in comparison with the general election two years before, gaining 12 per cent of the vote. In the big cities, where immigration was at the highest levels, the party polled between 15 and 20 per cent.

'A political earthquake,' declared the party chairman. The Progress Party was here to stay.

Hagen was an absolute master at setting groups against each other. He particularly favoured referring to the elderly on one hand and the immigrants on the other as examples of worthy and unworthy recipients of state subsidies. Through the 1990s the party demanded that some kind of migration accounting system be set up to establish the cost and calculate the long-term consequences of the growing number of immigrants from foreign cultures. The party spokesman on immigration policy, Øystein Hedstrøm, took the line that the

influx of refugees was eroding people's morality as taxpayers because
they were unwilling to make contributions that went to finance
immigration. Many asylum seekers were not prepared to work
because they could live well on financial support from the state, he
said. What was more, the foreigners provoked in the Norwegians
feelings such as 'frustration, indignation, bitterness, fear and anxiety
that could lead to psychosomatic illnesses causing absence from work
and instability at home'. He claimed that hygienic standards in the
shops, restaurants and stalls run by foreigners were so poor that they
could make customers ill, which again would have an economic
impact on society.

Hedstrøm foresaw that the rising levels of immigration would lead
to violence perpetrated by Norwegians. 'There is a great risk that
these negative emotions will find an outlet in violent reactions in the
not so distant future,' he predicted in 1995, at about the same time
as Anders Behring Breivik gave up tagging and weeded the immigrant
slang out of his vocabulary.

Before the election that year it emerged that Hedstrøm had close
contact with racist organisations such as the Fatherland Party and the
White Electoral Alliance. The party leadership muzzled him, but the
links did not appear to damage the party, which in Oslo had its best-
ever election and gained 21 per cent of the vote.

In 1996, the year before Breivik joined the Progress Party, it had
turned its rhetoric against immigrants in the direction of a critique
of Islam. In his speech to the party conference that year, Hagen
launched an attack on the imams. The state ought not to be supporting fundamentalism. 'The imams are against integration and
interpret the Qur'an in a way that is dangerous to the Muslims and
the new generation. They should not gain any power in this country.
It is a kind of racism that gives the imams in Norway power over
others. The imams require education in Norwegian practices and customs and training in how to behave here,' he claimed. In his opinion,
the Muslims had taken no decisive steps towards integration and the
growth of fundamentalism had frightened Norwegians. He cited the
demand for Muslim schools, segregated swimming lessons and

protests against religious education lessons based on Christianity, as well as the demonstrations against *The Satanic Verses*, and the attack in 1993 on the book's Norwegian publisher William Nygaard, who was shot several times in the chest and shoulder, but survived.

'Gangs are prowling the streets, stealing, going to discos in a group, fighting and committing rape in Oslo. The immigrant associations are fully aware of the situation but don't want to cooperate with the police for fear of being called informers. They have to protect their own. These bullies are not seen as criminals but as brave, bold heroes in this section of immigrant culture. If no one speaks out against this macho culture now, it could become a time-honoured tradition in our country.' This was the way Hagen sounded in the 1990s. 'When the imams preach that the Norwegians are infidels, there are automatic consequences. It means among other things that it is the duty of the Muslims not to pay taxes, that they can steal from the shops with no moral scruples and that they can tell lies.'

After al-Qaida's terrorist attacks in America on 11 September 2001 the Progress Party stepped up its rhetoric, in line with world opinion. Muslims were ruthless and dangerous. The Progress Party saw the world as George W. Bush did: us and them.

The party was flying high in the opinion polls. With the upturn in public support, the party wanted to expand its organisation. To reach out to more people, the party had to be visible at the local level and particularly among young people. That was when it decided to set up local branches, the ones that had appealed to Anders as party fortunes prospered.

He seldom spoke in plenary sessions. The few times he did address the floor, he gabbled nervously. He had written anything he said down in advance and read it in a monotone, without emotion.

He was not at home at the lectern. The internet was to be his territory.

The summer of 2002 was approaching. After an almost snowless winter and a glorious spring, the meteorologists said Norway could expect its hottest year in over a century.

As people sweated away in their offices, the parties' nomination battles were in full swing. There was vicious jostling for places on the lists for the city council elections the following year. Anders was staking everything on a political career, so he simply had to get nominated. He made himself as visible as possible and was an active contributor to the Progress Party Youth's new online debate forum.

'We needn't be ashamed of being ambitious!' he wrote one light night in May, in one of his first posts. 'We needn't be ashamed of setting goals and then reaching them! We needn't be ashamed of breaking with established norms to achieve something better!' Norway had such a loser mentality, he argued. A Norwegian would just stand there waiting, cap in hand. He would never put himself forward, but would follow the example set by our unassuming forefathers. This had to change, wrote Anders, using the new members of the royal family to illustrate his argument. In one of his first posts he expressed his support for Crown Prince Haakon's marriage to Mette-Marit, a single mother with a four-year-old son, and for Princess Märtha Louise's fiancé Ari Behn, an author whose books were steeped in drugs and dark, wild lifestyles. He praised the two new spouses for being individualists. Had they been rich, dull, conservative figures, no one would have criticised them, he wrote. No, Norway should learn from the US, where the key to success was: 1. You're the best. 2. You can make all your dreams come true. 3. The only limits are those you set yourself. 'Meanwhile, the wise goblins will sit on the hill and say something completely different: 1. Don't think you're anybody. 2. Don't imagine you can achieve anything. 3. Don't imagine anybody cares about you.'

The most powerful figure in Anders's circle was Jøran Kallmyr, leader of the Progress Party Youth in Oslo. Anders often added comments to Jøran's posts on the forum, eager to support and motivate, but seldom received an answer.

Anders, who had devised battle tactics for his toy soldiers as a boy, drawn maps and escape routes across Oslo in his time as a tagger and later sketched out business plans and marketing strategies, now drew up a chart of the Progress Party Youth organisation and planned his political future on paper.

To qualify for nomination to stand in the city council elections in 2003 the local branches had to submit suggestions to the nomination committee a year in advance, so now was the time to strike. The candidates under consideration were then called in for interview by the committee, which was led by a former diplomat, Hans Høegh Henrichsen.

Anders advised everybody to stand for election and wrote in May 2002 that he, Jøran Kallmyr and Lene Langemyr were preliminarily registered as candidates.

Jøran Kallmyr was the first of the three to be called in. 'He's made of stern stuff,' was Høegh Henrichsen's verdict. 'Enquiring, interested, alert,' he noted. The young man demonstrated a good understanding of Progress Party policies and could sustain an argument. A place on the list. Lene Langmyr was called in next. She was a controversial candidate; someone had sown seeds of doubt about how she conducted her life. The elderly diplomat made some discreet enquiries, turned up unannounced at her shop in Oslo one day, and then dismissed the rumours. He judged her to be 'a usable and interesting candidate'. Not all that strong academically, but she had drive, was enterprising and was full of fighting spirit, which he valued highly. Lene was examined on Progress Party policy by the party's grey-haired elders, and passed muster.

Anders was left waiting for a call.

He came up with several explanations for the time it was taking. The other parties were better at putting forward youth candidates, he complained. After all, he knew the elderly Høegh Henriksen from the Uranienborg-Majorstuen branch. Back then, Anders had even served as the deputy representative on the governing boards of the Majorstuen old people's home and Uranienborg School to maximise his chances.

'They're sure to call you in soon,' said Lene. 'Remember how many people they've got to get through.'

Lene and Anders made plans together. They wanted to apply for membership of the Oslo Pistol Club. They were both very interested in guns and spent a long time discussing different types.

In the military, Lene had grown familiar with everything from the standard AG-3 rifle to all sorts of machine guns, Glock pistols and the MP5 sub-machine gun. She was a good shot and could vividly remember the pride she had taken in mastering something hard, doing it well, coming up to scratch.

In Anders, she was surprised that someone who had not done their military service had such a good overview of a range of weapons. 'The army really ought to buy this type of machine gun,' he could say, and then elaborate on its range, applications and type of ammunition. Or he might show her something on the internet or in a magazine, commenting, 'This sub-machine gun's better than the one they're using now.' He had a vast store of detailed knowledge about a whole range of firearms.

Anders had been exempted from military service because he was registered as his mother's carer. After a serious herpes infection she had had a drain inserted in her head and she needed nursing for an extended period.

Lene was touched by the care Anders gave his mother. He told her how his mother was faring after her illness. She had changed since the surgical procedure, he said, become more absent-minded, more dis-organised and terribly depressed.

Anders had also told Lene about his mother's unhappy childhood, about his grandmother who went mad and the uncles his mother never wanted him to meet. He told her how self-sacrificing his mother had been when he was growing up, on her own with two children. But he also criticised her for having lost touch with her rela-tions. He would so much have liked a big family.

He must be a kind boy since he has such a warm relationship with his mother, thought Lene, though she could not shake off the feeling that it was all a bit odd. He must definitely have been the favourite and spoilt all his life, she decided.

Anders would never tell Lene anything about his father.

'He doesn't want any contact with his children,' was all Anders would say.

On the internet, Anders adopted a tone that was jovial yet intense. His writing was peppered with emoticons, exclamation marks and jokey remarks in brackets or quotation marks. He wrote a long list of things members ought to do if they wanted to be the next Carl Ivar Hagen or Siv Jensen, the young woman who had been elected vice-chairman and proved her resilience and ambition in a male-dominated party. 'Knowledge of selling and marketing is as important as knowledge of ideology and theoretical policy issues,' he wrote. It also helped to know something about psychology and law, be thoughtful and read a variety of newspapers. Anybody who had worked in sales would have a clear advantage: 'You have to be good at debating – be articulate, but talk about things in an accessible way.' He suggested starting with some practice in front of the mirror, and recording yourself as an aid to improving performance. If you wanted to be taken seriously you had to dress professionally, and there were occasions when it was better to sit there quietly than to say anything stupid 'in front of the grown-ups'. Teamwork was crucial, and 'if we, the capable new blood in the Progress Party Youth, don't assert ourselves in the main party other young people will come to prominence there.'

'Organisation freak,' groaned Jøran Kallmyr when he read what the deputy of the Oslo West branch had written. Behring's a total outsider, yet he sounds like one of the inner circle, he thought when he saw the way Anders was dispensing tips to people at the top.

It sounded familiar. *He was behaving like a king, but he was only a toy.*

In the course of his first summer's posting on the forum, Anders devoted more and more time to the subject of Islam. His tone was cautiously conciliatory. On 11 July 2002, when nearly everybody was away on holiday, he wrote, 'It's important to make the point that Islam is a great religion (on a level with Christianity) and that Muslims are generally good people (on a level with Christians).'

He stressed that it was 'certain aspects of negative cultures related to Islam that should be criticised, not Islam itself'. There was an essential difference, he explained, referring to the Italian journalist Oriana Fallaci, who claimed a secret Islamic invasion of Europe was under way. 'I wouldn't recommend anybody in the Progress Party Youth to fall in with this approach or they could be risking their political career,' he advised.

Later that day, the conflict in the Middle East made waves in the little pond of Norwegian youth politics. The Workers' Youth League – the Labour Party's youth organisation, known by the abbreviation AUF – formally accused the Israeli prime minister Ariel Sharon of a breach of international law and asked for him to be brought before a Norwegian court. The charges were to be murder, opening fire on ambulances and the destruction of property.

When Hans Høegh Henrichsen heard about the allegation, he immediately rang the Israeli embassy and asked for an audience for the leader of the Oslo Progress Party Youth, Jøran Kallmyr. The audience was granted. 'Now we'll be able to gather the material for a counter-attack!' Høegh Henrichsen told the young politician. The youth leader had the Israeli point of view explained to him, and adopted it as his own.

That afternoon, Jøran Kallmyr came down hard on the AUF, on the allegation and on Yasser Arafat in a post he called 'The anti-Semites of the AUF'.

Anders Behring did not let the opportunity of a discussion with Kallmyr pass him by.

'They're a pack of idiots! And they certainly haven't got a clue about the law,' he wrote of the AUF, adding that the police should fine them for making a false allegation. It was Jøran who mobilised the heavy artillery, Anders just agreed with what he wrote, and joked that the Progress Party Youth should make an allegation against Yasser Arafat.

Two weeks later, the Director of Public Prosecution dismissed the complaint on formal grounds. The International Criminal Court would be the appropriate legal authority for such a case.

The hot summer faded, autumnal weather came sweeping in and the wind whistled. It was the coldest autumn in living memory, and Anders still had not been called in for interview.

The chair of the nomination committee never read anything that Anders posted on the internet, but he had met him.

'He seems pleasant and reasonable,' was Høegh Henrichsen's assessment, 'but isn't he a bit vague?'

Anders Behring had failed to make any particular impression on the older man. He had only come to a couple of meetings and had not distinguished himself there. His name had been put into the ring along with a list of other names, but no one from Anders's local 'adult' branch – Majorstuen-Uranienborg – felt he was the right man. It was the local branch that had to interview and approve individuals from their district who were proposed to the nomination committee. For them it was the personal impression that counted, not anyone's empire-building on the internet.

He was not weighed and found wanting.

He was not even weighed.

He was never called for interview.

His name did not go on the list.

Just before Christmas, the nomination list was finalised. Two youth candidates were nominated. Jøran was on the list. Lene was on the list.

Anders's posts on the forum grew more negative. 'The sad thing about the political system in Norway is that it often isn't the most competent who get political power, but those who are best at networking.'

He told people that Jøran Kallmyr had promised to support his candidature, but had stabbed him in the back instead. That was what stopped him becoming a leader in the party, he explained to his online buddy PeeWee. 'Kallmyr went behind my back.'

'How the h . . . is the PPY supposed to recruit voters under 30 if they haven't any high-profile young parliamentarians???' he wrote in the new year, and, 'The way I see it, the central executive committee has been far too passive when it comes to developing a comprehensive youth strategy! Is there any kind of strategy at all??'

He was a nobody, and it was almost election time.

Jøran was voted onto the council and Lene was elected a substitute member. Soon, Jøran was appointed a secretary to a local government commissioner and later a commissioner, and Lene became a regular council member.

In one of his last posts in the summer of 2003, Anders predicted civil war once the Muslims were in the majority in Norway. The Islamisation of the West was alarming.

On that last point, many in the Progress Party agreed with him.

For his part, he had lost interest in the party. He stopped going along to the offices or to their social events. If they didn't want him, he didn't want them either. He moved on, out into the world. Without Jøran; without Lene.

'High Quality Fake Diplomas!!'

E Tenebris ad Lucem
From Darkness into Light

Motto of the St John Lodge
'Saint Olaus to the Three Pillars'

Sales of false diplomas had taken off. He made his first million.

He made his second million.

He was actually getting rich.

The money was pouring into accounts in tax havens like Antigua and Barbuda, St Vincent and the Bahamas. He had also opened accounts in Latvia and Estonia. That way, he could avoid paying tax in Norway. The banks offered him anonymous credit cards that meant he could make withdrawals from ATM machines in Oslo without his name being registered.

His mother helped him with this money laundering. He had asked her to open three bank accounts. There she deposited the cash her son gave her, before transferring it to him. Within a short space of time she had laundered four hundred thousand kroner.

He got the idea while he was still active in the Progress Party. It had struck him that there could be a market for false diplomas and he set up a website, *diplomaservices.com*, in the autumn of 2002.

His company, City Group, operated through addresses such as *best-fakediploma.com* and *superfakedegree.com*. They advertised 'Bachelor's, master's and doctorate diplomas available in the field of your choice'. Double exclamation marks were sprinkled across the pages. '***Receive a high quality fake diploma within 10 days!!***' ran the headline in bold italics. The cost was around a hundred dollars per diploma, and the customer was promised a full refund if he could find better print quality anywhere else. For those wanting a complete package of exam certificate plus graduation diploma from a particular university, there was a special-offer price of 295 dollars.

A young man in Indonesia drew up the diplomas to order and then emailed them to Anders in Oslo for approval. There were medical-school diplomas, doctorates and engineering qualifications, diplomas from organisations and societies, even prize certificates. Sometimes Anders did a first draft and then sent it to his employee in Asia, to whom he paid a monthly salary of seven hundred dollars.

The web pages brought in orders for several hundred diplomas a month. The company occupied most of Anders's time, apart from weekends, when he would be out on the town spending his money, freely at times but never recklessly. Anders had landed himself a nice circle of friends: young men from the West End, some from the School of Commerce, a classmate or two from primary-school days, a few others who had turned up along the way.

He had moved out of the collective in Maries gate and was now renting his own flat in Tidemands gate, not far from where he had lived with his fellow students. His mother came round to clean and tidy for him and took his washing home with her. For this Anders paid her in cash, a few thousand kroner a month.

The orders started piling up. His associate in Indonesia was not that fluent in English and there were quite a lot of corrections to be done. Anders needed somebody who could check the diplomas and add the finishing touches.

In the advertisement he placed through a government employment scheme, he said he was looking for someone to handle the graphics side. The only specification was experience of Photoshop and CorelDRAW, a graphic-design package. The applicant also had to be free to start at once.

Mads Madsen had only done a short course in drawing, design and colour at upper secondary school, but he was familiar with the two computer programs and fired off an application on spec.

In the very first days of 2005 he was invited to the offices of the E-Commerce Group, which was the new company name. The young man was offered the graphic designer job. But once his role was fully explained to him, he hesitated.

'Is it legal?'

'As long as we don't forge official stamps or anything like that, it's legal,' replied the besuited managing director. 'It's been tested in court in the US.'

He called them decorative diplomas. 'Your job is to check for spelling mistakes and evaluate the composition.'

On its website, E-Commerce Group covered itself legally by saying that the diplomas were intended as props in films and so on.

The truth was that they never asked customers, merely assumed the diplomas were for decorative purposes, or to replace documents that had been lost or destroyed. Anders had made a template for signatures, which Mads was to use. Anders called it a joke signature: it was not meant to imitate that of any actual university vice-chancellor and thus not illegal.

The salary offered was generous: Mads would get thirty thousand kroner a month. He proved to be quick and efficient.

One day, Anders asked him if he would rather work for cash. Mads could then avoid paying tax and keep more of the money for himself. The employee didn't want to. So he carried on receiving monthly pay slips stating the amount of tax paid.

After a while Anders asked him to dress more smartly, in a shirt and tie. Mads refused, and carried on wearing his jumper and jeans.

Then Anders started taunting his employee about being a vegetarian and tried to get him to come out for a decent meal. Mads said he was trying to leave the smallest possible footprint on earth when he was gone.

Anders became obsessed with catching Mads out, with discovering something unethical about him. 'If there's one thing I can't stand, it's a hypocrite,' he said.

Most of his acquaintances from the School of Commerce had now embarked on university and college courses. Magnus, one of his childhood friends, had become a firefighter, another was applying for jobs in the shipping industry. Lots of them were getting steady girl-friends, some even had partners they lived with, while others had strings of one-night stands. Anders did none of this, but he kept tabs on it all. One friend had been to bed with hundreds of women, he reckoned. He himself generally went home on his own. He didn't appeal to the girls and they didn't appeal to him. He complained to his friends that the Norwegian girls were too liberated and would never make good housewives. His friends laughed and told him to stop talking rubbish. Who wanted a housewife?

Then he did something his friends found rather strange. In December 2004 he ordered the contact details of ten women from a dating website in the Ukraine. In February the following year he ordered ten more. In all, he paid one hundred euros to the website, which featured the profiles of thousands of women from Eastern Europe.

When a female friend pointed out that acquiring a bride by mail order was not what boys of his age usually did, his other friends made light of it, saying he could be a bit odd sometimes.

The women he chose were blue-eyed and slim, with girlish figures. They were all younger than him, mostly teenagers.

He picked two photos from his most recent batch of downloads. One was dark-haired, the other blonde. He couldn't make his mind up, so he asked his mother.

When he showed her the two pictures, she pointed to the fairer one.

She was Natascha from Belarus.

He wrote and received an immediate reply. They emailed back and forth for a couple of weeks. In March he left the office under super-vision of Mads and took a trip to Minsk.

Natascha, who had grown up in a workers' district on the edge of the Belarus capital, was fascinated by the good-looking, well-mannered, nicely dressed Norwegian and liked what he had to say about himself: his education, his company, his status. The only thing was, she found it a bit hard to understand everything he said. Natascha didn't speak much English, and Anders used so many difficult words.

At home with her parents, he was served *blini* – Russian pancakes. He asked about radiation in the area and was careful not to consume too much locally produced food or contaminated water. He asked various people how many had died as a result of the radioactivity 'to get an overview of the hazards'.

On his return home a bare week later, he spoke enthusiastically of Natascha. She was blonde and stylish, he said.

Later in the spring he bought her a ticket so she could come and visit him in Oslo. His mother thought she was pretty and was very taken with her. 'It must be true love,' she told a friend, 'because it's the first time Anders has ever invited a girl round to meet his mother.' Anders had told his mother that Natascha lived in reduced circumstances in a very basic block of flats and was not used to anything else. Wenche thought that would be an advantage. 'Because a demanding girl won't do for Anders.'

She framed a picture she had taken of the couple when they all had dinner together and put it on the sideboard in her living room. 'Isn't it a bit too soon?' a friend who lived in the same block of flats had asked.

'Oh no, they're so much in love, you'll see,' Wenche had replied.

But it turned out that Natascha was not as easy to cope with as Anders had hoped.

His friends were sceptical about the Belarussian girl. All she wanted to do was go shopping and hand the bill to Anders, they said. She had probably been expecting something more than his little bachelor flat, Anders thought. Perhaps she was disappointed that he wasn't more extravagant in his spending habits.

For her part, she said the chemistry between them had gone and that he didn't respect her.

She called him a male chauvinist.

He called her a gold-digger.

Natascha was put on a plane home, and later married a church organist in a small town in America.

The person who was saddest about the break-up was Wenche.

When she finally took down the photo, a long time after Natascha's departure, she said Anders 'hadn't been able to afford to keep her'.

The fact that all Anders's friends were finding nice girlfriends while he was still on his own was a sore point with her.

The Natascha affair came as a blow to Anders. His vision of the ideal woman had turned out to be nothing but a dream. He was the type who would rather comment on the appearance of women in pictures, like Pamela Anderson, than on real girls he met. Women of flesh and blood were problematic. Some of his friends concluded he wasn't interested in the opposite sex.

One evening when he was out in town, he ran into his former partner from his time selling billboard space. Kristian was still working for the company that had bought up their mobile advertising idea. They stopped to chat at the bottom of Hegdehaugsveien, an exclusive shopping street which in the evenings was a social hub for yuppies and fashion babes. Kristian thought Anders looked a bit lost, a bit slumped inside that blazer of his, his face set beneath its foundation. They were both slightly inebriated. Kristian let slip something he had been thinking for a long time.

'Come out of the closet, Anders!'

Anders gave a strained laugh and pushed his friend away. Kristian refused to be shaken off, not wanting to drop the subject.

'You've got to come out, we're living in the twenty-first century, for God's sake!'

Anders twisted free. 'Ha,' he said. 'You're talking to the wrong person.'

Kristian had always thought Anders was gay, but it was the first

being ignominiously passed over, but he carried on paying his membership fees and he went to cast his vote. The party was still the place in which he felt most at home politically and it had a good election, winning 22 per cent of the vote.

But the Labour Party did better still and entered into negotiations to form a red–green coalition with the Socialist Left and the Centre Party. Together, the three parties formed a government platform that was the most radical in Europe. It signalled that it would put the brakes on all privatisation of state activities. The Socialist Left got the Ministry of Finance. The party stood for everything Anders Behring Breivik was against: stricter regulation of market forces, more control of the economy, bigger fines for financial misdemeanours and higher taxes on share profits.

He made it his principle to pay as little tax as possible. But when he was setting up E-Commerce Group that year, he did have to abide by some laws and regulations. He hired an auditor, which was a requirement when establishing a limited company with shareholders. The income from the diploma production was never reported to the authorities, but he could not conceal profits on selling shares.

He spent the autumn weighing up whether to stop doing the diplomas. It would be embarrassing if his full name came out in the media. Even if it transpired that his operation was not strictly illegal, it was still morally questionable, and he didn't want to make a living as a forger, he wanted to be a proper businessman. A proper businessman, rolling in money.

But it was hard to give up on shady dealings that generated so many kroner. So the man in Indonesia went on making examination certificates. Anders went on sending them out.

The snow came drifting down.

Christmas was approaching. Family time. Well, his family was rather meagre. His sister had married in Los Angeles a few years before and he had not seen her since the wedding, when his mother and sister clashed. Wenche complained that she had been instructed by her daughter to say she was a doctor.

So it would be just him and his mother on Christmas Eve as usual, the two of them opening presents and eating a festive meal. This year they would be at the flat in Hoffsveien, to which his mother had moved. But then, just a few days before the holiday, they were invited to Christmas dinner at the home of Wenche's second cousin, outside Oslo.

Wenche had only met Jan Behring on a few previous occasions, but now his wife had run into Wenche and realised that she and Anders would be celebrating Christmas alone. What a shame! They couldn't spend Christmas Eve in separate places when they were both so short of close family.

Wenche dressed, did her hair and put on make-up. Anders took trouble over his outfit too.

During the meal Anders noticed a candlestick standing on its own on a shelf in the living room.

'What's that?' he asked.

'Greek columns,' replied Jan Behring, a sparse, self-restrained man. 'A Doric, an Ionic and a Corinthian column.'

They were the symbols of the order of Freemasons he belonged to – the Pillars.

'Oh, I've always wanted to be a Freemason,' Anders exclaimed. 'It's always been my dream.' At thirteen he had gone to the Freemasons' Hall to find out how to become a member. He was told that the lower age limit was twenty-four. Now he was almost twenty-seven.

The Freemasons are the power elite, he told friends who thought it was weird of him to want to mingle with those old stuffed shirts. It was the ideal place to make contacts. You have to join if you want to get anywhere, he would say.

Here was his opportunity.

'Can you get me in?' he asked excitedly.

'Oh that would be amazing,' put in Wenche.

'Are you a Christian?' asked the cousin.

'Yes,' answered Anders.

Jan Behring was a cautious and pensive man who spoke in a rather slow and long-winded fashion. The brotherhood was based on Christian values, he explained. Membership improved and refined the individual. As a Freemason, one strove to become more humble, tolerant and compassionate – with style and dignity.

Anders had always lacked a father, grandfather, uncle or trustworthy family friend who could invite him in. To be proposed for membership you had to be invited by two brothers of the order who would remain your sponsors for the rest of your life, while two more people had to vouch for you.

Now he realised that he was related to someone who was a Freemason of the Eighth Degree!

As the evening drew to an end, Anders plucked up the courage to ask outright if this remote cousin, forty years his senior, would be his sponsor.

Behring hesitated. He did not know Anders well and did not feel able to recommend him just like that. But he lent him the Freemasons' book, the Masonic register containing the names of all the members. Anders could look through and see if he knew anyone in it who could act as his sponsor.

It was a mild Christmas in Oslo that year, with more sleet than snow. The streets turned grey, sprayed with slush that froze overnight. At home, Anders pored over the register and found barristers and judges, chief inspectors of police, renowned professors and businessmen. But no one remotely linked to him.

The Freemasons' website spoke of ancient symbols and rituals to which only a closed circle could be admitted. They were only revealed as you rose through the degrees. Truth did not come naked into the world. It came in symbols and images, it said.

'Every child deserves to win.'

This was the phrase with which Prime Minister Jens Stoltenberg began his New Year message that year. 'I'm talking about the sheer joy of succeeding at something,' he said in the address, broadcast on television. 'Many people are making plans in this festive season, dreaming dreams great and small. There are possibly more opportunities for making those dreams come true in Norway than in any other country. Our strong sense of community gives each one of us greater opportunities for seeking success and happiness. That is what constitutes the Norwegian dream – more opportunities for more people. For me, dreams are achieved through community.'

Greater equality created a more dynamic society, the Labour Party Prime Minister maintained.

For Anders, dreams were not achieved through community. He wanted to shine out above the grey mass.

So then it was 2006. Over the New Year holiday, Anders told his mother's second cousin that he had not found anyone he knew in the Freemasons' register. Jan Behring was then faced with conflicting loyalties and contacted the Chairman Master of the Pillars, the order of which he was a member. The Master said they could make an exception and ask Anders in for a chat to see what he was made of.

Later that winter, Anders was shown round the Armigeral Hall, the 'Knights' Hall' at the Freemasons' headquarters. It was a magnificent, high-roofed hall with stucco and murals on the ceiling and walls. Suits of armour and helmets were displayed between flags and banners. Knights on horseback and Crusaders in white mantles with red Maltese crosses on their chests were painted directly onto the walls. A lion in relief had the cross of St George hanging round its neck. The animal's tongue was painted red. In the cellars were the bones and skulls used in the Freemasons' ceremonies and rituals.

Anders was taken down into the depths, to the Pillars' little cubicle beneath the ceremonial hall. There he was questioned by the Master of the Lodge about his life and how he lived it. Anders replied politely, remaining rather quiet and reserved. The eagerness of Christmas Eve was now muted. His mother's cousin was rather surprised at this, but the Master of the Lodge thought the young man seemed to have a strong Christian faith and provided decent answers to his other questions too. His only cause for concern was that this Behring might be rather too unassuming and weak.

The Master of the Lodge promised to let Anders know the outcome. He said it might take some time.

Anders was kept waiting. His application had to go through a complicated process. He started to sense he would be turned down. Would he be refused entry to the brotherhood, wasn't he good enough?

The absence of a father weighed on Anders.

It was a lack that he sometimes felt quite acutely.

One day he decided to ring his father.

It was eleven years since they had spoken. Eleven years since he had last been arrested for tagging and his father had cut off all contact.

He rang the number. The receiver was lifted at the other end.

'Hello, it's Anders.'

His father said a surprised hello back, in his refined Nordland accent.

Anders told his father how well he was getting on, that he had his own IT company with employees all over the world. He said everything was great and he was considering further study at a university the US. He gave the impression that he was extremely content with life and that everything was going well, financially and socially.

They said goodbye, and promised that they would speak again soon.

It didn't happen. Anders never rang his father again.

Nor was his father ever to ring him. He had his own life to live. He was now married for the fourth time. He had no contact with any of his four children.

But maybe if Anders did something really great his father would see him, truly see him. He so much wanted his father to be proud of him. At least that was what he told his stepmother, his father's ex-wife number three, the one who had looked after him during the holidays in Normandy.

The winter proved tough; his self-esteem was sinking, his energy was gone. In February he stopped the diploma production with immediate effect. He could not cope with the prospect of being exposed in the media as a forger. So he started buying securities.

The stock market was sluggish and falling for most of the spring.

He lost a bit, made a bit, but never saw anything of the big, lucky lottery ticket he was hoping to draw. In May, share prices plummeted and stayed at rock bottom.

The totals in his accounts were shrinking. Most of his capital was now bound up in shares he couldn't sell without making big losses. He followed the stock and share prices in a feverish panic. Most of his portfolio was tied up in shares that had been suspended from sale.

When he sat down at the computer, what he liked best was to escape from reality.

Neither his annual report nor his accounts for the year were submitted in time to meet the deadline. When he finally sent them in, the auditor pulled him up for deficient accounting in both purchase and sale of shares.

Anders avoided his friends. The computer screen attracted him more and more. He swiftly typed in the addresses of the computer games he was involved in and could play for hours. If anyone called round or telephoned, they often had to wait until he had finished the level he was playing.

He could not be bothered to work out any more, his diet was poor, he no longer made the effort to dress up and go out into town; he'd had enough of partying with friends in that damn cattle market, as he called the social scene. 'Life's a rat race,' he told a friend. 'Dancing in never-ending circles to get rich. I can't do it any more.'

His cash reserves were dwindling. The rent for the decaying two-room flat in the fashionable street was fifteen thousand kroner. In a month or two he would have to start selling low-priced shares to cover his living costs. There was no fresh money coming in.

It had been his mother's idea. He could save lots of money by moving back home, she said. The room wasn't being used in any case. All he had to do was to take out a few bits of dining-room furniture she had put in there.

The summer when he was twenty-seven, he moved back in with his mother.

'It's only temporary,' he said.

'It'll be lovely,' she answered.

Choose Yourself a World

It was a good place to be. It was a perfect meritocracy.

If you were skilful and alert, you rose through the levels. If you persevered and carried out your tasks, you reaped the rewards.

Quite simply, you got what you deserved.

There were no inherited qualities or privileges. You chose your class and your race for yourself. It was your skills, and how you used them, that carried you up the hierarchy and towards your goal.

Everyone started from the same place, from the start.

You made yourself exactly as you wanted to be. You gave yourself a name and a story. You could be a man or a woman. You could be a human being or a troll, a dwarf or an elf, a gnome or an orc. That was your race.

Then there was class. You could choose to be warrior, priest, shaman, hunter or rogue. Or you could be one of the mages.

The hunters could get wild animals to fight for them while they stood back and fired their crossbows. The rogues could steal up on their opponents without being seen and attack them from behind with a dagger or axe. They were the best in hand-to-hand combat, while the priests could inflict the most damage from a distance. They had healing powers and used black magic. A mage had an arsenal of remedies that infused strength over time; a paladin knew magic spells that restored life instantly.

The druids could change themselves into bears and tigers, huge trees or rocks. They could summon tornadoes or dark clouds. The warlocks could call forth demons to sacrifice themselves in battle. The shamans could invoke air, earth and water, while the knights could use light to blind their opponents.

But a plus was always accompanied by a minus. If you were strong in one area, you were weak in another. Those able to dish out fire or ice could not take much themselves, whereas those who had only a club to fight with were hardier in battle.

Finally, you had to choose a profession. Blacksmith or alchemist, tailor or fisherman, skinner or cook. To know a craft well could be as valuable as swordplay or spellcraft. When you were not supplementing your own arsenal, you could make a profit supplementing someone else's.

The game could commence.

He was entering a world of colour. Sometimes the contrasts were subdued and misty, then all of a sudden the colours would crackle out at him. The landscape was constantly changing. A bolt of lightning would strike, a river burst its banks or red-hot lava threaten to fill the valley he was standing in.

The green was greener, the red redder, the dark darker, the light lighter. Everything had a meaning and a purpose. Every tool had its use. Every skill could be exploited. The landscape was charged with meaning.

Like everyone else, he started at zero in terms of qualities. From that point on he could earn points, which were given in percentages as he completed the tasks.

The qualities he had to improve to raise his percentage were strength, resilience, flexibility, courage and intelligence.

As a newcomer he was allocated simple tasks. It might be to harvest the crops of the field, make a spear, or barter to get himself an animal to ride. There were fast animals and slow ones. Some could fly, like the sandstone drake. He could also get himself a non-fighting pet that just followed him around the game.

Everything he wanted, he had to make or capture himself.

Sometimes there was gear for sale in auctions, or he could exchange things. Some tools were in the ownership of the enemy and then he had to beat his opponent and take what had been his.

It was laborious work. With patience came results. With time came assets.

The tasks grew more demanding. He was to kill a monster, find a hoard of treasure. Both of them might be concealed among the cliffs. Attractive castles could be surrounded by vampires, the plains around them transformed into enchanted battlefields.

Eventually it became impossible to complete the tasks alone. He had to cooperate with others, join a guild. The guild members had to have qualities that complemented each other. The strongest had to fight in the front line. The warriors and paladins had to draw the attention of the enemy so the more vulnerable, the mages and priests who had the power of healing, were not hurt.

There was an element of obligation too. If you didn't show up, if you weren't there, you let everybody down and the guild risked losing.

He gave himself the name *Andersnordic*. His gender was male and his race was human. His class was that of mage.

Andersnordic was tall and powerful, with a menacing, greyish face. His big body was dressed in a knight's outfit with precious stones sewn onto the chest and huge epaulettes on the shoulders. On his head he wore a tall, shining staff.

He relaxed his shoulders.

And pressed the keys.

The game drew him in and calmed him down. The system was easy to understand. There were no awkward categories like cool versus uncool. If you were clever enough, you were good enough. Absolutely anyone could be a success, all you had to do was be dedicated and logged in. Your reward came with time and experience, not like the volatile stock market, not like the risky chat-up scene.

Anders was good at collecting points and moved swiftly up the levels. The gamers played wearing headsets and communicated as they went along. The exchanges were largely about raids, allocation of roles and fighting tactics. They knew each other only as characters in the game – avatars – and not as their everyday selves.

Anders initially slotted into the newcomer role and was unassuming and quiet, not very active in discussions. As he rose through the hierarchy, he gradually changed. He became more affable, more talkative. As time went by he became known for his cheerfulness, as someone who could inspire others to contribute. Quite simply, he was well liked. 'A tonic to depression,' one of his fellow players called him.

Anders's mother was frustrated. This was not what she had expected of her son. Whenever she went into his room he just got annoyed and chased her out again. He scarcely had time to eat, was as quick as possible in the loo and the shower, hurried back to his room, shut the door and slept late. Life took on a routine determined by the game; his offline breaks were few.

He had stopped answering when anybody rang him on his mobile. He asked his mother to say he was out if any friends turned up at the door.

Thus he passed his early days at 18 Hoffsveien. It was a mild, sunny autumn. On the solitary birch outside his window the leaves turned first yellow, then brown, and then fell to the ground. The rain set in. The leaves lying in a circle round the tree were soon slimy and decaying. He, meanwhile, took a comfortable seat in the deep office chair each day and let his fingers do battle with the keyboard as the days darkened.

Christmas came again, and he was playing full-time. There were periods when he spent sixteen or seventeen hours a day at the computer. On New Year's Eve he spent the whole night logged on. Red-letter days were observed within the game. There were decorated trees at Christmas and fireworks at New Year.

These celebrations were yet another way for the game's manufacturer to replace real life and keep people logged on. In *World of Warcraft*, Blizzard had devised a game with no end.

It took Anders a little over six months of full-time playing to become the leader of the *Virtue* guild, which did its raiding on the European server Nordrasil.

Anders had been awarded the title *Justitiarius*. It was a title that took a long time and a lot of killing to achieve.

When Anders was on a raid, he was not to be disturbed on any account. *Virtue* had decided to mount its raids and conquests between seven and eleven o'clock in the evenings. Everyone was expected to take part. Most members of the guild played for around twelve hours a day, and a raid required a great deal of planning. They had to lay in provisions and make sure they had enough ammunition and weaponry. The better equipped they were, the greater their chances of beating other guilds in the battle to find the treasure or kill the vampires.

Andersnordic was good at motivating others and often got his fellow players to carry on performing even when they were getting tired and fed up. A bit longer, just a bit longer; he was known for never giving up.

'We've just got to finish this off, then we can get to bed,' he would say.

Sometimes the game came into conflict with real life, or the other way round.

One February morning in 2007, a letter came for him. He had been admitted to the First Degree of the St John Lodge and was invited to his first meeting at the Freemasons' headquarters. His mother was delighted.

The sponsor question had been solved. Wenche's second cousin would be his main sponsor, with primary responsibility for making a good Freemason of the boy. A secretary from the Pillars Lodge had undertaken to be his second sponsor.

Anders hadn't got time. He really hadn't got time.

It seemed so long ago. The admission interview in the vaults beneath the Armigeral Hall a year earlier was merely a faint memory.

But he couldn't say no to this. Good heavens, he'd been accepted as a Freemason!

Had it just been a question of logging off for a few hours and attending the meeting . . . But no, he had to kit himself out in full evening dress with a black waistcoat. That was the dress code for the initiation ceremony. He had to arrange all that and make an effort with his appearance before he could go out among people.

It was usual for the sponsor to come and collect the new member to take him to the solemn occasion, and the evening after his twenty-eighth birthday, which he had celebrated in *World of Warcraft*, Anders was called for by his mother's second cousin.

Anders got into the car. *Andersnordic* had made his excuses for the evening.

On the way to the Freemasons' headquarters, Anders started talking about the investitures of knights, about guilds and fraternities.

His relative was rather taken aback. Freemasonry was all about perfecting your own qualities, he explained.

Anders went quiet.

The Freemasons' headquarters was right by the parliament building. Inside the doors they were received by a Master of Ceremonies in a formal hat and white gloves, with a big sword hanging at his hip. In his hand he held a large staff, blue and black with a silver tip at each end.

Anders was the only one being admitted to the lodge that evening. Quite a number of brothers had come along to attend the ceremony. They greeted each other in accordance with the rituals they had all had to learn. Some wore rings to indicate which degree they belonged to, while others wore chains and crosses round their necks.

He was taken into a big room and the ceremony began. First, the Master of Ceremonies turned to Anders's two sponsors: *My brethren. On behalf of the lodge I am to convey to you its thanks for bringing this stranger to us, and accompanying him to the door of the lodge.*

Anders had to sign a document stating that he professed himself to the Christian faith and would never reveal the secrets of Freemasonry. Then he had a strip of cloth wound round his head. Now blindfolded, he had to repeat after the Master of Ceremonies:

Should I act against this my given Promise
I agree that my head be struck from my shoulders.
My heart expelled, my Tongue and Intestines torn out,
and all be thrown into the Depths of the Sea,
that my Body be burnt,
and its ashes scattered to the Air.

He was led round the room until he lost his sense of direction, then along corridors and down some steps. A door was opened and he was asked to sit down. The blindfold was removed, and he found himself alone in a tiny room that was painted black. In front of him was a table with a skull and crossbones on it. He was left there alone until someone came in and asked him several questions. Then he was blindfolded again and taken back to the big room, where he went through the rest of the initiation rituals.

He was a Brother of the First Degree.

Inside, but on the bottom rung.

All he wanted was to go home.

By the time he was dropped off at Hoffsveien, he was too late to join the raid. But there was still time to log on.

His mother's cousin had told him that the Pillars met every Wednesday and he would be happy to give him a lift. A sponsor had to make sure that the new member he had invited in attended meetings and study groups and took on guard duties.

Anders nodded. But he only attended one ordinary meeting in the course of the spring, and there he did nothing but crow. After the meeting, he remarked on a newcomer's behaviour and how poorly the initiate fitted in. And it had all been going so slowly, he moaned.

Jan Behring eventually stopped ringing Anders, even though Wenche asked him to persevere.

'He never goes out, just sits in his room on that internet thing,' she complained.

*

The goal for the spring was to be the top guild on the server, to lead the guild that succeeded in killing every monster the game could generate.

The guild members were located all over Europe and they played in English. As guild leader, Anders had a lot of responsibility. He had to make sure the players had the equipment they needed: provisions, swords, axes and shields. He had to make tactical choices and come up with battle strategies, but he also had to listen and be responsive to the other players' ideas.

In the course of that spring, *Andersnordic* grew less tolerant. He didn't care if he hurt people's feelings. When the game did not go his way, he was churlish. He would push, harry and nag.

This occasionally led to open dissent. One player thought he was taking the law into his own hands, calling him a bully and a control freak. Anders removed the player from the forum.

Some left of their own accord because he was too hardcore. He couldn't bear slackers, he said, and had no scruples about ejecting players if he didn't like them or thought they didn't work within the team. A player who dropped in on a Friday night with a glass of wine beside the keyboard and accidentally went down the wrong hill was not anyone he would want to take along on a raid.

Andersnordic preferred to throw people out late at night when the others were offline and could not protest. When the outcast logged back in, access to *Virtue* would be denied. Sometimes the other players would speak up for those who had been ousted, but the guild leader was implacable: this was serious, you couldn't just drop in for fun now and then. Players who had been involved since way before *Andersnordic* first logged in suddenly found themselves abandoned.

Slackers were generally people who had a life outside the game. A life that sometimes imposed its own demands, even obliging them to log out for long periods. The norm was to play for a few hours in the evening, after work. Most people couldn't sit up all night. As for Anders, he was living on his savings and his mother's food.

*

World of Warcraft is one of the most addictive games ever created, precisely because it is constructed on social lines. Players develop bonds with each other through their avatars, and the sense of solidarity can be strong. Every minute you spend away from the game means setting the others back slightly.

It allows you to enter a system that seems easy to grasp. If you can think strategically, success is achieved. You can measure your achievement in the minutest detail. Your goals are concrete. You get a virtual pat on the shoulder every time you log in, and your status is gradually enhanced as a result of time spent there. Everyone can succeed. Such is the online world.

Anders, who had wanted to be part of the power elite, was now one of the soldiers of *World of Warcraft*. From having been excited by the Freemasons' stately props, he was now fascinated by computer-generated suits of armour. From having been obsessed with making money, he was now a collector of *WoW* gold. From having been concerned with his appearance, he now lurked in his room, grubby and unkempt.

Anders, once so keen to build networks, no longer needed anybody but himself.

Then he was struck by hubris. Again. He changed server. To fight with the best.

He joined the guild known as *Unit* on the *Silvermoon* server. His guild was made up of newcomers, but on the official forums *Andersnordic* boasted that his crew would take over the server. They were simply the best.

'Who's that megalomaniac?' the Swedish player *Braxynglet*, ranked second on the server, asked his online peers.

At *Silvermoon*, Anders was a misfit from the start. They made fun of his style. They made fun of his name. It was odd that he used his real name – Anders – and that he hinted at his background – nordic. It was against the norm. They laughed at him, both behind his back and directly at him. He never seemed to catch it. He always responded nicely and in a friendly way, whatever they wrote.

Braxynglet despised newcomers who bragged. His way of putting this could sound like racism – a hatred of others, of outsiders. Anders took a liking to the Swede, never seeming to understand that *he* himself was the intruder, the foreigner, the immigrant. He spoke and acted on the forums as if he were one of the best, and sucked up to those at the top.

For a while, Braxynglet adopted the motto *Mohamed is gay*. Anders responded warmly, telling the Swede he was so cool, but still Anders was given the cold shoulder.

He was rejected by those who mattered.

He did not fit in. He was patient and persistent, but he never made it to the top of *World of Warcraft*. He was never among the Top 500 on the servers that mattered, and thus was never ranked.

He acted like a king, when he was only a toy.

Everything else was going to the dogs. When the 2006 accounts for E-Commerce Group were due with the auditor in 2007, board chairman Breivik was not contactable and the auditor resigned. The year after that, E-Commerce Group was compulsorily wound up. According to the bankruptcy report, the company had broken tax laws, share-trading laws and accounting laws.

Outside his room, life was unravelling.

But inside, the game went on.

Because the game had no end.

One night after a raid he stayed chatting to a player in his guild who was considering whether to pull out. He needed to get to grips with real life again, he said. Anders admitted he had thought the same. He was going to stop soon, he said.

But he didn't.

He stayed in his room.

It's only temporary, he had said. But he stayed in there for five years.

Five years in front of the screen.

A tonic to his depression.

Three Comrades

Give me the pure and the straight,
the men who are steady and strong
Those who have patience and will
never in life to go wrong . . .

Yes, give me the best amongst you,
and I shall give you all.
No one can know till victory is mine
how much to us shall fall.
It may be it means we shall save our earth.
To the best goes out my call.

Rudolf Nilsen, 'Revolusjonens røst'
(The Voice of the Revolution), 1926

'Mum, can I join the AUF?'

Tone stood there, receiver in hand. Simon had rung home at last.

'Mum, can you hear me? It only costs ten kroner!'

'So good to hear from you, Simon. I mean that's why we gave you the phone, right, so you could ring home!'

It was the winter of 2006 and Simon was thirteen and away on a trip, staying overnight in Tromsø for the first time. In Year 7 he had been elected to the student council at the secondary school in

Salangen. This year the county council organised a youth conference for northern Norway, and Simon was asked to represent his school. At the conference they discussed what improvements could be made to young people's lives in the north.

A teenage boy called Stian Johansen had talked about the AUF, the youth organisation of the Labour Party.

In the break, Simon went up to him. He introduced himself politely and carefully.

Baby face, thought the speaker

'I'd like to join the AUF,' said Simon.

Stian whipped out his membership pad and asked Simon to fill in his name and address. Recruiting new members was important. More members meant more influence and, crucially, more money in the party kitty. For every member in a political youth organisation, the state paid a contribution. Recruiting lots of people enhanced your status in the apparatus.

When Stian saw Simon's date of birth, he smiled. 'I can't sign you up – you've got to be fifteen. But if you get your parents' permission it's all right.'

Tone stood there in the kitchen, listening to the cheerful voice of her elder son. 'It's so much fun here, there've been lots of exciting discussions and debates, and the ones I agree with most are the lot from the AUF. Can I join? It only costs ten kroner!'

'Of course you can join the AUF, love,' laughed Tone.

'Okay, I'll fill in the form now and then bring it home with me, so you and Dad can sign it. I've met so many cool people, Mum! But I've got to hang up now.'

It wasn't exactly an expression of youthful rebellion on Simon's part for him to join the AUF. He had grown up in the labour move-ment: his father sat as a local councillor for the Labour Party.

Discussions round the dinner table were political, whether they were about the war in Afghanistan or drilling for oil in the sea around the Lofoten Islands. Simon was against both. The conversa-tion also revolved round more domestic issues, such as whether it was fair for Håvard to have to do penalty rounds the same length as

Simon when they had throw-snowball-at-log competitions in the garden. They had to run extra rounds when they missed the target, just like in biathlon. Simon and Håvard had inherited their father's competitive spirit. In athletics, Simon came high on the list of results in the high jump championships, and Håvard became the Norwegian champion in the boys' 1500 metres. To enlist the boys' help at home, Tone would often come up with competitions like 'Who can get to the bin with a rubbish sack first?' When they got to the skip at the top of the slope they opened the hatch and took aim from a distance.

But politics was even more exciting than sport. As a result of centralisation in Troms county and the falling numbers of children per year group in the north, each time there was a new budget to balance the politicians weighed up whether to close the upper secondary school in Salangen. Every year it fought for its life, and won. When Simon was in Year 8, he attended a county council meeting for the first time, to speak about why there should be no cuts to the school provision in the area.

Before long he was elected leader of the Salangen youth council. He devoted his energies there to campaigning for facilities for young people. In small towns and villages, sport often provided the only social life, and those who weren't sporty could find themselves left out. The central issue for him was trying to reopen the youth club that had closed down years before. The local council pledged to fund it as long as Simon could guarantee that the young people undertook the voluntary work of renovating and maintaining it. He gave his promise. The youngsters were given basement premises with a music room, dance floor, pool table and a little café they would run themselves. It would be a place to meet, for everybody. It just needed a bit of redecoration first.

'But Mum, how can I get people to come and help?' Simon asked.

'You need something to lure them in,' Tone suggested.

'Like what?'

'I could make pizza,' she offered.

Simon put up posters to advertise the working party, and by the time he got home from Velve, as the club was called, he was elated and splashed all over with red and cobalt blue paint.

'Loads of people volunteered, Mum! We ran out of paintbrushes!'

On his sixteenth birthday, 25 July 2008, Simon was old enough to become a member of the Norwegian Union of Municipal and General Employees. He joined that same day. His friends thought it was odd that he wanted union membership before he had a job.

'Everybody ought to join a union,' he argued. 'Even school pupils. The stronger we make the trade unions now, the better working life will be by the time we finish our education!' If they had a large enough pool of members, the unions could stamp down harder on shady practices in the world of work, because young people were often exploited, not paid the going rate for the job, or forced to accept poor working conditions. Employers broke laws on health and safety in the workplace and younger job applicants didn't always know their rights. That was why it was important for the trade union's summer patrol to go round the country checking up on conditions for young people.

The nicest surprise about membership was that it included several months' subscription to the left-wing newspaper *Klassekampen* – 'Class Struggle'. Simon read about the way the financial crisis was hitting the poorest people in developing countries, about social dumping and the unemployment explosion in Europe. Critical of those in power, the paper debated all the topics that interested him.

'Dad, you must read it!' he said. 'This paper's great! It tells you about stuff in a totally different way from anywhere else.'

When the summer holidays were over and he started in his first year at Sjøvegan Upper Secondary, a school under threat of closure, he wanted to do more than subscribe to *Klassekampen*. It wasn't enough to think about socialist answers to society's problems on your own. He rang the party office in Tromsø and asked how he could start a branch of the AUF in Salangen.

'Give notice of a founding meeting and then we can come and help you recruit members,' came the answer.

Simon put up notices all round the school:

INAUGURAL MEETING FOR
SALANGEN WORKERS' YOUTH LEAGUE.
In the Cultural Centre.

One evening in mid-September, three boys drove over from Tromsø. One was the leader of the Troms AUF, Brage Sollund, whom Simon had talked to on the phone. The second was the best recruiter in the county, named Geir Kåre Nilssen. With them they had a skinny Year 10 boy with glasses and a brace on his teeth. His name was Viljar Hanssen.

Over Tone's tacos they drew up their plan of action.

'Right Simon, this is what we'll do tomorrow,' said Geir Kåre. 'You go straight up to the prettiest girl in the school. It's vital we get her on board, because in most schools she's the one who decides what's cool or not. Then we'll sign up her friends, and once that's done we'll move on to the boys. Okay?'

Simon nodded.

'We'll start with the tough guys. They're always the hardest to reach, so if we can get them, this could be really big. Then it's all easy because the rest will follow.'

Simon nodded again.

'I've got a formula for you,' Brage said. 'AUF = 90% social + 10% politics.'

Brage had brought along a book to help Simon prepare for the meeting, a history of the AUF called *The Salt of the Party*. Brage read out a passage about when the legendary Einar Gerhardsen was leader of the Workers' Youth League: 'In spring 1921, Gerhardsen made it a condition of standing for re-election as chairman that there be no more dances. Study activities were to be intensified "to make every member of the group a conscious communist". His condition was accepted, but the outcome indicate that revolutionary consciousness remained lacking at grass-roots level. At the general meeting six months later, only thirty-six members remained of the original 322, a slump of almost ninety per cent!'

The boys laughed.

No, Simon wouldn't forget the social side.

They rang the local paper, which promised to come to the inaugural meeting, they planned which issues Salangen AUF would focus on, and they ended up on mattresses under warm quilts in the basement sitting room, joking the night away.

The recruiting session was timed for the lunch break.

'Okay Simon, the floor is yours,' said Geir Kåre, giving his new friend a pat on the shoulder.

A few seconds' hesitation, and Simon strode up to the prettiest girl at Sjøvegan.

'AUF?' she queried. 'For ten kroner?'

Then she smiled. 'Go on then,' and wrote her name on his pad.

Viljar came with him, and the boys went from one group of pretty girls to the next.

The membership pad was filling up. Soon they had asked everyone in the school playground and the canteen. Viljar was impressed.

'He's got a way with words, that Simon! Everybody joins,' he said to Brage and Geir Kåre.

The things Simon focused on when he spoke to each new group were: no to closure of Sjøvegan School, and yes to hot school lunches. Cheaper bus fares for young people. Things that most students agreed on. But to achieve them, they needed the AUF, Simon said, and the AUF needed them. It was as simple as that.

'You're very persuasive!' Viljar said to his fellow party member, one year his senior, when the lunch break was over. 'Salangen's golden boy. The local prince,' declared the lad from Tromsø with a laugh. 'They would have joined anything, as long as it was with you,' he teased.

Viljar was right, because everyone liked Simon. Whatever he suggested, you wanted to be a part of it. He was cheerful, he was cool, he had style. The girls in the school canteen were always aware of it when *that Simon* walked in.

In the course of the day eighty new members were signed up. Geir
Kåre and Brage had never seen anything like it. Simon basked in the
glory of his success.

'But I did talk to them beforehand, you know,' he admitted. He
had made the most of the time at break, before football matches or
at athletics training, on the way to school or in the canteen queue.
They had all known they had to bring ten kroner to school with them
that day. Simon had wanted to be as well prepared as possible when
the townies from Tromsø turned up with their membership pads.

'Ha ha,' said Viljar. 'So you'd warmed them up in advance, eh?'

He in turn had been recruited by Brage, who came up to him at
a youth conference when Viljar was thirteen and asked: 'Hi, have you
heard of the AUF?'

'Yes.'

'Good, I'm its leader.'

The local paper, *Salangen News*, had already announced the same
morning that 'Friday the 19th of September 2008 will be a historic
day in the community of Salangen. A local branch of the Workers'
Youth League is to be set up. Simon Sæbø is heading the initiative.'

The Tromsø lads made sure there were bowls of sweets on the
tables at the start of the meeting. Simon was unanimously elected
leader, a friend of his called Johan Haugland was appointed his deputy
and a committee was selected. The brand-new leader told the local
paper he was going to fight for extended opening hours for the youth
club, and activities like 'football matches on the big screen, pool tournaments and an inaugural outing up to the hunting and fishing cabin
at Sagvannet.' The paper provided the detail that there would be
dinner at the cabin on Friday and Saturday, but participants had to
take food with them for other meals. The local branch would hold
regular meetings in coming weeks, the paper promised, and rounded
off the piece with Simon's mobile number in case there were any further questions.

Their meeting place was to become the Sæbøs' blue house in
Heiaveien. Tone would fry up some mince, add taco spices and heat
the shells in the oven. She would put out dishes of sweetcorn,

chopped tomatoes and grated cheese. Other times she made her own pizza. If Simon forgot to buy in banners, marker pens, paper or anything else they needed, his mother had usually already done it. Inspirational leader he may have been, Simon was a logistical nightmare. Luckily, he had a very organised mother.

The young people demonstrated in support of the school, against what mankind was doing to the climate, in favour of the youth club and against drilling for oil in the Arctic. They held 'get to know each other' evenings, concerts and seminars. Simon had overcome his childhood stage fright. Now he was keen to be the compère when they staged cultural events in the town. After a demonstration against racism, the under-eighteens from the asylum seekers' reception centre were invited to the youth club. The refugees had never felt entirely welcome there before, feeling it was 'the Norwegians' place'. But when big posters went up at the reception centre saying 'Welcome to Velve' they came, first hesitantly, then in big groups. Simon even tried to recruit some of them to the AUF. The fact that they had not yet been granted leave to stay was of no consequence, they could just give their address as 'Sjøvegan Asylum Centre'. He'd treat them to the ten kroner.

———

The minibar was emptied before they got there. The hotel always took care of that before the delegates to the county youth parliament checked in. The county administration made the demand whenever accommodation was provided for unaccompanied minors.

On the floor was the crumpled plastic bag that they had brought the beer in. Empty bottles were already lining up by the door.

There were three of them, all mates. Simon and Viljar sat on the bed, Anders Kristiansen in the easy chair. They were comrades-in-arms from the AUF. Before the conference started, they always held their own sectional meeting. The county had invited young people from different political parties, culturally active youngsters, environmentalists, and a few individual high fliers with no political affiliation. There was also to be a geographical spread, and a gender balance.

Anders Kristiansen was the driving force in the gang of three. He was the one who brought them back to politics whenever Simon and Viljar started joking and messing around, or talking about girls.

'Listen you two, about the road safety plan: I've got a few comments. Look . . . ' he might say, and then they tuned back in.

If they disagreed about anything, they would always turn to Anders and ask, 'What do you think?'

And then they would do it the way Anders wanted. In actual fact all three of them were used to getting their way, but Anders was the first among equals.

He was six months younger than Simon and came from the neighbouring municipality of Bardu, home to Norway's largest military garrison. Just like Simon, he started a local AUF branch when he was fifteen, and was elected its leader. He was the most practical of the three, the one who always took charge of the tickets if they were going anywhere and kept tabs on the paperwork for meetings, not least the agenda.

'Troms county is far too centralised,' Anders was saying now. 'Everything that counts happens in Tromsø. We must spread activities across the county, devolve power; only then we can keep the population figures up in the more rural areas.'

'We've got to get the "Home for fifty kroner" resolution passed,' said Simon, who had come by bus from Salangen to Tromsø that same afternoon, a journey of three hours. Troms spreads over an extended area, and people live long distances from each other. For young people, the bus is the best means of transport. But a journey requiring lots of changes could cost a lot. The proposition was that young people would be able to go as far as they wanted in one direction for fifty kroner.

'You and your buses,' laughed city boy Viljar. Until he moved to Svalbard when his father – an expert in Arctic birdlife – got a job there, he used to boast that he had hardly even been across Tromsø Bridge. 'I see you need to get to the big city now and then for a breath of air!' he said laughingly to Simon. Though he now lived among polar bears and snowmobiles on Svalbard, they still saw him as a typical Tromsø type – with it and brimming with self-confidence.

'The bus is important, all the same,' Anders said firmly, with the documents and minutes from the previous meeting in front of him.

Anders Kristiansen liked to keep account of things from an early age. Aged just one, he would stand by the fence keeping all the passers-by updated: 'Mummy at work. Daddy at home.' And he liked to make sure everybody was all right. When his mother washed Mousey, his cuddly toy, and hung it out to dry on the clothes line in the garden, he came rushing up to her.

'Not by the ears, Mummy! Not by the ears!' Once the pegs had been taken off Mousey's ears, Anders said gravely: 'You mustn't ever hang anybody by the ears, Mummy. Nobody can stand that.'

When Anders started at nursery school, he was already interested in work and taxes, and how everything was shared out. 'Where does money come from?' the boy asked. He wanted explanations of everything and to know how things functioned, from the lawnmower and his father's kitchen knife to who was in charge of whom. Who was the boss where his father worked, and where his mother worked? Who was the boss at home? Who really decided things?

When he was five and found out there was somebody called the Prime Minister, who decided most things, he said in his thick Bardu accent, 'When I'm big, I'm going to be Prime Minister.'

If he was in doubt about the slightest thing, he ran round to their neighbour. Because she had an encyclopedia. Vigdis worked long days in the canteen at the military base in Bardufoss. Whenever Anders came to see her she gave him a glass of squash and made coffee for herself. Then they sat down side by side on the sofa with their noses in the book. One word led to another and the little boy and old lady soaked up new ideas and definitions.

When confirmation was approaching for the year group above his, Anders asked:

'What does atheist mean?'

'Someone who doesn't believe in God,' came Vigdis's brisk reply. She didn't need to look that one up.

'Well then, I'm an atheist and a pacifist,' the thirteen-year-old told her.

Vigdis tutted in dismay. Faith in God was a serious matter in the village.

But Anders stood his ground. When his classmates were preparing for confirmation the following year, Anders took a unilateral decision not to be part of it. His maternal grandfather, a strict Lutheran Pietist from Narvik, said straight out that he was not happy with Anders's choice. According to the Pietists, harsh punishment in Hell awaited those who turned their faces away from God.

'It must be pretty damned empty in Heaven then,' Anders's mother observed drily when she heard what the old man had said. There were all too many things for which you could get sent to Hell in Narvik, and Gerd Kristiansen had heard her fair share of such talk when she was a child. She supported her son and refused to believe anyone from Narvik was guarding the gates to the Heavenly Kingdom. Anders said that if he had had faith in any higher power he would have believed as much in Allah and Buddha as in God the Father.

Life on earth was what concerned him. The here and now. 'They've got to listen to us,' Anders had been saying since he was a child. 'We're part of society too! Why are there only grown-ups on the local council?'

Anders Kristiansen was of course chosen to lead the Bardu student council. Just as Simon Sæbø on the other side of the municipal boundary and Viljar Hanssen of Svalbard were.

The county youth parliament was made for them.

Now they sat there, the three comrades, representing their council districts and putting forward their views over a few beers, trying to reach a consensus on their strategy for the meeting. Before the night was over, they always reached agreement about the most important issues they would be voting on. Then Viljar and Anders had to make sure they woke Simon the next morning, so he didn't miss the ballot. Simon was a very sound sleeper.

That evening they were talking about more than just buses; they were talking about power.

The county youth council in Troms was led by a girl from the Progress Party Youth. She was pretty, quick-witted and popular. But the three comrades were planning to outmanoeuvre her and stage a coup. Just before the ballot they were going to propose a motion from the floor that Anders Kristiansen should become leader. With all his excellent qualities, victory lay glittering ahead of them.

It was all Viljar's idea. He was an ardent anti-racist and saw the Progress Party as a bunch of brownshirts, not representative of general opinion in the youth council.

This was the plan: Just before the vote, Viljar would stand up and propose his comrade. Nobody would be expecting another candidate. Then they would all go up in turn and speak warmly of Anders. Viljar, the one of the three who really had a way with words, would talk about Anders as a political phenomenon from the sparsely populated district of Bardu, where he had shown more initiative than anybody else, not only as an AUF leader but also as chair of the student council.

He tried out the wording on his friends.

'It's not just that the local people mean a lot to Anders, but that Anders means an awful lot to the local people,' he said with passion, and went on: 'Anders's list of achievements is as long as our coastline.'

The three comrades had also roped in Johan Haugland, deputy leader of Salangen AUF, for their coup. He was going to talk about the main distinctions between the Progress Party and the Labour Party, and thus between the two candidates.

'And lastly we want you to inspire the girls, Simon,' directed Viljar. 'Say whatever you like, as long as you melt their hearts. You've got to make them feel that with Anders as leader, the council will really come to life. Say something like: Anders is not only my best friend, he can also be your best friend,' suggested Viljar. 'Or ask them: Do you want to be led by some bloody racist?'

'That's over the top,' said Anders.

'How about: We want a leader who likes dark people as much as pale ones,' Viljar persisted.

'Pack it in,' muttered Anders.

Simon was swinging on his chair in the corner of the room. 'No, it'll be fine,' he said. He had started making notes. 'Anyway, don't worry, Anders, I'll judge the mood when I get up there. I'll think of something, and it'll be good!' Simon wasn't the sort to go in for meticulous planning, preferring to think on his feet.

The little round table in the hotel room was covered in a clutter of empty beer bottles, *snus* tins, documents and scribbled notes.

Anders started to yawn. He generally did when anything dragged on into the small hours. So he went off to bed while Simon and Viljar took a quick look in the mirror.

Then they hit the town. Laughing, they slipped into the Blårock Café even though they were several years below the age limit. Over a beer they talked about girls, sports, girls, clothes, girls, life and girls. Simon had a girlfriend, but had his eye on a few girls for Viljar. 'Check her out, check her out,' he said and then vanished, reappearing with a girl and saying, 'Have you met Viljar?' Then he moved off, further into the club, and was gone again.

The night before the coup, they stayed on there until closing time and ended up at an after-party. They got back to the hotel just as the breakfast room opened. Stuff happens. They locked themselves into the room they were sharing, showered in turn and started doing their hair. It was the hair that took the time. They stood side by side in front of the bathroom mirror with towels round their hips and the requisite amount of Renati hair wax in their hands. The wax had to be rubbed in from the back, moving up and over. The hair at the sides had to be styled in to their cheeks, while the hair at the back was shaped in a wave round the head, finishing above one eye. It took a heck of a lot of effort to make the whole thing look casual.

Their clothes were chosen with great care too. Simon favoured the style the kids went for, T-shirts with prints and leather thong jewellery around his neck and wrists. Viljar went for a more classic look, grey trousers and a grey cardigan with a black T-shirt underneath.

In the breakfast room Anders Kristiansen was sitting over a substantial plate of bacon and eggs. He shook his head when he saw

Simon and Viljar coming in, their eyes gleaming. They often kept going round the clock at the youth conferences. Now, they wolfed down a big breakfast to calm their nerves before the coup.

But the whole scheme came to nothing anyway. When Viljar made his proposal from the floor, the rules said that only one person was allowed to argue the candidate's case. So, the others did not get to deliver their carefully crafted words of praise.

Viljar couldn't do it alone. It was a shambles. They were a gang, they were meant to do it together. He couldn't pull it off on his own.

'Shit,' said Viljar afterwards.

'You'll get her next time Anders!' said Simon.

'Course I will,' smiled Anders. 'Next year she won't stand a chance!'

He would go at it for all he was worth. While Simon and Viljar were involved in all sorts of things, Anders stuck to just the one: politics. He wasn't sporty, he didn't mess about with his hair or waste time on clothes, nor was he into computer games. The closest he got to a hobby was keeping up with *The West Wing* or sitting in the hut he'd built in the garden, watching *Sex and the City* with a girl friend. He would shout 'Mum, come and watch!' when *Desperate Housewives* started. 'I'd rather have some desperate men,' his mother called back before she came in with a plate of waffles and cloudberry jam.

Childhood was the subject currently uppermost in Anders's mind. He was working with the county governor on 'The Giant Leap', a project to establish how Troms County was complying with the UN Convention on the Rights of the Child, and how children and young people could be more involved in the decision-making process. He was collaborating with the children's ombudsman in plans for the Youth Parliament, and brooding at the same time about the stance he should take on Norway's military involvement in Afghanistan. He was the one of them who – as Viljar put it – 'talked to the grown-ups'.

———

'That was amazing,' said Simon.

The three comrades were all at their computers, Skyping each other. Viljar in Svalbard, Anders in Bardu and Simon in Salangen.

'Magic,' added Viljar.

'Did you hear the way he repeated the words, took up the thread again to finish off? He, like, moved on from the whole subject and then brought it out again towards the end,' said Anders.

'Timing,' said Simon.

'Pauses,' said Viljar.

'Empathy,' said Anders.

The three comrades had all read various editions of *Famous Speeches*. They had now experienced a man of their own time with the same level of rhetorical skill.

'He's recreating the magic of Martin Luther King,' said Viljar.

It was Barack Obama they were taking about. They had been listening to one of his first speeches in the election campaign of 2008, and they were hooked.

Autumn came and northern Norway's season of darkness arrived. In the US, tension was running high.

'Mum, can you ask if I can have a day off school on Wednesday?'

Anders was keen to watch the news broadcasts all through election night, but then he would not be fit for school the next day.

'It's actually not fair,' argued the fifteen-year-old. 'Other people get time off to go to training sessions and matches and camps. Why do they get authorised absence to do sport stuff, which is their hobby, but my hobby, politics, doesn't count? Why's it any different for me?'

Anders's mother suggested he write a letter to the headteacher, putting his case forward. Anders wrote about the momentous Obama–McCain election and how important the outcome was for the whole world, including Bardu. He got his day off. And the nickname Little Obama from his paternal grandfather in Lavangen.

On the first Tuesday evening of November 2008, election day on the other side of the Atlantic, the three comrades were on their sofas in their living rooms, Skyping as they waited for the polling stations to close and the votes to be counted, state by state.

'America,' Anders said dreamily. 'If Obama wins, shall we take a trip over there when we leave school? I could work at the local old people's home and save up.'

'Count me in!' shouted Simon from Salangen. 'Let's hire a car and drive coast to coast!'

'We can buy a car on the east coast, take Route 66 and sell it at a profit when we get to the west coast!' suggested Viljar. 'A Mustang, whaddya reckon? Or a Pontiac Firebird, or an old Corvette?'

Long before the sparse daylight began to show itself on the horizon, the three comrades in their darkened living rooms were jubilant. It felt like such a huge event. A black president, a Democrat, someone with experience of ordinary life, not some rich, privileged type. To the three teenagers miles north of the Arctic Circle on the other side of the Atlantic, at such a distance from the Chicago crowds, Obama somehow felt like one of them.

One day they'd get there, to America, come what may.

Daybreak found Viljar and Simon asleep in front of their television sets. This time it was Anders who stayed awake round the clock.

Change was possible!

––––––––

One April morning the year after the US election, when the snow still lay deep on the ground round Sjøvegan School, Simon was eating his standard breakfast at his desk. Four slices of bread from a plastic bag and a bottle of strawberry jam to squeeze onto them. He was always too tired to eat at home, and stumbled the short walk down to the school like a sleepwalker. His body only started to wake up towards the end of the first lesson. Then he was always ravenous and would devour his bread and jam in the short break before the next lesson. On this particular morning, as he was polishing off the last slice his mobile rang. He wiped his mouth and put the phone to his ear.

'Someone's had to drop out of congress. Can you step in?'

'What?'

'Well you're a deputy, and Jan's cow's fallen sick so he can't make it. We've got to have a full delegation from Troms.'

'Do you mean the Labour Party National Congress?'

'Yes. Bit slow on the uptake, aren't you?'

'I'll have to ask Dad.'

'Make sure you don't miss the plane. It leaves Bardufoss at eleven-thirty!'

Simon quickly gathered up his books, pencils and jam bottle from the desk and told the teacher.

'I'm going to be a delegate to the Labour Party National Congress and I'll have to ask for time off.'

Then he rang his father. 'What should I say?'

Gunnar checked with his boss if he could take time off from work to drive his son to the airport. Of course the boy should go! You couldn't even call it skipping school. Gunnar had never been anywhere near the National Congress himself, and now his son was to be a delegate, at just sixteen and a half. Clumps of trees flashed by as Gunnar sped along the road to Bardufoss.

'What a stroke of luck, Dad,' exclaimed Simon when the flight to Oslo was announced. 'A sick cow!'

On arrival in Oslo he went straight to Youngstorget. The event was being held at the Congress Centre – The House of the People – the big building that occupied one whole side of the square, all the way along to Møllergata.

'Simon Sæbø,' he said at the table where they were registering delegates.

He was issued with a name badge and an accreditation card to wear round his neck – *Delegate, Troms. Labour Party National Congress 2009* – and a sheaf of papers, a programme, proposals of new resolutions, a songbook.

He went up the wide staircase to the main hall, slipping past all the old hands who were standing there chatting. Before boarding the plane he had sent a text about the sick cow to Viljar and Little Obama.

'Go get 'em,' Viljar replied.

'Show them who Simon Sæbø is,' texted Anders.

The congress was the party's top decision-making body. This was where policy would be carved out for the next parliamentary term.

The red–green coalition had been in charge since 2005. The financial crisis came the autumn before Simon's congress debut. In Norway, unemployment was rising for the first time in years. 'The Labour Party has lost its vision' was a view increasingly heard. 'It's become a party of administration no longer able to inspire people,' the newspaper commentators complained. They wanted some new blood.

Simon, Anders and Viljar were the new blood. And here was Simon, sitting star-struck in the row of seats for the Troms delegates, looking about him. There were people he had only ever seen on TV. There was Gro Harlem Brundtland, laughing loudly. She was celebrating her seventieth birthday and was to be honoured with speeches and good wishes from both Hillary Clinton and the UN Secretary-General. There were the powerful Martin Kolberg, the ubiquitous Trond Giske and good-humoured Hadia Tajik.

If there was anything Simon wanted to know, he simply asked Brage Sollund. The nineteen-year-old who had come over when Simon started the AUF branch in Salangen was also a first-timer at the congress, but he had more experience in the party. They looked so smart sitting there in nice shirts and dark jackets. They had both styled their fringes over to one side, Brage's several shades lighter than Simon's.

The congress was declared open. Simon put on his reading glasses. All the paperwork was in the folder in front of him. It was a bit late to start looking at it now. He would have to get to grips with things as they went along.

There was a lot at stake, with a general election coming up in the autumn. Prime Minister and Labour Party leader Jens Stoltenberg had to make people believe that the government's social project was going to carry on. The opinion polls were showing that voters were far from convinced.

There was a round of applause for Jens Stoltenberg as he went to the lectern. All round the country fellow party members were following the speech on the internet.

'The first thing to say is: this crisis is global! We have been brutally reminded how small the world is,' began the man who was an economist by profession.

'Reagan said in his First Inaugural Address: "Government is not the solution to our problem; government is the problem." Margaret Thatcher went as far to say, "There is no such thing as society." This led to three decades hailing the unregulated market. And the cultivation of greed.'

The Prime Minister looked straight at his audience.

'What went wrong? Well, comrades, when the American investment bank Lehman Brothers collapsed, it was not just a bank going broke, it was a political ideology going bankrupt. The failure of market liberalism. It ended decades of naive, uncritical faith in the market looking after itself. It does not!'

The previous autumn, as Simon was setting up the Salangen AUF, Stoltenberg's government implemented measures based on a Keynesian stabilisation model. The banks were given the money they needed, export industry got increased guarantees and money was earmarked for investment at home. There were tax concessions for business and industry, and maintenance work in the municipalities was brought forward to keep employment levels from slumping.

It was to prove effective. Admittedly, Norway had been better prepared than most countries thanks to its considerable income from oil and gas, and unemployment rose to no more than a little above 3 per cent. Lending rates went down, as did inflation. Robust state regulation of banks, insurance companies and financial institutions meant the Prime Minister had more means at his disposal than his counterparts around Europe. As Stoltenberg repeatedly reminded everyone throughout the crisis, 'The market is a good servant, but a bad master.'

'The market cannot rule, it has to be ruled. The market is not self-regulating. It has to be regulated,' declared Stoltenberg.

'Four more years!' yelled some people in the audience.

'Four more years!' yelled Simon. It was a history lesson, a sociology lesson and an introduction to rhetoric all in one.

In the break, Simon went over to the table where bottles of Farris mineral water were on offer. 'Free Farris!' he had pointed out to Brage earlier. Two men were coming towards him.

'Here's the youngest delegate at conference,' one said to the other. Simon straightened up.

'Hello, I'm Jens. Good to meet you,' said the Prime Minister.

'Simon Sæbø, from Salangen.'

'So you're from Troms . . . ' began Stoltenberg.

Simon had no time for small talk. With the Prime Minister in front of him, he had to strike while the iron was hot. He spoke with passion about the fish-farming industry in the Salang fjord where the net pens were crowded with salmon.

'But the framework agreement for fish farmers . . . ' he continued, elaborating on the problems facing the industry. In the AUF they called him the Fisheries Minister.

Simon won a pat on the shoulder and a 'Keep it up!'

Somebody took a photo. The Prime Minister and the Fisheries Minister, something to send to Anders and Viljar!

At the congress dinner, Simon was impressed by grown-up life – the posh food, the red wine, the witty speeches and the ladies in evening dresses. Afterwards, everybody went out into town. The bars and cafés round Youngstorget filled up with delegates from the nineteen counties of Norway. Simon went with the Troms delegation to one of them, Justisen.

Brage got in, the people behind Brage got in. Simon was stopped.

'ID! It's over-twenties only here!'

The sixteen-year-old looked up at an intimidating chest and brandished the card he had round his neck.

'See this? Delegate from Troms county to the Labour Party Congress. You think Troms county would let under-age kids run the show?'

The doorman waved him into the glorious darkness. The lads found themselves sharing a table over some beers with the leading lady of the Justice Committee in Parliament.

'This is what I want to do!' he texted to his comrades.

Politics was fun. Life was brilliant.

Writings

He called it the fart room.

The ceiling was painted white, the walls were papered in a geometric design. Embossed triangles, squares and circles ran from floor to ceiling. The wallpaper had hung there for a long time and started to yellow. It was a narrow box of a room with an opening at each end. A single bed ran along under the window.

The brick-built apartment block stood at a junction in a former industrial area in Skøyen. Anders's room looked out at the back. From the window he could jump down onto the grassy area between the blocks if he wanted, because his mother had bought a ground-floor flat. In the middle of the grass, in the middle of his field of vision if he turned his head away from the screen, stood the big birch tree. If he stood up, he could just about see the end of his mother's balcony. There was an artificial thuja in a red pot, and two window boxes hanging from the rail. In these his mother had planted plastic roses in bark chips the colour of soil. When she bought them, the roses were white and pale pink, but age and the elements had faded them. The petals had turned grey.

This was the view from the window of his room.

It was an internet hermit's room. The black leather swivel chair was soft, deep and accommodating. Just the right height for the screen. There was some IKEA shelving where he kept paper and ink cartridges. On the floor beside the printer were two safes.

The only objects telling another story were three bold pictures on the wall. They were faces, painted with the sharply delineated shadow technique of the graffiti artist. The faces were grey, the backgrounds dramatic orange or bright turquoise. They were the work of Coderock, a Norwegian artist with roots in graffiti. Once, he had been so proud of owning them, boasting that they had been painted specially for him.

If he left the room he could go left, turn the handle of the front door, go down a short set of steps and be out in Hoffsveien, where the pavement was separated from the road by a narrow verge with trees. On the other side of the road were a Coop, a flower shop and a café. His mother went to the café every day to meet up with her neighbours, drink coffee and smoke.

But generally when Anders left his room he turned right, into his mother's flat.

Whenever he wanted to eat something; to get a glass of water; to go out onto the balcony for a smoke, or needed the loo: always to the right.

He also turned right to take a shower. For that he had to go through another room, his mother's bedroom. At the foot end of her double bed a door opened into a tiny bathroom with a shower. Beside the shower cabinet, its frosted glass decorated with lilies, was a wash-basin, and above that a mirror with a built-in fluorescent light. There was a generous overhead light that did not cast any shadows. It gave anyone standing at the mirror a good view of their face.

Hanging on the wall was a white shelf unit divided into two sections, one for him and one for her. Standing in front of the mirror like that, there was just room to turn round without bumping against the washing machine in the corner. Everything that was not strictly necessary, like dirty-washing baskets and piles of towels, had to be kept in their rooms. After a shower, the steam had to be aired out through his mother's bedroom.

Back in his room, he would don some of the clothes that were folded up or on hangers in the fitted wardrobe that was painted a shade of pale blue, the sort that was popular just after the war.

He had little use for his coat. His room was two steps from the front door, but he seldom turned to the left and opened it.

It's only temporary, he said when he moved from Tidemands gate in the summer of 2006.

'He's hibernating,' said Magnus, the childhood friend who'd become a fire fighter. He was sorry that Anders had disappeared from his life. Magnus was working full-time and shared a flat with his girl-friend as Anders moved back home and was swallowed up by the magical world of the mages. 'It's as if his life has fallen apart,' Magnus's girlfriend remarked.

A year into his hibernation, Anders had one of his rare encounters with friends. He told them he was collecting texts.

'What for?' they asked.

'For a book about the Islamisation of Europe.'

'Can't you spend your time on something useful instead?' Magnus asked.

It was important that somebody took on the task, Anders replied.

His friends didn't believe what he said about the book. They thought he had become a compulsive gamer and worried about him. A few carried on ringing to tell him about parties and pre-parties for some time after he went into hibernation.

After two years in his room, in the summer of 2008, he suddenly felt like being sociable and rang his friends. *Andersnordic* logged off from the games; so did the other avatars he had created, like *Conservatism* and *Conservative*. All at once he was out and about, order-ing the sweet drinks he preferred. 'Ladies' drinks,' his friends teased. But he didn't care. He had never liked beer.

Anders had changed. He had developed a one-track mind.

From always having countless irons in the fire, he had turned into someone engrossed in just one thing. Having launched so many busi-ness ideas, he was now monothematic.

'He's in a tunnel,' said Magnus. Hoping he would soon see the light at the other end.

That summer, Anders delivered long lectures on the Islamisation of Europe.

'The Muslims are waging demographic war,' he said. 'We're living in *dhimmitude* and being conned by *al-Taqiyya*.'

'Eh?' said his friends.

'The Muslims will take power in Europe because they have so many bloody children,' Anders explained. 'They pretend to be sub-ordinating themselves, but they'll soon be in the majority. Look at the statistics . . . '

The words poured out of him.

'The Labour Party has ruined our country. It's feminised the state and made it into a matriarchy,' he told his mates. 'And more than any-thing, it's made it a place where it's impossible to get rich. The Labour Party's let the Muslims occupy . . . '

He started repeating himself. They generally let him go on for a while before they asked him to change the subject. His friends glossed over his peculiarities, the strange behaviour and extreme topics of conversation, because it was good that he was at least getting out. It surely wouldn't be long before he was back to his old self.

When his friends finally told him to shut up, he generally stopped talking. He could not cope with the transition from didactic mono-loguing to ordinary chatting. He could only talk about what his friends called his 'gloomy outlook on the world'.

'Do you think anyone's going to be interested in reading your book?' asked one of his friends.

Anders just smiled.

In spite of everything, Anders's friends were impressed by all the knowledge he had amassed. He liked discussing the Qur'an with Pakistani taxi drivers and 'knew it better than the Muslims did them-selves', his friends joked. Anders's vocabulary was peppered with Arabic expressions and foreign words. His friends grew accustomed to concepts like multiculturalism, cultural Marxism and Islamism.

Anders had found a new world. It had been lying there waiting for him, close beside the world of gaming.

He could sit in his room, in the same deep, black chair, with the same screen in front of him. He could click his way into Gates of

Vienna instead of *World of Warcraft*. Into Stormfront instead of *Age of Conan*. Jihad Watch instead of *Call of Duty*.

One website led to another. He found the sites engrossing, compelling, bursting with new information. Gates of Vienna had an aura of proud, European history about it, with its many colour pictures of great battles of the past. There were Biblical quotations, urbane discussions. Stormfront had a harsher, more brutal style, referencing fascist propaganda of the 1930s. The website called itself the voice of the new white minority that was ready to fight, and its emblem bore the motto 'White Pride, World Wide'.

Jihad Watch went in for criticism of Islam and adorned its web pages with Islamic symbols. Books promoted on the site were likely to have the words 'Islam' and 'war' in the title. At the top of the homepage, a green crescent and a pair of dark eyes stared out from behind a chequered Middle Eastern scarf.

Whether it was couched in refined terms or cruder ones, the message was the same. Crushing the influence of Islam in the West.

The websites had a strong sense of solidarity, of 'us'. It's us against the interlopers. Us as a group under threat. Us as the chosen people.

Us against them. Us against your lot.

He didn't even have to do anything to be one of them; there was no need to try to impress anyone. All he had to do was join the mailing list to get the newsletters, or click onto the site to follow the debates. Sometimes they requested donations, to be shared out between the contributors, but nobody demanded anything of him.

Criticism was reserved for others: the state, feminists, Islamists, socialists and politically correct Western leaders. It was the injustices inflicted on Europeans in the past, it was the mass immigration in the present; it was beheadings and castrated knights, mass rape, the destruction of the white race.

The massacre of the European people had to be stopped!

He had found his niche. Again.

The *New York Times* best-selling author Robert Spencer, who founded the Jihad Watch site, was one of his favourites. So was Pamela Geller, who ran the blog Atlas Shrugs. He paid close attention to what the two Americans wrote. Bat Ye'or, alias Gisèle Littman, was another of the stars in this firmament. Born into a Jewish family in Cairo, she had languished as a subservient subject of Muslim society. Her family left Egypt after the Suez Crisis, and she later wrote *Eurabia: The Euro–Arab Axis*. Presiding over it all as moderator of Gates of Vienna was the American Edward S. May, using his pseudonym Baron Bodissey.

But the one who shone most brightly of all was a character calling himself Fjordman. He was an apocalyptic figure prone to spreading prophecies of doom. And he was Norwegian. Anders devoured everything that 'The dark prophet of Norway' wrote, downloading it for storage. 'When I was born, Norway was 100% white,' Fjordman wrote on Gates of Vienna. 'If I reach a very old age and am still living here, I may be in a minority in my own country.'

There he had it. The truth, revealed in uncensored form. Fjordman wrote about Muslim men raping Scandinavian women, his analyses spanning the centuries as he discussed everything from Plato to Orwell. He predicted the ruination of Europe if the current trend continued and thought, as did Bat Ye'or, that the political elites had thrown in their lot with Muslim leaders in order to destroy European culture and transform the continent to a Muslim Eurabia.

Someone had to offer resistance.

There in the fart room, Anders felt a strong sense of kinship with Fjordman, who came across as uncompromising, brilliant and well-read. Everything Anders wanted to be.

In October 2008, using the profile *Year 2183*, he tried to make contact with Fjordman via the Gates of Vienna website.

'When will your book be available for distribution, Fjordman?' he asked, and then added, 'I'm writing a book on my own,' before concluding with 'Keep up the good work mate. You are a true hero of Europe.'

No answer was forthcoming from his role model. Five days later, he adopted a more critical tone.

'To Fjordman and others who are competent on this area,' he began. 'I've noticed from earlier essays that your solution is to attempt to democratically halt immigration completely and perhaps launch an anti-sharia campaign, or just wait until the system implodes in a civil war.

'I disagree,' he went on, criticising the others on the forum, such as Spencer and Bat Ye'or, for not daring to use the D-word. Deportation. Fjordman had only spoken up about stemming the Islamic tide by stopping Muslim immigration to Europe. What about the Muslims already in our country, asked Anders. Before long, half the population of Europe would be Muslim, he predicted, giving figures to illustrate the increasing demographic distortion in countries such as Kosovo and Lebanon, where the Muslim population was growing rapidly while the number of Christians fell.

'The above is an illustration from my coming book (it will be free to distribute btw)' he wrote of the statistics he had provided, and then reiterated that it was cowardly not to use the D-word. 'I assume because it is considered a fascist method in nature, which would undermine your work?' he wrote to Fjordman.

Deporting all Muslims was the only rational solution, he continued, because even if immigration were halted the Muslims already in Europe would have so many children that they would become the majority.

He never received a reply from the top names in the field, not from Robert Spencer, nor from Bat Ye'or, nor from Fjordman.

How could he make himself heard?

On the evening of 13 February 2009, there was a ring at the door. His mother opened it.

'He doesn't want visitors,' she said.

'We just thought . . . '

Three friends had decided to try to get Anders to come out. It was his thirtieth birthday. The birthday boy was sitting behind the door of his room, a few metres from the front door, and could hear everything they said.

His mother's second cousin had not completely given up on him, either. As Anders' sponsor, it was his duty to follow through with the relation he had introduced into the Masonic lodge. But each time he rang, Anders claimed to be busy with his book.

'What's that book of yours about?'

'It's a book about conservatism,' Anders replied.

'All right.'

'And about the Crusaders, the Battle of Vienna in 1683 . . . '

'Oh, well,' said Jan Behring.

On one occasion, Anders was obliged to attend. The fraternity was holding its annual family lodge meeting, at which members would sit with those they were related to, regardless of degree. Anders simply had to go along. It was a long ceremony; he lost valuable hours at the screen. It was no longer computer games drawing him in, but those texts. They took up all the space.

Some two hours later, the rituals had finally finished and everyone stood up and went out to the lobby. Anders followed them and waited for his older companion to go to the cloakroom, put on his coat and drive him home. When he finally offered to fetch the coats himself, the cousin told him this was just a break. The ceremony was only half over.

Anders could stand no more, and left the Armigeral Hall.

He must be disappointed that there aren't more young men here, thought his relative.

Anders also withdrew from virtual friends he had been close to. Some hardcore players urged him to come back to *World of Warcraft*. 'Things are going okay in the guild but new mage sucks compared to you,' wrote a guy on his team. Several sent messages asking him to start playing again.

He was generally logged out of the games these days. He had stopped paying his monthly subscription to some of them, so he would not be tempted to join one more battle, one more raid, one more fight.

One day when he went out to buy a part for the computer, he ran into an old friend in the street. Kristian, with whom he had shared a business and who, on their last encounter late at night in the city, had accused him of being a closet homosexual.

'What are you up to now?' asked Kristian.

'I'm writing a book,' said Anders.

'Great,' said Kristian. He would finally have a use for all those swanky foreign words of his. But it was a bit weird, all the same, he thought. Anders had been primarily interested in earning money, as much as possible, as fast as possible. How could he make any money out of something as obscure as this? Crusaders? Islam?

Sometimes Anders consulted document.no, a Norwegian website run by former Marxist-Leninist Hans Rustad, who over the years had become a cultural conservative, distinctly critical of Islam. Document.no kept careful track of the latest news. Its debate forum attracted a steady stream of visitors.

A week before the general election, due to be held on 14 September 2009, the username Anders B posted his first comment on document.no. It was about why the media ignored Muslim riots. There was 'an increasing trend in Western Europe towards acceptance of the media hushing things up'. He used the unrest in French towns around Bastille Day, 14 July, as an example. *Le Monde* and other French newspapers had refused to write about the riots, he claimed. But the quotes he used were part of a different story, namely that it was the French local authorities who had refused to answer questions from *Le Monde*, citing 'official instructions'.

This sort of quotation out of context was to become a hallmark. Twisting and turning things to make them suit Anders B.

Responses poured in. Everyone replying to him on document.no that day took what he had written at face value. The response whetted his appetite. That first afternoon as a contributor to document.no he dipped into two other subjects: the killing of whites in South Africa – 'a systematic, racially motivated genocide' – and multiculturalism as an anti-European ideology of hatred with the aim of destroying European culture and identity as well as Christianity.

Now he was in his stride. He recommended everybody following the thread to read Fjordman's book *Defeating Eurabia* so they would realise where Europe was heading. All those who dared to criticise

multiculturalism were branded fascists and racists, a political correctness permitting no alternative view. 'The Progress Party is one
victim of this intolerance,' he concluded just before midnight. His
threads continued with a life of their own.

Inspired, the following morning he wrote an open letter to
Fjordman, a year after trying to reach him on Gates of Vienna. This
time he posted it in the comment section of document.no.

> Fjordman,
> I've now worked full-time for over three years on a solution-
> oriented work (compendium written in English). I have tried to
> concentrate on areas a little to one side of your main focus. A lot
> of the information I have gathered is not known to most people,
> including you.
> If you email me at year2083@gmail.com I will send an electronic
> copy when I have finished it.

Two days later he received a reply.

> Hello, this is Fjordman. You wanted to get hold of me?

Anders B answered straight away:

> The book is ready but it will take a few months to prepare the
> practicalities for dispatch, will send it partially electronically.
> Defeating Eurabia is brilliant but it's going to take time for books
> like these to penetrate the censorship effectively. I've chosen free
> distribution as a counter strategy.

There was silence from Fjordman.

Wenche, on the other hand, heard plenty about 'the fjord man', as she
called him. Every day over dinner she got a little update. The words
he used to describe the fjord man were 'clever', 'my idol', 'such a
good writer'. Hans Rustad was also part of the dinner talk. But

Anders's mother grasped the fact that the fjord man was number one. The one called Hans was a bit more cautious than the fjord man.

But sometimes she felt she'd had enough of Doomsday.

'Can't we just be satisfied with the way things are?'

Red or blue?

Would the Labour Party continue its mismanagement of the country?

A week after Anders's debut on document.no, at nine o'clock on election-day morning, Anders suggested that the powers of good pool their resources to create a national newspaper to 'wake Norwegians out of their coma'. On his thread, lots of contributors suggested likely collaborators in the project. Names and organisations were tossed out and then shot down. Anders gave an impression of tolerance and readiness to compromise.

'We're not in a position to pick and choose our partners,' he wrote.

Just as in his days on the Progress Party Youth forum, when he was keen to form a youth politics platfrom on the right wing, he now envisaged a community of varying shades of opinion, but all pulling in roughly the same direction.

'I know lots of people in the Progress Party and some of those with influence want to develop *Progress*, the party's paper. I also know of some culturally conservative investors. How about working to consolidate *Progress* with document.no + get funding from strategic investors? Call the paper *Conservative*,' he wrote at 11 a.m.

At half past he added a PS: 'I can also help by bringing in some funding for the project from my lodge.'

As the polling stations closed that evening, the project appeared to be up and running. He wrote that he could set up a meeting with Trygve Hegnar, founder of the business and investment magazine *Kapital*, and Geir Mo, General Secretary of the Progress Party, to present this solution to them. 'This election and the coverage given to it show us definitively that we can't go on without a national mouthpiece.'

By the time the polling stations had been closed for an hour and a half Anders had drawn up a business plan, which he put on the site's discussion area. There was Strategy no. 1, which he called the low-brow model. It would have standard news, a few financial items and plenty of 'lowbrow features', like sex and pin-up girls. The problem with that was that you would lose a large number of conservative, Christian readers. Strategy no. 2, which he estimated would gener-ate circulation of about a third that of no. 1, would have a good deal of financial content and minimal 'lowbrow features'. And then there was Strategy no. 3, a hybrid of 1 and 2. With a substantial amount of financial content he was convinced it had the potential to poach a lot of readers from the business papers.

'The main aim is an increase in political influence by means of unofficial support for the Progress Party and the Conservatives,' he declared.

At midnight he saw the result of the election. It was depressing.

Fifteen hundred kilometres further north, Anders Kristiansen was jubilant. 'Four more years!' He had dipped into his savings so he could stay at a hotel in Tromsø and join Labour's election-night vigil. They'd done it! Viljar was up in Svalbard with his parents and younger brother, Torje; the Sæbø family was celebrating in Salangen. The Norwegian people had spoken and wanted the red–green coalition of Jens Stoltenberg to carry on.

The three comrades had not cast votes themselves. Viljar and Anders were still only sixteen. Simon had just turned seventeen. But next time, at the 2011 elections, they would finally be old enough to vote!

'Norwegian journalists won their war against the Progress Party,' Anders B wrote that night. 'They were able to bring down the vote by 6 per cent after four weeks of concerted warfare.' It was the media's blockade of news about the Muslim riots in France, Britain and Sweden that 'set the seal on our fate and cost the right-wing par-ties election victory'.

He nonetheless awoke the next day with his fighting spirit undampened and wrote an email to Hans Rustad about the need for a culturally conservative newspaper. Within the hour he had a reply from his role model.

'There is no doubt that your analysis is correct. If we are to win the election in 2013, we need more effective media. This puts the Progress Party at a real disadvantage. It gets pushed around and there's no third force to mobilise,' wrote Rustad.

Anders replied at once that the first thing he would do was 'to arrange a meeting between myself and Geir Mo', to discuss the Progress Party's view of the matter.

Months passed and he heard nothing from the General Secretary of the Progress Party. Nor did he ever quite bring himself to contact the editor of *Kapital*. He did not approach any of the investors he had boasted that he could contact so easily, nor was his lodge ever informed of his newspaper initiative. The only thing he did was to ask a print shop how much it would cost to print a glossy monthly magazine.

In November he started 'email farming'. Via Facebook accounts, he issued invitations to cultural conservatives and critics of immigration all over the world to become his friend. It was time-consuming, because there was a limit to how many invitations one could send per day. Fifty friend requests went out from each account every day.

About half accepted.

He had set up his profiles in such a way that it would be quite natural for cultural conservatives to accept his invitation. But he steered clear of any who seemed too extreme and deleted all those who had dubious symbols on their websites. He did not want any neo-Nazis as friends.

It was people's email addresses he wanted. After a few months, he had a database of eight thousand addresses.

Only at the end of January 2010 did he receive an answer from the Progress Party; a rejection from the parliamentary group. They wished him the best of luck with his newspaper project, but could not promise anything beyond giving interviews.

Anders wrote to Hans Rustad in disappointment. He also informed him that his book was finished.

I shall be leaving for book-promo before the end of February and may be away up to 6 mths. Regards Anders.

The Book

He began with a quotation.

'The men the European public admires most extravagantly are the most daring liars; the men they detest most violently are those who try to tell them the truth.'

He continued with a plagiarism.

'Most Europeans look back at the 1950s as a good time. Our homes were safe, to the point where many people did not bother to lock their doors. Public schools were generally excellent, and their problems were things like talking in class and running in the halls. Most men treated women like ladies, and most ladies devoted their time and effort to making good homes, rearing their children well and helping their communities through volunteer work. Children grew up in two-parent households, and the mother was there to meet the child when he came home from school.'

He had no inhibitions about stealing for the good of the cause. He credited hardly anyone. They were all subsumed into a higher entity: *Andrew Berwick*.

What was going wrong with Europe?

Andrew Berwick blamed it on the ideology of Political Correctness which, he wrote, was the same as cultural Marxism — Marxism transferred from the economic to the cultural sphere. He wanted to recapture the values of the 1950s, when women were housewives and not soldiers, children were not born outside wedlock and homosexuality was not glorified.

'Those who would defeat cultural Marxism must defy it,' urged Andrew Berwick. 'They must shout from the rooftops the realities it seeks to suppress, such as our opposition to sharia, the Islamisation of our countries, the fact that violent crimes are disproportionately committed by Muslims and that most cases of Aids are voluntary, acquired from immoral acts.'

One of the prominent features of cultural Marxism is feminism, wrote Berwick. It is ubiquitous and all-consuming:

> It is in television, where nearly every major offering has a female 'power figure' and the plots and characters emphasise inferiority of the male and superiority of the female. It is in the military, where expanding opportunity for women, even in combat positions, has been accompanied by double standards and then lowered the standards, as well as a decline in enlistment of young men, while 'warriors' in the services are leaving in droves. It is in government-mandated employment preferences and practices that benefit women and use 'sexual harassment' charges to keep men in line. It is in public schools, where 'self-awareness' and 'self-esteem' are increasingly promoted while academic learning declines. And sadly, we see that several European countries allow and fund free distribution of contraceptive pills combined with liberal abortion policies.

He went on: 'The man of today is expected to be a touchy-feely sub-species who bows to the radical feminist agenda.'

It was great to sit there cutting and pasting. Lots of the stuff he had been brooding about, but had not put into concrete form, was all thought out for him.

'Who dares, wins,' he wrote at the end of the introduction.

'We are deceived by our own governments into thinking that Christian and Islamic civilisation are of equal value,' he wrote. Obviously, they were not.

The book veered between polemic and pedagogy. He listed the five pillars of Islam – faith, prayer, fasting, pilgrimage and the giving of alms – at times presenting the Qur'an as though he were a primary school RE teacher: Allah's commandments to Muhammad via the Archangel Gabriel; the great battles for Islam; the taking of Mecca and introduction of sharia.

But then he got to jihad – the Muslims' duty to wage holy war – and he explained the Arabic term *al-Taqiyya*, which translates as dissimulation and in Islam means that Muslims can conceal their faith if it would put them in mortal danger to confess to it. Berwick claimed this was a Muslim tactic to hide their ambition of taking power in Europe. Until they struck. He explained the term *dhimmi*: non-Muslims living under Islamic rule, who are protected and allowed to exercise their own faith as long as they pay a tax, *jizia*, and do not raise any objections. This was the future lying ahead for Christians.

He used the Arabic terms to prove the Muslims had a plan to conquer the West and to kill Jews and Christians. The Repentance verse of the Qur'an was part of the proof: *kill the polytheists wherever you find them, arrest them, imprison them, besiege them, and lie in wait for them at every site of ambush!*

The verse was much more effective without the word *polytheists*. Then you could write that the verse was about Jews and Christians, when it really referred to sects that worshipped multiple gods in old Arabia. It also had more impact if you put *kill them* last.

He often quoted Robert Spencer, the man behind Jihad Watch. Spencer had dissected the Qur'an into its component parts, taking them out of context to show how violent and full of hate it was. Berwick subscribed to that understanding of the Muslim holy book.

He hastened on, jumping backwards and forwards in time. The Crusaders in the twelfth and thirteenth centuries, the extermination of the Christian minority in Lebanon in the twentieth century, the Armenian genocide in 1915, the different dynasties of the seventh century. Towards the end of the book he got to the Battle of Vienna in 1683, the start of the Ottoman downfall in Europe. The battle was

a prophetic parallel to his own book, which he had given the title
2083 – A European Declaration of Independence. Four hundred years
after the famous battle, the Muslims would be vanquished and out of
Europe for ever.

'You shall know the truth and the truth shall make you mad.' With this
quotation from Aldous Huxley's dystopian *Brave New World* Berwick
opened the second part of the book, which he called *Europe Burning*.
Starting with quotations added authority, so he threw in various bits
of Orwell and Churchill too. He only had to google 'famous quotations' and so many good ones came up.

The first hundred pages were essays by Fjordman with titles like
'The Eurabia Code', 'Boycott the United Nations', 'How the
Feminists' War Against Boys Paved the Way for Islam', 'What is the
Cause of Low Birth Rates?' and 'The Fatherless Civilisation'. The
themes overlapped with things Berwick wrote himself. It was cut-
and-paste, stolen and shared. A lot of it was sheer repetition. One
thing that could not be clarified too often was: why we can never
trust those who call themselves moderate Muslims.

Because they are deceiving us.

The Qur'an usually furnished the proof Berwick needed, as in sura
8, verse 12: *Remember when God revealed to the angels: 'I am with you, so
grant the believers resolve. I shall cast terror into the hearts of the unbelievers. So strike above the necks, and strike their very finger!'* He really liked
using that particular sura, called al-Anfal. It was the sura Saddam
Hussein had used to name the genocide of the Kurds in the 1980s. In
Berwick's reading, the unbelievers were the Christians; in the Ba'ath
Party's they were the Kurds.

Then he complained a little. It was, after all, quite a laborious task
he had taken upon himself. 'Occasionally I get annoyed over the fact
that I am compelled to spend significant amounts of my time refut-
ing Islam, an ideology that is flawed to the core and should be totally
irrelevant in the twenty-first century.'

But he *had* to do it, because the actual number of Muslims in
Europe was being kept secret by the authorities. There were far more

than they said and, more importantly, those numbers were increasing all the time, through births and mass immigration. This assertion was supported by more Fjordman essays and quotations from assorted experts, and finally proved by the Qur'an.

Berwick also endorsed Bat Ye'or's theory that EU leaders had opened their doors to mass immigration of Muslims in exchange for peace, cheap oil and access to markets in the Arab world, the so-called Eurabia theory. He adopted her expression 'freedom or *dhimmitude*'. Freedom or subjugation.

In the middle of his critique of Islam, Berwick abruptly threw in some comments on how a blog could be turned into a newspaper. He ridiculed all those who were not bold enough to take the risk.

'I have spoken to numerous successful and less successful right-wing blog/newssite/Facebook "reporters" over the years and the general opinion seems to be that the creation and distribution of a paper-magazine/newspaper is so incredibly difficult and problematic. I can honestly not understand why people feel this way.'

He then offered a three-step design with a planning phase, the development of a subscriber base and use of bloggers' texts as material to fill the pages. The only thing to be cautious about was 'hate speech', because racist magazines were bound to be banned.

At the very end of Book 2 he was critical of Fjordman, Spencer and Bat Ye'or in the chapter 'Future deportations of Muslims from Europe'.

It was the same question he had asked them to answer on Gates of Vienna. About the D-word. They didn't dare raise the subject of deportation because it would ruin their reputations, wrote Berwick. 'If these writers are too scared to propagate a conservative revolution and armed resistance, then other writers will have to.'

Berwick felt himself called.

———

The chat went on about the weather, the neighbours, the children and other matters at the smokers' table of the café outside the Coop.

'Anders is writing a book,' Wenche said.

'Oh is he?' said the others. 'What about?'

'Something historical,' replied his mother. 'It's a bit above my head.'

The neighbours nodded.

'It's going to be in English,' Wenche went on. The book would go all the way back to 600 BC, she explained. So everything was covered, as Anders put it. It was going to be about all the wars, everything that had happened.

Anders's mother was quite worried about his future, in actual fact. She had even told him she could go with him to the job centre. They would be able to help him to find out what sort of job could suit him.

She once told him she thought he would make a good policeman with ideas like his, decent and fair.

'For that I'd need to have taken some different choices in life,' Anders had answered then.

'He's good with computers, he's good at history . . . ' his mother mused. 'But really I've always wished he could be a doctor,' she said to her friends at the café. The nicest thing of all, she thought, would be for Anders to be a Red Cross doctor caring for starving children in Africa and helping people. Maybe Zambia, she suggested.

When he told her he wanted to be an author, she said, 'That sounds grand!'

She remembered his very first proper job, when he was seventeen. He had got a job with a company called Acta, where he sold shares to rich people.

'Rubbish,' Anders's sister had said afterwards. 'He's not selling shares, he's selling magazines.'

This had made Wenche sit down and wonder whether Anders felt that he wasn't good enough.

At the smokers' table where the sun rays never reached, they had learnt not to bring up the subject of Anders. They had a tacit understanding that if Wenche wanted to talk about him she would, and then they could join in, but they never asked the first question. They knew he was just sitting there in his room, engrossed in his games.

If they made some comment about compulsive gaming being a form of illness, she might say they were only jealous because she had a good, kind son like Anders.

The sons of several of the women at the café had finished courses in law or economics; some had already qualified as lawyers. Others worked in banks and finance.

Some had children. And when the ladies started talking about their grandchildren, Wenche pursed her lips.

Anders had told his mother to stop nagging him about getting a proper job. But it was even worse when she went on about how he ought to get a girlfriend.

'Why not find a nice little single mother then?' Wenche asked.

'I must have my own children,' Anders replied.

He said he wanted seven.

How Can I Get Your Life?

The buses were already waiting. They quickly filled with passengers from the ferry who had onward journeys along the peninsula. At rush hour the ferries ran every twenty minutes. On the way to Oslo, on the way back from Oslo – the short crossing on *Huldra* or *Smørbukk* could be a peaceful interlude or a chance for a chat.

If you hadn't been able to sit with who you wanted on the ferry, there was always a second chance on the bus.

One day Bano deposited herself in the seat next to a slender woman with an elegant short haircut. It was no accident.

'Hello,' said Bano with a broad grin.

The blonde woman in her early forties returned the girl's greeting. The teenager stopped chewing gum and started to speak.

'I know you're a member of the Labour Party. I am too,' said Bano. 'I'm a local politician just like you.' Bano was fifteen and had just joined the AUF.

Nina Sandberg was the Labour Party's mayoral candidate in Nesodden. What a spring of joy, was the first thing she thought when Bano sat down beside her.

'I'm supporting you,' Bano confided. 'So are my sister and mother.'

Then she got off the bus, while Nina Sandberg continued her journey to her farmhouse at the southern end of Nesodden.

*

Bayan and Mustafa tried from the moment they arrived to be part of Norwegian society. First they had to learn Norwegian, so they could look for jobs. Initially Bayan cried when she saw people on their way to work in the mornings. How she missed her accountancy job in Erbil! Mustafa, who had been a mechanical engineer, looked for engineering jobs. Water and drainage specialist, he wrote.

It got him nowhere.

He went to the social security office on Akersgata in Oslo.

'I'll take anything,' he told the woman behind the counter.

The adviser helped him improve the standard of his applications. She corrected his written Norwegian and suggested he take a language course to improve his chances. Then they sat talking for a while.

'Why did you come here?' she asked.

Mustafa said nothing.

'To Norway, I mean,' she went on.

Her question hung in the air.

'I don't know,' said Mustafa.

Life had become a blur. The days passed by in idleness. He felt something had slipped away; he had lost something, himself, his self-confidence and the status that his education and professional experience had conferred on him. He had only a hazy understanding of Norwegian and felt excluded.

The only thing that made him feel alive was the children, seeing them take root and grow, even if the girls were finding it a bit hard to settle at school. One of the teachers had told him that his daughters did not play with the other children, only with each other.

'Have you told them they're not allowed to play with the others?' she enquired.

Bayan and Mustafa would not have such things said about them! They signed the girls up for ballet, gymnastics and handball. Ali, who was now in a kindergarten, had already begun football training.

They themselves attended matches, shows and tournaments, and volunteered for community tasks. At first the Rashid children took their own chicken sausages along to eat at sporting events, but one day they simply didn't bring them. Kurdistan felt further and further away.

The children went to church with the rest of their school class at Christmas, and Bayan hung advent stars in the windows like everyone else. Bano said she was a devout Muslim, but when somebody asked her if she was Sunni or Shia, she did not know. 'I believe there's a God,' she said. 'I don't know what He's called, that's all.' And after attending church with her class, she said, 'If God knows there is only Him, there's no need to say it through the priest.'

As pupils from a minority background, the Rashid children were excused from lessons in New Norwegian, the country's second official language, which is based on rural dialects. But the proposal only made Bano indignant. 'If you get a letter in New Norwegian, you have to answer it in New Norwegian,' she asserted, quoting the general rule. When the teacher praised the fluency of a composition she had written, she was cross. 'Why say that to me in particular? I started New Norwegian the same time as everybody else in the class.'

If her parents moaned at her or weren't happy with something she had done, she would retort that lots of immigrant parents had to go and fetch their children from the police station.

'Mum, we're not like the ones who don't want to integrate. The future for us means good jobs, coming home to nice dinners and opening the fridge to find it's full. You complain about the cost of sandwich fillings and us staying in the shower too long, but Mum, at least we always have food and water,' she would say consolingly whenever her mother was worried about making ends meet. 'We're not ashamed of having a messy house because the main thing is that we children aren't being neglected. And our sofa and dining table are just as nice as everyone else's.'

It was important to be 'like everyone else'. The family had to have the same furniture, the same clothes and the same kind of sandwiches in their packed lunches. That is to say, the same or better. Bano was so pleased when her mother bought her sister a Bergans jacket. 'Mum, only Lara and one other person in her class have got a Bergans jacket. The others have just got the ordinary brands. I'm so proud she's got an expensive jacket!' she exclaimed to Bayan, who had been lucky enough to find the smart jacket in a sale.

Mustafa's applications had finally borne fruit. The social security office rang and offered him a temporary caretaker job at Grindbakken school in the west of Oslo. And just then, Bayan got a work experience place as a nursery assistant, which after a few weeks turned into a part-time job. But their wages did not allow for any luxuries.

Bano then did an abrupt about-turn and decided the family was buying too much.

'We're buying happiness,' she said. She told her classmates the same thing and imposed a shopping ban. No one was to buy clothes, chocolate or even a roll in the canteen for a week. Her friends found it easier to buy things surreptitiously than to argue with her. Bano was so stubborn.

Bayan and Mustafa called their oldest daughter their guide to Norwegian society.

'When you go to visit other people, the first thing you have to say is "What a lovely house you've got!"' Bano advised them. 'Houses are what count in Norway.'

'The best thing you can do is buy your own house,' she insisted. When they bought a terraced house, Mustafa was very pleased to get it for less than the valuation, because all the other houses in the street had sold for more than the asking price.

'But Dad,' said Lara, 'why do you think the Norwegians didn't bid more for the house? We must have been cheated.'

Hmm, thought Mustafa. The house proved to have various defects, like damp in the basement, and it required a lot of renovation. But he was a mechanical engineer after all and doggedly set to work.

Bano was day-dreaming about how they would do up the basement so the three children could have their own living room, bedrooms and even a little office. Things could always get better. She complained, for example, about the kitchen floor being two different colours. When Mustafa tried to sand and polish the floor it took him so long that he had to return the sander before he had finished. The sitting room had no skirting boards and there were wires hanging loose in her bedroom.

'You ought to be pleased with your room, Bano,' her father said. 'You've got the best room, much bigger than Lara and Ali's.'

Craving conformity, she reproached her parents for her name. Bano, what sort of name was that? Nobody else had it. When they told her they had contemplated calling her Maria, she complained even more.

'Oh, Maria, why didn't you call me that? I know several people called Maria! I could have been like everyone else.'

Their residence permit kept on being renewed on humanitarian grounds, but only for a year at a time. It wore the family down, not knowing if they would be able to stay in Norway. They were part of a group known as Temporary Residents with No Right to Family Reunification.

When the time came for Bano to start secondary school, and they still had not heard if they would be allowed to stay, she decided to take matters into her own hands. She was the family member best able to follow the news and she kept them all up to date with events. She was going to put the family's situation to the Norwegian state, she decided, and looked up the government's contact details in the telephone book. She rang the number of the local government department and asked for the minister.

They did not put her through.

'You have to be eighteen to talk to the minister,' the eleven-year-old later told her parents. 'The department said so.'

Then in 2005, when Bano turned twelve, Lara ten and Ali seven, they were finally granted citizenship, along with several hundred other Iraqi Kurds. The head of the Norwegian Directorate of Immigration subsequently had to resign when it emerged that the directorate had exceeded its remit and issued too many residence permits. The Rashids were among the lucky ones. And so, in February 2009, after ten years in Norway, the whole family became Norwegian citizens.

Bayan made a special meal and bought nougat ice cream, and they were all allowed to eat as much as they wanted.

*

Sport was an important part of becoming one of the others. Bano spent many hours on the bench at handball matches because she was clumsy and missed the ball so often. But one day, flat-footed and a little overweight, she thundered through the opposition's defences and scored. From that point on, there was no stopping her. She loved being on the attack, snatching the ball and scoring goals. After each goal the trainer would shout, 'Home, Bano, home!' But defending was too boring.

Bano had no time for anything boring. But if there was something to be won, she turned up. When there was a competition among the pupils of the Nesodden schools to see who knew their peninsula best, she did her research on local history. Bano, the outsider, got through to the final.

She wanted to be best on the court, best in the class and as well dressed as everyone else. She wanted to join the gang of popular girls and be as Norwegian as the Norwegians.

But a new interest was gradually taking over.

'You've been with me for the handball all these years, now you've got to come into the Labour Party with me,' Bano told her parents when she joined the AUF in Year 10.

Bayan obliged her and when Women for Nina was set up, a campaign to elect Nina Sandberg – the woman on the bus – as mayor, Bano, Lara and Bayan all joined.

The commitment Bano had shown on the handball court now transferred itself to the AUF. She eventually became leader of the little local group on Nesodden.

When she was seventeen, she had her first piece published in the daily *Aftenposten*. In it, she expressed her concern about the Progress Party and its leader Siv Jensen's use of the term 'Islamisation by stealth'.

'I know full well that Siv Jensen only came up with this term as a scare tactic. She is well aware that we have had immigration here for thousands of years and it all worked out fine,' she began, adding that the vast majority of people who move to a country adapt to its culture and way of life. 'It just takes a little time. If Jensen really is afraid of Muslims, she should look at the birthrate among Muslim women in Norway. It has fallen significantly. This is an example of the way people who live in Norway adapt to Norway.'

She asked people to see immigrants as a strength instead, and make full use of their resources. 'Oslo would doubtless grind to a halt if anyone opted for an immigrant-free day,' she wrote.

'The second-largest party in the country not only discriminates against me. The Progress Party also allows itself to discriminate against employees, women, the long-term sick and gays. Most people fall into one of those categories. Do most people really think that as long as the price of petrol comes down a bit, they can put up with a bit of discrimination?'

The signature *Bano Rashid (17), Nesodden AUF* was to feature several times on the youth pages of *Aftenposten*. 'Put pictures into people's heads as you write,' Hadia Tajik, a talented young politician of Pakistani descent, had taught her in an AUF course. Bano tried to.

There was another matter close to her heart.

'No one in the whole world has been able to convince me women are the weaker sex,' Bano wrote. 'It is no coincidence that 80 per cent of Norway's top leaders are men and that Norwegian women only earn eighty-five kroner for every hundred earned by men. This despite the fact that 60 per cent of Norwegian students are women. These are figures that we find hard to swallow, living in the best country in the world.'

She also had some advice to offer her sisters. 'Unlike traditional feminists I do not think it is a question of we girls sticking together. We girls must divide up! It is not actually a great tactical move to gang together. It only makes us fearful of everything and everybody outside the gang. We must move forward on our own. We must have the confidence to look up to the woman at the top, and allow ourselves to think we are amazing.'

Towards the end of the summer, Bano was invited to go to Alvdal by her friend Erle and her mother Rikke Lind. They took the train into the mountains and then walked for hours over the fells to the old hunting cabin. There, life was simple. They fetched water from the creek and cooked at a wood-burning stove. Bano was overjoyed, always keen to do the longest treks, reach the highest summits. In the evenings, which had started drawing in now midsummer was behind them, Rikke let the girls have a small glass of red wine each. They sat talking late into the night. Bano kept turning the conversation toward politics, to Erle's annoyance. Her mother held a post as under-secretary in the Ministry of Trade and Industry. She was the one who had suggested Bano and Erle join the AUF. But whereas Erle soon lost interest, Bano became local leader.

'The fact that we no longer have a woman Prime Minister is making itself felt nowadays,' said Rikke. 'Gro did things much more consciously. She was good at inspiring us, her younger colleagues.'

She told Bano and Erle about the times she had met Gro, and how good the older feminist had been at seeing other women and pulling them up with her.

This made Bano thoughtful.

'Rikke, how can I get your life?' she asked.

'Oh, it's hard work, you know!'

'I'm not joking. How can I be like you? I want a house as big as yours, a good job like yours, friends as interesting as yours,' Bano went on. Rikke and her husband gave wonderful parties at their big house by the sea on Nesodden. And Bano was never shy about asking things she wondered about, like how much they earned and what their house cost.

'Well then Bano, I'll tell you,' answered Rikke. 'A good education, that's the most important thing.'

'What should I study, then?'

'Law or political science. Take all the courses you can, make the most of learning for free. Take debating technique, leadership of meetings, rhetoric.'

That summer evening they made plans for Bano's life. She should get herself nominated to stand in the local elections in Nesodden in 2011, Rikke suggested.

'Do you really mean it?' Bano could not contain her enthusiasm.

Rikke nodded. Her own mother had made a class journey, leaving a strict Christian home behind and moving alone to Oslo, where she became a radical lawyer, the first one in the family to go through higher education.

'But Bano, why do you keep going on about being like Mum? You'd never be satisfied with being an under-secretary!' declared Erle.

They smiled.

Bano wanted everything, Lara often said. Not enough, but everything.

'Who's the most important person in the country?' Bano asked. 'Who gets to decide most?'

'The Prime Minister,' responded Rikke.

'Perhaps it's not realistic to try to be Prime Minister,' pondered Bano. 'But it would be realistic to be Minister of Equality. Then I can liberate women from oppression!'

The August night felt as soft as velvet. Dark wine lingered in the glasses. Bano was growing up.

Don't Make Friends With Anyone Before You Get There!

The community liaison officer in Salangen looked through her lists.

The minors among the asylum seekers were placed in reception classes at Sjøvegan School. Many of them made poor progress. They struggled with several subjects, particularly Norwegian, as they had little contact with the local population. The centre for asylum seekers was virtually a separate world up on the hill, way up by the skiing trails.

It was not that the asylum seekers were unwelcome. Attitudes to the refugees had steadily improved after a shaky start.

When the stream of refugees into Norway suddenly increased in the second half of the 1980s, the authorities were quite unprepared. Accommodation was suddenly required for several thousand individuals. Efforts were made to identify disused buildings. Ski resorts and tourist centres that had fallen out of favour were considered suitable, and the mountains filled with people from Africa and Asia.

If any of the refugees felt like prisoners in remote isolation and ran away from these hotels, the Norwegians reacted in a variety of ways. Some shrugged and said hah, so that's how they thank us! 'We take our holidays there, but it's not good enough for them, oh no!' Others were more understanding: 'They've fled from war zones, after all, so they might be traumatised and panicked by the wide open spaces.'

A centre for asylum seekers opened in Salangen in 1989. It was not long before the first refugees ran away and headed south, refusing to come back. The Somalis set little store by the northern lights or the wonderful opportunities for skiing among the willows in the forests above the centre.

No, they stayed in their rooms, hung about in the corridors or sat on the stairs smoking. Soon there was trouble. First between the Tamils and Somalis. Then between the Iranians and Kosovo Albanians. Arguments, pushing and shoving escalated into stabbings and threats to set fire to the centre.

The local press offered continuous coverage of the conflicts. There was finally something in the district worth reporting on. The towns-people followed events from a distance.

When the centre had been open for a few months there was the first scuffle between *us* and *them*. Fists, pool cues and knives were used.

A brawl outside the pub in Salangen led to criminal proceedings against both the Norwegians and refugees involved. Thirty people were formally interviewed in connection with the case; the county sheriff took a dim view of fighting.

'Our investigations reveal that Norwegian youngsters have been play-acting to blacken the reputation of the asylum seekers,' declared the sheriff. 'It's part of young men's lives to prove themselves in front of girls,' said his subordinate.

The young Norwegians told the local press that the asylum seek-ers had surrounded them, beaten them up and held bread knives to their throats. The refugees, for their part, claimed the partying Norwegians had threatened them, saying they would get killed if they did not leave the pub.

'There's a lynch-mob mentality in town now,' one of the protag-onists told the local paper. 'I think the safest thing would be to send the asylum seekers away from Sjøvegan as soon as possible.' The young man was pictured from behind, with a denim jacket and mullet hairstyle.

'Racial hatred in Sjøvegan,' wrote *Nordlys*. 'Asylum war in

Salangen' ran the headline in *Troms Folkeblad*. Arne Myrdal of the Stop Immigration Party rang the interviewees to offer support.

'Young Norwegians will have to show they have been brought up better than the asylum seekers,' said the town's mayor, adding that it might have been a mistake 'to let the asylum seekers straight out into Norwegian society' as soon as they arrived.

'The reception centres should be in bigger towns,' asserted two school pupils interviewed by the local press. Salangen simply was not large enough for an asylum seekers' centre.

Sjøvegan Upper Secondary School tried to defuse what *Nordlys* called 'the racial hatred that has also found a breeding ground in Salangen'. The school arranged a public debate between local residents, asylum seekers and the council. One of the young Norwegians on the panel addressed the refugees in the hall: 'You immigrants bring diseases, violence and drugs with you. Why do you come here? Is it just to get a better life?'

A girl rose from her seat and said she thought there must be something wrong with the Norwegian boys' self-image. Were they afraid the foreigners would come and take their girls from them?

People went home. The town had divided into two camps.

Something had to be done. Events were organised. There were get-to-know-you evenings and football matches to help people bond. The asylum centre invited people in for cultural evenings at which the refugees performed dances and songs for the locals, while the residents of Salangen in turn provided children's choirs, traditional fiddle concerts and the Sami singer Mari Boine, who merges the indigenous music of her roots with jazz and rock. An evening course was started for volunteer befrienders, who were to be the link between the refugees and the permanent residents.

Twenty years after the first asylum seekers reached Salangen, community liaison officer Lene Lyngedal Nordmo was going through her lists. Norway had by now developed its system for receiving refugees. Two decades had taught the authorities something.

Those who were young today had grown up with the asylum

centre. The refugees had become part of daily life in Salangen. That is to say, they were there and yet they weren't. Despite the passing of time, divisions between life at the centre and life in the town remained watertight.

Lene set her ambitions higher. Peace and quiet were not enough; she wanted to see the refugees included in Norwegian society. But it wasn't easy, because most of them did not want to be up here. They wanted to go to Oslo.

For a time, Lene had responsibility for minors who were there on limited leave to remain. This meant they would be sent out of Norway the day they turned eighteen. As a consequence, they saw no point in learning Norwegian. This was a difficult group to deal with, often depressed and sometimes resorting to aggression.

Before 2008, under-eighteens were always granted residence in Norway. That led to a dramatic increase in minors seeking asylum in the country. Tighter restrictions were imposed. Limited leave to remain was the step taken by the red–green coalition to limit immigration. In practice, it meant that anyone over fifteen on entering Norway, and at least sixteen when the decision was made, was only granted temporary rights of residence. As soon as they reached eighteen they had to leave the country. If they did not go voluntarily they were deported, many on the very day they turned eighteen.

In Salangen there were about thirty individual under-eighteens who had been granted residence in Norway. As Lene moved her pen up and down the sheet of paper, her bangles jingled. She wondered what to do to motivate her refugees to learn.

Well, she did know what they wanted more than anything.

A young Afghan had come into her office one day.

'I would like to have a friend,' he said.

She gave him a sad look.

'You know what, there's lots I can help you with. Just not that.'

Even though the youth club had put up posters and invited the asylum seekers to Velve, it didn't really help. The two groups still ended up sitting at separate tables. Some of the local girls felt the asylum seekers stared too much, and adult refugees way above the club's age limit started to come along too. A few of the asylum seekers sold drugs and smoked hash there, and the young Norwegians gradually stopped coming. The foreigners took over the club.

And they were no nearer integration.

Lene sighed. The only time the girls of the area had flocked up to the centre was just after the war in Kosovo, because they thought the young Kosovars were so good-looking.

If the young refugees were to have an active future in Norway and not remain stuck on benefits, it was crucial they did well at school. They had been put in classes of their own and received extra support with their homework so they could keep up. Lene had an idea: if she could get kids of the refugees' own age to help them with their homework, it would work better than the adult befrienders she had been using.

Her sheet of paper filled up with names of young people in the area who she thought would be suitable. As a mother of teenagers herself, she had a fair idea who they all were.

She rang the first person on her list, a boy who lived near by.

'Hi, Simon here,' came the quick reply at the other end.

'Could you pop round to the office for a minute?' Lene asked.

She applied some fresh lipstick and was standing by the window as he arrived. Simon had just passed his test and was driving round in an old red Ford Sierra. He swung recklessly into the council office car park, parked the car across three spaces, jumped out, slammed the door shut and sauntered across the forecourt. Everything about him signalled that he owned the world.

'How amazing to see you driving a car,' smiled Lene as he came in.

Then she told him why she had asked him to come. Was he free on Monday to Thursday evenings, between six and nine?

'Four evenings a week? But I've got school and football, and skiing and the AUF and . . . ' Simon was about to start his final year at upper secondary school.

'How about three evenings, then?' asked Lene. 'We need some good homework buddies. People who can inspire others to learn.'

Three evenings, he could do that. He of all people did not want to miss out on being part of the council's integration work. He stood up to go; he had to get to football practice.

Lene had drawn up a list of those she thought would work well together. Simon would be paired with three different people, one each evening. A boy from Somalia, a boy from Afghanistan and a girl from Ethiopia.

A few days later she rang him again.

'Could you just drop in with your tax details?' she said.

'Tax details?' exclaimed Simon. 'Am I getting paid for this?'

It was a great job, in fact. Not very much homework was done, though.

'How can I get to know some Norwegian girls?' was one of the first things Mehdi asked him.

'Well, it's like this . . . ' said Simon with a smile. The three hours passed in a flash.

Mehdi turned up faithfully to every Monday-evening session. The two boys were the same age, born only a few months apart. Simon into his family of teachers in Kirkenes, Mehdi into a farming family in Wardak Province, Afghanistan.

His grandfather had been a major tribal leader in the wide circle round the old king Zahir Shah, who was deposed in a communist-supported coup in 1973. That was the start of the family's downfall. The next catastrophe was the Soviet invasion of 1979, which led to the killing of 1.5 million Afghans.

In 1992, the year Mehdi was born, civil war broke out between warlords hungry for power. After four years the men with the black turbans were the victors. Mehdi came from the Hazara people; the Taliban showed no mercy to the Hazaras and engaged in ethnic cleansing of towns and villages.

Like most people in Wardak, Mehdi's parents could neither read nor write. They kept animals, but much of their grazing land was taken from them by the Taliban. Mehdi and his brother were sent to the *madrasah* while their four sisters were kept at home.

'When you can read, people respect you,' Mehdi's father told him. 'Read and grow wise.' At school they had their heads filled first and foremost with religion. The teachers were an extended arm of the Taliban.

The boys learned about the godless foreigners who had occupied their country. The foreigners wanted to destroy Afghan culture, to crush Islam. 'In Europe, the women go about half naked,' they were told.

But Mehdi did not entirely trust his teachers. He had grown up with stories of what the Pashtuns had done to his people in the past. They wanted to be rid of the Hazaras and took their land, he had heard. He also knew that in earlier times people in the region had worshipped Buddha. He had heard that the Taliban had blown up two enormous thousand-year-old Buddha statues in the neighbouring province of Bamyan because they were naked. They wanted to destroy everything that was not in line with the true teaching of Islam.

Just before Mehdi's ninth birthday, two planes crashed into the World Trade Center in New York. Barely a month after the terrorist attack, America began its bombing raids on his country. The Taliban fled from Wardak Province to Pakistan and the Hazaras could hold up their heads once more. But within a few years the Islamists were trickling back and inciting the people to resist the Western occupiers. They started recruiting soldiers from among the local farmers to fight the international forces. From 2008 onwards Wardak Province was again under de facto Taliban control. The men with the black turbans advanced across the country. They came to recruit Mehdi and his brother. Their father refused. But he knew that if they had come once, they would always come back. How long could he go on refusing?

He sold land and cattle.

'Go,' he said. 'Go to Europe. Find a better life than the one we have here. War could break out again, any time now. In Europe, there's no war,' his father said. 'People are given everything they need there, you can go to school, you get books . . . it's a *democracy* there.'

It was a word Mehdi had heard many times on the radio. But he had no idea what it meant.

Before long the two brothers were sitting on the back of a truck on their way to Kabul. From there, they took a bus to the border with Pakistan. Then they walked, drove and took to the saddle, reaching Iran, Turkey, Greece . . .

'Don't talk to anyone on the trip,' their father had impressed on them. 'Don't make friends with anyone before you get there.'

Mehdi told his story to Simon in dribs and drabs over the course of the year.

Squeezed under the driver's seat of a long-distance lorry, he had finally reached Oslo.

'It is a big place with nice cars, lots of girls and beautiful buildings like the Oslo City shopping centre,' Mehdi told Simon. 'The thing I longed to see was what the women looked like,' he smiled. His dreams had been of discos, ladies and dancing.

For a couple of weeks they were in paradise. But in November 2009, when Mehdi was seventeen, the brothers were sent to an asylum centre in Finnsnes, a small place north of Salangen.

It was dark and dismal. They felt trapped. Both suffered from severe depression and regretted having ever made the journey. At least in Afghanistan there was sun.

The brothers were in perpetual conflict with the staff and sabotaged the centre's usual procedures. They were meant to keep their room clean and scrub the corridor once a week. They refused to do so. At home, their mother and sisters had done all the cleaning. It was beneath their dignity; it was humiliating.

Mehdi's brother threw down the scrubbing brush and emptied a bucket of water over a female assistant at the centre. Was she going to stand there watching him scrub the floor? Why couldn't she do it herself?

It was all unfair and so bloody stupid. But whenever they rang their parents, they told them how great everything was, what a nice place they lived in, how much they had learned at school. They wanted their parents to believe their money had been well spent.

Eventually the elder brother was sent south and Mehdi got a place at the asylum centre in Salangen. Life seemed less of a trial. Even if it was not like hanging out in Oslo City and watching the girls, maybe things would still work out for him up here in the north.

But, 'The Norwegian girls are scared of me,' Mehdi complained.

Simon advised him to go easy. Let things take their time.

Easy enough for him to say. From Monday to Monday he disappeared out of Mehdi's life to all his other activities: to conferences, duties and tasks, football practice, skiing and ski jumping, his family and girlfriend. While Mehdi waited for Simon from 9 p.m. each Monday to 6 p.m. the following Monday.

For Simon it was a job, for Mehdi it was clutching at straws.

After the last homework session of the summer, Simon took him along to Millionfisken, the annual festival where you could win a million kroner if you caught a fish of a certain size, decided by Lloyd's of London. Nobody had ever won the million.

'If I hold hands with someone, does it mean she's my girlfriend?' asked Mehdi. Simon just laughed.

'How many beers will I have to drink before my head feels hot?' Mehdi went on.

'I reckon you'll have to find that out for yourself,' answered Simon.

After four beers, Mehdi was pinching girls' bottoms, pointing at Simon and grinning.

'Not like that Mehdi. Not like that!' Simon shook his head. But Mehdi did not hear. It was the first time since he came to Salangen that he just felt happy, thoroughly happy. He was a young guy at a festival and he didn't want to be anywhere else. He felt so cool being with Simon. So cool and hot and happy.

'Don't make friends with anyone before you get there,' his father had said.

Well, now he was there.

Patriots and Tyrants

It was a declaration of war.

A very exhausting declaration of war. The same phrases came over and over again. Scattered around in the text. Sometimes they were identical, sometimes words had been changed. Some of the phrases he had polished for a while, whereas others came tumbling one after another. He repeated his arguments. His tips and advice remained the same from one page to the next. The purpose of the text was to inspire fighting spirit, to fire up the reader.

No one would be able to remain indifferent! No one would be able to ignore him now, duck out of answering and avoid him. Indifference ranked among the worst sins. Many great men had said that, in many impressive ways. He had quoted and requoted their words.

His attention had been caught by a Thomas Jefferson quote, which he repeated six times in the last part of his book, each time as if it were the first. 'The tree of liberty must be refreshed from time to time with the blood of patriots and tyrants. The tree of liberty must be refreshed from time to time with the blood of patriots and tyrants. The tree of liberty . . . '

Many would have to bleed before society was drilled the way he wanted it. The last part of his book was bloody. It was more malicious, more ruthless than the first two, where he had largely pasted in texts that were already in circulation on the web. This was his own. His manifesto, or his will and testament.

The murders were planned along the way. The campaign took shape as he wrote. He had various ideas about who he would kill and how. A bomb at the journalists' annual conference? And some concerted shooting afterwards? Ninety-eight per cent of them were multiculturalists, and it was their fault the Progress Party had collapsed at the last election. Or a car bomb in Youngstorget when thousands of communists and cultural Marxists gathered on 1 May to march through the streets of Oslo. Maybe disguise himself as a fireman and hurl grenades and use a flame thrower in the auditorium at the Labour Party National Congress at the House of the People? He could park a car packed with explosives outside, timed to go off just as the delegates swarmed out to escape the flames. Those who survived would be branded. Badly scarred cultural Marxists would serve as living examples of what ultimately happens to traitors. People would realise you cannot commit high treason and go uncensured.

'The Phase for Dialogue is Over' he called the opening chapter of Book 3. He rattled off a list of the accused. There were cultural Marxists, multiculturalists, suicide humanists, capitalist-globalist politicians, state leaders and parliamentarians. There were journalists, editors, teachers, professors, university leaders, publishers, radio commentators, writers, comic-strip creators, artists, technical experts, scientists, doctors and church leaders who had knowingly committed crimes against their own people. The charge was that they had been complicit in the cultural genocide of the native inhabitants of Europe and in foreign invasion and colonisation of Europe by systematically allowing Muslim demographic warfare. This they had done by silently condoning the rape of between half a million and a million European women and actively supporting feminism, emotionalism, egalitarianism and Islamism.

Punishment would be administered according to the crimes they had committed and the class they belonged to. 'A' traitors were leaders of political parties, trade unions, cultural institutions and the media. They would be sentenced to death. 'B' traitors were less important cultural Marxists. They would also be sentenced to death, but could in certain circumstances have their punishment reduced. 'C' traitors wielded little influence themselves, but aided and abetted traitors in the two higher categories. They would receive fines and prison sentences. All multiculturalists would be pardoned if they capitulated to the Knights Templar before 1 January 2020.

This was also the date on which the deportation of Muslims would begin. To avoid expatriation, Muslims would have to convert to Christianity and be baptised with a new Christian forename, middle name and surname. They would be forbidden from using their mother tongues of Farsi, Urdu, Arabic and Somali. All mosques would be demolished, all traces of Islamic culture in Europe eradicated, even places of historical interest. No ex-Muslim couple would be permitted to have more than two children, and there would be a strict ban on telephoning, emailing or exchanging letters with Muslims outside Europe. For two generations after their conversion, the travel of ex-Muslims to countries that had populations of which more than a fifth were Muslim would be prohibited.

But in spite of all that: 'DO NOT for the love of God aim your rage and frustration at Muslims.' If a pipe is leaking in your bathroom, what do you do? 'It's not very complicated after all. You go to the source of the problem, the leak itself! You DON'T mop it up until after you have fixed the actual leak. Needless to say, our regime is the leak, the Muslims are the water.'

The declaration of war was set out pedantically, with the resistance struggle divided into phases. At the time of writing, the author was in phase 1 of the civil war that was to last until 2030. In that phase, the campaign was to consist of shock attacks carried out by autonomously functioning secret cells that were not in contact with one another. In phase 2, planned to last from 2030 to 2070, more advanced resistance fronts would emerge. This phase would also see preparations for final coups against the governments in power in Europe. In the third phase, post-2070, the execution of traitors in categories 'A' and 'B' would start and a culturally conservative agenda was to be initiated. From 2083 there would be peace; the revolutionary brigades of cultural conservatives would have won the civil war and the ideal society could be built.

The Knights Templar was the organisation nominated to lead both the civil war and construction of the new society. Anyone could become a member. Those who took up arms and began to fight would automatically become part of the brotherhood, part of a network of cells spread across Europe with no central command. Andrew Berwick himself held the highest rank in the organisation – *Justicious Knight Commander*. He was the one who, at the inaugural meeting in London in 2002, had been asked to write the organisation's manifesto, as he possessed special abilities and prerequisites for the task.

This meant he was also the one who decided the enrolment rituals for new members, rituals they could perform by themselves if they liked. All they needed was a darkened room, a large stone as an altar, a wax candle, a skull or perhaps a replica, and a sword. The candle was supposed to represent God and the light of Christ. The text they were to recite could simply be printed out from the manifesto.

Honours would be awarded, depending how many traitors one had killed. These honours had titles like *Distinguished Destroyer of Cultural Marxism* and *Distinguished Saboteur Master*. There was also an award for *Intellectual Excellence*. Berwick had pasted in pictures of uniform decorations from the Order of Freemasons and various branches of the armed forces, and offered hints as to where on the internet these were available. They only cost a few dollars, so the Knights Templar could easily make their own uniforms.

At last he had a use for what he had learned in needlework lessons at Smested Primary School. He wrote that the compulsory teaching of knitting and needlework had a utopian goal: equality between the sexes.

'In retrospect, however, I am grateful for having received this insight into sewing and stitching as this knowledge is an essential skill when constructing and assembling modern ballistic armours . . . It is quite ironic and even hilarious that a skill intended to feminise European boys can and will be used to re-implement the patriarchy.'

'Be creative,' he advised his readers when explaining the different ways of killing traitors. To cause a particularly painful death you could use bullets filled with pure nicotine.

He dealt in depth with information like how to buy guns from the Russian mafia or from outlaw motorcycle clubs, how to send anthrax through the post, use chemical weapons or spread radiation.

There were long lists of clever tricks and manoeuvres. 'Always mask your real goals, by using the ruse of a fake goal that everyone takes for granted, until the real goal is achieved. Strike where the enemy least expects it. Make a sound in the east, then strike in the west.'

If the enemy was too strong, or too well protected, as heads of government often are, 'then attack something he holds dear'. Somewhere or other there will be a chink in his armour, a weakness that can be exploited. 'Hide a knife behind a smile.' Infiltration can be the easiest way to get close to a difficult target: 'Getting a job at the youth camp connected to the largest political party is one way of doing this. The Prime Minister usually visits during summer season.'

'Be a chameleon, put on a disguise,' he continued, suggesting that his readers acquire a police uniform so they could move around with weapons unchallenged.

The very first thing a newly dubbed Knight Templar had to think about was good financial planning. You could have a job, earn money, take out loans or acquire several credit cards and use them to the limit.

The battle demanded the utmost of everyone, and to stay motivated it was legitimate to use 'good food, sexual stimuli, meditation'. Anything was permitted, so long as it worked. But he did worry about the poor combat skills of modern men. Most were useless both at taking aim and at firing. 'Urban Europeans like us, ouch ☺!' he complained, suggesting computer games such as *Call of Duty: Modern Warfare* as a good alternative to joining a shooting club.

To avoid being caught with incriminating evidence, he advised changing your hard disk several times during the planning stage. Equipment connected with the various phases should be buried or destroyed. Planning was everything: familiarity with the terrain, detailed timetables and reserve strategies in case anything went wrong.

It was a fact that most attempted acts of terrorism failed. They were insufficiently planned, the bomb did not go off or the protagonists injured themselves or were exposed. The last of these was to be avoided at all costs and the author suggested making use of social taboos. 'Say you've started playing *World of Warcraft* and have got a bit too hooked on the game. Say you feel ashamed of the fact and don't really want to talk about it. Then the person you have confided in will feel you have let him into your innermost secrets and stop asking questions. Or say you have come out as gay. Your ego is likely to take a dent unless you are secure in your own heterosexuality, because they will actually believe you are gay. But at least they will stop digging and wondering why you have changed, and why they don't see you so often.' Berwick himself had a number of friends who thought he was gay, he wrote, and that was 'hilarious, because he was most definitely 100% hetero!'

Behind the ruthless tone there was a hint of something friendlier, a chilly smile. The last part of the manifesto, in contrast to the first two, was addressed to *someone*. It had a recipient, an intended reader. Not the man in the street, not just anybody, but someone who was already on his side or on the verge of tipping over into his camp. He was at pains to show consideration, offering advice on how to counter fear and loneliness, and recommending songs and sweets as aids to motivation.

He was a guild leader again. With full oversight of his own players, opponents and terrain. If you got cold feet, all you had to do was think of the European women, between half a million and a million of them, who had been raped by Muslims, and carry on.

'In many ways, morality has lost its meaning in our struggle,' he wrote. 'Some innocent will die in our operations as they are simply at the wrong place at the wrong time. Get used to the idea.'

He devoted a chapter to 'Killing Women on the Field of Battle'. The majority of cultural Marxists and suicide humanists were women, and female soldiers fighting to preserve the system would not hesitate to kill you in battle. 'You must therefore embrace and familiarise yourself with the concept of killing women, even very attractive women.'

It was important to put your manifesto up on the internet before you went into action. And equally important to be mentally prepared. 'Once you decide to strike, it is better to kill too many than not enough, or you risk reducing the desired ideological impact of the strike. Explain what you have done (in an announcement distributed prior to the operation) and make certain that everyone understands that we, the free peoples of Europe, are going to strike again and again.'

A Knight Templar should not only be a one-man army; he also had to be a one-man marketing agency. Recruitment material had to look attractive and professional, and it was worth spending some money on marketing. 'Sexy projections of females sell and inspire, in peace-time and during war,' he advised. You should also equip yourself with a personal picture gallery, because if you were arrested, the police would only release 'retarded-looking photos' of you.

When getting ready to have the pictures taken, you had to think about style, 'to look your best'. Spend a few hours on the tanning bed. Work out hard for at least seven days beforehand. Have your hair cut. Use a professional make-up artist. 'Yes, this sounds gay to big badass warriors like us, but we must look our best for the shoot,' he wrote. 'Put on your best clothes and take several changes with you to the studio, like a suit and tie, some casual wear and, for preference, some kind of military outfit. But do not take any weapons or anything that might reveal that you are a resistance fighter.'

The way you presented yourself was important, both in life and in death. Andrew Berwick had also prepared a series of recommended epitaphs for gravestones such as 'Born into Marxist slavery on XX.XX.19XX. Died as a martyr fighting the Marxist criminal regime.' One of his other proposals was a paraphrase of Churchill's 'We shall never surrender': 'Martyrdom before *dhimmitude*! Never surrender.' You were free to add decoration to your stone; he suggested angels, pillars, arrows, birds, lions, skeletons, snakes, crowns, skulls, leaves or branches.

It was also important to give yourself a martyr's gift, something you really wanted. He himself had laid down three bottles of Château Kirwan 1979. As his martyrdom was approaching, he had taken one of them to a Christmas dinner with his half-siblings, the second to a friend's party. He would save the last one for his final martyr's celebration 'and enjoy it with the two high-class model whores I intend to rent prior to the mission'. He claimed that you had to be pragmatic in the face of martyrdom and allow 'the primal aspects of man' to take priority over 'misguided piety'.

If you died in battle, your name would be remembered for hundreds of years. Your story would be told to coming generations and your death would help to boost morale in the resistance movement. You would be remembered as one of the courageous crusaders who said: enough is enough.

If, on the other hand, you survived and ended up under arrest because power still had not been seized from the cultural Marxists, it was up to you to exploit your situation. A trial provided an excellent opportunity and a fitting arena for a Knight Templar to denounce the Marxist world hegemony. Berwick cautioned that on such an occasion you had to speak on behalf of the Knights Templar as a whole, not as yourself. You had to demand to be released, and for your country's regime to be brought before a tribunal of national patriotic forces.

'By the time you are done presenting your demands, the judges and the trial audience will probably laugh their asses off and mock you for being ridiculous. You must ignore this and stay firm and focused. You will then achieve the status of a living martyr.' This influential position would allow you to establish a pan-European prison alliance of militant nationalists. Prison was a first-rate arena for winning supporters and recruiting people for the campaign.

*

And then: the finale. When the civil war was over, the ideal society would be constructed to protect European genes. Factories of surrogate mothers would be set up in low-cost countries and each mother would be expected to produce ten or so blond, blue-eyed children. The possibility of developing an artificial uterus would also be explored.

Parents who were not suitable to look after their children could place them with patriotic foster parents who would be allowed to have up to twelve children. The most crucial concern was that of replenishing the Nordic gene pool. He explained that 'If you go black, there is no turning back.' Blue eyes were a recessive gene and it was important to prevent this threatened eye colour from steady eradication, otherwise there would be hardly any blond, blue-eyed individuals left on the planet.

The new society would be chaste. Sexual abstinence before marriage would be the norm. Divorce would be seen as a breach of contract and would be penalised. The patriarchy had to be rebuilt. Fathers would always be given custody of their children in cases of parents splitting up.

Free zones would have to be set up to avoid rebellion and revolt. Every country could have its Las Vegas, where those incapable of containing themselves could live. Here there would be free sex, free marijuana and uninhibited partying. Liberal, apolitical types could live there. Berwick stressed that even if all Marxists were liberals, not all liberals were Marxists.

Once a day he was torn away from his writing. He had to emerge from his room into life at 18 Hoffsveien.

The eating space in the kitchen was cramped. Their knees almost collided. If they wanted they could take their meals into the living room, where the dining table stood just inside the door to the tiny balcony, beneath two prints by Norwegian artist Vebjørn Sand and a reproduction of the *Mona Lisa*.

His mother talked about things people had told her, rumours she had heard. He talked about the world with which he was obsessed. The book he was writing. Norway, Europe, Islam, the world. His mother did not really like him when he was talking about his book, he was so intense. She eventually started avoiding all subjects that might turn the conversation to politics.

But Anders just ploughed on; after all, he only had his mother to talk to. Wenche sometimes thought: this is nonsense, this is madness and it's got to stop. Things used to be so nice, now he just went on about his book. He suddenly started calling her a feminist with Marxist tendencies, her of all people, who had always voted for the Progress Party.

Talking to his mother, he left out the violence. The great thing was that he didn't have to worry about her snooping about on his computer. She would not even know how to open his files. His sister, on the other hand, would have realised that something was going on if she had come to visit. But she did not come. Still, on the other side of the Atlantic she was worried and wrote in a letter to her mother, 'Mum, that's not normal! He's thirty years old but all he does is sit in his room!'

Wenche, who was now receiving disability benefits, had her head filled with her son's ideas. Across the outdoor café table by the Coop she would suddenly say that Norway should turn itself into an absolute dictatorship. Democracy was bankrupt. The others, a motley bunch who happened to be free in the daytime, would gape at her for a moment before getting back to their coffee refills and pleasant chatter.

Wenche had also grown gradually more opposed to immigration, but often no more so than the others in the café. Whenever it was election time she would go along to the Progress Party's stand by the shopping centre. Sometimes she spent the whole morning there, talking to the campaigners handing out leaflets with their message about a bluer Norway.

Some days she dreaded going home. Her son had started suffering from wild mood swings and he sometimes reacted so violently to little things, or he would be distant, abrupt and surly. He accused her of talking to too many people who could 'infect us'. When he was like that he did not want to eat in the kitchen but asked her to bring his meals to his room, putting the empty plate outside his door afterwards. He put his hands over his face when he needed to leave his room to go to the toilet. At times he even wore a facemask.

But then he would kiss her cheek all of a sudden. Or he would sit down so close to her on the sofa that she found it hard to breathe. At times like that she felt he was suffocating her, like when he was a child, when he was so clingy and could never leave her in peace. It was as if he was never really sure where to sit on the sofa and was sometimes too close, sometimes too far away.

Wenche was now single again. She had thrown out the retired captain. When Anders found out it was over, he bought her a vibrator.

'That's taking consideration a bit far,' she said, and told him her sex life was behind her now.

But Anders kept on asking her if she had tried out the gift.

Wenche often wondered if he was going to move out soon, but she never said anything. She put up with him. He put up with her.

The Progress Party and document.no had rejected him. Fjordman had given him the cold shoulder. From now on he was on his own.

Alone in his deep, soft, accommodating chair. Alone in front of the screen. He kept the blind pulled down over his window. The world was shut out.

It was time to emerge from his cave. High time, in fact.

He had carefully calculated how to keep himself afloat financially once he had made all the necessary purchases. The schedule was tight.

He wanted to make a bomb. That meant he would have to move. For the bomb he would need fertiliser, and to buy fertiliser he had to have a smallholding. The year before, in May 2009, he had set up a one-man business called Breivik Geofarm, operating from 18 Hoffsveien. He registered the company with the Norwegian register of business enterprises, giving its objectives as 'buying, selling and management of shares, project development including acquisition and development of real estate'.

In the course of the spring of 2010 he started buying equipment on the internet. The first thing he bought was a Pelican case from America.

'What do you want that for?' Wenche asked as he took the case, which he had informed her was bulletproof, into his room.

'In case anyone breaks into the car,' he answered.

In May he ordered smoke grenades, laser gunsights and spike strips that would shred the tyres of anyone who tried to chase him. Later he ordered flashing blue lights, a GPS, silencers and firearm magazines.

He took control of the keys to their storage spaces in the attic and the basement. The attic spaces were only divided by wire mesh, so everything had to be well packed up. In the basement their storage space had a sturdy door, but there was a lot of coming and going down there; people used the communal space for bikes, skis and toboggans.

When summer came he started to look for some kind of farm. He had picked out the local council districts of Eda and Torsby in Värmland, just across the Swedish border. *Seeking an isolated/ vacant/abandoned farm*, he put in the subject line of an email he sent to the councils' official email addresses, to Värmland county council and to about ten estate agents in the area. He wrote the letter in a peculiar Swedo-Norwegian.

Hello,

My name is Anders Behring and I have decided to spend the next two years writing a book about share strategies, primarily technical analysis and psychology as related to share trading. With this in view I am trying to find a quiet, isolated location in Torsby district, a disused or abandoned small farm or similar premises.

He stressed that it had to have a *barn/garage/shed* and an *isolated/ remote* location.

The following day an employee of Torsby district council wrote back: *Hello Anders, it's great to hear that you want to come to our district.* One of the estate agents wrote *Good luck with the book!*

But nobody could find a property to suit the Norwegian.

He put the farm project on the back burner for a while; there was so much else to do. Above all, he had to finish his book. The book was the most important thing of all.

It was crucial for him to take control of the narrative of his own life. Where should he start?

He devoted a few lines to his childhood. 'I had a privileged upbringing with responsible and intelligent people around me,' he wrote in the final section of his manifesto under the chapter heading 'Interview with a Justiciar Knight Commander of the PCCTS, Knights Templar'. Some might consider an interview of this kind irrelevant, he wrote, but personally he would have appreciated the opportunity to read such an interview with a resistance fighter.

So there he sat in the fart room between the Coderock artwork and the IKEA shelves, posing questions and thinking up answers. He had no negative childhood experiences at all, he wrote. 'I guess I came from a typical Norwegian middle-class family.'

But the idealised picture soon shattered, the fragments strewn all over the short account of the people he grew up with.

First his father.

'I have not spoken to my father since he isolated himself when I was fifteen (he wasn't very happy about my graffiti phase from thirteen to sixteen). He has four children but has cut contact with all of them so it is pretty clear whose fault that was. I don't carry grudge but a couple of my half-siblings do. The thing is that he is just not very good with people.'

He went on to libel his stepfather: 'Tore, my stepfather, worked as a major in the Norwegian military and is now retired. I still have contact with him although now he spends most of his time (retirement) with prostitutes in Thailand. He is a very primitive sexual beast, but at the same time a very likeable and good guy.'

Then his sister. 'My half-sister, Elisabeth, was infected by chlamydia after having more than forty sexual partners [. . .] Her chlamydia went untreated and she became one of several million US/European women who were suffering from pelvic inflammatory disease caused by untreated gonorrhea and chlamydia which leads to infertility. As she lives in the US, costs relating to this were not covered by the state.'

Finally his mother, and his stepfather again: 'My mother was infected with genital herpes by her boyfriend (my stepfather), Tore, when she was forty-eight. Tore, who was a captain in the Norwegian Army, had more than five hundred sexual partners and my mother knew this but suffered from lack of good judgement and morals due to several factors.' He thrust the knife in deep and twisted it. 'The herpes infection went to her brain and caused meningitis', so she had to have an operation to insert a drain in her head because the infection kept recurring. He wrote that his mother had to take early retirement as a result, and her quality of life had been drastically reduced. 'She now has the intellectual capacity of a ten-year-old.'

His mother had not only brought shame on herself, she had brought shame on him and on the whole family – 'a family that was broken in the first place due to the secondary effects of the feministic, sexual revolution'.

Morality's executioner was ready at the guillotine. The members of his family had each been assigned their share of blame for society's decline and now it was his childhood friend Ahmed's turn.

His classmate, the Pakistani doctor's son from the wealthy neighbourhood of Oslo West, never became truly integrated, ergo integration was not possible. Ahmed had Urdu classes as a child and started attending the mosque when he was twelve. Berwick described how one of the boys he played football with, who later became a business partner, was robbed and beaten up by Ahmed and his Pakistani gang. The Knight Templar invented a story that Ahmed had been involved in a gang rape in Frogner Park. 'These people sometimes raped the so-called "potato whores",' he wrote. Such things had opened his eyes to the Muslim threat.

He accused his childhood friend of having cheered out loud every time a Scud missile was fired at the Americans during the first Gulf War in 1991. The boys were not quite twelve at the time. 'His total

lack of respect for my culture actually sparked my interest and passion for it. Thanks to him I gradually developed a passion for my own
cultural identity.'

He boasted of his close ties with the two most powerful gangs in
Oslo at that time, called the A gang and the B gang. Everything was
framed in Islamic terms. He described the gangs' raids on Oslo West
to impose their authority on the *kuffar* – the non-believers – and collect *jizia* – tax – in the form of phones, cash or sunglasses. The
Muslim gangs taunted, robbed and beat up the ethnic Norwegian
youngsters who lacked the right connections. Anders had ensured
his own freedom of movement by entering into an alliance.

'Alliances with the right people guaranteed safe passage everywhere without the risk of being subdued and robbed, beaten or
harassed.'

Why did you have so many non-ethnic Norwegian friends?

'If I ever got in trouble I expected my friends to back me 100 per
cent without submitting or running away, as I would for them. Very
few ethnic Norwegians shared these principles. They would either
"sissy out", allow themselves to be subdued or run away when facing
a threat.'

Those who stood up for each other were either Muslims or skin-
heads. Back then, he preferred the Muslims to the militant whites.

Then they fell out. Anders wrote that he had been knocked down
without warning by a huge Pakistani outside Majorstua station and
believed Ahmed had ordered the attack. 'This concluded, for my part,
my friendship with him and I re-connected with my old friends.
However, this restricted my territorial freedoms, as I was no longer
under the protection of the Oslo Ummah. From now on we would
have to arm ourselves whenever we went to parties in case Muslim
gangs showed up, and we usually chose to stay in our neighbourhoods
in Oslo West.'

Fifteen years after being frozen out of the graffiti community he
tidied up his younger years, adding a new gloss. He could finally shine
the way he wanted, write over the bits he did not like. 'At fifteen, I was
the most active tagger (graffiti artist) in Oslo as several people in the

old school hip-hop community can attest to.' He called himself one of the most influential hip-hoppers of Oslo West, a focal point, 'the glue that held the gang together'. He referred to his friends by their tag names and their real ones interchangeably. 'Morg, Wick and Spok were everywhere. The fact that hundreds of kids our own age all over Oslo West and even Oslo East looked up to us was one of the driving forces I guess.' He described the way they would go out on graffiti raids at night, their rucksacks full of spray cans, and bomb the city with tags, pieces and crew names. If you wanted girls or respect it was all about being a hip-hopper, he recalled in this reconstruction of his life.

Girls had in truth played little part in Anders's youth. He simply was not popular. He had wondered why, his friends remembered. The only time he had a girlfriend in his school years was the summer when he was fifteen. They went swimming, kissed a few times, sat in the sun. But Anders had made the 'wrong' choice, a girl the others thought ugly, 'with a boyish figure and freckles'.

When the outcast tagger came to present his story to the world, he touched it up with silver glitter and sparkling spray paint. It had to be flawless. That was why, even here in the Declaration of War, he was obliged to explain why he had stopped hanging out with Spok and Wick in Year 9.

He had wanted to focus on school, and what was more he didn't want to do drugs. His mates, meanwhile, decided to stay in the tagging community and were drawn increasingly into criminality and drug use – according to the interviewee's inventions.

He counted the tagging community among the enemy in the coming civil war.

'Many of these groups claim to be tolerant and anti-fascist, but yet I have never met anyone as hypocritical, racist and fascist as the people whom I used to call friends and allies. The media glorifies them while they wreak havoc across the city, rob and plunder. Yet any attempts their victims do to consolidate are harshly condemned by all aspects of the cultural establishment as racism and Nazism. I have witnessed the double standards and hypocrisy with my own eyes, it is hard to ignore. I was one of the protected "potatoes", having friends and allies in the jihadi–racist gangs such as the A and B gang and many other Muslim gangs.'

The hip-hop movement was hijacked by 'Marxist-Jihadi youth', disguised by labels like SOS racism, Youth against Racism and Blitz. Meanwhile, young Norwegians were brought up to be 'suicidally tolerant' and thus unprepared for violence from Muslims. 'This system makes me sick.'

His next milieu – the Progress Party – received similar treatment. He described himself as one of the stars, about to be added to the party's list for the city council elections in 2003. But he had been sold down the river by another rising star of his own age.

'At the time I was more popular than Jøran Kallmyr. I don't blame him for backstabbing me like that, though. After all, he had invested so much more of his time in the organisation than I had.'

In retrospect it all seemed crystal clear. He had left the Progress Party because he had realised he could not change the system by democratic means.

He finished with one line about Lene Langemyr. He had once had a dark-skinned girlfriend.

It wasn't easy. Being editor, publisher, writer, interviewer and interviewee at the same time.

He copied the style from profiles of celebrities, in which they were expected to answer a series of questions about themselves like 'describe yourself in five words'.

Optimistic, pragmatic, ambitious, creative, hardworking.
Sports: snowboarding, fitness, bodybuilding, spinning, running.
Sport on TV: only women's beach volleyball.
Food: all cultures have excellent dishes.
Brand: Lacoste.
Perfume: Chanel Platinum Égoïste.

One day his mother knocked on his door to give him a message, but stopped short when she saw the large weapon propped in the corner of his wardrobe.

'Are you going to keep that shotgun in your room?' she asked. 'I really don't like it.' He had told her he had also ordered a rifle, and one day he showed her a big black pistol.

'You can't live here with all those weapons,' she went on.

Anders muttered something about an approaching civil war.

His mother left him to it; life with her son was becoming more and more claustrophobic. She often felt sorry for him, shut in there or messing around talking nonsense.

What had he got in all those black bags of his, heavy as lead? He was filling the basement storage area with the oddest things. Once she had found two rucksacks full of stones just inside the door of his room, along with four heavy cans.

Anders got cross when she asked.

When he told her he was planning to run a farm, Wenche had said, 'Good for you!'

But she was surprised. He had always been so impractical. It was nice, all the same, to be able to tell her friends at the café that Anders was finally going to do something with his life.

All the cans and containers, cartons and boxes were equipment he needed for the farm. He would have to take it there in several stages.

Once he put on a set of white overalls, which he called a survival suit. Sometimes he went round in a black waistcoat with lots of pockets. 'For my hunting licence test,' he answered when she asked.

One day, when he emerged from his room in a military jacket with lots of emblems on it, she thought: That's it. I give up. He does so many weird things . . .

He had bought the uniform the same month he registered Breivik Geofarm with the register of business enterprises. Using needle and thread, gold braid, ribbon, emblems of various orders, bandoliers and insignias he had made it into a real gala outfit.

Now it hung in a suit cover in the pale blue wardrobe. He wasn't taking it with him to the farm.

The other uniform was ready as well. Some of it was from sportswear shops, some from suppliers of military and paramilitary kit, like the army boots, the helmet with visor, the body armour – inserts and arm guards, a bulletproof vest, a neck protector – a Soviet gas mask and plastic-strip handcuffs. In March 2011 he had sourced the last thing he needed from an internet dealer in Germany: black combat trousers like the Norwegian police wore, at fifty-eight euros.

A few days before his move to the farm, he came out from his room.

'Mum, I'm scared.'

'Goodness me, what of?'

'I'm scared of doing something I might not master.'

She wanted to comfort him.

'You'll be a great farmer,' she said.

Not Just an Outfit

Across the fjord, Bano was sitting at the computer screen, looking for a special costume. She hit the keys hard and fast, clicking from one outfit to the next.

She had saved up her earnings from her summer job at Food & Beverage at the Tusenfryd amusement park, where she and Lara had spent the school holidays as hamburger chefs. As well as flipping burgers and filling paper cups with cola they had spent their days stealing glances at their handsome boss, who was one of the reasons Bano applied for a job at the café where her younger sister had worked the summer before. At the end of the season, Bano won the Worker of the Year award, selected from among all the employees at the park's food and drink outlets. She was quick-witted and deft-fingered. When she made up her mind to do something, it was done in a flash.

Bano smiled more than most, laughed louder and more often. Lara was more reticent. 'Now I know which one's which,' said one boy who had always muddled them up. 'The one who smiles all the time is Bano. Lara's the serious one.'

Lara had spent the money she had earned at H&M, while Bano's was in a savings account. She was searching for something specific.

Ever since she first experienced 17 May, Norway's National Day, as a seven-year-old, she had wanted a *bunad*, a traditional Norwegian folk costume. She had pestered her mother, who hunted all round town at second-hand clothes shops and finally found two girls' costumes at the UFF charity shop. The sisters had long since grown out of them.

Bano wanted a *bunad* she could wear for the rest of her life and pass down to the next generation, like the ones her friends had. Most of them had been given theirs as presents at their confirmation, and Bano had tried on their costumes and admired them. Having one specially made was far too expensive, so she looked for second-hand costumes among the classified ads on the buyers' and sellers' websites. It had to be one she liked and could afford, and the right size for someone who was 1.62 metres tall.

There was one that caught her eye. From Trysil, it said. It was made of black wool and had garlands of red and yellow flowers embroidered round the hem of the skirt and on the bodice. It came with a starched white blouse, a little brooch, a pair of cufflinks and a small embroidered bag to wear at the waist. The seller lived in the Skøyen district of Oslo.

Mustafa came with her. From the ferry they could see the silhouette of the whole city, from east to west. Cranes and scaffolding bore witness to the constant expansion of the city on the fjord. The whole side of the fjord was going to be linked together by a promenade several miles long, Bano had read. What a wonderful idea!

The ferry took them to Aker Brygge. From there they took the number 12 tram to Solli and changed to the number 13. They got off by Hoffsveien.

It was as if the costume had been made for her. Ten thousand kroner changed hands.

On the ferry home she sat with it on her lap. As usual, she couldn't stop talking, and as usual, her father listened and nodded. She jabbered on about affording a bigger silver brooch after this year's summer job, because this one was only child-sized. And then she'd want the special shoes with buckles.

Bano jogged up the steep slope to the housing area up by the edge of the forest. She went straight to her room on the ground floor, donned the traditional costume with its roots in Norway's nine-teenth-century National Romanticism and swept into the living room.

'*Mashalla ka joani*, Bano!' her mother exclaimed, her eyes filling with tears. 'How lovely you look!'

From then until National Day, Bano repeatedly tried on her cos-tume, turning this way and that in front of the mirror, before she would finally wear it for everyone to see. The teenager declared to her younger sister that it was the sexiest thing a woman could put on. She loved traditional festivals and celebrations. Norwegian National Day, with all its passion and fervour, was her favourite.

The day before, she polished her shoes and buckles, ironed her blouse and washed her hair. Her costume was hanging up, all ready to put on. She went to bed in a mood of exhilaration, but doubts came crowding in overnight.

'I've no right to wear this,' she said to her mother. She stood on the stairs, half-dressed, as the morning sun struggled to break through the clouds.

'What nonsense! Now come and let me plait your hair,' her mother said dismissively.

But Bano stood her ground. 'A *bunad* is meant to be from the place you come from. Your history is meant to come from there, your family, you're supposed to *be* from there. You can't just buy it on the internet.'

Bano leant over the banisters. On the table in the living room stood a vase with some green birch leaves and a Norwegian flag stuck into it.

'The *bunad* is yours,' her father asserted, looking down at her. 'You bought it.'

'What if anyone asks?' objected Bano. 'Think if anyone asks where it's from! And when I say Trysil, they'll ask why I'm wearing a Trysil *bunad*. I don't even know anyone in Trysil!'

Bano had explained to her parents all about folk costumes. There were lots of rules. You weren't allowed to change them or jazz them up, or clutter them with jewellery. Ideally you would inherit the costume from your grandmother. The next best way was to be given it for your confirmation.

An inherited costume was precisely what Bano had bought. The woman selling it had been left costumes by both her grandmothers, and since she had no daughter of her own she thought she might as well sell one of them.

Bano's maternal grandmother was from Kirkuk, her paternal grandmother from Erbil. Bano had always been proud of her Kurdish origins and took a keen interest in the Kurds' struggle for their own culture and nation. She talked largely Kurdish to her parents, whereas her younger siblings tended to answer them in Norwegian. But here, now, on 17 May, it was Norway's independence she wanted to celebrate.

Suddenly it had a hollow ring to it.

'So I don't know,' she faltered. 'I don't really have the right to wear it.'

'Now you just listen,' said her father. 'If anyone asks, then say that you had a great-great-great-great-great-grandmother who fell in love with a Norwegian Viking who was on a raid in Baghdad. To escape the honour killing that would be her fate for falling in love with a non-believer, she had to run away with him,' he said. 'To Trysil!'

Bano had to smile. She gave her father a hug and went back down to her room, and carefully finished getting dressed, before her mother plaited ribbons into the wavy, chestnut-brown hair that reached nearly to her waist. Bano drank her morning cup of tea carefully to keep her blouse clean. So did Lara, who was wearing a new white lacy dress from a popular chain store. It was a dress that her mother both disliked and liked. Disliked because it was so short. Liked because its neckline was *not* low cut.

The two sisters, so alike except that Lara had ended up with long legs and Bano with a big bust. They had the same eyes, the same long brown hair. Now they emerged onto the front steps of their terraced house, one in a proper traditional costume, the other in a revealing miniskirt. Little Ali was in a suit, as was Mustafa, and Bayan had put on a simple dress. They were all wearing national-day rosettes in the Norwegian colours – red, white and blue.

As the sisters walked side by side down the path to the main road they could already hear the brass bands. Bano gave her younger sister a serious look. 'This *bunad* is going to be passed down,' she said, stroking the beautiful embroidery, 'to whichever of us has a daughter first. That girl is going to inherit it.'

Lara smiled. Typical of Bano to have it all planned out.

'And you can borrow it when I'm a *russ*,' promised Bano. In the last year at upper secondary you were known as a *russ*, from the Latin *depositurus*, 'one who is going to deposit' – in their case, exam papers.

Bano was thinking ahead to the school graduation celebrations the following year and had already started to save up with her gang of girlfriends for an old van to decorate. She had been put in charge of the finances and had opened a savings account for the group, so everything would be transparent and above board. There were already eight thousand kroner in it. In the course of the year she would take her driving test. How she was looking forward to putting on the red *russ* overalls and cap next year!

A *russ* van drove past them. There were two teenage girls on top, clinging on to the roof. Her mother stared at them open-mouthed, shaking her head of curls that were just starting to go grey, and gave her elder daughter a stern look.

'Bano, you're not to do that when you're a *russ*! Those girls could fall and hurt themselves!'

'Don't worry Mum, I won't,' said Bano and smiled.

Her mother was not reassured and gave a heavy sigh.

'You know that, Mum,' said Bano. 'By the time I'm a *russ* I'll have my licence. So I'll be at the wheel, not on the roof!'

Soon the whole peninsula would see her costume. The new silver brooch glistened on her breast. Its pin was stuck through the fine, white fabric of her blouse, level with her heart.

The President's Speech

The grass was turning green but the trees were still without leaves.

The air temperature had risen above zero but on the shadier slopes and along the mountainsides around the village there was still snow, browny-grey with dust and soil. This far north, spring only crept up on winter slowly.

There was a murmur beneath the snow. Hardy plants were starting to send out shoots. Soon everything would blossom into a short, intense summer, bathed in light.

Throughout the winter, beautiful ice patterns had formed on the surface of the sea. The salty waves had frozen into little mountains of ice, waiting to be set free. In the night-time cold the ice in the fjord compacted, and in the spring sunshine it expanded. Rifts formed as the ice crazed and thin cracks spread at speed, making the ice tremble. The vibrations emitted a deep sound, a heavy rumble. It was the ice singing.

A procession of children made its way into the field in front of the sports hall. Their faces were hot and rosy-cheeked from marching through the village chanting and carrying flags. They had laid wreaths at the memorial stones raised for those from Salangen who had been lost at sea, and in memory of those fallen in the Second World War.

There were bands, there were choirs, there were dignitaries.

Some families were dressed in sturdy traditional costumes from the deep valleys or narrow fjords of Norway, all with warm woollen underwear. Others were wearing the colourful *kofte* or long jerkin of the Sami people, complete with reindeer-skin moccasins and a knife in the belt. The pastor was in a full-length white robe with gold embroidered edging, while the Scottish head of the asylum seekers' centre stood there in a purple tartan kilt and lace-up shoes, with a camera dangling round his neck and legs planted wide apart. The younger asylum seekers from Afghanistan clustered together in a group on their own, as did the Somalis and the Chechens. That year, the residents of Sjøvegan State Asylum Centre had carried their own banner in the procession. It was sky blue, with appliqué designs depicting the changing seasons, summer and winter, midnight sun and polar night, grass and snow, a silver fox and a leaping salmon. The whole thing was crowned with a Norwegian flag. Like the rest of the village, the asylum seekers were wearing the best clothes they had, and from the lectern a voice sang of 'how good and beautiful Norway is'.

A listless gang dressed in red, looking rather the worse for wear, stood out from the rest in the square. Their heads were pounding. Their eyes were slits. There they huddled, some lying down, stifling yawns, a couple even asleep. Their red boiler suits were covered in dirt, seagull droppings and beer. These were the *russ*, the final-year students who were leaving Sjøvegan upper secondary school. Most of them had been up all night and many had been partying since the first day of May. They had danced and drunk, necked and vomited. Some had found a boyfriend or girlfriend, while others had lost theirs. Only the drivers had stayed sober. They had all taken it in turns to drive, one night each, in the clapped-out old vans that got even more scratched and dented as the *russ* season drew to a close.

Now the leavers were gathered with the rest of the town for the first time. Not yelling from open van windows as they screeched by, but assembled with the rest here on the sports field, where they had been running about not so many years ago, trying to wheedle ice creams and treating the *russ* like rock stars.

Now all they had to do was last out until the final item on the agenda: the *russ* president's speech.

They pulled their red caps over their ears; the alcohol was breaking down in their bodies and they were freezing. They all had their names on the peaks of their caps, names to live up to or be ashamed of, given to them by the name committee at the start of the festivities. Their nicknames didn't feel quite so funny now, among that crowd of solid fellow citizens, where the speeches and poetry readings inevitably conjured up a ceremonial mood. Baptism was the worst bit of the *russ* season. What power they suddenly wielded, those teenagers in the name committee, when they sat in judgement on their fellow students. It showed what a fine line there can be between teasing and bullying. A few drops of seawater on your forehead and the verdict was delivered right there on the pebbly shore, in white letters on the shiny black peak of your cap, some of them so rude you couldn't show your cap at home. After the baptism one boy was left sitting on the beach, saying he would throw himself into the sea, in despair at being given the name *Hole-in-One* – a reference to an abortive sexual encounter in a red VW Golf that the whole school knew about. It was the *russ* president who decided the name had to go. He scraped the lettering off the peak with a blunt stone, took the soaking wet boy and his cap home to Heiaveien in the middle of the night, found some paint and began writing a new name with an unsteady hand. The name was to be Einstein. He started with the E, but then had an even better idea. $E = mc^2$ was just right for a brainy type.

The name committee was furious; this was blatant abuse of power on the part of the president. Baptism was their business. But they let the boy keep his cap with Einstein's formula on the peak.

Simon had been the obvious choice when the *russ* came to choose their president; most people were surprised that anybody else even bothered to stand against him, doomed to defeat as they must be. Simon won, naturally, while the runner-up was put in charge of the *russ* revue.

So there he was now, *that Simon*, looking pale with dark rings under his eyes, waiting for the neatly turned out boy from the lower secondary school to finish his poem. His own hair was stiff with gel beneath his red cap and his fingers felt numb.

Down in the crowd Tone, Gunnar and Håvard were waiting. Simon's parents had been far from happy when he came home the previous autumn and told them he's been elected president. 'There goes his *russ* season,' they sighed. For they knew that Simon got so involved in everything, in joys and sorrows, his own and others', and as president he was bound to get drawn into disputes, caught between a rock and a hard place, between the school management and the demanding *russ*. The bitterest clash of all was over something as minor as a hundred kroner.

The *russ* had worked and collected money to donate to the paediatric department at Tromsø's University Hospital. There turned out to be some money left over, amounting to a hundred kroner per *russ*, and the committee proposed that everyone would receive it in the form of a discount on the cost of the coach they were taking to a party in the neigbouring village of Finnsnes. Simon thought that was wrong, and that the money should rather go to the school's project in Cambodia, where they were helping to sponsor a clean-water project for poor rural communities. 'We earned it' clashed with 'Cambodia needs it more'. Positions that would later harden into political divisions created factions and cliques. Nobody was prepared to give in.

In the end, Simon got his way. As he usually did.

But now it was nearly over. It was his turn at the microphone.

His hoarse voice rang out across the square.

'We have been celebrating the completion of our years of study, something that has required hard work day and night!'

Rousing cheers from the *russ*.

'We are, if not reborn, then at least re-baptised over here at Brandy Bend,' he bellowed to renewed howls.

'But there's no disgrace in a name,' Simon went on; he knew when it was time to bury the hatchet. 'They named me J. F. Kennedy. He was a president like me, you know. But unfortunately he got shot in Dallas.'

Simon smiled out over his audience.

'I'm too much of an optimist to sit waiting for the same fate!'

His parents grinned with relief. Gunnar had persuaded Simon to take the time to write his speech out properly, rather than just scribbling a few notes as he generally did. This was going really well!

From the podium Simon cautioned against bullying, in daily life, at school and above all on the internet, where the pillorying of those unable to defend themselves 'could have far-reaching consequences'. He ended with how much money they had raised, their contribution to the water aid project in Cambodia and the campaign against the closure of Sjøvegan Upper Secondary School.

Then he paid tribute to the Constitution and his homeland, and the school band struck up the Norwegian national anthem, 'Yes, we love this country'.

Hundreds of voices were raised and blown out to sea by the wind. As the final notes faded, the square came to life. Parents and young children moved on to their local parties with cake and games, the old folk headed back to their care home, the lonely returned to empty houses and the asylum seekers plodded back up the steep hill to their centre. Their sky-blue banner with the silver fox and the Norwegian flag would be stowed away in a box room until it was time to take it out again, unroll it and press it for another 17 May.

The *russ* were off to slump in their rooms. In rooms that still harboured half-forgotten memories of a time when they were pink or pale blue. Spiderman and Britney Spears stickers still adorned the walls; football posters hung side by side with district champion certificates and school timetables. Some of the rooms were even home to a few overlooked soft toys, and their owners could carry on being children for just a little while longer, for one more short summer.

Most of them would gradually disperse from this town of scarcely two thousand inhabitants, with one clothes shop, a chemist, a sports hall and an asylum-seekers' centre. They would go out into the world, get down to their studies or do their military service. Some would stay on and work at the supermarket or the care home, and others didn't quite know what to do, there were too many options, so they would take a gap year to think it over.

Simon dutifully accompanied his parents and Håvard to the local party in Upper Salangen, where they had once lived, next door to his grandparents. Now he was the hero; just imagine, the *russ* president himself had put in an appearance. He played along and stayed in his role, while the children competed for his attention.

The midnight sun was just three days away. In the months to come, the sun would never set.

The Sæbø family turned into the drive of the blue house on the bend, just below the church, where the key was always under the doormat. Simon stumbled into his room, pulled off his *russ* overalls and collapsed into bed. By the window looking out over the fjord, the red and yellow Manchester United logo painted on the wall stood out boldly. To shield himself from the bright evening light he had closed the curtains. The design on the fabric was of a boy with a skateboard under one arm and a football under the other.

Still, it was not entirely dark. Above his bed shone a heart. It was made out of fluorescent stars. Stars his girlfriend had stuck on his ceiling one evening.

A few more weeks of school and then summer stretched ahead, shiny and glorious.

He had got himself a job in the churchyard, just up the hill behind the house. All he had to do was cross the garden, step over the fence and walk a little way along the road, then he could go in through the gate by the church. His job would be to cut the grass, weed and water and keep the graves tidy throughout the summer holidays, apart from a couple of weeks, for which he had other plans. It would make a nice change to potter round the peaceful churchyard, be outside, feel the sun and get away from the classroom.

So, at last: over the summer, real life would begin. JFK had it all mapped out.

In one of the books on his shelf there was a quotation: 'Ask not what your country can do for you, ask what you can do for your country.'

One day he was going to make speeches like Kennedy too.

Poison

A thousand kilometres further south, in one of Norway's thickest forests, a man stood in an open yard, boiling up sulphuric acid. The clear, viscous liquid was bubbling on an improvised hotplate and a stench of rotten eggs hung in the air. He was in the lee of a red-painted barn and could not be seen from the road. An electric cable, ten metres long, trailed to a socket inside the barn.

The farm consisted of a white-painted house, the barn, a summer cowshed, farmhands' quarters and a red storehouse raised on pillars, plus a garage. It lay on the eastern side of the Glomma river and looked out over dense forest to the east, while the view to the west was of green pasture and fields. The coltsfoot was blooming at the edges of the ditches and white wood anemones carpeted the dark ground beneath the fir trees.

Vålstua, built around 1750, was the first smallholding attached to the larger farm of Vål, a bit further down the wide river. Some ground and a small patch of forest went with it, but it was quite a few years since the place had been properly farmed. The owner was in prison for having run a hash plantation there. Presumably he had thought it was easy to hide away in the country, people said, shaking their heads. But no, if there was one place where the locals kept their eyes open it was here, and everybody knew there had been funny business going on at Vålstua. You hardly ever saw the people who lived there, yet there had been feverish activity in the outbuildings. People noticed things like that.

Before he began his sentence, the owner advertised the farm for rent on various websites. A young man from Oslo got in touch. He was going to start sugar beet production, he said. When he came to look round, he told the owner that he had completed three thousand hours of self-tuition in agronomy, and knew someone at the agricultural college at Ås. The farm was idyllic, and the place got the sun late into the evening, the owner responded. Afterwards he told his girlfriend he'd been surprised that the well-dressed young West Ender did not say a word about the beautiful views and scarcely bothered to look at the main farmhouse.

They agreed on a rent of ten thousand kroner a month. The owner wished his new tenant the best of luck and went off to serve his sentence of a couple of years.

The sound of drums and trumpets carried from the nearby hamlets. A light morning mist lay over the landscape, but sunny intervals were forecast for later in the day.

No 17 May celebration would be complete without some mild admonitions from the local paper. This year, *Østlendingen* had advised local residents not to buy confetti spray, which contained harmful solvents. Customs had stopped large quantities of it at the Swedish border in the run-up to National Day, the paper reported. And the *russ* had been banned from bringing water pistols to their procession in case they frightened children, prompting vehement protests from the *russ*.

These were the topics of conversation as the children played and the older people took wood anemones and wreaths of birch leaves to their family graves in the churchyard, in accordance with local tradition.

There was one news item that cast a slight shadow over the festivities. The previous night, a *russ* van belonging to a girl from an immigrant background had been daubed with swastikas. Nobody wanted that sort of thing here.

The man at Vålstua was too preoccupied by his bubbling sulphuric acid to have any particular thoughts about National Day. The small-holding was in any case too far from the nearest village for the school bands or the honking horns of the *russ* to disturb him. His pale blue eyes stared through a respirator mask, fixed on the sulphuric acid. He was wearing yellow rubber gloves and a heavy-duty protective apron bought from a supplier of laboratory wear. His ash-blond hair, cut short, revealed a slightly grubby brow. His skin had a greyish tinge, the typical complexion of a northerner who has spent a long winter indoors and was now squinting at the sun for the first time.

The hotplate was standing on a cast-off TV stand he had brought out into the yard. He turned up the heat as high as it would go and the acid soon came to the boil. His aim was to reduce the water content to increase its concentration. The farmhouse was littered with scraps of paper covered in numbers and calculations. He had worked out that it would take him three days and nights to reduce the roughly thirty litres of sulphuric acid from 30% to 90% concentration.

After an hour and a half the steam, initially all but invisible in the overcast weather, started to change character. It gradually turned into white smoke, then grey, and at the end of two hours the smoke was so thick and black that he was worried the neighbours would see it and pulled the plug. The smoke continued to billow for a while and he decided that from now on he would work at night, so as not to attract unwanted attention.

He had obtained the acid from various car dealers. At one breaker's yard he bought seven litres of 30% sulphuric acid. From a used-car dealer he bought four car batteries that contained a total of six litres of acid, and Exide Sønnak, a wholesaler to car repair shops, was able to supply another twenty-five litres. They had sold out of small cans, so it aroused no suspicion when he bought a large one. But the salesman was concerned for his customer's safety and how he was going to secure the container of the highly corrosive fluid for transport. Well, if he'd had a crash, he wouldn't need a new mask for Halloween, he joked in his diary once he was safely back home.

Buying in all the chemicals had been the most critical phase, in fact, with the greatest risk of discovery. When he started ordering the elements for making the bomb in October 2010 – the previous autumn – he was still living with his mother in Oslo. He had often been scared. If he bungled this and came to the attention of the authorities he would be done for, neutralised before he could carry out the operation.

He'd had to overcome his anxiety before he could cope with making his purchases and had started a course of anabolic steroids while also intensifying his bodybuilding regime. He'd downloaded some new vocal trance music and bought Blizzard's latest expansion pack for *World of Warcraft*, the newly launched *Cataclysm*, which he allowed himself to play to get his courage up. There, he was on home ground, among friends and enemies, on territory he had mastered, where his score was always rising.

With a bit of post hoc rationalisation he judged this combination of anti-anxiety measures, in addition to three weekly walks that were an opportunity for 'meditation and indoctrination', to have raised his morale and motivation to a whole new level. Or so he wrote in the log, which he later incorporated into the third and final part of his book.

Making a bomb was not easy. He had studied various instructions on the internet, from detailed dissertations to practical explosion experiments on YouTube. Several had been put up by laboratories and amateur chemists, some by al-Qaida and other militant organisations.

He gave the delivery address for the chemicals he ordered as 18 Hoffsveien. Via eBay he ordered powdered sulphur from the US, which was described on the carriage declaration as 'yellow artist paint dust'. He ordered sodium nitrite from a company in Poland and sodium nitrate from a chemist's shop in Skøyen. He made sure to have plausible cover stories. The powdered sulphur was for cleaning out an aquarium; the sodium nitrate for treating meat: a few teaspoons of it mixed with salt and spices and rubbed into an elk carcass would slow the growth of bacteria and help the meat keep its colour when frozen – a method in general use among elk hunters.

The orders were swiftly dispatched and the goods started piling up in his room, in the basement and up in the attic at Hoffsveien. Ethanol, acetone, caustic soda, flasks, glasses, bottles, funnels, thermometers and facemasks. He ordered powdered aluminium from Poland, telling the supplier that he wanted it for mixing with boat varnish to make it less permeable to UV radiation and that his company dealt in 'coating solutions for the maritime sector'.

He bought a fuse several metres in length. For the New Year celebrations, he would say if anybody asked. There were thousands of fireworks enthusiasts all round Europe who ordered that sort of thing for their displays. You could also learn how to make your own fuses from the various pyrotechnics forums on the internet, but it was safest to buy one.

It was crucial that it would be long enough. One centimetre equated to one second, so if you needed five minutes to get away you had to buy a three-metre fuse.

He also needed several kilos of aspirin, from which to extract acetylsalicylic acid. It was good timing to be buying headache tablets in December, at the height of the party season. He had worked out that he needed a couple of hundred packets. Cash registers automatically blocked sales staff from selling more than two packets to each customer, but he found out that there was a score of chemists' shops within walking distance of Hoffsveien. He reckoned he would be able to get round them all in one day and took the tram to the Central Train Station. From there, he did an east-to-west circuit of all the chemists', four to five times in the course of the winter at intervals of one to two weeks, until he had as much aspirin as he needed. Initially he bought the most expensive brands, but he soon switched to the generic alternatives. He was perpetually nervous that the pharmacists would get suspicious and he dressed smartly, in conservative clothes with discreet designer logos, so the red flag would not go up.

December was a good month in every way. The post office was so overburdened with all the Christmas parcels that it had reduced capacity for checking the contents of his orders of chemicals.

*

He bought protein powder to increase his muscle mass and milk this-
tle to strengthen his liver and mitigate the damage the steroids were
doing to it. He also laid in supplies of powders and pills to boost his
energy when carrying out the operation. He started attending shooting classes at Oslo Pistol Club so he could get a firearms licence, and
completed the required fifteen hours of training between November
2010 and January 2011. Two weeks into the new year he submitted
an application to buy a semi-automatic Glock 17. He also took lessons to improve his rifle skills, particularly at distances of over a
hundred metres. The shooting-based computer game *Call of Duty:
Modern Warfare* had also improved his firing accuracy, he thought, and
over the winter he bought laser sights from a variety of gun dealers,
along with large quantities of ammunition.

From China he ordered liquid nicotine. His bullets would be filled
with the poison. He could get everything he needed for this at the
hardware shop: a little drill for making a hole in the bullets, a pair of
cutters to take the tips off, a set of files and some superglue to seal
them up afterwards.

He bought a semi-automatic Storm Ruger rifle, the Mini-14
model, and a trigger that would make rapid firing easier. At the end
of January he received notification from Intersport in Bogstadsveien
that a silencer he had ordered could not be supplied; all private
orders had been cancelled because of a bulk military order. He did
not want to risk a non-automatic silencer: it could overheat and
explode during rapid fire, which could destroy the rifle. In the log he
managed to turn this into a 'bonus', a word he was fond of using:
'Without a silencer I can fix a bayonet to the rifle instead. Marxist on
a Stick will soon be the exclusive Knights Templar Europe trade-
mark.' Without further ado he ordered a bayonet from Match Supply
in the US, which was identified on the customs declaration as sports
equipment.

To document the process and help market the compendium, he
had bought a camera, and planned to use Photoshop to compensate
for his lack of photographic skill.

In the log he carefully wrote out his shopping list, encouraging all interested parties to follow his example: 'There is absolutely NO GOOD REASON for not getting this equipment out of fear you will be found out. All that is holding you back is unjustified anxiety and laziness! The only reason that could justify your fear is having an Islamic name!'

On 13 February 2011 he turned thirty-two, and two days after his birthday, which he did not celebrate, he started editing the film that was to 'market the compendium' he was in the process of compiling. He downloaded images from anti-Islamic websites and added music he liked, dramatic and emotive. Twelve days later he was satisfied with his film. He noted in his log: 'I would love to make it even better but I can't really afford to invest any more time into this trailer which might never see the light of day . . . ' He added: 'Was planning to hire a low-cost Asian movie guy through scriptlance.com but I have to conserve my funds.'

By February, his weight had gone up from 86 to 93 kilos and he had never felt in better shape. He was 50 per cent stronger, he thought, and this would undoubtedly prove useful, he underlined in his log.

In the spring, just before he moved away from home, he received a letter from the Freemasons' lodge with an offer of promotion to degree 4 and 5 even though he had hardly attended any meetings. He replied that he was not available, because he was away travelling for extended periods. He no longer needed the lodge that he had once implored to admit him. He had created his own lodge, where he made the rules.

The letting contract had been signed on 5 April, and the very next day the new farmer at Vålstua contacted the Norwegian Agricultural Producers' Register to inform them of changes at Breivik Geofarm. The business address was to be changed from Oslo to the district of Åmot. The farm's change of use to the production of root crops and tubers would have to be registered. The farm would have to have a new business code, and he needed a producer number in order to get fertiliser.

He was now so hyped up that he abandoned his usual caution and let his impatience for formal approval from the Producers' Register show, to the extent that the official dealing with his case began to wonder. In mid-April, the official carried out a background check on Breivik.

'He keeps on pestering . . . Is there anything on him?' he queried in an email to his boss, requesting a check on the tenant at Vålstua. Nothing showed up, and a week later confirmation was sent out that the change of use had been approved.

On 4 May Anders hired a Fiat Doblò from Avis and moved out of his mother's flat. He had ordered six tonnes of fertiliser on credit. The bags were delivered the day he moved in at Vålstua. As agreed, half of it was driven into the barn, the other half unloaded beside some birch trees on the property.

That first day on the farm, he constructed the metal framework of the bomb. The next day he started crushing the aspirin tablets to extract the acetylsalicylic acid. The internet advised him to use a pestle and mortar, but within a couple of hours his hands were aching terribly and he had pulverised only a small portion of the tablets. There had to be another way. He put a large sheet of plastic on the floor of the barn and started crushing them with a twenty-kilo dumb-bell he used for weight training. Four hours later, he had crushed a hundred and fifty packets of aspirin.

Many of the instructions were defective. He experimented and failed, tried different things and took a creative approach. He went to IKEA and bought three toilet brushes with steel holders to use as detonator containers. He planned to seal them with aluminium discs cut to shape, or screws and coins. From China he bought sixty water-proof bags ideal for storing and transporting chemicals.

When it came to extracting the acetylsalicylic acid from the pow-dered aspirin, none of the instructions he tried seemed to work and he ended up with useless salicylic acid. He trawled the internet des-perately and dejection set in. 'If I couldn't even synthesise the first phase of the easiest booster how on earth would I manage to syn-thesise DDNP?! My world crashed that day and I tried to develop an alternative plan,' he wrote in his log. To raise his spirits he went to a restaurant in the local town of Rena and treated himself to a three-course meal. Then he watched a few episodes of *The Shield*.

His mood swings were rapid and sharp. The steroids were affecting his mental state as well as his muscles. He could push himself more but he could also go to pieces without warning. But he always pulled himself together again, aware of the pressure of time.

None of the methods he had found online, primarily laboratory experiments from various universities, had enabled him to extract the acid concentration he needed. The next day proved fruitless too. He went out to the restaurant again in the evening to give himself a morale boost and ponder a new plan. 'I appear to be fundamentally fucked if I cannot manage to find a solution soon,' he wrote in his log on Saturday evening, 7 May.

When he woke up on Sunday morning, he went straight on to the internet. After several hours he found a YouTube video with very few previous hits. It showed an unconventional method for extracting the acid he wanted. The guy in the video used a suction pump and a dehumidifier in a laboratory, and succeeded where all the other chemists on the web had failed.

On Monday morning Anders tried doing the same himself, using coffee filters and natural air-drying rather than lab equipment. Despite not being entirely sure that it was in fact purified acetylsalicylic acid he had produced, he decided he had no option but to stake everything on the method. A calculated risk, he wrote in the log, since he could not know the quality of the product he had made. He used Tuesday to make the ice required for the extraction process. He filled the freezer with ice-cube bags, and had to make sure each layer had frozen before he added the next, so the bags would not tear under the weight of the next layer. He spent the whole week filtering.

'I just love Eurovision,' he noted in the log on Saturday 14 May, awarding himself a night off to watch the final of the song contest. He had watched all the semi-finals. 'My country has a crap, politically correct contribution as always. An asylum seeker from Kenya, performing a bongo song, very representative of Europe and my country . . . In any case, I hope Germany wins.'

Azerbaijan won.

The day before Norwegian National Day the magnetic stirrer, a special hotplate for heating unstable fluids, stopped working. 'Fuck, Chinese piece of shit equipment, I should have rather paid more to get good European quality machinery!' he wrote, and ordered another one. It would take too long to produce picric acid and DDNP without a magnetic stirrer.

That evening he completed the extraction of the acid he needed from the last aspirin tablets, using a spatula to get the remains of the crystallised material out of the coffee filters. He spread it on plastic, and with the help of an oil heater raised the temperature in the room to thirty degrees to dry the acetylsalicylic acid.

The bubbling sulphuric acid enveloped the yard in a dim blanket of gas. He turned off the hotplates and let them cool, hung his lab apron and gas mask in the barn and went in to make something to eat. He liked to eat well. Food was a comfort and a reward.

He sat in the farmhouse as evening drew in. There was no question of going out among other people. He kept a polite distance from the neighbours. 'Welcome to our village,' the woman who lived nearest had said cheerily the first time they met, holding out her hand, but luckily she had never come to visit. He was on nodding terms with the rest. He had made sure to give the impression that Vålstua was not a place to drop round for coffee.

In the surrounding hamlets, National Day was drawing to a close. Silver brooches and cuff links were put away in pretty boxes lined with cotton wool or velvet, starched blouses were thrown into the washing machine and traditional costumes were brushed and hung away in the wardrobe. Children's faces were scrubbed clean of ice cream and ketchup, and the national anthem and all those marches could finally take a rest in the music cases of the school band. The delicate wood anemones started to hang their heads in their vases, and at 9 p.m. everyone lowered their Norwegian flags.

Most people agreed that the 17 May celebrations in their valley had been as good as last year, well, apart from the fact that the red, white and blue bunting had not gone up along the pedestrian precinct in the local town. The metal hooks on the walls of the buildings were bare and some thought it was the district council's responsibility, others that it was the business community's. The following day, *Østlendingen* would try to get to the bottom of it and apportion blame where it was due.

The hamlet-dwellers had not sensed the smell of sulphur hanging over the delicate green shoots in the fields. None of *Østlendingen*'s newshounds had seen the clouds of black smoke, and none of the neighbours on the banks of the Glomma had wondered why the West End boy from Oslo had stayed at home on National Day.

As darkness began to fall he went back out. He turned the hotplate to its top setting and put the container on it. The thick black smoke would start billowing up again around midnight, but by then it would be as dark as it gets in Østerdalen in mid-May, and for a few hours the smoke would be indistinguishable from the night.

Below the farm, the cold waters of the Glomma rushed onward. The river had a powerful force to it, swollen by the meltwater it was carrying down from the mountains. Wherever you were on the farm, you could hear its roar. When he took over the place at the start of May there were still a few chunks of ice sailing by, having broken off from the ice fields north of Glombrua. The spring flood usually lasted far into June. It would be July before the river calmed. Then it grew idle and drowsy, scarcely bothering to flow at all in the summer heat.

But it was still a long time until July.

The Chemist's Log

Maybe it was the sulphur vapour, maybe it was the steroids, but he had grown more careless, in fact almost fearless. It was tedious having to stand there keeping an eye on the boiling sulphuric acid. This was the third day in a row he had been watching over it. He had to let it boil away for many hours and reach a concentration of more than 70% before it started to give off the dense black smoke; now he didn't bother waiting until nightfall. The acid followed its own rhythm and took no account of night or day.

The fridge was empty and he needed to do some shopping. But he could not afford to waste valuable boiling time by turning off the hotplate. He was behind schedule, so decided to take a chance and briefly desert the bubbling acid. He could turn the hotplate to a low setting, after all. He was in the hallway putting on his lab gear and protective goggles to go out and turn the temperature down when he glanced out of the window. A neighbour was outside.

He tore off the apron and calmly went out.

'Good morning,' he said, cautiously cheerful.

The neighbour asked about a BMW. The farm owner, the one who was in prison, had a car in the upper barn and the neighbour had promised to fix it for him by the time he got out.

That really was close. He was still shaking as he tried to make a genial impression, chatting and giving the neighbour enough petrol to drive the car away.

Later he advised the readers of his log: you ought to try to generate as much goodwill as possible from your neighbours. 'The goodwill will be returned indirectly by them not probing and investigating. If you get visits from neighbours, be polite and friendly, offer them sandwiches and coffee, unless it will jeopardise the operation.'

It seemed like too much of a risk to leave the sulphuric acid boiling while he was out after all, so he postponed operations until the evening. He had to buy food, so he went into the village and bought red meat, bread and sweets, and made himself a large meal when he got back to the farm. Once it was dark he went outside, and in the course of the night he reduced all the sulphuric acid.

The following day he went to Oslo to fetch some packages. The post office had sent his mother notification of several parcels to be collected. He went back to the farm with distilled water, microballoons and a set of dumbbells.

Half an hour from home, he gave a start when he saw a car parked at the side of the road. An unmarked police car, he thought. Closer to the farm he saw a car that could be another police vehicle. I'm about to be arrested, he thought. A short distance before the driveway to the farm, he turned off his engine and lit a cigarette. Was it all over now? There might already be a big police team waiting for him at Vålstua. All his weapons were in the farmhouse. Should he flee? But where to?

Once he had stubbed out the cigarette he started the car and drove slowly along to the farm with his fog lights on, so he would have an advantage if the police were in front of him.

The barn door was standing wide open. Somebody was there! They doubtless had the place surrounded and were closing in on him, or perhaps they were waiting in the main building. He got out of the car and approached the farmhouse. Locked himself in, fetched his Glock and searched the house and barn for surveillance equipment. Apart from the wind, all was quiet. Perhaps they had gone. Perhaps they had installed cameras.

'Paranoia can be a good thing, or it can be a curse,' he wrote in his diary. It must have been the wind that wrenched the barn door open. He swore never to let paranoia get the better of him again. If they came to get him there was nothing he could do in any case, so there was no point worrying.

The tender growth in the surrounding countryside was greener and more intense with every passing day. The birds were on their nests and the cherry trees were in bloom. While there was lots of activity in the fields all around, his own land lay fallow. Clover and timothy flourished in the rich soil, giving off a sweetish scent. Still, the smell of something rotten hung over the farm at Vålstua.

He had six tonnes of fertiliser. Half of it non-detonable, ordered so as not to arouse suspicion. Now, he was going to transfer three tonnes of it to fifty-kilo bags, pick them up with the forklift truck, take them over to the barn and heave them on to a handcart, and then wheel them in. Though he had only managed to move a fraction of the fertiliser, he was exhausted after the first day.

Fertiliser is delivered in pellet form, each pellet coated in a water-repellent material. To make it detonable, it has to be soaked in diesel. So the pellets had to be crushed in order to become explosive.

He cleaned the barn floor and spread the contents of one of the fertiliser bags evenly across it. Then he rolled his heaviest dumbbell over the fertiliser and shovelled up the crushed pellets before they could absorb any moisture from the air. He had worked it all out on paper and estimated that he would be able to crush fifty kilos in twenty minutes.

His plan failed. The method did not work. The first bag took him two hours, and the fertiliser absorbed moisture much faster than he had expected. The pellets ended up only partially crushed, and his back was soon aching from rolling the dumbbell to and fro across the floor.

'Fuck, why can't anything go as planned???? And the dumbbell set cost me a total of 750 euro and now it has proven to be worthless . . . what do I do now?' He decided to raise his spirits with a three-course meal in Rena. There he remembered something he had read about 'a Marxist terrorist traitor in the early 70s. I believe he was called Baader or it could have been Meinhof, terror prostitutes for the Soviets and the loyal *dhimmi* whores of the Islamic Ummah', who had used electric mixers to crush the pellets at home in their apartment. Breivik decided to try out the Marxists' method. If a 1970s mixer could do it, the more modern types should definitely be able to.

The next day he went to various suppliers and bought twelve different mixers and blenders, some on stands and some hand-held, to test which sort worked best. Half of them were unusable. The shape of the container prevented the pellets from going round, or the blades were not sharp enough. But one brand proved effective – Electrolux. Practically all the pellets got crushed and besides, it had a higher speed than the others and could process a good half-kilo of fertiliser pellets in thirty seconds. The next day he went to three different towns and bought six blenders of the same model.

It was three days until the end of May. The days passed in transferring the fertiliser to smaller bags and preparing it for pulverisation.

By the last day of May he was so shattered that he had to rest. He could hardly move his fingers and worried the damage might be permanent. The whole day was spent in bed. He would have to make some adjustments; three bags of fertiliser would have to do, not five as originally planned. It was simply too much for one person. So the explosive charge would just have to be smaller.

On 1 June he still did not feel able to get back to the job, and stayed at his PC, updating the log. On 2 June he also stayed in, surfing the web. Suddenly he heard a car drive up to the property. He peered out through the curtains. A man got out of the car and began taking photos of the farm. Breivik went out into the yard. The man said he had come to take some shots of the Glomma in spate. He's lying, thought Breivik instinctively. His body language gave him away. He must be a policeman.

He offered him coffee but the man declined, and Breivik suggested they go down to the riverbank to get the best pictures. The man nodded, but carried on taking pictures of the yard area. 'Landscape photography,' he explained. It made Breivik uneasy.

But he had no choice. He had to go on with his preparations.

That evening he rang his mother and said an undercover detective had turned up to take pictures of the farmyard. His mother thought that all sounded very peculiar. He also told her about creepy sounds. There was a creaking that really spooked him out.

'When can I come and visit?' his mother asked. She had enquired several times, but it was never convenient. He said that he was worn out and the ground was very stony. It was so stony that he would have to grow timothy-grass. She could not always follow what he said any more. This was not a good time to come, either. He wanted to get everything finished first, he said.

He had four blenders going simultaneously. They made such a noise that he went back to working at nights, as he would never hear if anybody happened to come by. Every time he had crushed enough pellets for a fifty-kilo bag, he poured diesel over them, making sure it soaked in evenly. He then sealed the double-layered bags from China with tape and set them aside.

He worked mechanically, all the while calculating and recalculating the time it was taking and adjusting the plan in accordance with his working pace. He soon got into a routine. He generally took only forty minutes per sack now, his record was thirty-two. He was making progress. There were ten bags piled in the corner. Twenty bags. Two of the blenders broke. He replaced them with new ones.

Saturday 4 June. Six bags. Sunday 5 June. Four bags. Two more blenders fell apart. Monday 6 June. Bought two new blenders.

That afternoon, he reached the end of the third sack. He had now crushed 1600 kilos of fertiliser pellets and soaked them in diesel. There was fertiliser dust everywhere. His green workwear had turned grey. 'Surely I am going to die from cancer within twelve months as I must have gotten a lot of this crap into my lungs even though I used a 3M mask . . . ' he wrote in the log, adding: 'Watching *The Shield*, a couple of episodes a day on average. I downloaded all seven seasons at the beginning of May.'

Next phase: to synthesise picric acid, also known as Mother of Satan. He had all the equipment and chemicals he needed. They were easily obtainable, he wrote in the log, 'unless you're called Abdullah Rashid Muhammed'.

To make the bomb go off he had to have a primary and a secondary explosive. The primary one was DDNP – diazodinitrophenol – the secondary was picric acid. He would have to synthesise both of them from scratch.

A car pulled up outside. Too many goddamned visitors. It was a neighbour who wanted to buy the clover and timothy that had grown on his fallow land. Breivik explained that for various reasons he had not been able to harrow his fields, but that he was intending to grow potatoes and vegetables. The neighbour was surprised to hear his plan and said it was pretty futile growing vegetables in the stony soil round the farm.

Breivik started talking about a farm he wanted to buy in Røros instead. 'It's even harder growing veg in the cold ground up there,' the neighbour pointed out.

They took a stroll down to the field, and Breivik was afraid his neighbour might see the fume hood fan sticking out of the living room window. They agreed on a price. The farmer would come back two weeks later to harvest the crop, which had grown wild on nothing but rain and sunshine.

Weird kind of guy, the neighbour mused on his way home. The new tenant had listened politely, almost servilely, to all his objections. He clearly hadn't a clue about farming.

Breivik carried on producing picric acid. Once the first batch was done he put fifty grams of the powder in the oven to make it ready to test it. If correctly made, it should ignite when he tried to set it alight. Nothing happened. The log was strewn with expletives. He'd followed the instructions, hadn't he? 'Could the compound I have manufactured be inert???? Unfortunate circumstances rams cock in the arse once again . . . ! I start to have serious doubts and my morale starts to shatter . . .'

As dusk approached on Saturday 11 June, heavy clouds came in over the farm. High in the air a thunderstorm was brewing, and big drops of rain came drumming down onto the roof. There was a sudden crash, lightning flashed across the sky, the computer gave a bang and the power went off. When the electricity came back on, the PC was dead.

Breivik sat down to pray. It was a long time since he had called to God. 'I explained to God,' he wrote in his diary, 'that unless he wanted the Marxist-Islamic alliance and the certain Islamic takeover of Europe to completely annihilate European Christendom within the next hundred years he must ensure that the warriors fighting for the preservation of European Christendom prevail. He must ensure that I succeed with my mission and as such; contribute to inspire thousands of other revolutionary conservative nationalists, anti-communists and anti-Islamists throughout the European world.'

The PC was still dead.

Two days later he made a test bomb and took it to a remote part of the forest, a few kilometres from the farm. There was still thunder in the air, which was good, because nobody would think twice about a loud bang. He lit the fuse and waited. 'It was probably the longest ten seconds I have ever endured . . . ' he wrote afterwards.

The little lump exploded.

He drove off straight away, in case anybody came to investigate. He headed to Elverum to celebrate with a slap-up meal. He drove home via the detonation site to study the small crater. The DDNP had exploded as it should, but the dried picric acid had largely failed to detonate. He would have to purify it still further.

In mid-June his financial mask began to slip. Ten of his credit card bills were due and he had received formal reminders about various other amounts he owed. If it went as far as debt recovery and his creditworthiness was in doubt, he would not be able to hire a car and it would be well nigh impossible to carry out the plan. The biggest unpaid bill was for the fertiliser, but nor had he paid last month's rent on the farm. The bills for the fume hood fan, the hotplate stirrer and the spare fan he had not even used were now due. He had just one week to find almost eighty thousand kroner. As well as withdrawing as much cash as he could from those ten credit card accounts, he would also have to ring the farming cooperative and ask for extra time to settle their bill.

He managed to defer payment for half the fertiliser, and wrote in his log that he could 'keep my head above water until mid-July'.

His activities at Vålstua were extremely hazardous. The barn was full of chemicals, the liquids were unstable and his working process was experimental. He had scarcely any safety measures. Sometimes he freaked out when he read about security precautions and all the eventualities that could lead to explosions. Contact with air was dangerous; contact with metal, concrete and plastic could increase static electricity and cause a detonation. So could friction and impact, and proximity to petrol, diesel and electric sockets. He was scared of what would happen to him if the explosive material went off. 'The blast wave/flame would probably cauterise my wounds, resulting in an extended and extremely painful death.' He made sure to keep the Glock to hand in his working area, so if he survived an explosion but lost his arms he could still shoot himself in the head by pulling the trigger with his toes.

Everything was covered in a layer of grey aluminium powder. The strong fluids and acids were gradually staining and eating into the floors and furniture.

After a long night's work towards the end of June, he woke up at eleven the next morning to find that he had received a text message. It was from the girlfriend of the convicted hash-grower and had been sent an hour and a half before. She wrote that she was on her way to pick up some stuff from the barn. In that case, she could be there within the half-hour.

It would take him at least twelve hours to clear up and make the barn presentable, dismantle his equipment, sweep up and clean the place. That meant he would have no choice but to kill her on arrival and then evacuate the farm. He rang her. Luckily she had not yet left. They arranged that she would come two days later. He used the two days for thorough cleaning and tidying. He had to move all the equipment down into the 'spider cellar' full of cobwebs, hide the damaged tabletops under cloths and the floors with rugs. It set him back by at least two days.

She arrived late in the evening and wanted to stay the night. Breivik got up early the next morning to check whether she was snooping round. If she got suspicious, he would have to kill her. She was hard to read, so when she had packed up and was ready to leave he offered her a bite to eat so he could try to glean a bit more about what she had seen.

He also tested out a few of the ideas from his book on her, but no, she did not want to discuss politics. He poured her more coffee. They chatted. She did not seem to have noticed anything. He could let her live.

The farm stank of chemicals: 'it smells like fresh egg fart,' he wrote in the log. He had to shut the windows to help the liquid reach room temperature more quickly and he worried about his health and everything he had inhaled.

Then his network interface card shorted again and he was without a PC. He ordered a new card and carried on with the production of DDNP. Once he had purified the last batch of picric acid, he went off to Elverum and bought three portions of Chinese takeaway, beef with noodles and fried rice. 'Yummy! I took an early night as I didn't have a PC.'

The next day he went to pick up the new network interface card and started paying bills. When he had paid nine out of the ten credit card bills there was another power cut and the computer short-circuited. Seconds later he heard a clap of thunder. 'What the hell, not again!!! And it isn't even raining!!' How was it possible to be so unlucky, he asked in his log, just two hours after he had repaired the PC after the last stroke of lightning? He watched an episode of the TV series *Rome* and tucked into the last portion of Chinese takeaway to help him over his setback.

The following day he filtered crystals out of the picric acid. There were fewer than he had reckoned on. He had to be more accurate and decided to take some time out. He gave himself Sunday evening off to go to the Rena festival but did not think much of the choice of local foods on offer – organic kid meat, smoked sausage, crispbread, cheese and honey – so he took himself off to Elverum for some more Chinese takeaway.

'There was a relatively hot girl in the restaurant today, checking me out,' he wrote in the log afterwards. 'Refined individuals like myself are a rare commodity here so I notice I do get a lot of attention. It's the way I dress and look. They are mostly unrefined/uncultivated people living here. I wear mostly the best pieces from my former life, which consists of very expensive brand clothing, Lacoste sweaters, piqués etc. People can see from a mile away that I'm not from around here.'

He certainly did get noticed. The girls in the hairdresser's where he once had a cut found him good-looking, while the man in the computer store decided he was gay. The Kurdish man in the kebab shop thought he was the nicest Norwegian he had ever met.

One of his flasks had started to crack and was leaking and dripping. It had been a big mistake only to buy two of those flasks and not four or five. This apparently trivial thing, the fact that he had bought too few flasks, cost him three or four days. By his own calculations he should have been ready by now. Ludicrous.

It was actually rather boring work with a lot of waiting about. Once he had extracted the acid he had to wait four hours for it to cool from boiling point to room temperature, then another twelve hours until it cooled to fridge temperature, and finally another twelve to eighteen hours for it to warm up by four degrees to room temperature again. This meant that it took about forty hours in all to make one batch of DDNP. If only he had six flasks instead of just two!

For the second time since he moved to the farm, he set out on a training run. First he gulped down a big protein shake to maximise what he got out of the workout, then he fixed a rucksack filled with stones on his back, another on his front, and carried a five-litre container filled with water in each hand. He lasted twenty minutes.

It was taking so much longer to make the bomb than he had planned. Nor did he quite know how to finish it off. The internet was awash with different ways of doing it. He took a scientific approach and questioned the suggested methods, evaluating and discarding as he went.

In the evening he relaxed with the vampire series *True Blood* or an episode of *Dexter*, the show about a serial killer. It annoyed him that all these series he watched were so keen to promote multicultural-ism, but 'such is life for the time being', he wrote.

Back in the early spring he had been struck by the number of creepy-crawlies on the farm. He could not stand them. Now they had bred and were more or less invading the farm. There must be colonies of spiders in the walls. One evening when he decided to treat him-self to some sweets while he watched another episode, there was a spider in with the chocolate. He screamed. Spiders had crawled inside the gloves he wore when he was purifying his chemicals. 'I freaked out . . . After that I started killing every little insect in view.'

Some of his friends had started talking about coming to see him. Magnus had wanted to drop by when he came to see his girlfriend, who was on holiday near by. Anders had been careful not to give his friends an address in case they just turned up. *They* would realise that something was going on. But on the other hand, he could not just sever all contact. 'Complete isolation and asocial behaviour can also defeat the whole purpose if you end up losing the love for the people you have sworn to protect. Because why would you bless your people with the ultimate gift of love if every single person hates you?' he mused in the log.

'I'm in Oslo this weekend,' Anders said when Magnus rang. 'But why don't you come at the end of July?'

It was clearly not a farmer who had moved in at Vålstua. The grass was never cut, a windowpane had come loose, smashed and been left on the ground, while two wood battens had fallen off the barn wall. Three trees had blown down as well. But he simply had no energy to keep up with repairs. He had more than enough to do creating destruction.

The neighbours gradually started to notice things. Why had he driven half the fertiliser straight into the barn? It was for spreading on the fields and was usually stored outside. What was more, he had put up a gate with a lock. When one of the neighbours commented on this, he said it was council regulations. That was strange, because nobody else had heard anything about the regulations. But life went on, people forgot, the year went on turning and summer came.

He started losing weight. His steroids were nearly all gone. He would have to go to Oslo for more. He could combine this with testing the route he had devised for the day of the operation. The second day of July, he took the E18 past Oslo and then the E16 towards Hønefoss. Before long he had the Tyrifjord on his left-hand side. He spotted an unobtrusive sign for the track to the island of Utøya. He drove down the steep hill, parked on the jetty and went over to the boat that was moored there. He had read on the AUF website that it was called the MS *Thorbjørn*, named after Thorbjørn Jagland, a former Labour Party Prime Minister.

He looked out over the sound. Until now he had only read about the island, seen pictures of it. Thought about it.

Now there it lay, green and peaceful.

He studied the old landing craft, considering whether bullets would penetrate its hull. He entered the coordinates into his GPS and familiarised himself with the roads in the vicinity. He also put in the coordinates of the nearby landing stage at Utvika. He called his destination points WoW1 and WoW2. If the police happened to stop him, he would say he was considering hiring Utøya to arrange a computer gaming conference there.

Back in Oslo, he went to the Elixia gym in Sjølyst, close to his mother's flat. In its bright premises with big windows and a view over a shopping precinct he went through his usual programme. He was surprised that he could lift as much weight as before he moved to Østerdalen; he had done hardly any training, after all. It must be the bomb manufacture that had kept him in shape. He felt exhilarated but then, halfway through the session, his head started to swim and he had to break off.

He bought enough anabolic steroids for twenty more days. He favoured Winstrol, a synthetic derivative of the hormone testosterone. He knew it was doing his guts no good and he felt particularly concerned about his liver. Later that evening he took his mother out for dinner at an Indian restaurant. He said he was worried about liver damage. His mother found that an odd thing to be anxious about. Hadn't he turned very strange all round recently? Strange and stressed.

'There are spiders seeping out of the walls up there,' he told his mother over the Indian meal. 'They're in my bed, they're everywhere.'

'If you clean and vacuum properly,' his mother said, 'you'll soon get rid of them.'

'The place is full of beetles, spiders and other flying and crawling things,' he went on. A spider-ridden hell.

'Well in that case I don't think it's worth ten thousand kroner a month,' his mother replied. She was surprised at how worked up it made him to talk about the insects. A bundle of nerves, that was what he had become. It was very strange; she had imagined life on the farm would calm him down. He had told her how beautiful it was up there, and that he had a lovely view of the Glomma.

Suddenly he looked sad.

'I've grown so ugly,' he said to his mother. 'Look at my face!'

'But you look normal.'

'No, I've got ugly,' he whimpered. He said he was thinking of having plastic surgery. At the very least, he wanted veneers on his teeth.

Anders paid and drove his mother home. They had a cigarette on the balcony.

'Don't stand so close to me,' he said suddenly. 'People might think I'm retarded.'

It sent a shiver through her. He had said something similar once before, when they were walking along the street together. He had

asked her to walk a few steps behind him, so people would not think
he was mentally defective. And when the owner of Vålstua came to
the flat in Hoffsveien for the signing of the tenancy agreement he had
asked her to go out so the man would not think he lived with his
mother.

They finished their cigarettes. He did not stay over.

It was a light night. He left Oslo and drove back to the farm.

He had grown more aggressive since running out of steroids. It was
a state he would be glad to recreate if the need arose, because it
seemed to suppress fear very efficiently. He asked himself how he
could manipulate his body into it. 'I wonder if it is possible to acquire
specialised "aggressiveness" pills on the market. It would probably be
extremely useful in select military operations, especially when combined with steroids and ECA stack . . . ! It would turn you into a
superhuman one-man army for two hours!' he wrote.

The next day he dug up the Pelican case, which he had buried in
the woods in a spot plagued by mosquitoes where nobody would
want to stay for long. With the car full of weaponry he drove back
down the drive to Vålstua and waved to his neighbour, who had just
started to harvest the crop of timothy and clover.

On the days that followed, he got his equipment ready. He
replaced the hollow-tipped bullets with lead-tipped ones – 'the most
suitable for the purpose of inflicting maximum damage to vermin',
because the hollow tips did not always expand as they were supposed
to. He also packed a case of the clothes he would be wearing. He had
got hold of a long-sleeved compression top from a sportswear supplier and sewn a police badge onto it. The black top had some yellow
stitching, but he went over it with black felt pen. He discovered he
had already packed in his case a load of Winstrol, the steroids known
as *Russians*. Good, that meant he had more than he had thought. He
also had some ECA stack in there, a combination of ephedrine, caffeine and aspirin. 'I realise that if I am apprehended with all this
equipment I will have serious problems trying to explain the intended
usage . . .'

He prepared the bags of ammonium nitrate and powdered aluminium, and shifted them from the spider cellar to the workbench in the barn. He felt something tickling his nose and screamed when he discovered a big black spider inside his mask. He was usually very careful to check there were no creepy-crawlies in his gloves, clothing and mask, but this one had sneaked in undetected.

Outside, the neighbour was still at it. He had said it would take six hours to cut the clover, but he had taken three days so far. It was holding things up at the farm. The nitromethane that Breivik now had to mix in to the powdered aluminium was highly explosive and he was not keen to do that indoors. When would the wretched neighbour be finished?

'You're not to come without ringing first,' Breivik yelled when he found the neighbour standing in the yard one day.

'That won't work if I'm to look after your fields,' the neighbour retorted angrily. Here in the country, you just popped by. If you saw that your neighbour was in then you told him what your business was.

The city boy always locked the door after him. He kept the curtains closed.

The first ANFO bomb was made by students at the University of Wisconsin in 1970, in protest against the university collaborating with the authorities during the Vietnam War. A physics researcher was killed. Later the IRA, ETA and al-Qaida all followed the same instructions. They were also used by Timothy McVeigh in 1995, when 168 people were killed in Oklahoma City.

Anders had studied them all.

What remained now was to blend the ammonium nitrate – the artificial fertiliser – with the aluminium powder, which would intensify the force of the explosion. It made a terrible amount of dust. He was covered all over in aluminium dust, which spread with him wherever he went. He had a special set of clothes and shoes to wear inside the barn. He had bought a protective suit from a British professor of mathematics who was selling off surplus stock, but he could never bring himself to use it; he got so hot and sticky when he was hard at work. One day, when Anders had been working for six solid hours and had just gone inside to get something to eat, the neighbour turned up in the yard again. Breivik's face was covered in shimmering powdered aluminium and his hair was striped with grey. He hurried to the sink and rinsed off his face, but there was no time to do anything about his hair.

'If you like, I'm happy to clear away the stones from your field so you can start growing your vegetables,' suggested the neighbour, standing on the doorstep. He also offered to apply the fertiliser so the land was ready for cultivation. He could hire a couple of men and have it done within a week. Breivik had already bought the fertiliser, hadn't he?

'I've changed my plans,' Breivik replied tersely, and sent the neighbour away. Later that evening, when he was watching another episode of *True Blood*, a car with four men drove into the yard.

The neighbour must have realised what he was up to with the fertiliser and tipped them off!

It was only four Poles looking for work.

Actually, he would have loved to have the Poles to help him mix the fertiliser with the aluminium powder; it was hard going. One little bag in two hours! He considered using the electric cement mixer he had bought second-hand. But he was worried that the friction of the motion and the contact with the metal could cause the mixer to short-circuit. In the worst-case scenario, this could generate sparks, which might cause a detonation. But all the same, mixing by hand was so time-consuming that he had to risk it. If he was going to pull off this operation he would have to at least halve the time required for mixing. 'In any case; let me die another day . . . ' he wrote in the log.

It turned out to work without any problems. As usual he had been far too concerned about safety, he concluded. The mixer was not particularly efficient, however. It left lots of lumps and he still had to use his hands, but now he was able to log a rate of ninety minutes per bag, with the aim of reducing it to sixty. Even so, it was hard work for just one person and he was starting to understand why Timothy McVeigh had only made a 600-kilo bomb. He must have come up against the same problems and learned the hard way. The tenant at Vålstua nonetheless felt he had slowed down over the past week, and resolved to pick up the pace.

He had now been at the farm for seventy days. On 1 June he hired a van from Avis, went shopping and apologised for it in his log.

'Considering the fact that I am currently working on the most dreadful task, I bought a lot of exquisite food and candy today.' He had to recharge his batteries and boost his morale before returning to his strenuous mixing work every morning. 'Good food and candy is a central aspect of my reward system, which keeps me going. It has proven efficient so far.' Whenever he was dreading a task, be it extreme hard labour or something involving risk of injury or death, he downed a can of Red Bull, a noXplode shake or an ECA stack to help him cope with throwing himself into the job.

Mixing powdered aluminium, microballoons and fertiliser was the worst task so far. The dust even stuck to the inside of his mask, because he had run out of filters. Once he got started he could not even take cigarette breaks. 'I literally turn into the tin man, with a layer of aluminium dust all over me.'

Towards the middle of July he started feeling sick and dizzy, and feared it could be the result of diesel poisoning. His work clothes had soaked up a lot of diesel. Such poisoning was not fatal, but it weakened you for a time and could lead to kidney failure. To counterbalance all the crap he had ingested these past months, he took vitamin and mineral pills with a herbal supplement that was supposed to strengthen the liver and kidneys. He felt worse and worse, and decided to wear the protective suit while mixing the last four bags. He should have done this from the start, because it turned out to work very well, apart from the fact that his T-shirt and boxers were drenched in sweat by the time he finished.

Every day he took his dose of steroids and drank four protein shakes to build as much muscle as possible. It was important to have the physical advantage.

On Friday 15 July he went to Rena to catch the train to Oslo, where he would pick up the hire car he had ordered. There were a few people at the station waiting for the 15.03 to Hamar, where you had to change if you were going to the capital. An elderly man on his way to Elverum to fetch a computer that had been in for repair was standing by himself on the platform.

Anders went up to him and asked if the train was expected on time. He told the man he ran a farm near by. The train arrived. Anders boarded it, and the man got on behind him. As he was passing the young man hailed him and invited him to sit with him.

Anders got straight to the point.

'Islam is in the process of taking over Europe,' he said. Muslims had been killing Christians throughout history. You could call it genocide.

The elderly man listened with interest. The boy was bright and well read, he thought, though their taste in reading matter clearly differed. The man pointed out that many Muslims had also been also killed in the name of religion in the Crusades. He counted as a political veteran, he said, and told the younger man about taking part in the first demonstration against the Vietnam War, in Los Angeles in 1964.

'So you must be a communist!' exclaimed Anders. He was a Christian himself, he said.

The man replied that one should love one's neighbour and follow Jesus's example. Breivik became evasive. He was not interested in Jesus and love and caring and stuff like that, he said.

'I earned twenty-six million kroner before I was twenty-eight,' he said, and now he was using the money to support people behind the scenes who would throw the Muslims out of Norway.

As the train approached Elverum station, the old man stood up to get off but Anders grabbed him and held him. The man tried to twist free but failed, and the train pulled out of the station.

The ticket collector came along and Anders released his grip. The old man hastily grabbed up his jacket and bag and followed the ticket collector. All he told him was that that he had not got off at Elverum when he was meant to. He could get off at Løten and take the train back to Elverum, he was informed. The old man went to the exit and stood by the door for the rest of the journey to be sure of getting off in time. He was about to do so when the young man passed him a scrap of paper. On it were a name, a Hotmail address and a telephone number.

It was several hours until the next train back, so the old man ended up taking a taxi to Elverum. There he told friends about 'that idiot', as he called him. 'There was something burning him up from inside,' he said. 'I could hardly believe he was on the loose.' There was indeed something about the young man that made him hard to forget; the older man wondered whether he needed someone to talk to and rang the number. A little girl answered. He apologised and tried again. The same little girl answered. Oh well. Wrong number. Anders had actually written down his real number, but the man had read the zeros as sixes. He never tried to reach Anders at the other address he'd written down: anders.behring@hotmail.com.

Late that evening, Anders returned from Oslo in his hired van. He removed all the Avis logos from the bodywork with a drill bit designed for taking off dealership stickers, and rubbed over the sticky patches with acetone. There was still a faint outline of the hire firm's logo, but it would have to do. He started calculating the weight of the bomb, and whether the van would be able to carry it. The capacity of a Volkswagen Crafter was 1340 kilos, and now he had 900 kilos of fertiliser plus 50 kilos of internal charge. He assumed his own weight to be 130 kilos including weapons, ammunition and body armour. He was also planning to take a small motorbike weighing 80 kilos. That meant he still had about a hundred kilos' leeway.

Monday evening, 18 July: he took the last batches of picric acid and DDNP out of the oven. The bomb was ready. He packed the explosives in the sturdy sacks he had got from China and the internal charge was in two plastic bags. When it got dark he loaded it into the van. He had cut up a mattress and used three sections to pad a cardboard box. In this box he would transport the booster and the detonator, separate from the bomb. He put in the heavy case containing the rifle, pistol, shotgun and ammunition – more than three thousand bullets in all. Once he had satisfied himself that it all fitted and was in its proper place, he filled up both vehicles with diesel. In the morning he would strap everything down tightly.

He was ready to go.

That evening he took an extra dose of steroids.

But now he had to sleep. He was shattered. 'At this point I should be fearful, but I am too exhausted to think much about it,' he wrote in the log.

All We Could Dream Of

'Have you packed?'

The evening sun sent streaks of light across the living-room floor at Heiaveien. Simon stretched his long body and shook his head. Here on the floor was where Simon generally put out what he was taking with him when he went away. His first solo trips had been to football tournaments and track and field meetings. His parents had often accompanied him to the Norway Cup events. His father as trainer, his mother as a contact point and extra mum for all the little boys. Tone had carried on doing her son's packing for a long time, but then she decided they should do it together. Simon would come up with heaps of clothes which he laid out on the living-room floor: boxers in one pile, jerseys in another, shirts, trousers and socks, all in their separate piles. Then Tone would go round the various heaps like a judge, approving or rejecting. Simon usually put out too much; he always liked to have a choice, clothes-conscious as he was. He often stopped his younger brother on his way to the door with a 'You're not going out in *that*, are you?' and ordered him to change.

This late summer evening, the living-room floor was empty.

Simon's almost nineteen, Tone thought, and after the summer he'll be called up for his military service, I can't carry on sorting his things out for him. Soon he would be leaving the nest, going out into the big world. He had to learn to cope on his own.

She and Gunnar were just back from a fortnight in Turkey. It was their first holiday without the boys.

On one of their last evenings away, they had dinner at a restaurant by the beach.

'I'm just sitting here thinking,' Gunnar said, 'that if someone asked me whether there was one thing I wanted to change about my life, anything at all, I wouldn't be able to think of a single thing.'

Tone stroked his arm and smiled. 'Well, life has given us all we could dream of.' They had been together for over thirty years and were now in their late forties. Ever since they met on the dance floor that dark St Lucia night in Lavangen, they had known that this was the love of their life.

They sat there with their arms round each other. 'If there was one little thing, right this minute,' smiled Tone, 'it would be that we'd brought the boys with us and they were here now.'

They laughed. Gunnar nodded.

The boys had been offered the chance of a sunshine holiday, but they preferred to work. They both had summer jobs in the technical services department at Salangen District Council. Håvard's was cutting the grass and undergrowth on verges and in car parks, while Simon's was keeping the churchyard neat and tidy. He was expected to turn his hand to all sorts of odd jobs and maintenance. 'It's just that it's a bit awkward sometimes, Mum,' he said just before his parents left for Turkey, 'having to go round with that noisy mower when people are visiting graves and want to be left in peace.'

He usually got round it by finding something else to do for a while, like painting one of the toolsheds over by the new graves. The paint was red and he had already done three sides. He would do the fourth when he got back from Utøya.

All year he had had a part-time job as a reporter on *Troms Folkeblad* and the summer had brought with it more assignments than ever. 'Think I must have one of the coolest summer jobs in the whole of Troms!' he wrote on Facebook the time they sent him to cover the Millionfisken festival, with free access to all the concerts. That day he had also been honoured with a visit from Bardu, and his friend Anders

Kristiansen had gone round with him to interview people. It was one of the best days of the whole summer. Anders was more fun than ever, inspiring people to give entertaining answers. Perhaps he wanted to be a journalist.

By the time his parents were flying home from Turkey, Simon had updated his Facebook status again: 'Time to rush round and make sure there's domestic harmony when Mum and Dad get home. 14 days on our own has left its mark.'

So now the freshly mopped living-room floor was empty. It was nearly midnight and the sun hung like a ball just above the surface of the sea. Tone could hear Simon rummaging about downstairs and went down to check what he was doing. It was time the boy was in bed; he had to be up early tomorrow to catch the flight to Oslo.

She came into Simon's room just as he was zipping up the family's largest suitcase.

'Oh, have you packed your stuff in the suitcase, Simon?'

'Yes, it's practical. There's room for the tent, the ground pad and my clothes, all in the same case.'

'But it's huge; you'll never even get it into the tent, will you?'

Simon had borrowed a little two-person tent. He shrugged expansively and said, 'I'll cross that bridge when I come to it.'

Gunnar came in as well, to wish him a good trip. He expected he would still be asleep when they left the next morning. He looked at the big suitcase and shook his head.

He gave his son a goodnight hug and a few words of advice.

'Be yourself and stand up for what you believe in!'

It was a short night.

Early on Tuesday morning, Tone crept quietly out of the bed where Gunnar was still sleeping. She wondered how she was going to wake Simon; they had, as always, stayed up chatting too long last night.

She put on the coffee machine, got some food out ready and went downstairs, through the basement sitting room and into Simon's room. The pale morning light filtered through the blue curtains and their pattern of the boy with the football and skateboard.

The luminous heart above the bed, which at night shone with a greenish tinge, merged almost entirely into the ceiling in the early-morning light.

Simon was lying on his back with his arms flung straight out. His breathing was deep and even.

'Simon, time to wake up!' called Tone. 'You've got a plane to catch!'

Not a murmur.

'Simon!'

Not a grunt.

'Simon! You're off to Utøya!'

Tone stood there admiring the peaceful face of her tall elder son and decided she might just as well lie down beside him and wake him in a more gentle fashion. 'Simon,' she said, this time in a coaxing whisper. She stroked his shoulder and chest. It was tempting just to fall asleep there.

Simon had always been a cuddly boy; from an early age he had liked curling up beside his mother in bed and sleeping where she was. He could lie there for ages, close and cosy. Imagine him still being happy to snuggle up to his mum!

Tone had made herself comfortable on his arm. She pinched his chest, where just a few wisps of hair had started to grow. He wriggled slightly and went on sleeping. She lay there dozing for a moment before she looked at her watch and leapt up.

'Simon!'

She pulled him with all the strength she could muster.

He was in his usual morning daze; it would take at least an hour for him to wake up and that was an hour they did not have. He hauled himself into a sitting position in bed and put on his clothes as she passed them to him. He could not face eating anything, but Tone had made sure there were some slices of pizza left over from the one she had made the previous evening and put them in a bag in the outside pocket of his suitcase.

She wondered if he had packed everything he would need. It was the first time he would be going on a trip without her knowing exactly what he had with him. But there was no time to worry about that now.

The eighteen-year-old got into the driver's seat. He enjoyed driving, but this morning he pulled in at the first bus stop.

'You'll have to drive, Mum. I'm too tired.'

Tone smiled. Simon was dozing off, but then he came to with a start. 'Did I say I'd promised Mari Siljebråten a lift?'

Tone put her foot down a little. The birch forest was glimmering, pale and beautiful. For the first part of the journey they had a view over the fjord and later, as they approached Bardu, they could see up to the mountains of Troms. Simon had woken, and mother and son now talked about love. Simon and his girlfriend had just decided to split up, and Tone was the first person he had told. They had been drifting apart, and at the end of the summer he would go off for his military service in Stavanger and she would start her teacher training course in Tromsø. But what was love, really?

'Oh, you'll both find out in due course,' Tone said gently.

'I don't know if I want to carry on studying after I finish my military service, Mum,' he said.

'Of course you do,' said Tone. 'But there's no rush. Take one thing at a time: you've got your whole life ahead of you.'

Simon smiled. He was hungry for everything: experience, adventure, love.

As they came into Bardu they drove past Anders Kristiansen's green house, where his father was in the process of laying new flagstones in the drive. In the Kristiansens' garden there was a little hut with just one room, Anders's Cabin. In there he had a TV and a stereo and some bottles of tequila, his very own little party venue. Anders and his father had built it together, with decent foundations and properly insulated floor, walls and roof. His mother had made curtains for it. The cabin in the garden was to be somewhere the teenagers could be left in peace.

A bit further up the ridge, in what was called Bardu Beverly Hills, Tone turned in at Mari Siljebråten's house. Pretty, fair-haired and brimming with vitality, she was ready and waiting for them. She called goodbye to her mother and jumped into the back seat. Mari, a couple of years older than Simon, was the leader of the Troms delegation to Utøya that year.

'Gunnar Linaker and I have been arranging things like crazy for three days and I think we've covered it all, so now I can look forward to this properly!'

Gunnar, the son of the local priest, was the county secretary for AUF Troms and had grown up in the house next door to Mari. He was the one who always had an overview of all the youth organisation's activities. He booked the tickets and sorted out the departures of the Troms youngsters from three different airports, Bardufoss, Harstad and Tromsø. He had rung the parents of all the under-eighteens who had signed up in good time, to make sure they knew what would happen on Utøya. While Mari fretted, he stayed calm.

'Gunnar's gone on ahead, he's already on the island,' said Mari. 'But Hanne's waiting for us at the airport.'

Hanne was Gunnar's younger sister, and had also been active in the AUF since her early teens.

On their way to the airport at the Bardufoss military base the delegation leader received instructions from Tone.

'Can you make sure Simon gets some breakfast down him.'

'He'll get his bread and Nugatti, and maybe even a slice of gherkin on top,' laughed Mari. She was used to Simon forgetting to eat. And being picky about his food. Food was just fuel to him, but like a car he didn't run on just anything. At last year's summer camp in Russian Karelia, where he had represented Troms along with Anders and Iril from Bardu, they had been served nothing but cabbage soup. He had refused to eat vegetables for a long time afterwards.

'Remember to answer all your phone calls, Simon. Remember to answer all your texts. Otherwise I shall stop paying your phone bill.'

'Yes Mum, but my phone loses its charge so quickly it's generally not even on.'

Tone knew that. That was why she had bought him a new mobile phone. But it was a secret. It was to be for his nineteenth birthday on 25 July, barely a week from now. She had the cake all ready in the freezer. 'Simon's 19th', said the label on the plastic bag, and she would ice and decorate it on the day.

They were there.

Simon's mother hugged him. She gave one cheek a kiss, then the other. So it wouldn't be jealous, they always said.

Mari laughed at the pair of them.

'And would you like a mumhug, too?' Tone asked. Mari's two cheeks also got their kisses.

Tone stood watching them as they walked away. *God, what a handsome son I've got!*

His best mate had taken him to the solarium because he always looked so pale, and now he was tanned and fit.

He's so happy with all those girls, his mother thought as she watched the delegation gather at the entrance. It seemed to be all girls on that flight, which would suit him just fine, Tone chuckled to herself.

As they were going up the steps to the plane a crack opened in the clouds and there was a sudden brightness on the mountains beyond.

'I can see the sun and the sky, Simon,' Tone texted to her son.

'No need to rub it in, Mum.'

Rain and rough weather were forecast for further south.

Summer Fever

It was the sort of weather for lying at home under a warm blanket drinking tea. Lara made some thyme-leaf tea and brought it to Bano.

'Are you feeling any better?' she asked.

'Maybe a little bit,' answered Bano.

Lara had plied her elder sister with grapes, apples, honey, hot milky cocoa and cod liver oil. Now she was following her mother's tip that thyme was good for your throat. But she was also trying to cool down Bano's face, hand and feet with a damp cloth.

At eleven o'clock the previous evening Lara had rung her mother, who had gone with Ali and Mustafa to the Football Cup in Gothenburg. While father and son were at the championship, she was visiting relatives in nearby Borås.

'Have you got Lana's number?' asked Lara.

Lana was Bayan's sister. She lived in Erbil and was a doctor, a paediatric specialist.

'What do you want to talk to her for?' asked Bayan.

'You know Bano and I are supposed to be going to Utøya tomorrow, but Bano's almost lost her voice and her temperature isn't coming down. What can I do to make her better by tomorrow?'

'Lara, it's past midnight in Kurdistan, you can't ring Lana now! I'm coming home tomorrow. And anyway, you mustn't ring my sister and tell her you two are alone at home! What sort of mother will she think I am? I'm coming home.'

'No, Mum, you don't have to do that.'

'Yes I do!'

Bayan told Mustafa she would be going back the next day, whether Ali's team went through to the next round or not. The two of them had never got used to the relaxed attitude in Norway. They were anxious when they were not supervising in person and always feared the worst if the children were out and did not answer their mobiles. Bano was at home with a fever in the middle of summer; it must be something serious.

Bano grumbled to her sister.

'I don't think God wants me to go.'

'Stop talking rubbish. Of course you're going to be well enough!' Lara retorted. Bano had been so looking forward to Utøya. They had wanted to go the previous year, in fact, but then they had to go with the family to Kurdistan, a place where they could only bear to stay for a fortnight at a time. All the restrictions, all the looks, all the rules; no, they preferred life in Norway.

Lara massaged her elder sister's feet and neck. She had bought crisps and sweets, and tried to tempt her with all the exciting things that would be happening on Utøya. Bano could hardly stand up, so Lara packed for her: warm clothes, a sleeping bag, a ground pad.

They dozed off on the sofa, both of them.

'You're bound to be well enough to go tomorrow,' said Lara before she fell asleep.

First thing on Wednesday morning, Bayan caught the train from Gothenburg. Four hours later she took the tram from the railway station to Aker Brygge, then the ferry over to Nesoddtangen and the bus home to Oksvalkrysset, and by noon she was ready to take over the role of nurse. She came home to find the place a total mess. Not a glass had been washed since she left, not a plate, nothing. Bano had had enough of being ill, and Lara of looking after her.

Lara was ready to leave when her mother arrived.

'I'm sure you'll be better tomorrow!' she called to her elder sister before she slammed the door and went down to the bus stop. In Oslo she was going to meet up with the other AUF members arriving by plane and boat and train from all over Norway to continue the journey to Utøya.

She got to the island mid-afternoon, which meant she did not, after all, have to choose between the various seminars on offer, on subjects like refugee integration and drilling for oil in the Lofoten islands, as they were already over. All that was left now was a fashion show featuring the AUF leader Eskil Pedersen and his second-in-command Åsmund Aukrust. They would be on the catwalk modelling the new AUF clothing range of soft-feel T-shirts, sweatshirts and trousers. Then it was time for the football tournament to start and after that there was something in the programme called speed dating, before it was time for a quiz in the café. The late-night cinema started at midnight.

Lara got changed, ready for Akershus county's match. They lost.

She could not be bothered with the speed dating and went to lie down in the tent and read *Mornings in Jenin*. She wasn't having such a good time without Bano around. That was often the case. Bano made everything seem so much fun, sometimes even when it wasn't. How often had Lara found herself doing things because Bano had said they were *wicked* or *awesome*, but when she tried them for herself, they were nothing special?

Bano lay in her parents' double bed. She felt poorly, had earache and was tender all over. Her mother gave her some painkillers and brought warm cloths to hold over her aching ear. Bayan had gone out to the kitchen to make more tea when she heard a crash from the living room. The alarm clock was lying on the floor in pieces. Bano had thrown it from the bedroom.

'Its tick was driving me mad, Mum.'

'That's all right Bano. It doesn't matter.'

Bayan lay down beside her daughter in the bed. Everything was wrong. She was sick, she wasn't on Utøya and she had failed her driving test twice.

'Bah, I've spent so much money on it, and I've got to have my
licence by the time we're *russ* . . .'

Bano was in a hurry in life. She wanted it all, right away. The first
time she failed she had gone through a red light, the second time she
had turned the wrong way at a roundabout. When she was out in the
car with Mustafa to practise, they always ended up quarrelling. The
last time she had driven was the morning Mustafa was taking Ali and
Bayan to Gothenburg, while she was going to work at the Tusenfryd
amusement park. Bano was running late as usual, and on the winding section of road just before the Vinterbro junction she found
herself behind a lorry.

'I'm going to overtake!'

She moved into the opposite lane and sped up.

'Are you mad?' cried her father. Bano pulled into her lane in front
of the lorry, but a few seconds more and they would have crashed
into the car coming the other way. 'Your driving will kill us all!'

'You should be like my driving instructor,' Bano said. 'He never
makes any comments until I stop the car.'

Once they got to Tusenfryd and she was dashing off to change into
her work uniform, she shouted cheerfully: 'Don't forget to bring the
allowance of four litres of red wine back with you, it's much cheaper
in Sweden!'

Now Bano asked her mother to bring her laptop to her. There was
something she wanted to show her. As she was finding her way to it,
her spirits rose. That's how it was with Bano; it was never far between
the highs and the lows. She found what she was looking for.

'Mum, can we go to New York?'

For the first time, the family was planning to go away in the
autumn holidays and her parents were talking about Spain or Greece.
The girls preferred the idea of a city break.

Bano showed her mother the cheap tickets she had found and a
hostel 'that 'would cost almost nothing for the five of us'.

Lying there with her poorly daughter beside her, Bayan was in a
soft-hearted mood.

'All right Bano. Let's go. I'll pay.'

Bano hugged her.

'But you and Dad will have to tighten your belts and try to save a bit, okay?' her mother said. 'And you girls mustn't have such long showers!'

Bano stayed in bed on her laptop, looking at sites that told her about New York, the Statue of Liberty, Central Park and all the cool streets in the Village. Her mother wanted to show her some pictures she had taken of her relatives in Sweden.

'Look how lovely your cousins are. Almost as pretty as you, Bano!' said her mother, pointing. 'And those are their boyfriends.'

Bano's sad expression returned.

'Everybody's got boyfriends except me,' she complained. 'I've never had a boyfriend, and now I'm eighteen!'

'There's a time for everything Bano, I'm sure you'll find one, of course you will, a beautiful girl like you! And you meet so many people, after all.'

'Yes, but never a boyfriend.'

'Well you've got your last year in upper secondary now, and then you'll go to university and you're bound to meet somebody there. And what about that nice boy in your class I asked about before?'

'Ugh, don't bring him up again.'

Bano rested her head on her father's pillow. Her delight at the holiday plans seemed to have evaporated, leaving only the sadness, and she turned to her mother.

'Just think, I might never have a boyfriend in my whole life!'

'Stop talking nonsense Bano!'

'Mum, just think if I die single . . . '

———

That same Wednesday, the tenant at Vålstua farm had driven the Volkswagen Crafter, laden with explosives, to Oslo. He was on the verge of passing out from exhaustion, having slept so little in recent nights.

Calm and steady, so he would not be stopped and checked. Calm and steady, so the bomb would be safe.

It had taken a total of nine hours to dry the last batches of picric acid and DDNP in the oven. He had thought he could do it much faster, now he was even further behind schedule.

He had also tested the fuse. The most effective method, he had read, was to insert it in a narrow surgical tube. The fuse he wanted to test as part of his final preparations was seventy-five centimetres long. That meant it would take seventy-five seconds before the explosives detonated. The fuse burnt to the end in two seconds. 'Damn, I'm glad I checked this beforehand,' he wrote. Two seconds would not have given him enough time to escape the explosion. No tube round the fuse, then.

Once in central Oslo, he parked the van at the Olsen's Widow garden centre. He had made a logo for a water-treatment company and put it on the front so people would not wonder about, and possibly report, the bad smell coming from the vehicle. Then he invited his mother out to dinner, and took an early night in the fart room.

On Thursday morning he dressed in a fawn blazer and dark trousers before taking the train back to Rena. There he rang a taxi company for a cab to take him back to the farm.

'Is that the place where there was a hash plantation?' asked the driver manning the phone that morning.

Breivik confirmed this, and in the car he asked the local man if the case was all cleared up now.

'Yes, the police won't be turning up there again,' the Rena resident replied.

This driver had been to the farm many years earlier, when it was under previous ownership; there had been cows in the fields and the place was kept in good order. As he set down the well-dressed visitor from the city, he was taken aback to see how dilapidated and overgrown the farm had become.

'Well, welcome to our valley,' he said, and drove off.

I Love You

'I'm very much against it, Bano,' said Bayan.

'But I've GOT to see what it's like! Last year we were in Kurdistan, remember. Everybody says it's so cool!'

Bano had felt a bit better when she woke up on Thursday morning. Even though she had scarcely any voice, and certainly was not entirely well, she insisted on going out to the island.

'But you're sick, you ought to stay at home. And tomorrow Ali and Dad will be home, so you won't have to be bored with only me for company. If Ali loses his match today they might even be back this evening! Then we can all be nice and cosy here together, and you can get properly well.'

'Mum, I've never been to Utøya before, I've got to go!'

Then Lara rang. 'Jonas Gahr Støre's coming to speak, it'll be really exciting! Foreign affairs! There's going to be a Middle East debate on Israel and Palestine. You've got to come!'

'Sounds great!' exclaimed Bano. With half an eye on her mother she added, 'I'm better now. I'll come today.'

Her mother gave her an anxious look. But Bano had made up her mind.

'*Sibay, Daya, sibay Gro det!* Tomorrow, Mum, Gro's coming tomorrow! Just think, getting to hear Gro speak!'

Bano fetched the bag that Lara had packed for her. She was on her way out the door when her mother came up to her with the photos of their relations in Sweden. 'Take them to Utøya so Lara can see them too.'

'But *Daya*, we'll be back on Sunday,' laughed Bano. 'Lara can see them when she gets home. What if I lose them, or they get wet? I've got to go now. I have to catch the eleven o'clock boat. *Xoshim dawei, Daya!* I love you, Mum!'

'I love you, Bano,' answered her mother and gave her a kiss.

When Bano had signed up for the summer camp she had volunteered to be part of the working group. That meant you got free food and your fee was waived. It did not occur to her now to ask if she could opt out as she was not really well. She registered on the jetty before she went on board the MS *Thorbjørn*.

The sun was finally peeping through. Bano was wearing some thin trousers and a sleeveless blouse. When she arrived on the island the coordinator told her to go down to the outdoor stage and put up some tents ready for the Datarock concert that evening.

'Oh no,' she exclaimed when she was instructed to hold up the tent poles. Luckily she spotted Lara passing by.

'Lara!'

Her younger sister came over. 'Lara, can you hold these?' she asked. 'I forgot to shave under my arms, okay!'

So Lara was roped into the working party as well.

Once the tents were up, the sun vanished behind the tallest trees. It started to turn chilly. The grassy areas were still wet from the previous day's rain and the mosquitoes were out in force. The sisters went to the tent to get mosquito spray.

'Shit!' cried Bano. 'I've lost the key!'

'You locked the tent?' asked Lara incredulously.

'Well yes, when I was at the Hove festival loads of stuff got stolen from the tents.'

'But this is an AUF camp! Nobody would steal here,' said Lara.

Bano went off to look for something to open the big padlock with. Eventually she found a saw but it was really blunt, so she went back to the tool shed and asked the caretaker to see if he had any other suitable tools. She pointed to a chainsaw.

'You're planning to get into your tent with a chainsaw?' laughed the caretaker. In the end he found a file that she could use to open the lock.

'Bano, Bano!' It was just as Lara had been thinking as she lay alone in the tent the day before: there was always so much going on when Bano was around.

Lara wasn't in the party spirit. She just wanted to go to bed after the Datarock concert, while Bano and three other girls from the Akershus contingent were keen to do karaoke. One of them, sixteen-year-old Margrethe Bøyum Kløven, was the bass player in the girl band Blondies & Brownies, which had won the Junior Melodi Grand Prix song competition the year before, and she could really sing. *You know you love me, I know you care, just shout whenever, and I'll be there . . .* Now they were practising 'Baby' by Justin Bieber in the tent, so they could perform as a quartet in the karaoke.

The karaoke machine did not have any Justin Bieber songs, but there was lots of Michael Jackson, Margrethe's favourite. She knew all the words, and if she had brought her guitar she could have played the music too. Bano did the backing vocals in a hoarse voice. The girls came back to the tent in a giggly mood to get some more clothes; there was a cold wind blowing. Their heads were still full of Michael Jackson. *Before you judge me, try hard to love me, lalala . . . look within your heart then ask, have you seen my childhood?*

'Have you heard about Lovers' Path?' Bano asked the other girls excitedly. 'It's a path that goes all round the island, and you can see people groping each other.'

She laughed out loud at her own suggestion. They all sniggered. It was their first time on Utøya.

'Well girls,' said Bano. 'Shall we take a stroll along Lovers' Path?'

———

Anders Behring Breivik locked the door of the white farmhouse at Vålstua and drove away.

In the back of the Doblò, the booster and detonator were packed between bits of mattress. Detonators were extremely unstable, but the boxes were securely fastened. He had first put the fuse in a slim plastic container, then in the IKEA toilet brush holder. It was important to avoid friction or bumps while transporting these, otherwise the whole lot could detonate and blow the van sky high.

His weapons were all in the Pelican case. He had rebuilt them to make them exactly how he wanted, mounting the bayonet on the rifle and the laser sight on the pistol. With a knife he had carved names onto them in runic script. He called the pistol *Mjølnir* after Thor's hammer. *Mjølnir* hit everything Thor wanted it to and returned to him afterwards. Odin's spear *Gungnir*, after which he named his rifle, possessed the same powers.

His weapons, his uniform, the Knights Templar coin in his pocket: he had made them all his own by adapting and naming them.

As nightfall approached and dark clouds massed in the sky, he parked the Doblò alongside his VW Crafter outside the locked garden centre with its summer range of fruit bushes, roses and perennials. Behind it was the railway line that ran down to the south coast. On the other side of the road was an upmarket housing cooperative. The trees were quivering slightly in the breeze, a sign of a new weather front on its way in over Oslo.

He got out and locked the van. Exhausted, he dragged himself across Sigurd Iversens vei, down Harbitzalleen and over the junction at Hoffsveien. It was the hour before midnight.

His mother was still awake when he let himself in. He went out onto the balcony with her for a cigarette. Anders stood in silence, inhaling the smoke, and then suddenly looked at her.

'Mum, don't stand so close to me.'

She moved away.

He went to bed. The plan was to get up at three o'clock. He would have to, if he were to fit it all in. Gro Harlem Brundtland would start her speech at 11 a.m. To be sure of getting there in time to decapitate her, he had to be up before dawn.

He would capture the former Prime Minister at gunpoint and

force her down on her knees. There, on the ground, he would make her read a text he'd written about her betrayal. She would be forced to beg for her life and ask for forgiveness for destroying Norway. Then he would cut her head off. He would film the deed and put the video out on YouTube.

But he wouldn't be able to.

He realised it would not work. He simply had to sleep. If he was going to be in a fit state to carry out the operation at all, he had to be properly rested. It was going to demand everything of him: alertness, stamina and concentration.

He set the alarm for somewhere between seven and eight and fell asleep in the narrow bed under the window. Outside, the birch tree rustled its leaves. The wind was gathering.

————

They did not meet many others on the path; most people seemed to prefer companionship in the crowd at the outdoor stage to romantic trysts this evening.

They had met the previous year. 'Say hello to Simon,' a girlfriend of hers had said.

So handsome, Margrethe Rosbach had thought. And a little while later, Pity he's got a girlfriend.

They had spent quite a bit of time together, even so. Afterwards they had exchanged text messages now and then.

This year, as Simon stepped ashore on the island he sent her a text: 'I'm here.' When she did not reply at once, he wrote 'You come too.'

Now they were drifting round Lovers' Path. Simon had his *snus* tin in one hand. On the side where Margrethe was, his hand was free.

Simon from Salangen and Margrethe from Stavanger. She had long, soft hair and that burr to her 'r's. At the national youth congress in the spring he had tried to kiss her. But no, not then, they both had someone else.

Simon put another wad of *snus* under his lip. In the autumn he would be doing his military service at Camp Madla outside Stavanger, near where Margrethe lived.

What an evening it was!

They had been standing together at the Datarock concert. He had lifted her up onto the stage. They sang, they danced.

The July night was darkening. Bewitching, almost spooky, thought Margrethe. They wanted to make a circuit of the island after the concert. Halfway round they went down to the water and sat on some rocks out at Nakenodden. She borrowed his jersey. Midnight came and went, then it was one, then two.

A murmur went through the woods. The first raindrops wet the rocks out on the point. They pulled their clothes more tightly around them and turned back up to Lovers' Path.

A decaying fence ran alongside the path. Below, the Tyrifjord lay in darkness.

'Give me a piggyback!' said Simon on the slope up to the campsite. 'I'm done in!'

She laughed. But she did carry him up the last steep stretch. And dropped him where the northern contingent were based, right at the top of the campsite.

One kiss. Goodnight. She crept into her tent in the Rogaland camp, where the girl she was sharing with had long since gone to sleep. Simon crept into his.

The Troms camp had still not fallen silent. In one tent, Viljar was telling stories. As usual, he had not bothered to bring a sleeping bag or tent with him. He always sorted something out when he got there. His younger brother Torje was lying in another tent, listening to Metallica with his best friend Johannes, also from Svalbard. The two fourteen-year-olds had decided to stay up all night. The sound of their singing could be heard through the canvas. *Forever trust in who we are, and nothing else matters! Nothing else matters!*

From Mari Siljebråten's tent came the sound of laughter, while Anders Kristiansen, who was on supervision duty that night, tried to hush them all.

But without success. This was Utøya, after all.

As the night wore on it started raining harder. Lovers' Path emptied. Everyone sought refuge from the downpour.

Heavy raindrops beat on the tent canvas. Water seeped in through zips and vents, it soaked up through ground pads and into sleeping bags, which clung round the young bodies like wet wrappings.

Raindrops from the same clouds pelted down on the magnolias and unripe plums at the garden centre. They drummed on the roofs of the two vans parked outside.

But the mixture of fertiliser, diesel and aluminium lay dry and ready. The fuse nestled softly in a mattress.

Friday

The *Commander of the Norwegian anti-communist resistance movement* donned a brown Ralph Lauren polo shirt. Over that went a striped Lacoste jersey in subdued, earthy colours. He put on dark trousers and Puma trainers. In the kitchen he made three cheese and ham sandwiches. He ate one of them and put the others in a bag.

Back in his room he brought out a Telenor box with a new modem in it. He had bought the fastest one available. But it took time to install. First he had to go into Outlook and click his way through various procedures, and then restart the machine. At half past eight he sent himself an email from behbreiv@online.no with the title line *Test first time. Hello, Best regards, AB.*

The modem worked.

He prepared to send out the film he had compiled out of snippets and short videos from the internet, plus the all-important *2083. A European Declaration of Independence*. He had already keyed the eight thousand email addresses into the computer. All he had to do was press Send. But they couldn't get the email just yet. No one was to open the document until he was about to set off.

'I'm going to the computer shop,' he told his mother when he was ready. 'I need a couple of spare parts.'

That was his goodbye.

His mother said she was going out too. She'd take the tram into the city centre.

'Will you be having dinner here with me?' she asked.

'Sure,' he replied. He had told her he would stay until Sunday.

She planned to make spaghetti bolognese because Anders had always liked that. And then maybe they could have a nice snack later in the evening, like prawns and white bread.

Outside there was hardly a soul to be seen. It was raining, the sky was grey. The garden centre had just opened and there were only a few cars parked in front. He unlocked the Dobló, pushed aside the mattress in the cardboard box and took out the fuse. Then he got into the back of the Crafter to mount it on the explosives. With an angle grinder he had made a hole from the cab through to the load compartment so he could set off the detonation without getting out of the van. The fuse was held in place with tape, running back from the cab so it would not curl round on itself and catch fire, but burn down all the way into the charge itself.

He left the Crafter and its bomb parked at the garden centre, where they were advertising a special offer on thuja hedging. He locked the van and got into the Dobló, which was loaded with the Pelican case with all his equipment: handcuffs, plastic strip cuffs, a water bottle, his rifle, shotgun and ammunition. He drove through the deserted streets towards the city centre. He parked in the square at Hammersborg torg, just above the government quarter. He made sure to put plenty of money into the meter and leave his parking ticket clearly visible in the front windscreen. Then he took a brisk turn through the government quarter to check no new roadblocks had been put in place. Under his arm he had a black leather attaché case. He was carrying it so he blended into the setting, here in the bastion of bureaucracy. All the roads were as open and accessible as before. He passed the flower sellers at Stortorget and hurried towards the cathedral, where he hailed a taxi.

'When do people who work in the government offices tend to leave in the holiday period?' he asked.

'The first ones start going home about two,' replied the driver, a Pakistani in his forties.

'Which building in Oslo do you think is the most politically significant?' the passenger went on. The driver was just thinking about it when the man asked another question.

'What would you say is the optimal route from Skøyen to Hammersborg torg?'

It was half past twelve by the time he was back home in Hoffsveien.

At twenty to one, Gro Harlem Brundtland left the stage in the main meeting hall. She was hot and flushed after warming to her subject of the struggle for women's rights. It was many years since she had last visited Utøya, an island she had first been to as a little girl, just after the war. On that visit, the seven-year-old had sneaked out of her room in the evening and gone down to the campfire where the grown-ups were sitting. Her father had pretended not to see her, and she had stayed and listened to the songs of the labour movement, the laughter and talk. This time, she had spoken about her political life and all that had changed since she was born in the late 1930s. The changes had not been without cost, the liberation campaign had come at a price, women had stood at the barricades, they had been ridiculed and excluded. Gro warned the young AUF girls to be alert to the possibility of a backlash. Equality was something that had to be fought for every day, both globally and in your daily life.

Bano and Lara sat barefoot among hundreds of other young people in the damp, clammy hall and listened. Equality was one of the issues dearest to their hearts. They were particularly keen to make sure immigrant girls were fully included in society. The two sisters had had their own very physical experience of the limitations imposed on women. When they were on holiday in Kurdistan, they encountered restrictions of dress, behaviour and freedom of movement. They agreed that the struggle for equality should not stop at the Norwegian border.

It was time for lunch. After that, Gro was to meet some of the girls who were candidates in the local council elections coming up in two months' time. Akershus was one of the counties selected, and Bano was on the list of candidates for Nesodden!

'How can we make ourselves heard?' she asked.

'Be yourself!' said Gro. 'No one will hear any of you otherwise, still less trust you. That's the most important thing of all. If you're not yourself you just can't sustain it in the long term.'

Bano was listening attentively. She was soaking wet, and on her feet she had a pair of pink flip-flops.

When Gro had stepped ashore from the MS *Thorbjørn* in bright white trousers and new white trainers, in the most horrendous weather she had ever experienced on Utøya, one of the reception party on the jetty decided footwear like that would not survive the day. He asked the retired doctor her shoe size.

Then the cry went up: 'Find a pair of size 38 rubber boots!'

'She can have mine,' came a croaky voice from inside a tent. It was Bano, who instantly pulled off her green boots and put on her bright pink flip-flops instead.

She had rung home: 'Mum! Gro's got my wellies on!'

They kept Gro dry. Meanwhile, the young people on Utøya got wetter and wetter. The campsite below the café building turned into a mudbath and few of the tents could withstand the rain that forced its way through the canvas and dripped in on rucksacks, sleeping bags and changes of clothes. On the football pitch and by the volleyball net the grass was no longer green but dirty brown with trampled-in soil and mud. The football tournament had to be postponed because the pitch was not fit to play on. People had come to hear Gro in their last set of dry clothes. Eventually the hall grew so sweaty and sticky that they had to open the windows onto the rain outside.

Bano rang her mother again after the meeting with the former Prime Minister.

'I talked to Gro, Mum, I talked to a living legend!'

'But Bano, you've scarcely any voice!'

'It doesn't matter, it's such fun here,' Bano exclaimed in return.

'Try not to make yourself even worse. Do dress warmly,' her mother begged. 'And ask Gro to autograph your boots!'

A TV reporter who had come over to Utøya with Gro asked the AUF girls what Gro meant to them.

'She's the best,' answered Bano, standing in the rain in her rubber flip-flops.

'Even better than Jens Stoltenberg?'

Bano thought about it.

'Well, if this was a rock festival and they were bands, Gro's name would be top of the bill, with Jens underneath,' she laughed croakily.

I believe this will be my last entry. It is now Fri July 22nd, 12.51.
Sincere regards,
Andrew Berwick, Justiciar Knight Commander.

He was back in the fart room after his taxi-ride home, and was about to send out the film and his manifesto. But the computer kept on getting stuck. Then it stopped working altogether, before he had managed to send anything. Finally the file began to move, the marker creeping forward. It seemed to have sent to some people at least, but then it got stuck again and he had to restart the computer.

A feeling of panic spread through his body. So many years of planning, and then it went wrong!

He stared at the screen.

At last the machine cranked itself up and started sending.

Western Patriot, read the heading. Then he introduced the work as a set of 'advanced ideological, practical, tactical, organisational and rhetorical solutions and strategies'.

I do not want any compensation for the work as it is a gift to you, as a fellow patriot. In fact, I ask only for one favour of you: I ask that you distribute this book to everyone you know. Please do not think that others will take care of it. Sorry to be blunt, but it does not work that way. If we, the Western European Resistance fail or become apathetic, then Western Europe will fall, and your liberties with it . . .

He checked the time.

The email with *The Islamisation of Western Europe and the Status of the European Resistance Movements* in the subject line must have got through to at least some of the addresses? All the staff would soon be leaving the government quarter.

He had planned to destroy the hard disk after sending off the manifesto, but now he would have to leave the machine working away without him.

He got ready to leave the room. The computer, the two safes, Coderock on the walls, the light blue wardrobe, the single bed. At a quarter to three he went out of his room, turned left, opened the front door and slammed it shut behind him.

In the fart room, the computer and modem droned on. Once the manifesto had been sent to a thousand email addresses, everything ground to a halt. Telenor's spam filter had detected that the upper limit for the number of messages that could be sent per day had been reached.

On the screen, a window was open in the web browser. It showed the day's programme for the AUF on Utøya.

Down to the junction, along past the old industrial buildings of the electrical plant, past the bronze statue of a naked girl with her arms in the air. He briskly covered the ground on his usual route to the garden centre. He did not meet anyone he knew.

He unlocked the van and climbed into the back. Inside were the strong plastic bags from China in which he had packed the explosives. He got changed beside the bomb. Off came Ralph Lauren, Lacoste and Puma. He pulled the black compression top over his head and fixed the plastic police insignia onto the sleeves, then strapped on the bulletproof vest. He pulled on the black trousers with the reflective strips and fastened the pistol holster to his thigh. Lastly, he put on the heavy black boots with spurs at the heels.

Before opening the van door to get out, he looked round carefully. This was a moment of vulnerability. If anyone saw him getting out of the back of the van in full police uniform, they might start to wonder. But he saw nobody. Skøyen seemed deserted on that chilly grey Friday in July; most people round here were away at their summer cottages or holiday homes. He closed the back door, went round the side of the vehicle and climbed into the driving seat.

At just the same time, Gro was taking a seat in the cabin aboard the

MS *Thorbjørn* to leave the island. Beside her sat her granddaughter Julie, daughter of her late son Jørgen. Julie was active in the AUF and had wanted to stay on after Gro's address, but with the weather turning ever wetter she decided to go home with her grandmother. With them was the parliamentarian Hadia Tajik, the young woman of Pakistani origin who once had given Bano a course on rhetoric. She had come over to hear Gro speak, and left with her in the horrendous weather.

Gro got away. She got off the boat at the jetty on the mainland, where her car stood waiting.

Anders Behring Breivik took the same route he had taken earlier in the day. On the way to the E18 there was a traffic jam. A tractor had driven off the road at the exit to the Viking ship museum, and part of the road was blocked off, with two uniformed police officers in attendance.

He looked straight ahead. Think if they spotted his police uniform at the wheel of the grey van! They would stop him and notice his fake insignia. Then it would all be over before it had started.

But it wasn't.

He drove past the roadblock.

It continued.

In the city centre he turned into Grubbegata, which was a one-way street with government buildings on both sides. It was seven years since the authorities had taken the decision to close it. But the measure had done so many bureaucratic rounds that it had still not been implemented. At a quarter past three he stopped outside the Ministry of Fisheries and Coastal Affairs. He got out and put the blue light on top of the van. He climbed back in; he was scared.

He could simply leave it. Just drive past.

He started the van. And drove calmly towards the Tower Block.

By his calculations, the fuse would take six minutes to set off the bomb. Plenty of time to get away, but also time for somebody to cut it and prevent detonation. Ought he to light it right away, several hundred metres from the building? He could not decide. And then he was there.

There were no barriers to prevent the van driving right up to the seventeen-storey building that housed the Ministry of Justice and the Prime Minister's office. There was a *No Entry* sign hanging on a chain between two pillars, but there was plenty of space to drive round it.

When he turned up towards the reception area, he saw that there were a couple of cars blocking the ideal place to park. To maximise the pressure wave in one direction he had packed the 950-kilo bomb so there were several hundred kilos more explosive on one side. The two cars would force him to park the other way round. The explosive force would blast outwards from the building, rather than into it.

The aim was to make the building collapse. He had calculated that if he managed to destroy the first row of the pillars holding up the building, the whole thing would come down. The Prime Minister's office at the top and everything below it.

He parked right outside the reception area, close to the building. Fear was starting to take a grip. His hands were shaking. To try to suppress the fear and calm himself down he focused on the plan, which he had run over in his head hundreds of times. He had seen the sequence of events unfold in his mind over and over again. Now he had to rely on his training and stick to the plan.

He took out his lighter. His hands continued to shake. Still seated at the wheel, he turned and reached backwards to light the fuse protruding through the hole from the load compartment.

The fuse caught light immediately, emitting sparks. It crackled its way towards the bags of fertiliser.

Now there was no way back.

He had been braced to die the instant he lit the fuse. The Analfo gas could escape through the hole and make the van explode. Slightly nonplussed when this did not happen, he grabbed his keys and got out, forgetting his mobile phone on the dashboard. He locked the car and looked round. Planning the operation, he had imagined that armed agents would come running up and he would have to kill them. But nobody came. He still undid the holster on his thigh, took out *Mjølnir* and crossed the road with the pistol in his right hand.

*

The lower basement level, two floors below the Tower Block, was where the security control centre was located. From there, a couple of security guards monitored the government quarter via multiple screens. The guards did not notice the van parked by the exit.

A few minutes after Breivik lit the fuse, one of the receptionists in the Tower Block informed them there was a wrongly parked van outside the entrance. One of the guards rewound the film from the relevant camera back a few minutes and pressed play. He watched the images of a van slowly driving up and saw a uniformed man, whom he assumed to be some guard, leave the van and disappear from the screen.

They were used to illegal parking. Delivery vehicles were often parked in the wrong place, as were the cars of people popping in on brief business. According to the regulations, the reception parking area was only for the use of official cars collecting or dropping off the Prime Minister and his ministers. But the rule was not enforced.

Off camera, roadworks obliged the uniformed man to cross over to the opposite pavement. There he met a young man with a bunch of red roses. The man gave the police officer a curious look and the pistol caught his eye.

Breivik swiftly weighed up whether the man in front of him was a security agent who would have to be shot. He decided he was a civilian and let him live.

They passed each other and then each turned round to look back, their eyes meeting. They both walked on, and turned again. By then, Breivik had his visor down.

The man with the roses slowed almost to a halt. He was surprised to see the police officer get into a delivery van. It was also rather odd that he drove out into Møllergata against the flow of traffic. In fact, so strange that he got out his mobile and tapped in the van's make and registration number — *Fiat Doblò VH 24605* — before he went on.

Down in the security control centre, the duty officer was using the cameras to try to locate the driver. He seemed to have gone in the direction of the Ministry of Education. But the cameras there revealed nothing. The guard switched his attention back to the illegally parked van and zoomed in on the number plate.

By then, Breivik was already on his way out of Møllergata, where he turned right to drive down to the sea and into the Opera Tunnel, where the motorway ran under the fjord. He set the van's GPS to the coordinates he had programmed in when he was examining the hull of the MS *Thorbjørn*.

The security guard in the government quarter decided to ring the Driver and Vehicle Licensing Agency to ask for the name and telephone number of the van's owner. That was what they usually did, so they could ring the driver and ask him to move his vehicle.

A young man came up the little access way from Møllergata towards the fountain at Einar Gerhardsen's Square. He was wearing a white shirt and had a laptop case slung across his back. The young lawyer was not at work today, but he had just finished a report on customs agreements between the EU and the developing world and wanted to show it to his team. 'Just email it,' said his colleague in the legal department, but Jon Vegard Lervåg wanted to hand it over in person, so he could wish everybody a good summer holiday at the same time. He had just got married, and over the weekend he and his young wife would be going home across the mountains to the coastal town of Ålesund to tell their parents the good news – they were expecting their first child.

The man crossed Grubbegata. He was fit and agile, an active hill runner who favoured the steep mountains of Western Norway. He was thirty-two, the same age as the man who had just left the government quarter and was now on his way to the motorway tunnel. They were born in the same month of the same year; only four days separated them. Four days and infinity.

Jon Vegard Lervåg was a member of a group of law-clinic volunteers and of Amnesty International. Anders Behring Breivik was a member of the Knights Templar and Oslo Pistol Club. Jon Vegard, who was a competent classical guitarist, was looking forward to a

Prince concert the following evening and to his trip home on Sunday. He was looking forward to becoming a father in February. Four days separated them, and eternity.

As Jon Vegard came abreast of the van it exploded into a sea of flame. He was thrown sideways by a pressure wave so powerful that he was killed instantly, even before the splinters of glass and metal hit him.

The time was 15.25.22.

Two young women, lawyers at the Ministry who were standing behind the van, were also lifted into the air by the pressure wave, engulfed in the sea of flame and thrown to the ground. They too were killed instantly. Two receptionists in the Tower Block were thrown out of their seats, over the counter and out into the square. Glass blew into the building, doors were smashed, window ledges became jagged spears of wood and shards of metal red-hot knifepoints. Everything was hurled either into the building or out over the square, street and fountain, where eight now lay dead or dying. Around them lay numerous injured people, knocked unconscious by the pressure wave or with deep cuts.

Sheets of paper descended. Gently, almost floating in the wind, they fluttered down over the scene of destruction.

Fragments of Jon Vegard's body flew through the air and spread along the façade of the Tower Block. Only one hand landed intact on the ground. On one of his fingers his wedding ring remained unscathed.

'What was that?' said the Prime Minister when he heard the bang.

Jens Stoltenberg was sitting at his desk, talking on the phone. That morning, he had decided to work from his residence in Parkveien, behind the Royal Palace. It was the holiday period and quiet, so there had been no need to go into the office in the Tower Block. He was preparing the speech he would be making on Utøya the next day. Its theme was the economy and the fight for full employment. His pet subjects.

When the bang came, he was on the phone to the president of the Parliament, Dag Terje Andersen, who was in a forest down south.

Thunder, thought the Prime Minister; the forecast was for stormy weather.

They carried on talking.

A secretary from the Prime Minister's office was in the reception area when the bomb went off. She was killed instantly by the pressure wave. Outside Stoltenberg's door in the Tower Block lay one of his security guards, knocked unconscious, while the PM's communications adviser ran out of his office on the fifteenth floor when the windows blew in. Blood was dripping onto his shoes. He put a hand to his head and his fingers turned red. There was a deep gouge across the back of his head and blood was welling through his copper-coloured hair. He ran back into the wreckage of the office for something to staunch the bleeding. He found a T-shirt in a bag and pressed it to the wound.

As he ran down the stairs he rang the Prime Minister on his direct line. 'Hi, it's Arvid. Are you okay?'

'Yes,' said Stoltenberg. He still had Andersen on the other line.

'You're not hurt?'

'No . . . '

As Arvid Samland made his escape down the partially dark, wrecked stairwell he told the Prime Minister what he could see. He and various other employees were trying to get out of the building. There was smoke and thick dust everywhere, fallen masonry and fittings were blocking sections of the steps and splinters of glass covered the staircase where Picasso's sand-blasted lines hung undamaged.

Beneath the block, the security guard had held the phone in his hand and was about to dial the Driver and Vehicle Licensing Agency when the bang came. The ceiling shuddered, all the monitors went black, lights and alarms started flashing, and water pipes sprang leaks. He rang the Oslo police district instead, and was thus the first person to alert them to the explosion.

Meanwhile, hundreds of people were running away from the Tower Block. Smoke was gushing out of the building and several storeys were on fire; the building could collapse at any moment or there could be another explosion. Others just stood there gaping. Or they got out their phones and rang home.

The security guard who had alerted the police stayed in front of his screens. He found his way back to the pictures of the van that had parked six minutes earlier. As soon as he had viewed the recording again, he rang the police for a second time.

'It's a vehicle that exploded,' he said, and told them about a man wearing a dark uniform who left the van minutes before it blew up.

Three guards came into the Prime Minister's office in Parkveien, put him into a bulletproof vest and ordered him to follow them to a secure room. The fact that the attack in the centre had been directed at the government building meant it was possible the Prime Minister's residence could also be a target.

Still, no armed guards were directed to protect the building.

Breivik had the radio on as he drove. He had not heard any blast.

Something had gone wrong; the fuse had not detonated the explosives. It had failed!

The Crafter should have blown up long since, he thought as the traffic came to a standstill in the Opera Tunnel.

A few hundred metres from Hammersborg, however, the Pelican cases had gone crashing over in the back of the van. Perhaps the explosion had happened just then, and he had not heard it because of the noise? Or . . . it occurred to him, perhaps it was actually the air pressure from the explosion that had made the cases fall over.

He drove on. Turned up the radio. A few minutes later the broadcast was interrupted with the news that there had been an explosion in the government quarter.

Yes! It had gone off.

The first police car reached the scene three minutes after the explosion. Ten ambulances were also dispatched. Several passers-by stopped to give first aid. Oslo University Hospital was put on major incident alert and the accident and emergency department prepared for many admissions. One of the firemen sent to the government quarter was Magnus, Anders's childhood friend, the one who had just called him at the farm about coming for a visit, who had worried, and wondered when his friend would emerge from his tunnel and be himself again.

Nine minutes after the explosion, a call came through on the police public hotline.

'Er, hello, Andreas Olsen here. I'm ringing because I saw something very suspicious as I was going past the government quarter.'

The operator said she could not take his tip-off then and there, and that it would be better if he called back. Olsen interrupted her and said he had observed a man in police uniform walking along with a pistol in his hand.

'I'm sorry, you do realise I can't take this now, but what's your name?'

'This is a concrete lead about a car,' Olsen insisted. He was the pedestrian with the bunch of roses who had seen Breivik walking up from the government quarter. He gave a brief account of what he had seen: a man with a crash helmet and pistol, who had 'something strange about him'. The man had left the area unaccompanied and got into a grey van with the registration number VH 24605.

The operator had just read the report from the security guard in the basement of the Tower Block, and put the two pieces of information together. She realised this was an important tip-off and noted it down on a yellow Post-it note.

She took the note with her to the joint operational centre and put it on the leader's desk. Although the chief of operations was busy on the phone, the operator thought she had made eye contact with her. Her impression was that the supervisor had registered that the note was important.

She went out.

The note sat there.

While a Fiat Doblò VH 24605 was stuck in the queue for the Opera Tunnel, the note sat there.

Untouched on the desk, in a room in chaos, it did not disturb anyone.

The Oslo police district did not have any shared alert procedures, so the chief of operations – who should have been leading the action – got out the telephone book. Once she had looked through the holiday rota detailing who was in charge of what over the summer break, she started ringing staff members one by one. Instead of taking the lead at the joint operational centre and coordinating action with the incident commanders in the field, she gave priority to calling individual officers in for duty. In the acute phase there was hardly any contact between the chief of operations and the on-scene commanders in charge of the secure and rescue operations in the government quarter.

Anders Behring Breivik was still in the queue to get into the Opera Tunnel. He was afraid the whole of Oslo was already shut off because of the bomb attack and that he would never get to the next phase of his plan.

Had he been the police chief, he would have blocked all the main arteries, he reasoned. Perhaps the security forces had already hermetically sealed off the capital.

But no roadblocks were set up, no roads were closed. It was not even considered. No attempt was made to stop the escape of a potential perpetrator. All available manpower was deployed to the government quarter and the rescue work there, including the elite emergency response unit that went by the name of Delta.

In the chaos there was still nobody to pick up the yellow note. None of the police on the streets were asked to look out for a Fiat Doblò delivery van with the registration number VH 24605, or a guard in a dark uniform in a civilian vehicle.

Breivik was still very close by. It took him a long time to get through the eastern city centre and the tunnel under the Oslofjord before he re-emerged at ground level in the western part of the centre. From the Opera Tunnel he drove past the US embassy, which was now swarming with security personnel. The police had taken up positions outside the embassy. He drove right past. Ha, they've assumed it's Islamic terrorism of course, he thought. He amused himself listening to the terror experts on the radio saying this pointed to al-Qaida.

The security mobilisation at the embassy pushed up his stress level a bit and he was afraid someone would react to the fact that he was wearing a helmet and uniform in a delivery van. He had to calm down. The crucial thing was not to crash. He passed the corner of the Royal Gardens, he crossed Parkveien, where the Prime Minister was in a secure room, and he drove up Bygdøy Allé with its exclusive shops. There were clusters of green horse chestnuts hanging on the huge trees. He was in his own district, his own biotope. He passed blocks of luxury flats, he drove past Fritzners gate where he had lived in the very first years of his life. A few streets away, on the other side of the avenue, was the flat he had rented in his twenties. He knew the streets here, the bars and the shops. He knew the escape routes and shortcuts. He now knew he would get out of the city; the police would never be able to close off all the roads to the west.

He sped out of Oslo.

As time went on, there were more reports from members of the public who had observed a man in uniform leaving the van a few minutes before it blew up. The security guards in several ministry buildings viewed the CCTV tapes that showed the sequence of events from different angles. They provided a description identical to the one given by Andreas Olsen.

But no alerts were sent out from the joint operational centre at the police headquarters in Oslo, neither to the force itself nor to the public via the media.

At 15.55, half an hour after the bomb had gone off, an operator happened to see the yellow note lying on the unit leader's desk. Twenty minutes had passed since Andreas Olsen reported his information. Now, they rang him back and asked him to go through it all again.

'And that was before the explosion?' asked the operator after Olsen had once again explained what he had seen.

'Five . . . '

'What did you say – it was?'

'It was five minutes before the explosion.'

'Are you sure he was in police uniform?'

'There was a police badge on the sleeve. I can't say whether it was a genuine police uniform. But I thought police, because I saw a helmet with one of those glass visors in front and he'd got a pistol out. So I wondered if there was some operation going on, because I thought the whole thing was . . . that is, something made me react.'

'But that was five minutes before the explosion?'

Olsen confirmed this again and gave a description: European appearance, in his thirties, about 1.80 metres tall. The operator became convinced that this was an important lead. 'Good observation. What was the registration number of that car?'

By the time they rang off, it was 16.02.

After the call, the operator marked the report as *Important* in the operation log and made sure it was accessible to all. She also filled in the on-scene commander, who asked her to pass the report on to a patrol from the emergency response squad. It was impossible to get through on the communication radio, so she found their mobile number and rang them.

At 16.03, Breivik passed the police station in Sandvika, on the E18. If the officers had been looking out of the windows, they would have seen the silver-grey van driving past on the main road. Sandvika had men ready and waiting, but did not know what to do with them and was awaiting a request for assistance from Oslo.

At 16.05 the operator in Oslo made a mobile phone call to the emergency response unit informing them of the man in a dark uniform driving a Fiat Doblò. She also gave them the registration number. The patrol said the description was too vague for any action to be taken.

At 16.09 the chief of operations in Asker and Bærum, the district through which Breivik was now driving, finally got through to Oslo police district to offer assistance. She was informed about the van and the possible perpetrator. At that point in time, the station at Asker and Bærum had three patrol cars at its disposal; the chief of operations rang the closest one and gave the description. This patrol was on its way to Ila prison to pick up a prisoner who was to be taken to Oslo.

The chief of operations asked them to postpone the prisoner transport because of the bomb in Oslo. She also alerted the two other patrols and read over the radio the type of vehicle, registration number and description. Then she once again contacted the patrol at Ila prison, which by then should have been free, and commanded it to go out on observation along the E18.

But the two policemen in the patrol car had chosen to ignore their orders. They had picked up the prisoner from the prison after all and were now on their way into Oslo. They had wanted to 'get the job out of the way', they said. In the operation log, the prisoner transport was marked Priority 5, the lowest level. The country's seat of government had been blown up yet the patrol decided to act on its own whim. Asker and Bærum's second patrol had been busy with a psychiatric assignment and had been given orders to leave it. That order was not obeyed either.

And this at the very moment Breivik was driving through their district, in a light-coloured Fiat Doblò VH 24605, just like the one the chief of operations had described to them over the radio. Two police patrols could have been positioned along the E18 and could have followed him. Nobody did. Breivik pushed on westwards.

To judge by the way the Oslo police was behaving, little indicated that Norway had just been the target of an act of terror, with an acute risk of secondary attacks. When other districts offered support, their offers were largely declined, even though many potential targets around Oslo remained unsecured. The Parliament requested reinforcements as there were no armed officers outside the main building. You will have to make do with your own guards, the head of the Oslo operational centre informed them. Just close off some of your buildings, the head of security at the Parliament was told. The Labour Party offices at Youngstorget asked for police guards; the House of the People asked for police guards. Their requests were turned down, with the advice to evacuate their premises.

Norway owns a single police helicopter. And in July, the helicopter service was on holiday. As a consequence of new savings measures, there was no emergency crew cover at the height of the summer. The first pilot nonetheless reported for duty right after hearing about the bomb on the news. He was told he was not needed.

Yet the emergency response unit requested use of the helicopter twice in the hour that followed. The squad was informed that the helicopter was unavailable, even though it was on the tarmac, fully operational and ready to fly. Nor did the police take any steps to mobilise military helicopters or make use of civilian helicopter companies.

After the bomb in Oslo, no immediate nationwide alert was sent out. A nationwide alert is issued to communicate information considered important to all the police districts in the country. When such an alert goes out, all police stations follow a standard procedure. In Asker and Bærum, this would have involved setting up a police roadblock on the E16 at Sollihøgda, towards which Anders Behring Breivik was currently heading.

When the duty manager at Kripos, the National Criminal Investigation Service, contacted the chief of operations of the Oslo police to ask if they could help in any way, the exchange ran as follows:

Oslo: Well, er, you could, that is, it might be interesting to maybe issue a warning, send out a national warning.
Kripos: Yes. What do you want it to say?
Oslo: No, that is, well it's interesting now because a van was spotted here, uh-huh. A small grey delivery van. VH 24605. So if you could send out, that is, a national warning that there's been an attack here, and then that the police districts are bearing it in mind.
Kripos: The van?
Oslo: Yes, and any other activity, because it could be interesting on routes to border crossings. Mmm, maybe alert the customs service, which is at most of the borders at least.

The conversation ended without the chief of operations clarifying that the van could be the vehicle of a potential perpetrator, that the individual driving it had been observed at the scene, and that he was wearing a police uniform and was armed.

The information provided by witnesses was not read out over any general communication wavelength, nor was it passed on to the media so that alerts could go out on radio and television. The Public Roads Authority in Oslo, which has a comprehensive network of cameras, was not alerted either. Despite the fact that the government quarter – Norway's most important seat of power had been blown to smithereens by a bomb, the terror-response plan was not implemented.

Nobody pressed the big button.

The resources available were not exploited.

Meanwhile, Breivik drove calmly on towards Sollihøgda. He kept to the speed limit. He did not want to overtake anyone, or be over-taken. He had to avoid anyone who might look into the van and think there was something not quite right about him.

At 16.16 he passed Sollihøgda. Down to his left lay the Tyrifjord.

Soon, he would be able to see Utøya.

———

You had to put your best people in defence.

And these last few summers on Utøya, Simon had been the work-horse of the Troms football team. Among the activists he was the fittest and most experienced team player; he was good at countering attacks, getting the ball and kicking it away up the pitch. He was also the one who got most annoyed with the slowcoaches. 'Get a move on!' or 'Run faster' he would shout. He did not approve of half-hearted efforts – that was no fun. You were here to win.

Brage and Geir Kåre played in the midfield, while Viljar made an impressive forward. He ran fast and scored the most goals. Once, late at night after a long party, he and Simon argued about who was actu-ally fastest, and they decided to race each other across the kilometre length of the Tromsø Bridge. Ready, steady, go! They ran, but admit-ted defeat after a few hundred metres. The effects of the party won out in the end.

They were happy to live not knowing who was fastest, and now Viljar had a hat-trick to celebrate – three goals in the same match.

Gunnar Linaker reigned supreme in goal. The Troms county secretary was a big, burly type who weighed over a hundred kilos but he threw himself around in all directions. He was so muddy after the match that Mari had to hose him down. He had also strained his groin, and rang a medical student friend in Tromsø. 'You'll have to lie down and rest until it stops hurting,' the friend advised. Not a chance. Troms had won all its matches so far and was the first team to qualify for the semi-finals. He would be playing in spite of the pain. They were going to win the tournament this year!

Anders Kristiansen was nowhere to be seen during the matches, not even as a spectator and cheerleader. They could have done with his enthusiasm and loud voice, but he had other duties to perform and was busy preparing the political programme. The eighteen-year-old had arrived at the island a few days before the others to attend a training course for the election campaign that was to start after the holidays. Anders was on the Labour Party list for the local council elections in Bardu and was hoping to win a seat in September. From late summer he was going to travel round to schools all over Troms to take part in election debates and it was important to polish up his arguments and his style. Debating was what he most enjoyed. He had recordings of several parliamentary debates that had been shown on TV, including those on the data storage directive and the postal services directive, and he made a careful study of how the various representatives put over their points, what worked and what did not, how you could defeat your opponent, ridicule him, render him harmless or undermine his credibility. How he was looking forward to the election campaign!

After the football match there were political seminars. They could choose between such topics as 'My dear brother in dark blue – the experience of Conservative government in Sweden' or 'Violence against women and children' or an update on climate negotiations.

Mari and Simon opted for something they knew nothing about, 'Western Sahara – Africa's last colony'. They learned about the Sahrawis' fight against the Moroccan occupation of their land while they were exiled to the most inhospitable desert areas, cut off by a wall over two thousand kilometres in length, in a place where over a million landmines maimed people and cattle every year. Freedom of expression was limited and there were disappearances and arbitrary imprisonments.

'We've got to get to work on this,' Mari whispered to Simon.

As the seminar was drawing to a close, disquiet spread through the room. Conversations were conducted in loud whispers while the human rights activist from Western Sahara carried on speaking. A boy stood up and interrupted the Sahrawi to say that there had been a big explosion in Oslo. He referred to his iPhone and what he had read on the internet. Many were frightened; a number of the camp participants from the Oslo area had parents who worked in or near the government quarter.

The seminar was abruptly ended by a boy who came to summon everyone to a meeting. It was to be held in the main hall, where they were now, so Mari and Simon stayed in their places. At the meeting, AUF leader Eskil Pedersen gave them the latest information on the explosion. But it was nothing more than they could read for themselves on their iPhones.

Monica Bøsei, a slight woman in her mid-forties, came onto the stage. 'Those who want to ring their parents can do so. Anyone who wants to talk can come and see us, we're here for you,' she said. Monica had been running the island on a day-to-day basis for twenty years, promoting the ideas of the labour movement and adding a few of her own. She had handled its finances, put down mousetraps and seen to the upkeep of the buildings. When she had been working there for a few years, they advertised for a caretaker. Jon Olsen, an AUF member her own age, got the job. And Monica. They fell in love, moved in together and had two daughters. When the AUF bought the MS *Thorbjørn* to use as a ferry, Jon became its captain.

This was due to be Monica's last summer on the island. Mother Utøya, as she was known, had got a job as director of the Maritime Museum and wanted to hand the baton over to somebody else. But for now she was here to take care of anxious young people. 'This

evening we'll light all the barbecues and you can have as many
sausages as you want,' she proposed, telling them Utøya was a long
way from Oslo and that it was the safest place for them rightnow.

Out of respect for the victims in the government quarter, the
Friday disco was cancelled, and because of the rain the football tournament was postponed. There was no pitch left to play on. Monica
recommended that the leaders of the county delegations gathered up
their groups to talk through what had happened.

Simon and Mari went out together and headed for the tents.

'We're not safe here,' said Simon.

'What?' exclaimed Mari.

'Well, if this is an attack on the Labour Party . . . ' he said.

'Now you just shut up!' Mari declared.

'I'm only saying that it's no coincidence they went for the government quarter. That means this is an attack on the Labour Party,
and we're part of the Labour Party. . . '

They came across Viljar. And Simon did not shut up.

'If this is political, Viljar, and against the government, we're not
safe here either.'

Viljar had just been talking to his mother and was wondering what
to tell his younger brother Torje. During Gro's talk the fourteen-year-
old had collapsed from lack of sleep after his all-night session
followed by the football tournament. Now he and Johannes were
asleep in their tent. Viljar and his mother had agreed it was best not
to wake him until after the meeting, and then to give him a toned-
down version. It must be time to get him up now.

Up in the Troms camp, Mari was delegating tasks. She set some of
the activists to buttering bread and making up fruit squash. She went
round pouring the sweet drink into plastic cups. When you've had
bad news, your blood sugar levels fall, she reasoned. So it was important for them to have a bite to eat now.

It was wet, grey and mucky. The whole campsite had turned into
a huge pool of mud. But soon they were all sitting round on whatever
they could find in the way of dry camping stools, boxes and tree
stumps.

'Take big breaths, stay calm,' Mari told herself. But it was beyond her.

———

Anders Behring Breivik was now driving through Nordre Buskerud, the police district to which Utøya belonged. In Hønefoss police station no one had yet received any instructions to look out for a silver-grey delivery van with a particular number plate.

He drove along the winding road from Sollihøgda, looking down at the Tyrifjord. There was an arrow pointing down the narrow road to the left. The sign said Utøya. Not that the driver needed the sign; the car's GPS had already told him this was the place to turn. Just before half past four, the van left the highway.

He did not want to drive down to the jetty yet, so he pulled into a small clearing a little way above it. This was how he had planned it; if he arrived in good time for the next crossing, he would stop in a place where he could be seen neither from the road nor from the jetty. The boat ran on the hour. He had checked the timetable on the AUF web pages, and the next boat was not until five.

He drank a little water and a Red Bull, and got out of the car to pee. The drawback with ECA was that it made you want to go. The steroids did not give you a high in themselves, but they thinned the blood so your heart got more oxygen. They helped you concentrate and speeded up your perception. Your visual skills were enhanced and your reaction times were shorter.

But now he had to wait, and that did not suit him.

While he was waiting, Kripos was formulating a nationwide alert about a potential perpetrator. Forty minutes after the vague phone conversation with the joint operations centre in Oslo, the one in which it was said that 'It might be interesting to maybe issue a warning', the alarm was sounded. It was one hour and eighteen minutes since the explosion, and one hour and nine minutes since Andreas Olsen had rung in to tip them off about the uniformed man with a pistol, and the number plate of his car.

```
Nationwide Alert - Explosion Potential
Bomb(s) in Central Oslo
All units requested to be on the alert for
a small grey van, possible reg. 24605. As
of now unknown relationship between
explosion and vehicle, but if it is
located, alert Desk or Oslo pending further
instructions. Units requested to exercise
relative caution in approaching the
vehicle.
Sincerely, Kripos Desk.
```

It was 16.43. There was nothing in the wording to indicate that the driver of this van, for which Kripos had incidentally omitted the initial letter code of the registration number, had been observed in a guard's or police uniform. What was more, only very few police stations actually received the alert. Many did not have the relevant communication equipment switched on, or the alarm signal was wrongly set.

This certainly applied to Nordre Buskerud police district, where Breivik was now located. The computer that was able to receive alarms was some distance from the three desks in general use. When the PC was not being used, its screen went dark. In order to check whether there had been any alarm calls, one had to go into Shared Files > Alarms > and then select the police district from the list of all the districts in the country. Only then could one see if any alerts had come into the police station.

Nobody did that at Hønefoss police station in Nordre Buskerud.

So, while the alarm was going out from Oslo and not being received by the police station a few kilometres away, the man with the pistol sat waiting in the van. The fjord was grey and sombre. The rain lashed the surface of the water. No boat arrived.

It would have to be here soon if it was to leave at five.

———

Simon was worried and wanted to ring home, but his phone needed charging. Julie Bremnes lent him hers. As the daughter of the musician and songwriter Lars Bremnes, she could usually never get anywhere near Anders, Simon and Viljar without the trio starting to squawk her father's lyrics: *Oh, if I could write in the heavens, yours is the name I would write!*

But not this time. At five to five, Simon rang his father in Salangen, where he was sitting watching the news with Håvard.

'Dad, what's the latest?'

'They say it's a bomb. *One* person confirmed dead so far,' answered Gunnar, and described the pictures he could see on the TV screen. 'They still don't know, Simon, it's just speculation.'

'It's important for us to get as much concrete information as we can. Ring me if you find out any more, then.'

'Yes I will,' answered Gunnar. 'All the best, then!'

Simon had sounded stressed. Gunnar settled back into his seat. Tone was sitting beside him, knitting.

At the same time, just across the water from their son, Breivik decided to drive down to the jetty to find out what had happened to the boat. He drove slowly down the steep dirt track to the landing stage. There were a few youngsters with rucksacks standing about. They watched him curiously as he parked. A young blond man with a security vest and a walkie-talkie came over to him. Breivik got out of the car and waved him away. He did not want the boy to come any closer.

'Routine check because of the bomb in the government quarter,' he told the young guard. 'Officers are being posted at various locations.' He paused. 'To make sure nothing more happens.'

The guard was a bit surprised when he heard this. It was strange for an armed police officer in uniform to arrive unaccompanied in a civilian vehicle. But there was probably a shortage of police cars in a situation like this, he reasoned.

'Where's the boat?' Breivik asked the AUF guard.

'Cancelled because of the explosion,' replied the nineteen-year-old.

The policeman asked him to call the boat over. 'There are two more men on their way from the security service,' he said, but he stressed that he wanted to get over as quickly as possible himself, to secure the area. The boy rang over to the island.

There was a car at the landing stage with its windows down and the news blaring out at high volume. Some teenagers stood hunched over as they tried to keep their mobiles out of the rain. They were making calls, sending texts and checking the internet on their iPhones. They all knew someone in Oslo, and most of them had been on the bus on their way to the island when the bomb went off. They were talking among themselves about who could be behind the attack. Al-Qaida seemed the likeliest candidate.

The young people had registered with the guards on the landing stage and their bags had been searched for alcohol and drugs – standard procedure at the summer camps. 'I've just got to check you haven't got any sawn-off shotguns or revolvers with you,' the volunteer guard from Norwegian People's Aid had said to them in an attempt to lighten the mood.

MS *Thorbjørn* put out from the jetty on Utøya and chugged towards the mainland. The uniformed man stood waiting by his van at the far side of the parking area. The AUF guard could see he was sorting out something in a case.

The rain was easing off as the captain steered towards the quay. His vessel was a military landing craft built back in the 1940s and used by Swedish navy commandos for a generation. The AUF had bought the boat cheaply fifteen years earlier. The hull, made of 10mm steel, was painted red to the waterline, and black up the sides. The windows of the wheelhouse were steaming up. The Norwegian flag on its roof hung wet and heavy.

Once he reached the mainland, the skipper lowered the front of the boat and the prow became a gangway. Monica Bøsei hurried ashore to meet the policeman on the landing stage.

'Why haven't we been informed of this?' she asked in some agitation.

'It's chaos in Oslo at the moment,' the policeman replied.

'Fine,' said Monica. She turned back to the boat, while the police-man went over to his van. He had to bring some equipment over, he had told her.

He came back dragging a heavy black case. He was holding a rifle. Monica approached him again. 'You can't bring that rifle onto the island. You'll frighten everybody,' she exclaimed. 'You'll have to keep it hidden, at least.'

This time it was the policeman who said 'Fine.'

He went back to his vehicle for something to cover the rifle. In the front seat he had the Benelli shotgun in a black bin liner. He took the powerful weapon out of the bag and left it lying there uncovered. He decided he was not going to need the shotgun after all.

The heavy plastic case on wheels gouged deep grooves in the gravel on its way to the boat. At the gangway, the policeman see-sawed it on board. The rifle was still only half covered, and Monica found another plastic bag in the wheelhouse to cover the stock.

The engine spluttered and the boat put out from the landing stage. Everyone had been counted and registered, all the luggage had been checked; well, except for the wheeled case. It had not occurred to anybody to check the representative of law and order.

Everything on board was wet after the rain and there was nowhere to sit or lean. The green paint of the deck had a sleek, slippery sheen to it. Raindrops massed on the ship's rail. It had turned a little brighter and the heavy rain had stopped; the sky was now more white than grey. It offered some prospect of a clear evening.

Monica wanted to talk. About the bomb, about what the police were doing and the officer's specific tasks. The uniformed man was taciturn, giving short, brusque answers while he drank thirstily from a CamelBak, a little backpack with a drinking tube. He seemed irri-table and did not look at the kids next to him on the deck. The waterproof case stood at his side, black and heavy.

He was a solid, broad-shouldered figure; he looked very tense. Feeling the seriousness of the moment, the young guard left on the landing stage had thought.

The crossing only took a few minutes. As the boat came alongside the jetty on Utøya, just after a quarter past five, the crewman threw the hawser, jumped out and tied up.

The skipper emerged from the wheelhouse to help with the case. Bomb-detection gear, he thought. The policeman asked if someone could drive it up to the main building. The captain offered to do it. He went to get the only vehicle on the island, heaved the case into its boot and drove off to the admin building a little way up the steep slope.

The youngsters who had been on the boat straggled up the gravel path with their rucksacks. Down at the jetty, the policeman was left with Monica. One of the guards on the island, a police officer called Trond Berntsen, came and shook the new arrival by the hand.

'Hello,' was the terse response of the man disguised as a policeman, who introduced himself as Martin Nilsen. That was the name of a friend of his, a name he ought to remember.

Before long the other guard on the island, Rune Havdal, came to join them. The AUF had hired two security guards, as the teenagers rarely spent the whole night asleep and some adult supervision was necessary to settle them down at times. The guards had the daytime off, and on this particular Friday they were meant to be taking their sons to the Tusenfryd amusement park, but with rough weather forecast, they had gone the previous day instead. Their boys, aged nine and eleven, were the island's mascots. They built tree houses and played hide-and-seek in the woods.

Trond Berntsen asked which police district the new arrival came from, and the man answered 'PST: Police Security Service, Grønland station.' Breivik was aware of stumbling over the police terminology, that these were codes he had not mastered. The guard continued questioning him about his assignment.

This man is the greatest threat on the island, thought Breivik. He is the one who could expose me.

He suddenly felt paralysed. His limbs felt heavy, his muscles stiffened, his nerves seemed numbed. He felt a sense of dread. He wasn't going to pull this off.

Berntsen went over to exchange a few words with one of the Norwegian People's Aid volunteers, a woman who had come over on the boat. 'Odd guy,' he said, referring to the policeman. But the woman, shaken by the bomb attack, was in a hurry to go up and join her colleagues in the camp. She merely nodded. Trond Berntsen turned back to the little group on the landing stage.

'When are the other two arriving?' he asked the bogus PST man.

Under his police outfit, his heart was pounding, he was sweating and his breathing was uneven.

I don't feel remotely like doing this, was the thought running through his head as he stood there with Monica Bøsei and the guards.

'They'll be here later,' he replied.

'Do you know Jørn?' Berntsen asked suddenly.

Breivik shrugged. It could be a trick question. There might not be a Jørn. Or perhaps Jørn was somebody that anyone who worked for the PST would be bound to know.

He had to take control of the situation or he would be done for. He pulled himself together and put an end to the interrogation by suggesting they go up to the main building. He could brief them on the bomb in Oslo there.

Berntsen gave him an appraising look and then nodded, leading the way up the grassy slope.

'A policeman's come over.'

Anders Kristiansen was standing in the Troms camp a little way from the others, who were sitting eating their bread and butter. He was a supervisor that Friday, equipped with a walkie-talkie and a high-visibility jacket. The news of the policeman's arrival had come over the radio.

'Oh good,' said somebody, relieved.

'The police want everyone to gather in the middle of the island,' Anders Kristiansen went on, once the instructions had come through.

The middle of the island, where's that? thought Mari. It was more or less exactly where they were now. In the Troms camp, at the camp-site.

So they stayed where they were.

*

'Now or never. It's now or never.'

The *Commander of the Norwegian anti-communist resistance movement* took a few steps up the slope behind Berntsen. On his feet he wore the black army boots. The spurs on the heels were hidden in the wet grass.

He had a firm grip on *Gungnir*, which was still covered by the black bin liner. *Mjølnir* was in the holster on his thigh.

His body was fighting against it, his muscles were twitching. He felt he would never be able to go through with it. A hundred voices in his head were screaming: Don't do it, don't do it, don't do it!

I must either let myself be caught now or carry through what I have planned, he thought as he reached the point where the hill grew steeper.

He forced his right hand down to his thigh, unfastened the holster, took hold of the pistol.

There was a bullet waiting in the chamber, seventeen more were ready in the magazine.

The case and the three thousand cartridges inside had been driven to the main building. It was behind the building, closed and locked. The key was in his pocket.

There were three people ahead of him, and two behind. If they started suspecting anything, they could overpower him.

So. Now. He slowly raised the Glock and pointed it at Berntsen.

'No!' cried Monica. 'You mustn't point it at him like that!'

He fired at the guard's head. Monica Bøsei turned but there was no time to run. A bullet hit her at close range.

The two were lying close together, where they had fallen. The killer straddled Berntsen and shot him twice more in the head, then fired two more shots at Monica. She lay face-down in the damp, newly mown grass.

The boat captain, who had parked the car and left the case in the boot, came round the corner of the building as Berntsen fell. Seconds later his eyes were fixed on the spot where his beloved had slumped to the ground.

He ran up over the hill, expecting to be shot in the back. 'Run for your lives!' he shouted to everyone he met.

Screams filled the air.

The killer was breathing rapidly.

From now on, everything would be easy.

His eyes, his body, his brain, his hand, they were all coordinated.

The other guard, Rune Havdal, was heading for the clump of trees. He was the next to be gunned down, first with a bullet in his back to incapacitate him, then murdered with a shot to the head.

The young people who had seen the executions were running in all directions.

The crewman on the boat shouted 'Christ, let's get out of here,' and tried to put the *Thorbjørn* in reverse.

The killer did not hurry. He walked steadily, following the biggest group of fleeing youngsters.

It was 17.22. He had been on the island for five minutes. He had plenty of time. The island was not large. The water lay glinting like a weapon of mass destruction. They were trapped now. He only had to scare them a little and they would throw themselves into the water and drown.

That was the way he had visualised it.

As the adrenalin pumped round his body he was suffused by a feeling of calm. His will had triumphed over his body. The barrier was down.

Lara had heard a bang. And then another. Then several more in rapid succession. She had been standing in front of the mirror in the bathroom block at one end of the campsite. The bathroom floor was warm to her numb feet. She had really only packed clothes for sunny weather and was so cold. She had taken off her sopping wet top and changed into a dry one, and was checking if it looked all right when she heard the loud reports.

Lara was born to the sound of gunfire. It was a part of everyday life in Erbil in the 1990s. She had been five when the family fled, from the bullets, the explosions, the tears of those left behind. Now that dreadful sound was here. Here.

Terrified screams cut through the air. She ran out to see what was happening. Outside, people were rushing past.

Where was Bano?

They had gone back to the tent together after the meeting. Lara wanted to stay near her elder sister. They had rung their parents from the tent and Mustafa had tried to reassure them. 'A bomb in Oslo? Well, that means the value of our house goes up. Now everybody will want to live in Nesodden instead,' he joked.

Bano had hung up her wet green top and black leggings to dry in the tent and put on dry jeans and the red Helly Hansen sailing jacket she had just bought with the earnings from her summer job. The jacket with the fluorescent yellow hood had cost almost a thousand kroner more than the model without a hood, but it was the one she wanted. It is important to look good if you want to be taken seriously, she had told Lara as she delightedly pulled on the wellies that Gro had borrowed earlier in the day.

The sisters had left the tent together. They had wanted to try to find out what was going on. What was all this about the bomb in Oslo? How bad was it? Then Lara had popped into the bathroom to change while Bano went straight on up to the café.

Bano always wanted to be where things were happening. And now there was a big crowd outside the café building. Of course Bano would go there.

'Do you need me for anything, Lara?' Bano had asked her outside the bathroom.

'No, I'm fine. I'll be right with you,' her little sister replied. She had wanted a few minutes to pull herself together. Suddenly she found herself crying. Had al-Qaida reached Norway?

Then she heard the shots.

Lots of those streaming past were heading for the café, others were running in the opposite direction. Was Bano still there? Or was she one of those running away?

Lara stood in the doorway. She did not know any of those rushing in the direction of the building, nor any of those coming away from it. Suddenly, without really thinking, she turned and ran the other way. Alone, up a steep slope covered in scrub and broad-leaved trees, she ran. Into the forest, in among the pine trees.

She kept on running, in her stockinged feet, over the soft moss between the trees, down the hill where it began to slope towards the shore, further round Lovers' Path before it got steep. Suddenly there were four boys with her, all running. They crossed the path and stopped at the water's edge, close to the pumping station – a grey brick hut providing water to the island.

'What's going on?' asked Lara.

Up at the top of the campsite, most of the Troms delegation was on its feet.

'We've all got to take deep breaths,' said Mari. 'No need to panic.'

'Stay calm, stay calm,' said Viljar. 'It'll be all right.'

'Bad joke, letting off firecrackers now,' said Geir Kåre Nilssen.

'Those aren't firecrackers,' said Simon.

Anders Kristiansen was listening to the communication radio and checking the tents at the same time. 'Everyone out of their tents,' he ordered.

Julie Bremnes from Harstad stood there, staring at Anders. It was the first time she had seen him so serious. He was alternately listening to the radio and taking the walkie-talkie from his ear to listen in the direction of the landing stage.

Simon, Anders and Viljar looked at each other, the comrades-in-arms, the three friends, the three musketeers of Troms.

'Stay here,' said Anders. 'I'll go and find out what's happening.'

'I'm coming too,' said Brage Sollund. The boy who had attended the Labour Party Congress with Simon two years earlier was now among the seniors on the island.

Anders Kristiansen stopped. New messages were coming over the radio.

'There's something wrong here,' he said in concern. Brage went off to find out.

Viljar was holding tight to his little brother Torje, who was wailing and wanted to run away. People were on the move all around them. The fourteen-year-old was kept there by his brother, three years his senior.

Mari ordered them to take each other's hands. The Troms ring stood firm, in spite of all the people running past them and up into the forest.

'Stay here,' Mari instructed those who wanted to run. 'The policeman said we were to gather in the middle of the island!' That had been the last clear message over the radio. Mari was preoccupied with trying to keep control over her group and shouted, 'No one's to move. Stand still! Stand still! The police are here, there's no need to panic.'

'I want to go home,' Torje whispered to Viljar.

As Brage came up to the café he saw two comrades fall to the ground. First one and then the other. Shot by a policeman! Brage dived into the bushes.

Then the uniformed man entered Mari's field of vision. She was looking in the direction of the café building and saw a girl with dark hair and a grey AUF sweatshirt walking towards the man. She saw the girl say something to him, but could not hear what. When the girl was a few steps away from him, the policeman raised his pistol and shot her.

At that, Mari yelled 'Run!'

'Run! Run!' she yelled to all those who had been holding hands.

Julie was standing between Simon and Anders, having decided that was the safest place.

'Run!' Simon shouted.

'Just run! Don't look back!' cried Anders.

Breivik opened fire on them with the rifle, from a range of thirty or forty metres.

The bullets scorched towards them at eight hundred metres a second. They splintered the trees, smashed into the trunks, hit bodies, a foot, an arm, a shoulder, a back. The young people stumbled, ran on, vanished among the trees.

Back at the campsite Gunnar Linaker, the king of keepers, was lying by a tree stump with his face pressed to the grass. The shot had entered his shoulder and gone through to the back of his head.

Eirin Kjær from Balsfjord tried to drag him with her. He was breathing heavily, very heavily, but she was not able to make any contact with him and she was not strong enough to pull him along.

I shouldn't have left Gunnar, I should have brought him with me, Eirin thought as she ran.

Once the campsite was empty, Breivik strode over to Gunnar and shot him in the neck. The bullet entered the back of his skull on the right-hand side and exited through his right temple. He lost consciousness. But his heart went on beating.

Gunnar's younger sister was lying a short distance from him. Hanne had tripped when the others ran for it; she had got up, started running and fallen into a thicket. Now she just lay there. She had not seen her elder brother being shot, and from where she was lying she could not see anybody. She had no idea her brother was flat on the ground just a few metres away, with massive head injuries.

Neo-Nazis, thought Mari as she ran beside Simon.

'Mari, Mari,' was all Simon said, looking at her.

'You were right, Simon,' Mari gasped. 'Come on!'

When she turned to him again, Simon was gone.

On Lovers' Path she found Anders Kristiansen. He was gabbling so fast it was hard to make out what he was saying. It was as if he could not string his sentences together properly, but then he said: 'I'll ring the police.'

'Yes, do that,' said Mari. 'Good idea.'

Viljar and Torje were running side by side. Torje got out his phone and rang their mother's number, and howled down the line: 'They're shooting us! They're shooting us!' Viljar took it from him. 'It's all right Mum, I'll take care of everybody,' he said as calmly as he could while running.

He rang off.

'Where's Johannes?' cried Torje. 'Johannes!'

His best friend was gone.

The brothers ran along Lovers' Path until they came to a bend where the rusty fence was broken and a log had been wedged across the gap. They skidded down until they got to a rocky ledge that they could hide under.

On the path Mari came across Tonje Brenna, the secretary-general of the AUF.

'What's happening?' Mari asked.

'I don't know. Lie low.'

I'm not bloody well staying anywhere near you, thought Mari. You're a more likely target than any of us.

People were running past each other, going back the way others had come. Utøya did not have many hiding places. It was mainly open spaces with newly mown grass, steep slopes or sparse areas of trees. In many places there was a sheer drop to the water and it was impossible to get down. Beyond the trees, the firing went on. A group of youngsters came to a stop on Lovers' Path, unsure of what to do.

Hønefoss police station had one officer in the operations centre. The station had been under financial pressure for the past year and the chief of police had implemented a series of cost-saving measures, including the introduction of single-person shifts in the operations centre.

In addition to the chief of operations there were five police officers on duty. The officers were watching the news broadcasts in the staff room and discussing whether to have their cars at the ready in case they were called in to assist the Oslo district. The chief of operations in Hønefoss rang her colleague in the capital, but there was no request for reinforcements, so they dropped the matter.

At 17.24 they received an emergency call. It initially went through to the medical emergencies call centre, but was then put through to the police. A man shouted that he was 'the boat driver out here' and that he would try to get to his boat. 'There's a man going round here, shooting,' he said. 'He's dressed as a policeman.'

It was a call from the captain of the MS *Thorbjørn*. 'He's got a machine gun!'

Jon Olsen had just seen his partner Monica being shot. Now he was looking for his elder daughter. 'Ring me if you need the ferry,' he finally got out.

There was a simultaneous call on the other emergency line. A boy blurted out that there was 'shooting everywhere', panic and chaos, and that people had run to 'the edges' of the island.

Suddenly there were red lights on all the incoming lines.

At 17.25, Anders Behring Breivik walked back across the campsite, where Gunnar was lying unconscious.

By then Breivik had killed three people at the landing stage, three by the main entrance, one at the campsite and two on the way there. Now he came round the corner of the long, brown wooden building that housed the café and the main hall, and skirted along the wall.

He wondered whether to go in. There was always a risk attached to entering a building. Someone could be standing behind the door and jump him, set a trap, overpower him. In *World of Warcraft*, the odds always went down if you entered the enemy stronghold.

'What's happening?' an AUF member called to him from a window. Several other heads appeared. This was their first sight of the man in police uniform.

'Somebody's shooting, so stay away from the windows!' the man told them. 'Lie down on the floor and I'll come and help you!'

A girl at the window was holding a pink mobile phone. She had just spoken to her father, a lorry driver who often made deliveries in the Oslo area. Luckily he was safe.

'Let me know if you lot are getting flooded out over there,' her father had said right before the shooting started, 'and I'll come and get you.'

'I'd rather you dropped off a pair of wellies if you happen to be passing, Dad,' Elisabeth answered. She had just finished Year 10 and it was her first time on Utøya. Her face was still that of a child.

'We've run out of dry clothes!' she had laughed.

*

Breivik went into the building. The walls were covered with posters of AUF slogans from over the years. In the corridor there were hundreds of shoes and boots, as no outdoor footwear was allowed in the meeting rooms.

He went calmly into the first room, known as the small hall. He paused for a moment in the doorway to get an overview. The youngsters looked at him, awaiting instructions.

He went over to a group and started shooting.

Several fell to the floor.

Ha, they're faking it, ran through his head. He calmly went round to each of them in turn and ended their lives with a shot to the head.

Some of the youngsters were screaming, standing still as if glued to the floor. They stared at him fixedly, unable to run away, escape, save themselves.

How weird that they're just standing there, thought Breivik. I've never seen that in a movie.

Then he aimed his pistol at them.

Some of them begged for their lives. 'Please don't shoot!'

But he always did.

He shot one girl in mid-scream. His pistol was almost touching her face. He fired into her open mouth. Her skull shattered, but her lips remained unharmed.

By the piano at the end of the room a girl was sitting on a piano stool, resting her head on the keyboard as if unconscious. He shot her in the head. Blood poured out and down between the keys. Standing by the piano, he noticed more kids, hiding behind the instrument. He stood over them, raised his arm and fired into the gap between the wall and the piano. Shot after shot, hit after hit.

Many hid their faces in their hands. The bullets splintered their hands before entering their heads. One of those hiding behind the piano was Ina Libak, a friend of Bano and Lara's from Akershus. A shot went through both her hands and another through the top of her arm. I can survive this, she thought to herself. The next shot got her in the jaw. This was more serious. Eyes closed, she crouched there, trying to hold her jaw in place. She could not see the man who was firing, but she could hear him breathing above them, hear him moving round the piano. Then she felt the impact in her chest. Shots like that kill you, she thought. There was a taste in her mouth she had never had before. Gunpowder. She lost feeling in her arms and thought her hands had been shot off. The taste of bullets mixed with another taste: blood welling in her mouth, over her chin, down over the hands that were holding her jaw in place.

Then the pistol gave a click. The magazine was empty. He had been careful not to fill it right up in case the bullets got stuck. He calmly changed magazines. It took a few seconds, long enough to throw yourself out of a window, get to the door, long enough to escape. Many tried, but there was a crush at the exits.

The bass player of Blondies & Brownies was trapped in the doorway between the small hall and the main hall while Breivik changed his magazine. There the slender, fair-haired girl was hit by one – two – three shots. She slumped to the floor. One of the shots had entered the back of her head on the left side, penetrating her skull and ripping into her brain. Her life ebbed away. There, between the two rooms, Margrethe's life ended. '*Before you judge me, try hard to love me. Look within your heart then ask, have you seen my childhood?*' she had sung with Bano at the karaoke the night before.

Breivik stepped over her. He entered the AUF's largest venue, the main hall, where Bano had been inspired by Gro, where the meeting about Western Sahara had made Mari and Simon want to get involved, where Monica Bøsei had tried to comfort the AUF youngsters with the prospect of lighting all the barbecues.

A boy was hiding behind a loudspeaker. Breivik saw him and opened fire. The boy ducked, several times. Breivik had his work cut out trying to hit him. He fired five or six shots and missed each time.

Frisky type, thought Breivik, then, finally, one of the bullets found its mark. It hit the boy in the head and he fell. To make sure he had finally got the better of his target, he fired twice more.

Elisabeth ran along by the wall; she was calling her father again.

Freddy Lie answered, and heard nothing but screams. His sixteen-year-old daughter was huddled down against the wall, crying into her phone, when Breivik came into the room.

Freddy, who only a few minutes earlier had offered to come and get Elisabeth and her older sister, was in his car. He couldn't do any-thing but listen. What was happening? Was she being attacked? Was she being raped?

The line went dead. When he rang his daughter back, he got a message to say the phone was switched off or had no signal.

The bullet had hit Elisabeth's ear canal, seared through her cra-nium and gone right into her brain and out the other ear. Only when it got to the pink phone cover did the bullet stop. The girl fell side-ways and Breivik shot her twice more. She lay there, no longer moving. Her long, wet blonde hair turned red with blood. Her grey jogging bottoms, her white T-shirt, everything was stained red. Soon her fingers would stiffen in their grip on the pink phone against her head.

Everyone sitting along the wall was shot. The killer used the same method as in the small hall. First he opened fire from a few metres away, then closed in and shot them all down.

I'm wasting ammunition, he told himself. On the other hand, it was an effective method.

The first target was always the head. But as soon as he started shooting, everybody hit the deck. It was difficult to follow what was going on. It wasn't always easy to hit them where he wanted. But he was getting better all the time. He had made sure to buy the best sighting system on the market for both *Gungnir* and *Mjølnir*.

Sometimes it was hard to tell if he had already hit the kids. The rifle made a very small hole, and if a person died instantly the blood stopped pumping, so it was not easy to decide who was dead and who was not. It was better to fire once too often if he was in doubt.

Breivik looked around the main hall. No movement. He went back through the small hall. No movement. He went out.

He had been inside for two to three minutes. It had taken him about a hundred seconds to kill thirteen people. Several were left critically injured. It was 17.29.

The killer crossed the campsite. He shot into a few tents, but it would take far too long to check them one by one, so he moved on.

The chief of operations at Hønefoss police station had started calling in reinforcements. Five minutes had elapsed since the first telephone call, and further calls were queued up on the line. There was no system to notify her staff in case of a crisis, but the officers all had one another's mobile numbers stored on their phones, and got in touch with the colleagues who were not away on holiday.

Four officers, two men and two women, ran into the equipment store to prepare for the operation. They put on protective gear, armed themselves and took communication radio equipment with them. A fifth officer, an older woman, stayed to relieve the chief of operations.

There was no plan in place for what the police operation was going to do. It was clear, however, that they would need a boat. The police boat, a red rubber dinghy, should be made ready.

Nobody thought of the MS *Thorbjørn*. The former military vessel could have taken a large force to the island within minutes. The distance by road from Hønefoss to the *Thorbjørn*'s jetty is thirteen kilometres. Optimally, the police officers could set foot on the island a little more than a quarter of an hour after leaving the station.

But the ferry, which had transported six hundred youngsters to the island in the last few days, was forgotten. The ferry that spent every summer shuttling between the island and the mainland was overlooked in all the hectic preparations.

After Jon Olsen had rung the police, he started searching for his daughter. A thought struck him: Colonel Gaddafi had announced that same week that he would send terrorists to the countries that had

bombed Libya. That must be what was happening! They were bound
to take hostages. He and Monica had talked between themselves several times about how perfect the island would be for holding
hostages.

He did a hasty circuit of the island and then came back to the landing stage where the ferry was tied up. He dashed on board.

In the wheelhouse he found the crewman and a couple of other
youngsters, hiding. Some others came running. Someone on the boat
was ringing the AUF leader, who had been in the admin building near
the landing stage when Breivik came ashore. Someone hammering,
Eskil Pedersen had thought when he heard the bangs over the sound
of the TV. Two of the AUF counsellors went down to check and one
of them came straight back. 'There's someone shooting,' he cried.
They locked the door and opened the veranda door on the first floor
to look out, but could see nothing.

The other counsellor ran down to the boat, and he was the one
ringing now. 'Get down here as fast as you can!'

'What's happened?' asked Eskil.

'Just run!' answered the counsellor.

Apart from the AUF leader, the captain and the crewman, six
people saved themselves by getting onto the boat. They were terrified. They had heard shots and screams. In his panic, the captain
reversed at full speed. He asked everybody to lie down, because the
gunman had telescopic sights, he had seen that much. The time was
17.30.

When they were halfway across, the captain straightened up and
wanted to turn round. He wanted to rescue more people – there was
room for far more than nine. Some youngsters had already jumped
into the cold water, trying to swim away from the island.

Monica was dead and their daughter was still on Utøya. The captain started thinking about a friend who lived near by and had been
in Afghanistan. He kept weapons at home. Perhaps they could get
some guns from him. Jon's thoughts were in turmoil, but the boat
held its usual course for the mooring point on the mainland. Then the
crewman remembered that the policeman had said he was expecting

two others. That meant the ferry landing stage was not safe. The captain was also afraid there could be terrorists there, and that they might seize the boat. They would have to dock somewhere else. The MS *Thorbjørn* changed direction, away from the jetty and out into the fjord.

Meanwhile, people were hiding down at the water's edge around the island. They saw the boat disappear from view. Eskil Pedersen received desperate texts from those still on the island and replied: 'Get away! Hide or swim!'

Then he rang the Labour Party leadership to alert them.

Lara was lying behind some rocks down at the shoreline, thinking about the chainsaw Bano had found the day before. That would have been good to attack and to defend oneself with, she thought. She had left her phone behind when she ran, and she so much wanted to talk to Bano. Bano was bound to have found a good place to hide. Maybe she was hiding in the cellar where the chainsaw was kept. That would be a great hideaway: the door could be bolted from the inside, and then you could pile things up against it so no one could get it open.

But Bano was not hiding indoors. She had been on the edge of the woods by the campsite when Breivik approached the café building. She was with some girls she did not know. Their names were Marte and Maria.

'If there really is a person shooting, then somebody's got to talk to him,' said one of them. 'We've got to ask him to stop,' said the other.

As AUF members they had grown up in a culture of words. The debate must be won. It is the strength of your argument that gives you power. The young people on Utøya this Friday were used to being heard.

'We won't die today, girls. We won't die today!' said Bano as they stood there by the trees. They could hear the shots, but did not know where they were coming from. It was only when they saw a boy being shot down by the café that they ran. Up the hill behind the campsite.

Over harebells and yellow bird's-foot trefoil, over heather and wild strawberries. They ran until they reached Lovers' Path.

On the path they met Anders Kristiansen. He was used to the sound of gunfire from the firing ranges at Bardufoss, where his father worked.

Now he was desperately ringing 112 for the emergency services. But they seemed permanently engaged. Finally he got through.

'There's shooting on Utøya!' he said. But because the local emergency switchboards were jammed, his call was put through to a police district where they still had not heard what was happening on the island. The eighteen-year-old was told he was mistaken. It wasn't shooting on Utøya, it was a bomb in Oslo.

Futile. Anders hung up.

They went further along the path. There were lots of them. They squatted down, poised to run. Beneath them, a long way below, the Tyrifjord lapped against the rocks. Some people were running by barefoot or in their stockinged feet.

On the path they were discussing whether it was genuine, or just some kind of joke.

'It just isn't funny to fool around like that,' said one girl.

'Maybe it's some sort of PR stunt,' a boy suggested.

The young people huddled down behind a slight rise in the ground. Sitting there, they could no longer see the café building where the last shots had gone off. That must mean that those firing could not see them either.

Then they heard heavy footsteps in the heather.

One boy suggested lying down in strange positions and pretending to be dead. It was too late to run away, after all.

Bano lay down on her side with one arm under her and the other thrown out at an angle. She had pulled the fluorescent yellow hood of the red sailing jacket half over her hair. On her feet she had the size 38 wellington boots.

Anders bent down beside her. He, who from his earliest years had always liked to have an overview, lay down on the ground. He who had learned rhetoric from Obama and was passionate about parliamentary debate found no more words. This eighteen-year-old who had fought wars in the forest with a gun carved out of wood now lay down to play dead. He put his arm around Bano.

The uniformed man had reached the slight rise, a few metres from them.

'Where the hell is he?' he asked.

Nobody answered.

He started at the right-hand end.

First he shot a boy.

Then he shot Bano.

Then he shot Anders.

The shots were fired at intervals of just a few seconds.

> Our dear little moon, shines down on those
> Who have no bed and have no home

The two girls who had been with Bano on the edge of the woods when it all started were near the end of the row. They were holding hands. A bedtime song was going round in Marte's head. It had come to her as she lay, listening as shot followed shot.

> May all the world's little ones sleep tonight
> May none of us cry, may none be forsaken

The song had soothed her when she was little and it soothed her now. She lay quite still, eyes closed.

Marte and Maria had only just joined the youth organisation and were on Utøya for the first time, to see whether it was the sort of thing for them. Their faces were turned to each other. They were wearing their new AUF sweatshirts. The flame logos on the chest were turned to the ground.

Marte stole an upward glance and saw a pair of muddy black army boots, and above them a chequered reflective band.

Then a bullet hit her best friend in the head. Maria's body jerked, and the twitching ran down into her hand.

Her grip slackened.

Seventeen years is not a long life, thought Marte.

Another shot rang out. It was as if a current ran through her body, as if someone was playing drums in her head. There was a glitter in front of her eyes.

Then everything faded out. The ground beneath her disappeared, and then all sound.

Blood ran down her face and covered the hands her head was resting on. So much blood. I'm dying now, she thought.

The boy beside her was shot several times; he reached out his hand and said, 'I'm dying.'

'Help, I'm dying, help me,' he begged.

But there was no one there to help him. Marte wanted to, but she could not move. He gave a jerk, but went on breathing. His breathing got quieter and quieter, until it stopped.

Breivik had put a bullet or two in each of them. Then he had gone back and shot them again. Those who had tried to get up were shot more times; one boy had five bullets in his body.

The weapons could be lethal over a distance of up to a couple of kilometres. Here, the gunman stood at the feet of his victims and aimed at their heads. The bullets expanded and fragmented when they made contact with tissue.

The killer was surprised by the sound emitted by people's heads when he shot them in the skull. It was a sort of *ah*, an exhalation, a breath. How interesting, he thought. I had no idea.

The sound did not always come, but usually it did; he wondered about it each time he killed a person.

Twenty-five spent cartridge cases were strewn around them, some on top of their bodies. Five from the pistol, twenty from the rifle.

The smell of blood, vomit and urine hung about the eleven on the path. Two minutes earlier, the smell had been of rain, earth and fear.

From somewhere in the middle of the group came a faint moaning. Before long there was nothing but little cheeps. And then there was silence.

Marte's brain was bleeding. Burnt gunpowder fouled the wound in her head. Then she too lost consciousness.

A few raindrops hit the ground.

'Psst, Ylva, come here so I can cover you.'

Simon sat crouched on Lovers' Path. Ylva Schwenke, one of the youngest girls from Troms, crept towards him. 'Come here,' whispered Simon, holding out his hand. He had been helping people get over the log. He was strong. They could hang on to him until they got a foothold and then let go and run to hide.

'Girls first,' he said gallantly. The shots were getting closer.

Two Troms girls came towards him, holding on to each other. Eirin Kjær was carrying Sofie Figenschou, who had been shot in the shoulder and stomach as she ran across the campsite. While the two were lifted down, the queue built up. Tonje Brenna, standing at the bottom to make sure people got down all right, needed assistance. Mari, who had been up on the path, went down to help. Simon gently lifted the badly wounded girl and passed her down.

This was a winding section of the path. Not far away, round a couple of bends, the killer kicked the eleven on the ground to make sure they were dead.

He was finished there. So he moved on along Lovers' Path.

The island was still.

Where had they all gone?

Then he saw a hole in the fence. A log wedged across it at an angle.

Mari saw the policeman coming.

That's the man who's shooting, he's the one shooting us, she thought the instant before she jumped. She slid down the cliff; her foot broke on landing. People were jumping over her. She lay down flat on the ground.

Simon came leaping down the cliff towards the water.

A voice called out.

'Simon!'

The voice reached the jumping boy in mid-leap. It was Margrethe, his companion on the romantic walk along Lovers' Path the night before.

'Come here!' she called.

Simon threw himself towards her. The rock ledge was full, but they managed to make space for him.

The murderer looked over the log and down the steep drop. He would not be able to get down to the water. It was easy to lose one's balance with all that gear, and he would have difficulty getting up again.

He caught sight of something brightly coloured behind a bush. Lying hidden in the scrub and undergrowth were more kids he could murder.

'I will kill you all, Marxists!' he shouted gleefully, raising *Gungnir*.

He shot three girls at the top of the cliff. None of them died instantly, but they soon bled to death.

Breivik saw a foot sticking out from under an overhanging rock and fired again. The shot hit the ankle. Simon screamed. He plunged from the rock ledge. Did he fall or did he jump? Those left sitting did not know. He flew down the cliff face, he hovered, he seemed to hang in the air, before a bullet caught him in the back.

He landed on a rock, without bracing himself, without a shout. His arms dangled down. His feet were barely touching the ground. His left hand was clenched round a *snus* tin. In his right hand, Margrethe's warmth would last for a little longer.

Then Viljar was shot.

Viljar and Torje had been sitting at the other end of the rock ledge as the shots came closer. They were squeezed further and further along until they were entirely unprotected. Torje wanted to go, Viljar wanted to stay. When the shots hit the cliff face above them, Torje jumped first.

The brothers landed at the water's edge.

The bullets came fast. Viljar took one in the shoulder and dropped to the ground. He stood up to run and was hit in the thigh. He fell again, and tried to get up. He lurched to his feet and was almost upright when he was hit once more and toppled back down.

There was a buzzing and whining in his ears as he knelt at the water's edge, and then another shot went right through his arm.

His little brother was howling.

'Torje! Get away!!' cried Viljar. Torje must not see him like this.

He tried to kick water at his brother to make him run away from the bullets.

He got up once again, and staggered. Blood was running down his body.

The fifth shot hit him in the eye and shattered his cranium. He keeled over. Five bullets had fragmented inside his body. The bullet in his head had splintered into little bits that were now embedded in his brain tissue. One bit had stopped just millimetres short of his brain stem. His shoulder and arm had been virtually shot away. Half his left hand had gone.

But it was Torje he was thinking of.

The little brother he should be looking after.

'Torje,' he whispered.

There was no answer from Torje.

Shots were raining down on the young people at the shoreline.

Ylva Schwenke, the fourteen-year-old that Simon had lifted down from the path, had been hit in both thighs and in the stomach. Then in the neck. She pressed her hand over the bullet wound as she cried out to her childhood friend who was lying right beside her.

'Viljar, I'm dying!'

'Oh no you're not,' he answered from the water's edge. He could no longer see.

In films you die when one bullet hits you, thought Ylva. How could she still be alive when she had been shot four times? It's impossible to survive that, she thought, and lay there waiting for the light.

But no light came. So she had to try to stem the bleeding instead.

'I think I've been shot in the eye.' It was Viljar.

She looked at him. 'Oh shit!' she said. That was all, because she didn't know what you say to someone who has been shot in the eye.

Eirin was lying a little further up. 'Please don't shoot, I don't want to die,' she had shouted when her leg gave way under her. A bullet was lodged in her knee. Then she was hit in the back. The bullet came out her front, and now there was blood spurting from her stomach. I'm going to bleed to death, she thought as she lay there on the shingle, coming to terms with it. They were definitely all going to die. The girl beside her had been shot in the shoulder and stomach, one lung and one arm, and was drifting in and out of consciousness. It was Cathrine, the elder sister of Elisabeth who had been shot through the ear while she was talking to their father on her pink phone.

A girl with deep wounds in her back and legs tried to use her arms to drag herself to some sort of cover. She slipped back into the water, where she lay coughing up blood. A couple of boys pulled her out of the water before retreating to their hiding places.

'Tell Dad I love him,' they heard her say.

The whole thing had taken the gunman two minutes.

It was 17.35.

He moved on.

Viljar lay at the water's edge, trying to orientate himself around his body. He discovered that his fingers were just hanging by some scraps of skin. He could see nothing out of one eye, and put his hand up to it. He could feel that there was something wrong with his head. He ran his hand over his skull and felt something soft. He was touching his brain. He took his hand away quickly.

Viljar's skull had been shattered.

Bits of his brain were outside his head.

But he was thinking. He was thinking that it was important to breathe, not to pass out, not to give up. He was thinking about things that made him happy. That he would go home to Svalbard and drive a snowmobile. He thought about a girl he wanted to kiss.

Then he went very cold and started to convulse. He was shaking. Consciousness came and went.

'This is going all right Simon, we'll get through this together,' he said to his friend who was hanging over the rock beside him.

Viljar was rambling. 'We can deal with it, Simon,' he said, and started to hum.

He told jokes, he sang, he called to Torje.

'Shush, he might come back and then he'll get us,' said the others around him.

But Viljar did not hear them.

Oh if I could write in the heavens, yours is the name I would write... sang Viljar.

And if my life were a sailing ship...

Torje had thought his brother was running along beside him, until he looked round and saw Viljar fall, get up and fall again. He stopped and cried out. Then he turned, ran out into the water and started to swim.

What Torje had seen was instantly wiped out of his mind. He would have no memory of the shots hitting his elder brother.

He swam along the edge of the island and found a large crevice in the limestone cliff. Standing in it, he had water up to his neck. He was there all alone at first, then others came to join him. Those swimming past heard a small, red-haired boy screaming.

'Where's Viljar? Where's Viljar?'

At 17.38, the first patrol left Hønefoss police station. Nobody at the station had a very clear idea of where Utøya was despite the fact that the island lay in their district and was visited every year by the Labour Prime Minister or party leader. Now they had checked it on the map.

The two officers in the first patrol had pistols and sub-machine guns and were wearing body armour. The tactical commander had ordered them to drive towards Utøya and 'observe'.

They went at full speed, blue lights flashing.

As they drove, Breivik was moving south across the island. He had now reloaded the Glock and the rifle several times. He had to avoid running out of ammunition in both weapons simultaneously. Sometimes he changed magazines even though he had a few rounds left. He had got through a lot of bullets, but he still had more.

He fired at someone swimming. Between the trees he spied two figures. A Norwegian man and an Arab woman, he would later call them. They looked very disorientated, he thought.

One of them was Johannes, Torje's best friend from Svalbard.

When the Troms contingent had scattered in panic, all fleeing in different directions, the others had lost track of Johannes. He had run towards the southern tip of the island and hidden there, then he had run back on his own, into the woods.

Breivik stood there quietly, waiting for them to come closer. He did not raise his weapon; that would only make them turn and run. No, he waited.

As Breivik raised his weapon, Johannes cried out to the girl.

'Run! Run!'

The bullets were faster. Three slammed into Johannes. Two into Gizem. Johannes was fourteen. Gizem had just turned seventeen.

––––––––

'Daddy! I want a hug!'

'No, not now, I haven't got time.'

'Cuddle,' shouted Eilif. But his father just snatched up his keys and police badge from the shelf by the door at home in Hønefoss. Håvard Gåsbakk put his foot down and raced to the police station, ignoring the red lights. As he swung into the station, he almost crashed into patrol number two, which was just on its way out of the car park.

The experienced police officer had been following the TV coverage of the explosion in Oslo. Gas tanks underneath the government quarter was his first thought. Then al-Qaida. Gåsbakk had been a member of Delta, the emergency response unit, before he and his family moved to Hønefoss, where police life revolved round thefts from the local supermarket and the occasional brawl. The most daring thing he ever did these days was to climb to the top of the forty-metre pine tree on his property, which gave him a view over the whole of the Tyrifjord.

As Nordre Buskerud started calling in reinforcements, he had a call from a friend, occupying the line.

'So terrorism's reached Norway now,' said Gåsbakk.

'Yes, your lot will have to mobilise round the local town hall!'

They chatted for a quarter of an hour. Only after he hung up, did Gåsbakk did notice that a colleague had rung and left a message on his answering machine: 'Come in to work. There's shooting on Utøya.'

The patrol on the way out of the car park spotted Gåsbakk arriving and informed the chief of operations that a more senior officer was now at the station and should take over as on-scene commander.

Gåsbakk dashed into the station, put on his uniform and body armour, unlocked the weapons room and saw a sniper rifle on a shelf. He took that in addition to his own MP5, because the local marksman was on holiday. He fetched radio equipment and the keys to one of the police cars. Now he had to get to the island as fast as he could.

He got in the police car, but it would not start. Dammit – flat battery. There was an emergency starter in the garage and he finally got the engine going. In common with all other police cars in Norway, this one had no data transmission display. All agreements, all communication, had to be oral. Amid the constant flow of messages on the communications radio his mobile kept ringing, from the same number. It rang and he rejected the call, it rang, he rejected, he kept on pressing the button until he finally had to take it and say, 'I don't give a toss about the raspberries. Don't ring again!' It was an old friend of his mother's who had picked some raspberries for them. They were ready for collection.

Håvard Gåsbakk took the road to Utøya.

At 17.42, as Gåsbakk listened to his phone message about the shooting on Utøya, a task force of twenty-six men left the capital. It was his old colleagues of the emergency response unit – Delta – redeployed from the government quarter, now heading for Utøya, thirty-eight kilometres away. These were heavy vehicles, the roads were wet from the rain and there was a lot of traffic. On the way, they overtook a series of ambulances that had been mobilised.

They also swept past Viljar and Torje's parents, who had not heard

anything from the boys since Torje cried on the phone and Viljar tried
to reassure them.

Their parents, Christin Kristoffersen and Sveinn Are Hanssen, had
come down from icy Svalbard for the holidays and were visiting
friends in Oslo while the boys were at the summer camp. They
exchanged looks as a convoy of heavy black vehicles with flashing blue
lights thundered by.

'What's *happening?*'

It was as if all the air had been forced out of them. It was hard to
breathe. The last vehicle left a swishing sound in its wake.

Just before Sollihøgda, the boys' parents were stopped. A roadblock was being set up, right in front of their car. Christin leapt out.

'My boys are on the island! Let us through!'

But it was no good. She tried to force herself past the roadblock.

'You won't get through here,' said the policeman. 'There are lots
more of us. And we're faster than you.'

Christin realised it would be impossible either to get past by car
or to run to Utøya on foot. She went back to the car, where Sveinn
Are was sitting quietly. Perhaps they would open the road soon. There
had still been nothing on the news about an incident on Utøya.

Mustafa had bought all the parts for the shower cabinet before he
took Ali to the football championship in Sweden. He usually shopped
where things were cheapest, and then assembled them himself to
make what he needed. At the hardware store in Ski he had had them
cut him a 70x120 centimetre sheet to hide the pipework at the side
of the cabinet. Bano had always complained that it did not look very
nice with the pipes showing.

The only thing still missing was a handle for the sliding door.
'Typical Dad work,' Bano would say if the shower was still unfinished
when the girls got back from Utøya. 'Those doors will never get
handles,' she would say. 'It's like all the jobs Dad does round the
house.'

The whole family complained about the bathroom. The bathtub
was old and stained, and the walls and floor were so ingrained with

grime after years of use that they had lost their original colour. Bayan tried to mop under the bath but she couldn't get to it; the floor was always wet and the ceiling was sagging with damp. Mustafa had installed an extractor fan but it did not help. His wife wanted to get a plumber in, but Mustafa was, after all, a mechanical engineer who specialised in water and drains, so that was out of the question.

He wanted to surprise the girls with a brand-new bathroom when they got back from Utøya. So on his return from Sweden, he went to the big store in Ski to buy a handle for the sliding door. That was where he was when he got the calls, first from Ali and then from Bano, about the bomb in Oslo.

Now he was on his way home with the shiny new handle.

The radio was on in the car.

They were talking about who could be behind the Oslo bomb when a text message came through to Mustafa's phone:

> Welove you more than anything in the world banoANDlara
> theres a man with a gunHere will ring when we are safe

It was tricky typing on the boy's phone; it did not have the same settings as hers. Lara had wondered whether to send the text, because she did not know where Bano was. She dared not tell her parents. So many shots, it never ended! And every single shot could be Bano. Lara and the four boys were still hiding in the bay beyond the little pumping station, where lots of the young people were now gathered.

Her father replied.

> what's happening?

A few minutes later, Lara texted again.

> Somebody shooting don't know where Bano is

Then her father wrote:

Can you ring me?

There was no answer. He sent another message.

I know it not true, you are not Bano or Lara

A new message from the same unknown number lit up his screen.

We love you so much. But somethings happened

It was 17.47.

At the same time, the joint operational centre in Oslo sent out a message to all units.

'01 with important message to all. In connection with both the explosion in the government quarter and the shooting on Utøya in Nordre Buskerud it has been observed that the suspect is wearing a police or security guard uniform – out.'

When the message went out over the radio, more than two hours had passed since Andreas Olsen, the guards in the government quarter and other eyewitnesses had first reported that the man was in uniform.

Five minutes later, at 17.52, the local patrol from Nordre Buskerud police station reached the MS *Thorbjørn* jetty. On the way there, the officers in the car had been informed by their chief of operations: 'Helicopter on its way, possibly also Delta.' They were told to exercise caution, and to wait for the police boat.

When they got out of the car they could hear the shots. They were being fired in a steady stream, controlled and distinct, from two different weapons, never simultaneous or from more than one place on the island at the same time. From this they deduced that it was a lone perpetrator.

The two policemen were standing on the jetty observing, as they had been ordered to do. Observe, and wait for the police boat. They were heavily armed. And they stood waiting, while the shots rang out on the other side of the strait.

Official police instructions are that when the situation is defined as 'shooting in progress', officers are obliged to make a direct intervention. No such actions were undertaken.

Utøya was six hundred metres away.

On a sunny day, there would have been lots of boats in the fjord. Today, it was empty. The boats lay moored close by. The local patrol made no attempt to fetch one to approach Utøya. They did nothing but listen to the shots.

Since there was a clear line of sight over to the island, the patrol was worried about being shot at. The officers took refuge behind a container on the jetty. Three minutes after arrival, at 17.55, the patrol reported that the rendezvous point would have to be moved up to the road. Eventually one of them went up to the road to direct the traffic and clear the way for the emergency response unit. The two officers lost connection.

Nordre Buskerud police district had a boat of its own, a red rubber dinghy, which was kept in a trailer outside the police station. But it was not kept in a state of readiness. The incident commander had to inflate the boat and put petrol in the engine. The Hønefoss fire service, on the other hand, had a large and steady boat ready and waiting at the quay by the fire station. They rang at an early stage and offered assistance, but their offer was turned down because the local police had their own boat. When the police station later rang back to ask to use the fire boat after all, they could not get through. The chief of operations rang the fire station again and again, but she was dialling the wrong number.

Neither the emergency response unit coming from Oslo nor Håvard Gåsbakk on his way from Hønefoss had been given any definite information about where to rendezvous. Gåsbakk, however, took it for granted that it would be at the MS *Thorbjørn* jetty, straight across from the island.

The Delta emergency response unit did not know where Utøya

was. The first patrol had GPS in its vehicle, but the small islands in the Tyrifjord were not named on the system. The Delta troops in the black cars tried to make contact with Nordre Buskerud police to get definite instructions about where to meet and to alert them to the fact that extra boats would be needed for their personnel. But the emergency network did not yet extend as far as Nordre Buskerud and analogue police radio coverage only worked until Sollihøgda, which was halfway there. Consequently, the telephone was the only form of communication open to them, but the switchboard of the local operations centre was jammed with incoming calls and did not answer the emergency response unit's call.

The lack of communication made it impossible to use the journey time to plan or coordinate the operation. When the Nordre Buskerud operations centre was finally informed that Delta was on its way, it was given no indication of how large a force it would be, or that it was coming by road. Right up until 18.00, the local chief of operations assumed the response unit was arriving by helicopter and would fly directly to Utøya.

When this was finally clarified, a fatal misunderstanding ensued. When Nordre Buskerud informed the response unit where to rendezvous, it said 'meet on the jetty'.

'Which jetty?' asked the Delta man. 'Do you mean the jetty at the golf course?' It was the only place he knew by the Tyrifjord.

The chief of operations at Hønefoss held the line while she turned to the chief of staff, who had just come into the station, and said, 'Delta says the rendezvous point is at the golf course.'

The chief of staff, on the phone to someone ringing from Utøya, merely nodded and the chief of operations said to Delta:

'Okay, let's say the golf course.'

The meeting point was thus moved to a location 3.6 kilometres from the island. The original spot where the patrol from Nordre Buskerud was observing, and where Håvard Gåsbakk was headed, was only six hundred metres from Utøya.

The occupants of the first vehicle in the response unit convoy had not been told that the meeting point had changed. At 18.01 they turned off the main road and followed the track down to Utvika Camping, next to MS *Torbjørn*'s jetty. The car drove down to the water, where there were several boats. If they had taken one of the boats moored there, they could have been over on the island within minutes. But here the driver received a radio message instructing him to turn round and go back up the track again. The cars behind did the same manoeuvre, leaving the jetty. Then they were up on the main road again, heading away from the island.

Gåsbakk had almost reached the *Thorbjørn*'s landing stage when he was instructed to turn round and drive to the golf course.

Breivik was killing an average of one person a minute.

He was standing by a low red building known as the schoolhouse. No doubt lots of them were hiding in there, he thought. He fired through the door and heard girls' screams. He tugged at the door, but on the other side was a man from Norwegian People's Aid, keeping the handle firmly in place. The room was full of people. Breivik gave up on the schoolhouse. The risk of trying to fight his way in was too great. In the Pelican case he had a can of diesel, which he had planned to pour round buildings and set light to them, so he could shoot people as they came out.

But he had no lighter on him, so he went back up to the café building to look for one.

He had now shot and killed forty people on the island. It was time to give himself up; that would increase his chances of surviving the operation. But he had left his mobile in the van with the bomb.

He did not find a lighter, but he found a mobile phone. He rang the emergency number, 112, and was put on hold. After several attempts he got an answer from the operation centre at Hønefoss. It was 18.01.

'Police emergency line.'

'Yes, good afternoon, my name is Commander Anders Behring Breivik of the Norwegian Anti-communist Resistance Movement.'

'Yes.'

'I'm on Utøya at the moment. I want to give myself up.'

'Okay, what number are you calling from?'

'I'm calling on a mobile.'

'You're calling from your mobile?'

'Well, it's not my mobile, another one . . . ' replied the man on Utøya, and the call cut out.

'Another one, what's your name? Hello . . . hello . . . !'

It was a mobile with no SIM card that Breivik had found, so the number did not come up on the screen at the local police station, and he was never called back.

He had better carry on, then. Along the path he met a dog that was running around crazily. He had not seen anyone to kill for a long time; where were they all?

He went along by the water. At the point they had named Stoltenberget he came across a few youngsters and shot and killed three. At the bathing area known as Bolsjevika he found another group, and killed five. The water's edge gradually became more inaccessible. He went inland again.

One little gang, lying flat in the tall grass, heard his footsteps. But they could not run, they could not get away, because they were holding a life in their hands.

Ina's life.

After Breivik had left the café building, Ina crawled from behind the piano. She managed to drag herself out of the hall, holding her jaw in place. When she got to the campsite she collapsed. Somebody lifted her over to the skateboard ramp just alongside.

'She's not going to make it,' Ina heard them whisper. Then one girl took the lead.

'We'll take a wound each,' she commanded. That was how they were sitting around her now, as they heard Breivik approaching, each pressing a stone to one of Ina's wounds. A woman from Norwegian People's Aid was lying on the ground with the injured girl resting on top of her, keeping her warm. But Ina was steadily losing blood.

One of the kids pressing stones to Ina's wounds had wanted to run and look for his sister, but was told: 'We need you here.' That's when they had seen the man in uniform behind the tall stems of grass. 'All lie bloody still,' said the girl who had taken charge.

He was going down Lovers' Path.

If he looked right, he would see them.

But he looked straight ahead.

He stopped at a little grey hut he thought must be an outside toilet. He balanced his way down the side of the hut carefully, because it was steep on both sides. He saw one person, then another, then more, a big group of them sitting there, pressed right up against the wall of the little pumping station. Breivik was still a short distance from them.

'Have you seen him?' he asked.

Nobody answered.

'Do you know where the last shots came from?' he asked.

Nobody moved.

'We haven't caught the gunman yet, but there's a boat down by the water ready to evacuate you. Can you gather together? You've got to come right away!'

A couple of girls got up hesitantly. They approached him tentatively. He looked at their faces; some looked relieved, others more sceptical.

'You've got to hurry up, before the terrorist comes. We haven't got him yet.'

A couple more young people stood up and came towards him.

'Have you got ID? Can you prove you're a real policeman?' one of them asked.

A seventeen-year-old from the Oslo suburbs was one of those making her way towards him. She saw him suddenly give way to irritation, as if frustrated that they were not coming fast enough. He fired a shot. Andrine threw herself into the water. From there, she saw that the girl who had been standing beside her was lying on the ground. Then she saw her best friend Thomas shot. First in the neck, then in the head.

A girl cried, 'Help, please!'

Breivik blasted her down. Then he mowed down those running up the steep slope.

Andrine felt sudden pressure against her chest. Her neck, her throat, her mouth were filling with blood. A bullet had entered her breast and stopped a few millimetres short of her spine; her lung was punctured. She lay in the shallow water, unable to breathe. She was drowning in blood. Her eyes were wide open. If I close them I shall die, she thought, fighting for air. She saw the man shoot everyone who had stayed by the pumping station. He went over to every single one of them and held his pistol a few centimetres from their heads. And fired and fired and fired.

Then the killer stopped. He looked round. Surveyed the prone bodies, turned and went up the slope. Then suddenly he swung back round. He stopped, smiled and raised his weapon again.

He aimed at her. He looked right at her. The shot went through her wellington boot and her foot. Bullets splashed into the water and ricocheted off the rocks all about her, sending chips of stone flying into her face.

He took aim at her again. Now I'm going to die, she thought. It's over.

Breivik pressed the trigger.

A boy leapt up.

Andrine thought she was dead when she saw the boy jump forward. He took one bullet – two bullets – three bullets that were meant for her. The first hit him in the hip. The next went into his back and out through his chest. The third crushed his head. He slumped down; he was dead.

He was Henrik Rasmussen from Hadsel in Nordland. Andrine did not know him. But he had been crouched on the slope, hiding, and had seen her hit repeatedly. So he jumped out in front of her.

Henrik had turned eighteen that February. The last thing he did before setting off to Utøya was to lead an anti-racism event in his home district.

'Hoho!' cheered Breivik.

Then he went. Andrine looked round her. They were all dead. Some were lying face down in the water, others curled into the foetal position. One skull had been cleft in two. The brain lay exposed.

Andrine waited to die. She waited for all the blood to run out of her. She wanted a white casket at her funeral, completely white. But how could she let people know?

She could not die. If she did, the sacrifice of the boy she did not know would have been in vain.

Lara had thrown herself into the cold water and started to swim when she heard the first shots from the pumping station. It was about quarter past six.

As she swam, she could hear shots and screams. Someone begged for their life. 'Please, don't shoot! I want to live!'

On this side of the island, the water had worn cavities into the limestone. She swam along to one of them but it was already full. She swam on, and was able to get into the next one. In there, she was hidden from all angles.

She saw boats in the channel beyond. Campers and people from the summer cottages dotted round the fjord's edge were pulling frozen, terrified youngsters out of the water.

Ina and her helpers had also heard the shots from the pumping station. Shots, screams, cries, shots. One of those compressing her wounds whispered, 'They're dying, they're dying, they're dying,' over and over again. Then it all went very quiet.

Ina's own strength was failing. She had lost a lot of blood. Lying there drowsily, she saw a raindrop glistening on a leaf.

Just imagine something being so beautiful, here, now, she thought.

In Salangen, Gunnar had the phone in his hand. Just after six he had seen a line of text running along the bottom of the TV screen. 'Shooting on Utøya', it said.

'Tone!'

'Tone!!! There's something on here about a shooting on Utøya.'

Simon's mum came rushing in. She burst into tears.

'My boy!' she cried.

'But you know, Tone, our Simon's a fast runner and a good swimmer, so he'll be fine,' Gunnar reassured her.

But panic had seized Tone. She had to gasp for breath.

'It's bound to be some disagreement between a couple of individuals. We mustn't worry, there's nothing to indicate Simon's involved. There are lots of people on the island, after all.'

But Tone was still anxious.

A few minutes passed. There was no more information about Utøya. 'I've got to find out about this,' muttered Gunnar and rang the number from which Simon had last called them.

'Hello, excuse me, this is Gunnar Sæbø, Simon's father,' he said. 'Simon just rang us from this phone.'

'There's a lunatic going round here shooting. I can't talk,' Julie Bremnes whispered back.

'But have you seen Simon?'

'Er, no, we were running together but then we spread out, I haven't seen Simon for a bit,' whispered the sixteen-year-old, who was lying in a bay a little beyond the steep slope. 'I'm hiding, I can't talk any more,'

'The girl was taking cover, she could only whisper,' Gunnar told Tone. 'We can't ring again, we can't ring any more. It might get someone hurt.' But they called the numbers rolling across the screen. Numbers for next of kin, it said. They never got through.

Tone stood there crying. 'My boy! My child!'

Gunnar rang the friends whose birthday party they had been invited to that Friday evening.

'We're going to be a bit late,' he said. 'We'll come as soon as we've made sure Simon's okay.'

'Now it's fucking kicked off.'

As the massacre at the pumping station was in progress, around thirty men from Delta, plus the local police, arrived at the bridge by the golf course.

Their banter was irreverent.

'Terror on Norwegian soil.'

'Yeah, it's started with a bang.'

They had been informed that their target was wearing a police uniform. Like the Taliban in Afghanistan, thought Gåsbakk. They were also fond of putting on police uniforms, to infiltrate the population before they attacked.

The message that this was, in all likelihood, a young, blond man in a police uniform had not reached them.

As Delta established itself at the rendezvous point, the police boat put in at a stone buttress just below the bridge. The heavily armed officers lost no time going aboard. They were eager to get on with the operation; they were in action mode now and wanted to get there the quickest possible way. 'That's about it,' called the boat driver. The red dinghy was registered to carry ten people, and the officers were heavy: each of them had about thirty kilos of equipment, on top of shields and battering rams. With just the driver on board, the bow was steady, but as the men moved about to go further back in the boat and make space for the others water came in over the sides, down into the bottom and over the fuel tank.

'I'm going to be part of this,' was the general attitude. 'We're going over to take him out. We're saving lives here.' Nobody wanted to be left behind. Nobody wanted to miss the action. With ten of them on board, the driver called a halt.

The boat was lifted from the rock it had been resting on. It suddenly sank so far down that the sides were just a hand's breadth above the water.

'Hit the gas, top speed!' called Håvard Gåsbakk as the boat puttered slowly along. 'Hit the gas!' he shouted again to the boat driver.

'I'm at full acceleration,' answered the driver. 'It doesn't go any faster.'

After a few hundred metres the engine started to sputter, before giving up completely. There they all sat, ten heavyweights armed to the teeth, in a rubber dinghy bobbing on the waves. Some of them started loosening their suits. If the boat sank, they would sink with it, forced down by the weight of their gear. They cursed. They cackled. They swore.

They heard the salvoes from the island.

A holidaymaker came to their rescue. He slowed down so the wash from his boat would not swamp the red rubber dinghy. It was lying so low in the water that any sudden manoeuvre could swamp it.

The heavily armed special forces officers were standing in water up to their knees and the fuel tank and fuel hose were floating around with the paddles and other equipment. The first thing to be heaved over into the camper's boat was a shield. Then the officers moved over into the boat one by one, while the boat owner transferred to the red rubber dinghy. Once in it, he had no option but to take to the oars.

One of the policemen raised a hand in the air and cried, 'Many thanks, comrade!' Then they headed for Utøya.

But again they made slow progress, because this boat, too, was overloaded.

Another craft came alongside, and four men jumped over into it.

Finally they picked up speed. Both boats accelerated. But all the transfers had wasted precious time.

Anders Behring Breivik was surprised that Delta had not turned up. He saw a helicopter circling overhead and thought it must be the police. He was amazed at how low it came, because he knew the helicopter had a thermal-imaging camera that could detect signs of life from a distance, even through vegetation. The helicopter was in a two-hundred-metre line of fire. He could have brought it down with ten shots, but that would mean revealing his location, if they had not already seen him. Why didn't they shoot him? Perhaps the helicopter was just reporting back to Delta on where to deploy when it reached the island.

A thought occurred to him. Did he in fact want to survive this? He thought of all the demonisation that was to come. He had everything he needed to kill himself, and if he was going to do it, he should do it now.

He weighed up his life for a moment.

He came down on the side of living.

He had to keep to the plan. Phase one was the manifesto, phase two was the bomb and Utøya, phase three was the trial.

All at once he felt a huge urge to survive. He thought about ways of surrendering, to ensure he would be able to continue to phase three. He feared it would be difficult to capitulate. Delta would execute him at the first opportunity.

He had no armour and there was not much ammunition left now. Seeing another abandoned mobile phone, he decided to ring the police again. It was 18.26. He had been on the island for over an hour. This time he got through quickly. But not to where he wanted. An error at a base station meant that all calls from NetCom accounts were transferred to Søndre Buskerud police district.

'Police emergency line.'

'Good afternoon, my name is Anders Behring Breivik.'

'Yes, hello.'

'I am Commander of the Norwegian resistance movement.'

'Yes, hello.'

'Can you put me through to the Delta operations manager?'

'Yes . . . where do you come in, and what's it about?'

'I'm on Utøya.'

'You're on Utøya, yes.'

'I have completed my operation, so I want to . . . give myself up.'

'You want to give yourself up, yes.'

'Yes.'

'What did you say your name was?'

'Anders Behring Breivik.'

'And you were a commander of . . . ?'

'Knights Templar Europe, the organisation is called, but we are organised in . . . the anti-communist resistance movement against the Islamisation of Europe and Norway.'

'Yes.'

'We have just carried out an operation on behalf of the Knights Templar.'

'Yes . . . '

'Europe and Norway.'

'Yes . . . '

'And in view of the fact that the operation is complete, then . . . it's acceptable to surrender to Delta.'

'You want to surrender to Delta?'

'Can you . . . can you put me through to the chief of operations at Delta?'

'Well, the thing is, you're talking to someone with, er, in a way, superior authority.'

'Okay, just find out what you need to and then call me on this phone here, all right?'

'Hmm, but what telephone number?'

'Brilliant, bye.'

'I haven't got that telephone number. Hello?'

Once more Breivik had called from a mobile without a working SIM card, one from which you could only make emergency calls. The operator therefore could not see the telephone number on the screen.

The *Commander of the anti-communist resistance movement against the Islamisation of Europe and Norway* decided to carry on until he was neutralised.

He went south. He followed the pebbles on the beach.

The fastest boat reached the island at 18.27. Four men from the emergency response unit were dropped off at the landing stage. Some AUF members came running up and pointed north, to Bolsjevika and Stoltenberget.

'He's there! He's there!'

That was the last place where Breivik had shot anyone. But since then he had come past the landing stage, via his base at the back of the main building, where he had rung 112, and then gone south.

Delta moved north while Breivik headed for the southern tip of the island.

As he approached the southern tip he saw a bunch of people partly hidden by bushes and undergrowth. They did not see him coming. He realised he had been here before. There were lots of dead and wounded bodies strewn on the ground. Some people were standing in the water, a little way out. The terrain was flat here, with no steep places or sheer cliffs; the island sloped gradually into the water.

A couple of girls noticed the uniformed man approaching.

'Oh, police! Police! Help us, help us!'

He walked calmly towards them.

'Which of you need help?' he asked. He went right up to them. Then he opened fire.

High above, it was all being filmed. The helicopter above the island did not belong to the police, as the killer had thought. It had been chartered by NRK, the Norwegian Broadcasting Corporation. The camera team had been filming above the government quarter when the desk editor told them to head to Utøya.

It was too far down for the cameraman to make out through his lens what he was filming. It was only later, when he saw the footage, that he realised he had been filming a massacre.

Breivik stood by the water and saw several people swimming out. A yellow speedboat came towards him. It stopped to pick up some of the swimmers. He fired a few shots, causing the boat to make a rapid turn and retreat over the fjord at speed, away from him, away from the island, away from the youngsters in the water.

Meanwhile, the boat containing Håvard Gåsbakk and five other officers was just putting in to the island. The six on board had heard the shots and seen the bullets hailing down into the water, so they knew which direction they would have to take.

One man stayed on the spot to secure the ferry landing stage, the others moved south in a five-man formation. First the man with the shield, then the others. They forced their way through bushes and scrub to get down to the water, but the undergrowth was so thick that they had to turn inland, up a little path through the woods, and then back down to where the shots were coming from.

Meanwhile, on the southern tip of the island a girl was hit twice in the head and once in the chest as the armed men were walking along the path. Another kid got a bullet through the neck while the men were jogging across open ground. A third, through her head while they were changing shield carrier. A fourth was shot twice in the back as the five men drew nearer. The fifth, a boy, was shot three times, first in the back to bring him down, then through the head and neck, and the men were still not there.

They were running along the gravel path.

We'll come under fire now. We'll be shot at, thought Gåsbakk. This is going to be a firefight. The father of two had still not seen any of the dead bodies on the island. The men's route was outside Breivik's sphere of operations. The murderer had avoided that stretch because it was in full view of the mainland and there was a risk of being shot.

I'd be crazy to raise my visor, thought Gåsbakk, but lifted it all the same. It was so steamed up in the damp weather that it was impossible to see clearly through it. He heard the rapid succession of shots, a heavy weapon in action.

The gloves are off for this one, he thought, looking down at his MP5 machine pistol, which was nothing compared with the weapon he could hear, something with much more power and range. He felt at a distinct disadvantage.

I should have given Eilif that cuddle, he thought. This could be my last run.

Breivik stood over the people he had killed. Beside him was a boy who looked 'too fucking young'.

'You killed my dad! You killed my dad!' cried the boy. 'You've got to stop shooting now. You've done enough killing! Leave us alone.'

Breivik looked down at him, and thought he looked awfully small for a teenager. Perhaps this one was not an indoctrinated cultural Marxist yet.

'It's going to be all right, it's going to be fine,' he told the small boy.

The boy did not move, but shouted: 'He let me live! He spared me!'

Breivik turned to go up to his base for more ammunition.

The five men came to the end of the path and swapped shield carrier again. They stood quietly. He must be very close by. They squatted down and secured their position. Listened. It was a while since they had heard a shot. There were no sounds to go on now. One of the Delta men started calling out.

'Shut up!' said Gåsbakk. It was unwise to call out until they knew where he was. 'Keep listening!'

They advanced again. After a hundred metres they came to a low, red building, the schoolhouse. They made for the south-west corner, keeping potential firing zones covered as they went.

All was quiet.

They saw a movement in the undergrowth, fifty metres away. Something reflective gave a glint. They lost sight of the figure. They crossed Lovers' Path. They advanced through the thicket from two directions. Then a man in police uniform was standing there ahead of them.

'Delta, Delta,' they shouted.

Now they'll shoot me, thought Breivik. But at the same time, they seemed a bit bewildered. They had probably expected a dark-skinned man, he thought.

'Armed police! Stand still! Hands up!' one of them shouted.

Breivik set down his rifle, propping it against a tree.

Then he turned and went towards the policemen, keeping both hands at his sides. He had earplugs in his ears, with a lead that went inside his vest and down his body.

'Lie down!' shouted one.

'Down on your knees!'

Several men were pointing their guns at him, with their fingers on the trigger.

'If you come any closer, we'll shoot!'

The Delta officers had noticed his bulging vest. Could it be a bomb belt? The leads of his iPod were hanging out. Would he finish them all? The men were preparing to shoot him.

'It's not a bomb belt! It's an equipment belt with ammunition!' shouted a Delta man from the flank.

'Lie down,' shouted one.

'On your knees!' roared another.

'Make up your minds, kneeling or lying?' responded Breivik.

'Down!'

He flopped down, first onto his knees and then his stomach.

Håvard Gåsbakk jumped straight on him, forced his hands round behind his back and put on the handcuffs. Another officer bound his legs with plastic strip cuffs.

From down there, with his body pressed to the ground, Breivik turned his head and looked up at Gåsbakk, who was now sitting astride his back.

'It's not you lot I'm after. I see you as my brothers. It's not you I've got to take out.'

'Have you got ID?'

'In my right pocket.'

A man took out his card and read his name and personal identification number over the radio.

'I'm not against you,' Breivik went on. 'This is politically motivated. The country is being invaded by foreigners, this is a *coup d'état*, this is the start of hell. It's going to get worse: the third cell has still not been activated.'

Then Gåsbakk noticed two dead bodies on the ground. The first two he had seen. It was Johannes and Gizem, who had been shot by Breivik in the woods.

'The Glock's in the holster,' said Breivik.

'I know,' Gåsbakk replied.

One officer took the pistol from his thigh. Another stood there throughout with his weapon raised, pointing at Breivik.

Gåsbakk looked Breivik in the eyes.

'For the sake of your conscience, answer now: are there any more of you? Where are they?'

Breivik looked up at him.

'There is only me,' he said. 'There is only me.'

There. Is. Only. Me.

When It's All Over

The living room in Heiaveien was filling up.

As the evening went on, the reports said seven had been killed. A bit later it was ten.

Gunnar couldn't get through on any of the telephone numbers going across the screen, and finally rang their local district sheriff. Maybe he had acquaintances in Buskerud police district.

Yes, in fact he did.

They sat there, transfixed by the pictures on the screen. They saw young people swimming in dark water. White bodies far below, filmed from the air. They were going fast, with powerful, dogged strokes. Some were swimming in groups. Others were on their own. They were on a steady course towards the mainland. They were all engaged in the same thing: getting away from the island.

The old sheriff rang Gunnar back. 'It's serious,' he said. But he had nothing more to tell them.

The sheriff had been putting things straight in the Salangen community for forty years, handing out speeding fines and clamping down on illegal fishing, enforcing the snowmobile ban on the mountain, upholding law and order ever since local residents and asylum seekers had clashed at the end of the 1980s.

Now he knocked on the door. 'I thought I ought to come,' he said, standing on the doorstep. 'In case there's anything I can do to help.'

He was going to try ringing some other direct lines, not those listed on the screen, and he would be on hand if they needed him for anything.

But all the lines were jammed.

Astrid, the girl who had lived next door to them in Upper Salangen, turned up too. She was three years older than Simon and had played with him since he was four years old. Astrid was always the director when they performed their New Year revue and pretty much counted as an older sister. This Friday, she had just poured herself a glass of wine and sat down in front of the television when she saw the report of the shooting on Utøya. She got straight in the car and drove to Heiaveien.

Relatives arrived, neighbours, friends. Everyone at the birthday party the Sæbøs were meant to be attending came through the door. They could not have any kind of celebration until Simon had rung to say everything was all right.

A newsflash ran across the TV screen. Some of the surviving youngsters said that far more had died than had been officially reported. As many as thirty or forty, estimated one AUF member.

Hearts in the living room began to race and hammer.

Every second Simon did not ring was a second of pain. The minutes soon became unbearable.

Someone made coffee and put out the cups. The birthday guests had brought some of the cakes.

A heavy pall of anxiety hung over the light living room.

The sun's rays were still shining through the big picture windows facing the fjord. The sun would not set that night, just move westwards along the horizon.

Tone had disappeared. It was a long time since anyone in the living room had seen her.

They found her in the little utility room that was mainly used for drying clothes. She was sitting there on the floor, rocking back and forth.

'Not my Simon. Not my Simon. Not my Simon!'

Tone was heedless of anything beyond herself. The pain was just too greedy; fear had gripped her. She had lost the use of her arms and legs, and was nothing but a heap on the floor. She could only conjure up a single image. Simon, a happy Simon, when she gave him a hug and two kisses at the airport.

Gunnar was talking to the police. He looks just like normal, thought Astrid. His voice was clear, never hesitant. He held the phone to his ear and turned to the window.

Then she saw his back. His shirt was soaking wet, with huge sweat rings under the arms.

Gunnar was pacing to and fro, from the TV to the veranda for a smoke, and then back again. Tone couldn't be left sitting there on the floor alone, some of them thought. They helped her up. She walked stiffly, moving mechanically with the support of two friends. She went out to Gunnar and asked for a cigarette. The only way to breathe was to smoke.

The fjord was twinkling in the evening light. The mountains behind were reflected on the water's surface.

A car suddenly came into sight on the main road. 'It'll go off the road!' said someone who was standing on the veranda with them.

The car was speeding along. It turned off the main road and up the steep driveway and pulled up on the open area outside the house. The door was thrust open. Kristine, football player and trainee teacher, Simon's girlfriend all the way through his teens, almost part of the household these past few years, was standing there on the gravel, looking up at Gunnar and Tone on the veranda. The girl was in floods of tears. She came rushing up the steps with a cry of anguish.

'Simon's dead! Simon's dead! Simon's dead!'

For a moment, everything went completely still in Heiaveien.

Then Simon's mother collapsed onto the veranda floor.

Kristine had been sitting at home, gradually getting more and more desperate at not making contact with Simon, and had rung all his friends. Ten times, twenty times, the same numbers over and over again. Brage Sollund finally answered. He had been hiding in the thicket he had thrown himself into after leaving the Troms camp to check what was happening. There he lay until the perpetrator was caught. He had not seen Simon himself, but he had heard what other people were saying.

'Tell me what you know about Simon,' said Kristine.

The words stuck in Brage's throat. He mumbled something while he wondered what he could say. He had to give her some sort of answer.

'You won't be seeing Simon again.'

Kristine gave a shriek. 'Are you sure? Are you sure?'

'I didn't see it happen, but Geir Kåre did . . . '

That was all Kristine remembered before she leapt into the car and drove to the Sæbø house.

Now she was sobbing. 'We'll never see Simon again,' she cried.

'He could have got it wrong,' said Gunnar. 'Maybe,' he added.

They had also heard reports that Simon was in hospital, that he had been rescued, that he had been shot in the foot. And after all, Brage had not seen Simon himself. Brage had been hiding somewhere else entirely.

But Simon's mother, the powerhouse of family love, had been drained of all her strength and dragged herself into the bedroom.

Håvard had gone off into his room to be on his own. He sat there in bed with his laptop and went into his elder brother's Facebook page, where he wrote a message.

Simon! Come back home!!!!

Down at the water's edge, Viljar had gone quiet.

He was lying in the foetal position. Completely still. He had stopped telling stories.

He had stopped singing, stopped cursing. His mumbling had also ceased.

There was no more sound coming from Viljar. The hood of his sweatshirt was red with blood. There was something hanging from his eye socket.

Margrethe Rosbach was huddled up on the ledge with her eyes fixed on a single spot. Down by the rocks.

She could feel nothing, no grief, no fear. Simon is dead, and soon we all will be, she thought. The people who were shooting, who kept on shooting, would come back and kill them all. The shots were so regular, so loud. Margrethe had lost her will to live; she did not bother to sit out of sight, she had given up. She had gone numb, up there on the rock ledge. Her phone kept lighting up. *Dad*, said the display, but she did not take his call.

It was over. This was the end.

Her last conversation with her father had finished before Simon fell. Simon had taken the phone out of Margrethe's hand and said, 'We've got to be quiet. We've got to hide.' Then he had put the phone down on the rock ledge. But he did not end the call. So her father in Stavanger had heard the two shots, two loud cracks, right in his ear. He had heard the screams. That was them being killed, he thought. One shot hitting Simon, the other Margrethe.

He did not know that one of them had taken both bullets.

A civilian boat with three heavily armed policemen in it came in towards the cliff.

They're going to shoot us now, thought Margrethe.

'Police! Police!' shouted the men.

The teenagers lying wounded on the shoreline thought, either we're saved now, or we're done for. There was no panic, nobody trying to flee, because if this lot were in league with that first man the odds against them were too great, the firepower too immense.

The men jumped ashore.

'Is anyone hurt here?' they called, and immediately set about bandaging those who could be saved.

Margrethe rushed down to Simon.

How cold he was!

The jersey she had borrowed the night before had ridden up over his back, as had his waterproof jacket, which was almost over his head. She pulled down the fleecy top and tucked his jacket more tightly round him, turning the hood down carefully so his face could be seen.

It was completely white. All the colour was gone. There was no blood. Nothing to indicate he had been shot. In the jacket and jersey there was just a small hole where the rifle shot had entered, and then a wound on his leg. It was as if he were asleep, and freezing.

Margrethe stroked his back, patted his shoulder. Put her arms round him. Clutched him.

Reality tore into her like a claw.

He was dead. And she was saved.

He was dead, and she would live.

The policemen had quickly identified the dead. A boy floating in the water, with four shots to his back and stomach. Dead. Simon, hanging lifeless over a rock. Dead. Viljar, lying at the water's edge with parts of his brain outside his skull. Dead.

Higher up the cliff, the three girls Breivik shot first. Dead. One had celebrated her fourteenth birthday five days earlier. The second, who was fifteen, had just been chosen as a confirmation course leader at her local church, where she also sang in the choir. The third, a sixteen-year-old, had come with Margrethe from Stavanger and the two had shared a tent. The three girls all bled to death before the rescue team got to them.

The policemen worked quickly and efficiently, concentrating on the youngsters they could save. Ylva, Eirin and Cathrine, their bodies riddled with bullets and splinters of bone and rock, were carried into boats. All three with severe internal bleeding.

'No!' Tonje Brenna cried as the police determined who was dead.

'He was talking just now! He isn't dead!' The AUF secretary-general pointed at Viljar. 'He was singing, not long ago.'

One of the rescuers squatted down by Viljar on the shoreline.

'He can't be dead!' cried Tonje.

Viljar was lying limply in the water. The policeman detected something.

A weak pulse.

And then a sound, an almost imperceptible sound.

'Here!' he shouted. 'There's life!'

The man had specialist training in first aid and battlefield medical

treatment; he had served in Afghanistan and had many years' experience. He produced a triangular scarf, which he worked under
Viljar's head. He carefully put parts of Viljar's brain back into his
head. He pieced together the bits of skull, paying meticulous attention so that no sharp corners went into the soft mass. He gently
packed up Viljar's head and knotted the scarf around it. With his brain
in its proper place, Viljar was carried to a waiting boat by some of the
survivors.

Viljar came round with his head in someone's lap in the middle of
the Tyrifjord. He looked at those with him and asked faintly:

'Where's Torje?'

They called out to her. The other teenagers were already in the boat.
It was the last one taking survivors from the cliff.

A policeman came over to Margrethe.

'You've got to come now.'

'We can't just leave him here.'

'He'll be looked after,' said the policeman.

An armed officer had been positioned there to guard the place.

'We have to take Simon with us!'

'The dead will be picked up later.'

Simon was so cold.

'I'm not going without Simon!'

'The island hasn't been secured yet. None of the living are allowed
to stay here.'

In the end, the policeman dragged her away. Simon was left hanging, as he had fallen, on the rock by the water. He had three dead girls
above him, a dead boy at the water's edge below him, and a policeman to look after him.

'The injured first! The injured first!'

Lara, icy cold, sat on the shore between the steep slope and the
pumping station. She was shivering after so long in the water. In her
cavity in the limestone she'd grown indifferent to everything, her
head had drooped onto her chest and she was convinced she was

going to be shot. She was too cold to care. But now . . . now they were saved.

Oh, how she needed Bano now. She wanted to be rocked, to be held, to be comforted. She needed to talk to her elder sister. Bano, who laughed at everything, who always found something good in even the worst things, who transformed the ordinary into a fairytale. And fairytales always have a happy ending.

Suddenly she could not stop screaming.

She howled, she yelled, louder than everyone around her. All the strength she had left was channelled into sound.

She gasped for breath, and collapsed in exhaustion.

Then she got a place in a boat.

'Don't look towards the island,' said the boat driver. 'Look straight ahead, don't turn round!'

Some looked anyway, and screamed.

All along the shore lay young people, some halfway out of the water, others on the rocks. In some places, the rock was stained red. Bloody clothes lay abandoned. There were so many clothes, so many shoes. Left by those who swam for it.

'I will never play *Call of Duty* again,' said a boy in Lara's boat.

They landed at Utvika Camping. On the beach, people met them with blankets and quilts.

They know what has happened out there! Lara was abruptly returned to the real world. It had actually happened!

She asked everybody she saw if they had seen Bano. 'Yes, she's alive,' one boy said. 'I think somebody said they'd spoken to her.' Another person thought they had seen her in a tent.

There were anguished cries, tears and panic. Some were in shock, moving mechanically, their gaze empty. Some had to be lifted ashore, and lay apathetically where they were put down. Others were terrified of everyone; their eyes said, 'Are you going to try to kill me, too?'

Up on the road, a line of cars stood ready, volunteers who drove the youngsters to the assembly point and then came back for more. But Lara did not want to leave until Bano was safely ashore. She knew her sister could not have arrived yet, because Bano would have waited for her if she had got here first.

Finally, three of Lara's friends made her come in a car with them. 'Everyone's supposed to assemble at Sundvolden Hotel,' they said. 'Bano's probably there.'

The car radio was on, and there was a report that the perpetrator was Norwegian.

In the car, somebody lent Lara a phone. She rang her father.

'We're on our way to fetch you,' he cried.

When news started to come through of the shooting on Utøya, all the neighbours had gathered at the Rashids'. They, too, tried ringing the numbers on the TV screen, but failed to get though. One of the neighbours had found out that a centre for next of kin had been set up at the Thon Hotel in Sandvika. Now they were in a taxi on their way there, because Mustafa was under too much nervous strain to drive himself. He and Bayan picked up Ali from the little field near by, where the fourteen-year-old had been play-ing football with some friends. They could look after him, the friends' parents said, but no, Ali wanted to come along to fetch his sisters.

'How are you?' Lara's father asked her.

Lara went quiet. 'Dad,' she said. 'Dad . . . I don't know where Bano is.'

'Aren't you with her?'

Lara wept.

They agreed that the first to hear anything from Bano would ring the other.

Ali was sitting in the back seat with Bayan. He tried to reassure his mother. 'You know how smart Bano is. She's the best at finding good places to hide. That's why nobody's found her yet!'

Their taxi driver was from Morocco and had a copy of the Qur'an in the dashboard. Bayan read the holy scripture and asked God to look after their elder daughter, their firstborn.

Mustafa sat in the front, muttering to himself.

God, there is no god but He, Living and Everlasting. Neither slumber

*overtakes Him nor sleep. To Him belongs what is in the heavens and what
is on earth.*

It was the same prayer, Ayat al-Kursi, that he had prayed in the boat
on the Khabur river between Iraq and Syria, the prayer he had turned
to as he lay sleepless during the civil war.

*He knows their present affairs and their past. And they do not grasp of His
knowledge except what He wills. His throne encompasses the heavens and the
earth; Preserving them is no burden to him. He is the Exalted, the Majestic.*

It was a long time since he had needed that prayer.

In Sandvika they had a long wait before they were informed that
everyone from Utøya had been sent to Sundvolden Hotel by the
Tyrifjord. Bano did not ring. Bayan wept and groaned. 'My child, my
child!' she sobbed.

One of the other mothers took care of her. 'It's going to be all
right,' said the slender woman, putting her arm round her. Her name
was Kirsten and she also had a child on the island, she said. His name
was Håvard, and he was the leader of the Oslo AUF. They had not
heard anything from their son for some hours now, either. He had
sent them the last message just after six, from his hiding place by the
pumping station. Kirsten offered them a lift in their family's car to
Sundvolden. But with Ali they were too many, so they took a taxi.

It was starting to get dark as they set off on the long circuit of the
Tyrifjord.

'Everything will be fine,' Bayan said to Ali as they got into another
back seat. 'We'll soon have both the girls with us.'

The taxi turned out of Sandvika, and Bayan looked at her son and
smiled. 'You'll see, Bano will ring soon and say: "I'm fine!"'

At Sundvolden Hotel, Lara could not share in the scenes of joy as
people were reunited. She went out into the rain in her already
sodden clothes. She had no more tears left, no more screams.

She waited in the car park outside for the buses and cars bringing
young people from Utøya. She scrutinised the vehicles, her eyes sur-
veying windows and doors and fixing on every figure to climb out in
front of her, then moving on.

There was a pale, red-headed boy with freckles standing at a slight distance. He was soaked through. Torje had stayed hidden in the hole in the rock at the waterline for a long time. When a boat came to rescue youngsters from the water, he swam towards it. He was almost there when shots began to whistle overhead. The boat beat a rapid retreat. Torje was left alone in the water. He swam back to the island and went ashore. He was too cold to swim out again to the hiding place. On several occasions, Torje was close to the gunman, but he always managed to get away or hide.

The fourteen-year-old rang his parents once the bus had brought him from the jetty. They were on their way. They had waited three hours at Sollihøgda and then they had decided to drive almost all the way round the Tyrifjord. They had rung, rung off, and rung again. Torje and Viljar grew younger and younger in their mother's mind as they drove. By the time they came into Sundvolden, she was seeing them as two tiny tots.

Torje was waiting for Viljar and Johannes. His big brother and his best friend.

Then someone told him no more buses would be coming.

'When Bano Rashid arrives, can you tell her this is our room number?'

Lara was exhausted with waiting, and since there were no more buses coming she'd gone in and asked for a room. They gave her a key. 'Bano's got long dark hair and, well, she looks like me. She's my older sister.'

She dragged herself over to the lift.

She's alive, thought Lara as she got up to the room. She had borrowed a computer at reception and had put a heart on Bano's Facebook page.

She must be alive, because if she were dead, I would feel it. And I don't feel as if she's dead, she said to herself.

In a room in the same wing of the hotel, Margrethe looked at the king-size bed.

This posh room! How she hated this posh room! It was all wrong.

'We'll get in the car and come for you,' her parents in Stavanger had said when she finally rang home to tell them she was alive.

'No, don't do that,' she had answered in a flat voice. 'I'll get myself home.'

Everything in the room was smooth and shiny. It was all ironed and pressed and polished. She pulled aside the cover, threw out the scatter cushions and lay down under the quilt. A soft, clean, warm quilt. That was when she broke down. She simply could not bear it.

To lie under the lovely quilt, while Simon was left lying out there, alone in the rain.

———

'There is only me,' he had said.

That was while Håvard Gåsbakk was still sitting astride him. It was a little after half past six in the evening. His body was pressed against the damp ground. His nose was in the wet grass, in fresh leaves, earth and moss. With his head bent to one side, he carried on talking.

'The third cell has still not been activated This is the start of hell! It's going to get worse.'

His voice was hard, militant.

Worse than this? Gåsbakk shivered. He reported over the radio that a nationwide alert should be issued, warning of a further attack.

Breivik looked up at Gåsbakk. 'I can tell you ninety-eight per cent, but I want to negotiate about the last two per cent.'

'You've said enough. Head down!' said Gåsbakk. He could hear the others in the team calling for medical packs and giving details of the dead and wounded.

'This is a *coup d'état*,' said the man lying beneath him, bound hand and foot.

Gåsbakk had to keep the man down and quiet, that was his task, not to negotiate with him.

He heard a thin voice, painful cries.

A little boy emerged through the trees. A dark-skinned teenager with blood on his chest held him by the hand. The child was sobbing. 'I want my dad, I want my dad!'

The man on the ground was breathing heavily. The chemical effect of all the stimulants was wearing off, but he was still high on what his own body was producing. He was high on the murders he had committed, the hormones it had released in him.

At times he coud not get enough air into his lungs and started hyperventilating, lying there on the ground between the schoolhouse and the southern tip of the island.

After half an hour or so, one of the Delta officers took over the apprehended man. Gåsbakk ran to the main building to help with the rescue work.

'What shall we do with the dead bodies?' came the question.

What should they do with the dead bodies?

Gåsbakk looked around him.

'Pull those on the shoreline up far enough to stop them floating out into the water, the others can stay where they are,' he replied into the radio.

Three men had arrived from the Organised Crime Section, Special Operations. Their most important task was to find out whether further attacks could be expected. It was vital to stop any further loss of life.

The initial interviews would be carried out on the island. Transporting Breivik to Oslo before the island was secured, before the rescue operation was complete, would tie up too much manpower.

Headquarters were set up in the white wooden building above the landing stage, where the camp administration and Mother Utøya had been based. This was where the AUF leader had been sitting to follow the TV news when the first shots rang out, three hours earlier.

Victims were still lying wounded on the island when two policemen from the emergency response unit brought the prisoner up the grassy slope to the HQ.

A short set of stone steps led up to the building. Wide, safe steps of old granite. Just beside them in the grass lay three bodies. Monica and the two security guards, fathers of the small boys who were now calling out for their dads.

The three interviewers stood waiting for Breivik outside the building. It was a quarter past eight when they took over his supervision from Delta, about an hour and a half after he had been apprehended. The Delta men also handed over a mobile phone and a jacket badge with a skull and crossbones on it. *Marxist Hunter*, the badge said. The lead interrogator unfastened the handcuffs keeping the killer's hands behind his back and cuffed them in front instead. 'You might just as well execute me here on the ground floor,' said Breivik when they ordered him upstairs.

'You're not going to be shot. We're going to talk to you,' said the lead interviewer.

Breivik looked at him.

'I'm going to die anyway,' he said, and explained that he had taken a great number of chemical substances. He was dehydrating and would die within two hours if he did not get something to drink.

They took him up to the first floor and put him in an armchair. In the room were a table, a large sofa, several armchairs and a few two-seater sofas. Breivik was given a bottle of fizzy drink.

The interviewers took a sofa each.

'You are suspected of murder. You are not obliged to explain yourself to the police, and you can—'

Breivik interrupted. 'That's okay. I can explain myself. In broad terms.'

He sat facing the table with his cuffed hands in his lap.

'I have sacrificed myself. I have no life after this. I may very well suffer and be tortured for the rest of my life. I shall never get out. My life ended when I ordained myself into the Knights Templar. But what is it you actually want to talk to me about? I'm surprised they haven't sent the secret services to interrogate me.'

'What were you trying to achieve here today? And is anything else going to happen?'

'We want to take power in Europe within sixty years. I am a commander of the Knights Templar. Our organisation was set up in London in 2002 with delegates from twelve countries.'

He stressed that they were not Nazis, and that they supported Israel. They were not racists, but they wanted political Islam out of Europe. It could be called a conservative revolution. 'But I've written a fifteen-hundred-page manifesto on this, I can't explain it all now,' he said.

'Is there anything else on the island?'

'No.'

'Explosive charges? Weapons?'

'No, that's over and done with.'

'Your car on the other side, is it booby-trapped?'

'No, but my shotgun's in there.'

'Are there others here apart from you?'

'No,' he said, but suddenly thought better of it. 'There's something else, but I won't tell you what, or where it is. I'm willing to negotiate with you. I want a proper arrangement, with something in return for the information.'

'Oh yes?'

'If you want to save three hundred lives, then listen to me carefully. But I would really have preferred to negotiate with the secret services.'

'Tell us what you know. Lots of innocent lives have been lost today,' said the interrogator.

'I wouldn't exactly call these innocent. They are extreme Marxists. Marxist spawn. It's the Labour Party, the youth wing. They're the ones with the power in Norway. They're the ones who have presided over the Islamisation of Norway.'

'Will any more lives be lost?'

'Of course. This is only the beginning. The civil war has started. I don't want Islam in Europe, and my fellow partisans share my views. We don't want Oslo to end up like Marseille, where Muslims have been in the majority since 2010. We want to fight for Oslo. My operation has succeeded one hundred per cent, which is why I'm giving myself up now. But the operation itself is not important. These are just the fireworks.'

He looked down at his hands. There was a bit of blood on one finger.

'Look, I'm hurt,' he said. 'This will have to be bandaged up. I've already lost a lot of blood.'

'You'll get no fucking plasters from me,' muttered the policeman who was taking messages between the interview room and the room next door, where they were in contact with the staff in Oslo.

'I can't afford to lose too much blood,' said Breivik. 'And I've lost half a litre already.' He claimed that the blood loss could make him pass out.

Sticking plasters were procured.

While the plasters were being applied, Breivik wondered why he was bleeding. He remembered something hitting his finger when he shot a victim in the head at close range. Something had flown into his finger and then popped out again. It must have been a bit of skull, he told the officers in the room.

The cut was logged as five millimetres long. The interrogation could continue.

'In return for my explanation, I want a PC with Word in prison. I want . . . '

He stumbled, stammering a little as if he suddenly did not know what to ask for. 'I have to have a more formal setting before I can put forth my demands. It has to be done in the proper way.'

Eventually, he decided he had three lists of demands. A simple one with requests that could easily be met; a second that they might also agree to – and that would actually be very attractive to the police; and then a third list that they probably would not accept.

'Out with it then. Start with the simple one!'

'My cell has fifteen thousand sympathisers in Norway, many of them inside the police. No one could possibly defend such bestial acts as those I have committed today, yet Islam is more brutal than my organisation! We are martyrs, we can be monsters, that's fine by us. Marxist youth, they're—'

A police officer came in and interrupted. 'The police are outside 18 Hoffsveien. Is your mother at home, and what does it say on the door?'

'It says Wenche Behring Breivik.'

Wenche had been at home when the bomb went off, and had neither heard it nor felt the pressure wave.

Earlier in the day, she'd taken a coffee break with her friends at the café and gone into the Coop to buy some mince. When she'd got home about two, Anders was back from the computer store. By half past two he was off again; there was something he had forgotten to buy.

'I'll have dinner ready when you get back!' she called after him.

She chopped onion, fried it with the mince, mixed in the tomato sauce and set the table. She wanted it all ready when her son got home. She would wait to put the water on for the spaghetti until she saw him at the door. She set the sauce to one side and started peeling the prawns they would have in the evening. She put the shells in the rubbish, tied up the bag and put it by the front door. Then she sat down and waited.

She was ravenous. Would he be back soon?

Two hours after he had gone out, she rang him. His phone was switched off. That was odd, he didn't usually turn off his phone.

Strange that he wasn't back yet. He'd only popped out to the computer store. Could he have dropped round to a friend's?

At five o'clock she rang him again. No answer.

Just after that, one of her friends rang and told her to switch on the TV. It was dreadful! She sat there watching the news and then went to put on the water for the pasta because she was so hungry. She ate a little.

At seven she rang Anders again. Where could he be? Could he have had a car accident?

It was a long time since she had had Anders at home. Since his move to the farm he had only spent one night there, well, apart from this night. She had asked him if he had found himself a nice milkmaid up there in the valley. Straight from the cowshed!

She was glued to the TV. Imagine Anders not being there with her, when these frightful things were happening.

First the bomb. And now: ten people killed on the island.

Between eight and nine she rang his phone several times. She was starting to get seriously worried. What could have happened? Could he have been hit by the bomb?

At 21.40, there was a call to her landline. She hurried to pick up the phone.

'This is the police. We request that you come out.'

'Oh no! Has something happened to Anders?'

She ran out of the flat.

Outside, she was met by flashing blue lights. There were several police cars in front of the entrance. Armed men with black jackets and visors had their weapons trained on her.

She had to hand over her keys, and was taken to a car. A police-woman took her by the arm.

'Your son has been arrested in connection with a serious criminal offence. You are wanted at the police station to make a witness state-ment.'

Wenche stared at her. This was insane.

'Does your son have access to firearms?' asked the policewoman.

'He's taken his hunting-licence test and belongs to a pistol club. He's got a Glock and a shotgun,' Wenche said, and added: 'The shot-gun's in the wardrobe in his bedroom.'

The car sped through empty streets.

'Does your son have any mental health problems?'

'What's he accused of?' blurted Wenche. 'Him of all people. He's so kind and considerate, and . . . '

The car drove into the garage at the main police station.

The assault force was still outside 18 Hoffsveien.

People were gaping from the windows of their flats. The whole neighbourhood was soon at the windows, phones in hand. They were all ringing each other: 'Look outside! Look outside!' On the televi-sion, which they all had on in the background, they would shortly see their own block live on the screen, and hear that the perpetrator was Norwegian, and thirty-two years of age.

Good God, it must be Wenche's Anders!

The flying squad was awaiting notification from Utøya before storming the flat.

'Are there explosives there?' Wenche's son was asked.

'No,' he replied. 'There's a PC in the fart room.'

That was how he put it. It was the first room they would come to, he said, and the only one of any interest. He had removed all his things from the loft and basement.

'There is one thing you have to be clear about,' he said abruptly. 'This has been the worst day of my life. Unfortunately, it was necessary. Hopefully the Labour Party will learn its lesson from this and stop the mass import of Muslims.'

'Will anyone else die today?'

'I don't want to comment on that. And I do need some more comfort in order to formulate my list of demands.'

'I find it rather strange that you didn't prepare your list in advance,' observed the lead interviewer.

'I'm in a lot of pain now, and I can't focus. I think a better location would help me.'

Breivik was informed that it was not currently possible to change location.

'You all see me as a monster, don't you?'

'We see you as a human being.'

'You're going to execute me. And all my family.'

'We are prepared to give your family protection if need be. For us, a life is a life. You will be treated exactly the same as everybody else.'

He said he had to go for a pee, and some officers accompanied him out.

'Now I've got my list of demands ready. Are you making a note of this?' he asked when he got back.

They assured him they were.

'I want to send and receive letters in prison.'

'You will, as soon as there is no longer any reason to block your correspondence and visits.'

'How long is correspondence normally blocked for?'

'That depends on the investigation, and it is hard to say in a murder case.'

'Murder case? This wasn't murder, it was political executions!' Breivik burst out. 'Knights Templar Europe has given me permission to execute category A, B and C traitors. For me – that is, for us – the Knights Templar is the highest political authority in Norway.'

He admitted that those he had killed on the island were category C traitors.

'Who decides which category people end up in?'

'I've set it all out in my book. Strictly speaking, we are not authorised to execute category C traitors. Now, about my demands . . . '

His second demand was to use the PC for a minimum of eight hours a day. It need not have internet access, but there had to be a printer. 'I am an intellectual. Not a warrior. My calling is to fight with the pen, but occasionally one has to use the sword.' Demand number three was access to Wikipedia. Demand number four was to serve his sentence with as few Muslims as possible. Demand number five was not to be given any halal meat.

The officers in the next room communicated his demands to the police chiefs in Oslo, and the interviewers informed him that the demands would very probably be met. But they added that if there was to be an agreement, he must now tell them whether anyone was going to be killed in the imminent future.

'Okay, if you agree to my most far-reaching list of demands I'm willing to hand over details of the two cells that right now, *as we speak*, are planning acts of terrorism against parties supporting multiculturalism.

'Go ahead.'

'Well then, the security services must present a proposal to the Justice Committee to bring in the death sentence, by hanging, in Norway, and to use waterboarding as a method of torture.'

Then he asked for a cigarette, and was given one. He asked for another drink and got that too.

'It's the media who are most to blame for what has happened today because they didn't publish my views. One thus has to get the message out by other means.' Then he suddenly said that the whole thing was tragic, and that his heart was weeping at what had happened that day.

'You are the commander so the responsibility is yours,' objected the interviewer.

'My responsibility is to save Norway. I take full responsibility for everything out here, and I'm proud of the operation. If you only knew what hard work it's been,' he said. 'It was bloody awful. I've been dreading this day for two years. . . '

The interrogation had already been going on for several hours when a team from Kripos arrived to carry out a preliminary examination of the accused. They took DNA and urine samples, and scrapings were taken from his clothes.

The officers produced a camera. But the *Commander of the Norwegian anti-communist resistance movement* objected to being photographed. He had already had pictures taken and had posted them on the internet. Now the police would take the sort of pictures he had warned about in his manifesto. Photos of an offender in handcuffs, with drooping shoulders. In the ones he had had taken at the studio he was in make-up and Photoshopped. They were portraits of him in his Freemasons' suit, in his Knights Templar uniform, in his chemical protection suit. He had pasted the pictures into the final pages of his manifesto. No, there would be no Utøya photographs with AUF posters in the background. He would not have that.

But he was no longer the one making the decisions.

In the picture later leaked to the press, Breivik is sitting in an armchair with his hands in his lap. His head is bowed, his eyes fixed on the floor.

His clothes were to be secured, as they would be used as evidence. The Kripos men got out a black sack.

'Get undressed.'

He refused.

They said he had to.

He refused again.

Then he suddenly leapt up and started tearing off his clothes.

'Stop, stop!'

His garments were to be removed one at a time, at Kripos's command. He could have explosives on him. Hidden weapons. It was the officers who would decide the order in which he was to remove the clothes, and when.

Finally he was standing there in a room of uniformed men in his underpants. He started posing, trying to look macho. Now he was all for having his picture taken. He looked into the camera and thrust out his chest. His hands were clasped at one hip while he held his body taut in a classic bodybuilding pose, to make his muscles bulge as much as possible.

For a moment, the policemen were nonplussed. In another setting, another crime, it might have been ridiculous, but here . . . it was grotesque, it was simply incomprehensible.

Who on earth were they dealing with here?

Breivik gave a nervous laugh. He had misjudged it. He could tell. The joke had fallen flat. The opportunity had presented itself out of the blue, and now that he was for once happy with his body, it had kind of been ready for a show. The Commander had temporarily forgotten himself.

He was issued with a disposable white jumpsuit and quickly put it on. The policemen found an old pair of shoes for him in the corridor. They could be the captain's, or perhaps they belonged to one of the guards. Whoever they belonged to, he did not like them. But they were all he got.

The interrogation could continue.

'You say we, so who are you, as a group?'

'In Norway I'm the overall leader of our organisation. I'm the commander here. I'm the judge as well. I'm the supreme authority here. The international Knights Templar can't micromanage its Norwegian commander. Today I sent out a document to thousands of militant nationalists. Some countries have got further than Norway. France, for example, will be taken over by my brothers within fifteen years, and once they have established a decent base it will be easy to get me released from prison.'

'You said you were set up as an organisation in London in 2002. Have you been working towards this goal ever since then?'

'To start with, I was a sleeping cell. I've never expressed extreme ideas until now. That's why the PST hasn't found me out. It's people like me we want to recruit, people who are suitable, but who haven't done anything to bring them to the attention of the police.'

He wanted to go out and pee again, and when he was brought back in he asked if anyone had any *snus*. Someone did. He was given a wad of *snus* and put it under his top lip.

It was past midnight.

'My operation will go on,' he said. 'But by means of the pen. History will judge me. But it's also a question of how the media judge me. I draw a distinction between success in the techniques of warfare and media success. The media certainly wants to portray me as a monster—'

'Is it your aim to be portrayed as a monster?'

'Not necessarily,' he replied briskly. 'The aim was not to be as brutal as I have been. When I evaluated people, I tried not to take the youngest. I took those who were older. There are moral boundaries, aren't there? Even if I perhaps didn't show that very clearly today.'

The night had reached its darkest point. Outside, the July night was chilly. A tent had been erected for the men who were now conducting a full search of the island.

'How long will it actually take for me to get a response to my first list of demands?' Breivik pestered them. 'If I don't get access to a PC with Word in prison, I shall terminate myself. If I have no chance of contributing to the struggle for the rest of my life, it will all be meaningless.'

'How many do you think you killed today?'

'Um, forty, or fifty. But they were executed, not murdered. The aim was to kill the party leaders of tomorrow. If the Labour Party alters its policy, I can guarantee there won't be any more attacks on

Norwegian soil. That is, I can practically guarantee it. Maybe I can guarantee it.'

The inspired thing about the choice of Utøya was that it was a knife blow to the heart of the Labour Party. 'Of course it's tragic if anyone has to die, but in the end it's the big picture that matters. Of course it would have been much easier, say, to just kill Jens Stoltenberg. That would call for about a month's surveillance. But for someone of my intellect and intelligence, it would be a waste of resources planning to kill only one person.'

An officer came in to inform them that the Oslo police chief had accepted his demands.

'Now you tell us what you promised to,' said the lead interviewer.

But the *commander* would not.

'I want written approval, signed by the public prosecutor.'

'You should keep your word and stop playing for time!' replied the interviewer.

———

Julie was in the hotel lobby at Sundvolden when she got the call.

Geir Kåre had told her what happened on the cliff. About Viljar getting shot in the eye, Eirin in the back, Ylva in the neck. He had been running down with Simon; he had been next to him when the shooting started. Geir Kåre had been lucky. All he had was a bullet hole in his windcheater.

'Simon can't be dead,' cried Julie when she heard about Simon landing on the rock. It all went black. She slumped to the floor. Simon, who that same morning had invited her over to his table in the canteen when he saw she was on her own. Simon, who gave her the best hugs. Simon, who was always singing her father's song.

As she picked herself up from the floor, her mobile rang. She took the call without looking to see who it was.

'Julie, have you heard anything about Simon?'

It was Gunnar Sæbø.

Julie froze.

'I . . . I don't know anything. He must be hiding somewhere.'

Gunnar thanked her and hung up.

It was night, the sun was up, and nobody slept. In a few hours' time Tone, Gunnar and Håvard would set out on the same journey Simon had made on Tuesday. The flight from Bardufoss to Oslo. And then on to the Tyrifjord.

Gunnar wanted to make one more call. He had been given Geir Kåre's number. Many people said he might know something. Gunnar went into a room on his own and tapped in the numbers one by one. Gunnar knew Geir Kåre well; he had been a frequent visitor to Heiaveien since that time he came with Brage and Viljar to help Simon set up the AUF branch in Salangen.

Geir Kåre was still standing in the lobby when he got the call. He pressed the answer key and heard a low voice.

'Hello, it's Gunnar, Simon's father.'

That was all Gunnar got to say.

Because Geir Kåre just cried.

He wept and could not stop.

He sobbed into the phone.

Gunnar sat very quietly at the other end.

Geir Kåre could not get the words out.

Gunnar was silent. He sat completely still.

'Geir Kåre,' Simon's father said at last, 'can you tell me what happened?'

Geir Kåre described what he had seen.

There was not a sound from the Salangen end. Then Gunnar cleared his throat.

'Is there any chance Simon could be alive?' he asked finally.

'Well I'm not a doctor—' replied Geir Kåre.

'Is there any possibility you could be wrong?'

'But I've been in the army, so I've seen . . . I mean, we were taught—'

'Could you be wrong?'

'I don't think so.'

'Perhaps there's a chance he's alive, all the same?'

'No, Gunnar, he was shot through the heart.'

Silence down the line.

'I saw him die, Gunnar.'

'Well, thank you for telling me,' said Simon's father.·

He put the phone down. He got up and went into the living room. Tone was sitting there. All the others were sitting there.

Gunnar didn't say a word. His legs carried him out onto the veranda.

————

'Your son is charged with acts of terrorism.'

They were sitting in a room at Oslo central police station. Wenche wanted to keep her jacket on because she was 'all to pieces with nerves'.

'Is there any proof?' she asked.

The interviewer confirmed that there was. 'Did you know anything about his plans?'

'I don't know anything. I don't know anything!'

'Tell us what you do know.'

'He said he'd finally got everything he had dreamt of. He dug the soil, he sowed grass and reaped it, and he'd learned to drive a tractor. When he got back yesterday evening he was shattered and just fell into bed. He said he was going to be at home here with me for three days, for a rest. I don't know how he could have anything to do with this. That's all I can tell you.'

Anders was sensible and clever, but had definite opinions, his mother said. He had lots of good friends, and solved other people's problems for them; everything he did, he did 100 per cent. 'He's a nice boy, warm and fond of his mum. Yes, as his mother I can only give him top marks.'

'What was it that Anders had definite opinions on?'

'He thinks so much has gone wrong with society. It should be stricter in Norway, people here have too much freedom. He thinks there should be more rules. The state church should be a proper state church, more forthright. The priests should be more like in the old days. I think the same. The Norwegian gospel won't count for anything soon. Anders thinks it's a bad thing that there's no teaching about Christianity in our schools any more. But then it's a bit difficult because we've got so many different people here. I grew up in the 1950s. It was stricter then. You got the cane if you didn't behave yourself. And you were expected to show consideration for other people. Anders wanted it to be like that. I miss it myself, having grown up with it.'

'Is there anybody Anders feels hatred towards?'

'Not hatred. Maybe dissatisfaction's a better word. But then so many people are dissatisfied, aren't they?'

'What is he dissatisfied with?'

'He's dissatisfied with the government. That's allowed, isn't it? He said the system was a shambles and they needed to change their policies a bit.'

For her part, she said, she thought society ought to take better care of the old, and the poor children, instead of stashing away all those billions abroad. 'But whenever he complained I would say, leave it, it's fine living in Norway, things are pretty good for us and the government's clever with money.'

She was asked about his weapons. The shotgun was in two pieces, she said, and therefore not dangerous. The Glock was big, dark and so heavy she needed both hands to hold it.

'He really enjoyed the pistol club. The supervisor told him he was good,' she said, and continued: 'If Anders does turn out to be involved in this terrible drama, I don't want my friends ever to know. Because then my life will be ruined, too. I hope you understand. There's no call for my friends to go judging Anders, even if I do. I can't bear the idea of losing contact with my friends . . . It can't be possible. My Anders who's such a good, kind boy.'

She started crying.

'Would you like some tissues?' they asked her.

She shook her head.

'And after we had such a nice time yesterday evening. Why would he want to attack a government building? It's just unthinkable. Why would he kill people on Utøya? I mean to say, he's a farmer in Elverum! He was so worn out and happy. This is awful. I think this might finish me off. It's almost like my own trial. I hope you don't see me as a bad mother. Here I am, more or less informing on my own son.'

'We very much appreciate the fact that you are helping us shed light on the case.'

'My son is as good as gold. If it does turn out to be Anders, he must have been unconscious when he did it. Could I go out for a cigarette?'

They let her go out. The interview continued on her return.

'How does he react if things go against him?'

'He makes sure nothing goes against him. He's always ahead of his problems.'

'How does he show his feelings?'

'He sometimes raises his voice, but generally he says things aren't worth crying over.'

'What's he like when he's happy?'

'Well, then he says he's happy. That's what I've always told him: you've got to say it. You've got to show it in your body language, put your feelings into words and be more extrovert. If ever we've got problems, we always sit down and talk about it. He's good at that.'

'What's he like when he's unhappy?'

'I've never seen him really unhappy. Because he's never been particularly unhappy. He's nice, and he's decent. He changes light bulbs, carries heavy things, does bits of painting and that, so I've always said I couldn't have a better son. He's not the sort to keep his feelings inside. He was a bit unhappy when he was about twelve or thirteen because he was so small, but I told him not to think about it, because he had so many great qualities. Then he became a bit more of an extrovert.'

She stopped, and was asked to go on.

'He's kind, he's never done anything to hurt his mother . . . this is a nightmare . . . if what you say is true . . . I feel as if I'm dying . . .

But nobody could possibly do all that on their own . . . it must be a gang . . . it can't be Anders anyway . . . he only got back yesterday . . . '

She fell silent for a moment. Maybe she should not say this, she went on, but what they said on the TV about that bomb had made her think. They had interviewed some expert who said how easy it was to make a bomb out of fertiliser. It had occurred to her that Anders had lots of cow dung. And when they said on TV that the man was white and had a pistol, she had thought, well, Anders has a pistol. But then she had told herself: No, I'm adding two and two to make five here, just because Anders hasn't come home. It couldn't be possible.

'But I don't want to say anything that might put my son in prison for fifty years. How do they treat a person who's suspected of something like that?'

'He's safe, and the police are taking care of him.'

'He said he was looking forward to his dinner . . . '

Wenche started crying. 'I shouldn't cry so much.'

'You go ahead,' said the interviewer.

'No, I'd rather cry when I get home,' she replied.

'Ought I to get angry, get furious, and ask why he did this to me? It's awful, terrible. I can't tell a single one of my friends, and it's sure to be in the paper and everything. It's almost worse than being . . . than being lesbian or homosexual! It's the very worst thing that could happen to a person. What will people say about me? They'll point at me and say: she's the mother of that man who killed those ten people on Utøya. . . '

She sobbed. 'How long will the sentence be if he's guilty? Will he be able to have visitors?'

The interviewer let her talk freely. 'He can't have planned this overnight, he must have been sitting up there, thinking.'

Wenche paused and looked at the woman interviewing her. 'Is it right what they say, that a mother can have an intuition, a sickening feeling? I think it is. I sat there, wanting him to see those terrible things on TV, and he didn't come home, and I thought . . . and I thought . . . oh no . . . '

She looked at the interviewer.

'I'm the unhappiest mother in Norway.'

———————

It was almost two in the morning. Lara had dozed in the bed, but she could not really sleep. She was afraid there was somebody standing outside her window. The sound of the shots was still ringing in her ears. She thought about Bano. Maybe she was downstairs.

The reception area was still full of people. There were parents with desperate expressions and red-rimmed eyes. There were also cries of joy, people embracing. There were parents who had come to pick up their children, cold, yes, wet, yes, traumatised and afraid, yes, but alive!

Lara was looking towards the entrance at the very moment her family arrived. Ali ran towards her in tears and hugged her. 'I'm so, so glad you're alive,' he whispered.

Her father came hurrying over too and folded her in his arms. He was shaking. He hugged her, kissed her, hugged her again.

'I'm so glad you're here,' he said, over and over again.

But her mother did not see her.

All she could see was the one who was not there.

———————

The interrogation at Utøya ended in the fourth hour after midnight. The accused was to be taken to the main police station in Oslo, from where his mother had just left.

They called up one of the volunteer boat drivers who had been ferrying the police to and fro between Utøya and the mainland all night. Breivik was taken out of the building in the white overalls and old shoes.

On his way down the wet grass with cuffed hands, he slipped.

A policeman grabbed hold of him so he could regain his balance.

'Are you all right?' asked the officer.

'Yes thanks,' Breivik replied.

He sat in the boat in silence on the way over. It was a dull, grey dawn.

The interrogation continued in the car on the way to Oslo. The officers asked Breivik to tell them honestly whether any more attacks were planned. He answered that: 'If I give you that, I'll have nothing.'

'It's important to curb people's fears now,' objected the police. Breivik retorted that it was up to the powers of law and order to make people feel safe.

'It's beyond our power to reassure the Norwegian people now, so you have achieved that effect.'

Breivik grinned.

'That's what they call terror, isn't it?'

———

All over the island, sounds were ringing out. The opening notes of a symphony, a Justin Bieber song, the signature tune of *The Sopranos*, or just standard ringtones. Many of the phones were set to silent, because their owners had been trying to hide and did not want to be given away by their phones. Now their mobiles were lighting up soundlessly in the darkness. Some through a blanket, in a pocket, in a stiffened hand.

They were calls that would never be answered.

Only the police officers set to watch over the dead could hear the tunes or see the displays, lighting up over and over again.

Mum

Mum

Mum

Mum

Until the batteries gave up, one after another.

On Facebook, people were sharing their hopes and fears. Håvard followed the messages flooding onto Simon's page.

COME ON Simon Sæbø!

Fighter!
Get in touch!
Come back hoooooome!!!!
I have hope.

Simon was not lying out in the rain any longer. As the result of a misunderstanding, the rescue team had started to take some of the dead off the island, transporting them over to the mainland, where the civil defence force had put up a tent.

The young police officer from Nordre Buskerud who had stayed over at the *Thorbjørn*'s jetty throughout the massacre, counting the shots but never trying to interfere, was now taking part in the rescue operation. He had been part of the team that patched up Viljar's head and helped carry him off the island and into a boat.

Once all the living had been taken to the mainland, he turned to the dead.

He went over to the tall, thin boy dangling over a rock. The boy's face was totally white and his muscles had begun to stiffen. His left hand was clutching a *snus* tin.

The policeman took hold of him. He gripped his shoulders. As he lifted the boy from the rock it came.

The blood.

It came gushing out.

All the blood that had been pooling in Simon's chest cavity came flooding over the policeman. Blood that had been kept in by the pressure of the rock sprayed his face and drenched his hair; it ran down his uniform and onto his boots, and stained his hands red.

It was precisely as much blood as could fit in a strong young chest.

Does Your Child Have Any Distinguishing Features?

On Saturday morning, Jens Stoltenberg took the shortest possible route to Sundvolden. He climbed into a helicopter at Akershus Fortress and fastened his seatbelt. The machine rose into the air.

All through the evening and night he had been in emergency meetings: the police had briefed him; PST had briefed him. Norway had been exposed to a terrorist attack from the inside. One by one his secretaries of state had come to see him at his residence, to which his staff had moved after his office in the Tower Block was reduced to rubble. Bedrooms were turned into offices, armchairs served as beds. The long wooden dining table accommodated a growing number of computers, mobile phones and notebooks. Most of his ministers were on holiday when the bomb exploded; a lot of them at summer homes the length and breadth of Norway, in the mountains, in the woods, by the sea, and they assembled gradually, depending on how far they had to come.

Stoltenberg initially did not want to believe it.

He clung to the hope that it was a gas leak. He was exasperated at being confined to the secure room. But it was the police, not the leader of the country, who decided such matters. He wanted to get out and set to work. In there, news from the outside world came via a couple of mobile phones. At times he was left sitting in the room on his own.

The first intimation that something dreadful was happening at the AUF summer camp had come in a text message at a quarter to six from the Minister of Culture Anniken Huitfeldt, herself a former AUF leader. 'Shooting incident on Utøya. Some dead, I hear.'

The Prime Minister was kept constantly updated on the worsening situation. He received the disquieting reports of the increasing number of deaths before they reached the news media. By about ten o'clock on Friday evening, still only seven deaths had been reported. Around midnight, a figure of ten was issued.

Then came the shock announcement at between three and four the next morning: more than eighty killed.

Towards morning Norway's chief of police Øystein Mæland, who had also been best man at Stoltenberg's wedding, confirmed a total of eighty-four.

As the helicopter came in over the Tyrifjord, the Prime Minister asked the pilot to take a sweep over Utøya. He knew every point and bay of the island, he knew which flowers would be spreading their fragrance in late July, where there was sun and where there was shade, where Lover's Path was at its most romantic. The year before, he and his father Thorvald had had one of the points named in their honour as a thank-you for donating to Utøya the royalties from the book they wrote together. The point was called Stoltenberget. The previous day, three young people had been killed there.

Jens Stoltenberg was fifteen the first time he came to Utøya. That was in 1974. The AUF was in the doldrums after a divisive split in the Labour movement over EEC membership two years earlier, with the mother party campaigning wholeheartedly for YES, while the youth wing clearly came out in favour of 'Vote NO'. The EEC was ruled by capital, the AUF argued. The Labour Party lost a lot of its votes to the more left-wing Socialist Electoral Alliance in the election the year after the referendum and had to try to pick up the pieces. The entire AUF was quite unpopular with the Labour Party leadership, particularly for its standpoint on foreign policy: the young radicals' stance on issues like the Vietnam War, support of the PLO in Palestine, criticism of apartheid in South Africa and opposition to NATO.

Utøya was also at a low point. The island was a heavy burden on the AUF budget and the secretary of the organisation declared that he wished the whole island would sink into the fjord so they would be rid of it. It was overrun by water voles, the buildings were rotting and there was no proper maintenance. In 1973, a German business-man had put 1.5 million kroner on the table to buy the whole island, which had been a gift to the AUF from the trade unions in 1950.

But then the AUF took the decision to really make something of the heart-shaped island. To tempt people to the summer camp in 1974, the members' newspaper wrote of a state it called 'Devoted to Utøya' and held out the prospect of community singing, political workshops, sun, summer and new issues to campaign on.

The teenage Jens Stoltenberg was one of those who rapidly became devoted to Utøya, and since his first trip in 1974 there had only been two years when he had missed a visit. This year would have been his thirty-fifth summer.

As the pilot swung across the island the Prime Minister stared down. He saw numerous white spots on the ground. In some places they lay like strings of pearls along the shoreline. Every pearl was a blanket. Every blanket was a human life.

It was impossible to take in.

He had been told what had happened, he had seen the number, but it was a number the economist simply could not grasp. He had dealt with numbers and statistics all his working life but he was not accus-tomed to counting life, to counting death.

They sat in silence. The only sound as the helicopter landed was the whirring of the rotor blades.

The Prime Minister, dressed in a black suit and tie, entered the hotel lobby. He was taken through reception to the bar area, a place that made him think of drinks in tall glasses. Nobody was there now. They were all in the banqueting hall, up a few steps from the bar. The chief of the Hønefoss police station and a man from the Criminal

Investigation Service's ID group were up on the stage. They were giving information about the last group of young people to be identified as alive.

Sitting in the hall were the Sæbø family from Salangen, the Kristiansen family from Bardu, the Rashid family from Nesodden and some hundred other families, next of kin of the missing.

The police officers on the stage had a list of thirteen names. These were young people who had been missing but had now been identified, alive but injured, at hospitals all over southern Norway.

Their names were read out one by one.

Every name was greeted with joy by one family, and growing anxiety by the rest.

Stoltenberg and those with him stood at the back of the hall. The Prime Minister surveyed the napes of necks. The shoulders. The backs. The sheer number of them. The number of parents. Younger siblings sitting next to a mother or father, leaning close. He could see those trembling, or shaking, and those sitting utterly, utterly still.

There are too few names and too many parents, Stoltenberg thought.

He knew many of those sitting in the hall; he knew their children. He had followed some of them from birth, others from the time they first spoke at the Labour Party congress. He had argued vehemently against some of them in the question of EU membership, he now being an adult in the YES camp, while they were the young radicals. Monica Bøsei – Mother Utøya – who was confirmed dead, had been a close friend.

With every name that was read out, the chances were reduced for the parents still sitting there. Those who hoped to hear that their offspring were among the critically injured. Because that would mean they were alive.

The last name was read out. Eighty-four was no longer a number, it was a catastrophe. There was no more hope; there were no more injured survivors.

Stoltenberg had to struggle to keep upright. Soon they would all be coming past him on their way out of the hall.

Then a police officer came in with a note, which he handed to one of the men on the stage. They had been notified of one final survivor at a small hospital in Ringerike. The patient had now been sent to the larger Ullevål University hospital in Oslo.

Stoltenberg held his breath.

There was one last chance.

'It is a girl,' read the man on the stage.

The parents of boys are out of hope now, thought Stoltenberg.

It was unbearable. He himself had two children the same age as those on Utøya, a boy and a girl.

The parents of girls glimpsed a ray of hope.

'. . . between fourteen and twenty, about 1.62 metres tall . . . '

'Oh God, it's Bano!' exulted Bayan under her breath.

'. . . with dark hair . . . '

'It's Bano!'

It all tallied: the height, the age, the hair colour!

'. . . and blue eyes.'

Lara looked at her mother. Her heart sank.

'Contact lenses,' whispered Bayan. 'She must have been wearing blue contact lenses!'

'She has a distinctive scar on her neck.'

'It's her,' whispered another mother. 'It's Ylva.' She was crying. 'It has to be Ylva!'

Ylva – Viljar and Torje's childhood friend – had been lifted by Simon over the log and then shot four times just seconds after Simon. She had still not been able to say her name.

Ylva's mother turned and looked at Stoltenberg, whom she had known for some years. She came towards him. Behind her, the meeting was breaking up.

Stoltenberg was overwhelmed. He embraced her and was about to say, 'That's wonderful!'

But just as he found his voice, his eyes met those of another mother. Her last hope was gone. Her gaze burned into him.

'Those eyes. Those eyes,' he said later. 'It was like the entrance to hell.'

He held his tongue and gave Ylva's mother a pat on the back instead.

Jens Stoltenberg is a man who only believes in matters that can be proved. This atheist rarely throws big words around. He seldom talks in images and allegories, and all his life he has been direct, concrete, a little hard-edged and abrupt. But in his encounter with all those lives cut short, through those who loved them more than anything, vocabulary had to expand and broaden; the word hell acquired a concrete meaning.

He went out to the bar. There was bright daylight outside. In here the desperate stood among disco balls and mirrored walls. It was hot and sticky, and a pungent smell spread through the room.

Stoltenberg went over to the nearest group of seats. There a daughter was missing. In the next one it was a son. In the third they told him their son had kept on calling, and then suddenly there were no more calls. A father had heard screams down the phone, then silence. One youngster had swum with a wounded friend on his back. A girl who had not really meant to take part this year had gone to Utøya anyway; now she was missing.

Missing gradually came to mean deceased.

Stoltenberg knelt down beside people who were not capable of getting up from their seats. He hugged, he cried. He folded people in his arms, he patted and comforted them. It was an intense sensation: all those people, all those bodies, faces in shock, young folk telling him they had cried 'Kill me, kill me, I can't bear this any longer,' when the response unit arrived.

There was scarcely a hand's breadth between the groups of seats. I can't get through this, thought Stoltenberg. There are too many of them. The number that was no longer a number overpowered him.

On the way out, numerous microphones were thrust into his face. He pulled himself together and talked, in Norwegian and English, about consideration, fellowship and warmth. While the local reporters were most preoccupied with Stoltenberg's feelings and the fact that the royal family had arrived, the foreign journalists asked searching questions about the country's state of preparedness for terrorist attacks.

'Do you have confidence in the police and the security apparatus, Mr Stoltenberg?' asked an American reporter.

'Yes, I do,' said the Prime Minister.

But today, feelings were his strongest point. 'Utøya is the paradise of my youth and yesterday it was turned into a hell.'

That was how it was.

After the meeting in the banqueting hall, Gunnar had to find Geir Kåre.

The Sæbø family had got seats on a flight from Bardufoss early that morning. Viggo and Gerd Kristiansen were on the same plane. They knew nothing, nothing at all, about their son. Nobody had seen Anders after he ran from the campsite. Roald and Inger Linaker had also flown with them. They had found out that their son was in hospital, badly hurt. They had no idea how badly.

Håvard had been given a sleeping pill before take-off, and he fell asleep. Tone and Gunnar sat clasping hands.

Simon had been shot, they realised that. He would have called otherwise. He must be on an operating table somewhere. That was why he could not call.

Before leaving Salangen they had sent pictures of him to the emergency ward at Ullevål, where the most critically injured had been flown. The hospital had asked if there was any distinguishing feature they could look for.

'Distinguishing feature? Tone! Does Simon have any distinguishing features?'

Tears ran down Tone's cheeks. 'Distinguishing features?'

She wanted to answer that they should look for a beautiful boy. The most beautiful of all.

Then she remembered the mole on his chest.

Once they had registered at Sundvolden, Tone gave her DNA; a cotton-bud swab in her mouth, that was it. The parents were asked again about Simon's distinguishing features: had he any scars, piercings, tattoos, distinctive clothing or hair? They had to fill in a yellow form called an *ante mortem*, to make it easier for the police to find Simon. This was something everybody had to do, the two of them agreed. The form was to help to identify Simon if they found him alive, but terribly injured.

Back at reception, they once again looked very thoroughly through all the lists of survivors that were up on the walls.

'I *must* find Geir Kåre. I'm sure he knows something. Do you want to come with me?'

No, Tone did not want to. She wanted to sit at a table in a corner and wait for him. She could not bring herself to talk to someone who knew.

Gunnar found Geir Kåre.

Geir Kåre took him in his arms. Held him.

Until then, Gunnar had clung to a tiny hope.

But Geir Kåre had seen everything.

Gunnar wandered in a daze across the terrace of café tables and parasols. He crossed the road and went down to the water. There he had to stop.

He couldn't get any air. It all went black. There was no air reaching his lungs. He stood there fighting uncontrollably for breath. His chest constricted.

His thoughts choked him, stabbed him and sank. Certainty took hold. His loss was so vivid to him, and memories flooded in. And everything that would not become memories.

There on the shore, Gunnar wept.

It came home to him now.

It was so final. We won't see Simon again.

Then he went up to Tone.

And told her.

A priest came over to them and sat down by Håvard, who had been going about like a sleepwalker ever since he locked himself into his room the previous evening. He sat there stiffly, shut away inside himself.

'Do you want to tell me about your brother?' asked the priest.

Håvard nodded.

There were skilled people going among them: priests, psychologists and people from the Red Cross. The King and Queen were there, the Crown Prince and Crown Princess. They were discreet, circumspect, warm. Besides Stoltenberg, a number of his ministers were also circulating. Anniken Huitfeldt, the Minister of Culture, came over to their table.

'Who are you here for?' she asked.

'Simon Sæbø,' said Gunnar, his voice giving way.

'Oh, the one who saved so many!' the Minister exclaimed.

'What's that?' Gunnar gave her a quizzical look.

'Yes, he was the one who helped people down from the path and gave away his own place!' said the minister.

What? Had he sacrificed his own life?

Gunnar was bewildered. What was she saying?

A boy who could have been alive, but wasn't. Is that what she was saying?

Had he chosen others' lives over his own?

More people came up and told him the same thing, or variations on it.

That Simon had saved lots of people at the cliff's edge.

A new sadness stampeded over them.

An unspeakable sadness.

He could have been alive! It was his own fault!

In Ullevål hospital, Viljar Hanssen was fighting for his life, while Gunnar Linaker, the goalkeeper of the Troms football team, had given up. That is, his body had given up. The king of keepers was still breathing when the police lifted him from the ground at the campsite, where he had been shot in the act of shouting 'Run!' to the rest of the Troms camp. He was still breathing when they took him down to a boat. On the way over the strait, his breathing stopped, but the rescue team got it going again. In the helicopter, they connected him to a respirator.

He was on the machine when his parents arrived from the airport. The doctor explained that if they took him off it, he would not live. The first shot had hit him in the back and gone on up the back of his neck and head, where it had expanded. The second had gone straight into the back of his head. He was knocked out by the first shot, the doctor said, but it had not penetrated the cerebellum, so he had carried on breathing. But now, there was no longer any blood supply to the brain.

'It's so unfair! It's so unfair!' cried his sister Hanne in the sterile hospital room. She had first recognised her brother by the tattoo on his leg when they were carrying him off the island, covered by a blanket.

His family all sat round him, saying goodbye. They had been asked to make some difficult decisions. It was left up to them to decide on the moment of his death.

That afternoon, his life-support machine was turned off.

But just before that, his heart was removed and would be transplanted into someone else's body.

The three said a prayer.

Their grief was vast and black. But they were grateful that they had been able to say their farewells to Gunnar while he was still warm.

And that his heart would still beat.

In another wing, Viljar lay in a coma.

His mother had spent the whole night ringing round to hospitals all over Norway. She had rung places as far north as Trondheim. But nobody could give her the assurance she sought, that her son was with them and alive.

At Sundvollen, the others from the cliff had told them what they knew. They had seen Viljar shot in the head, straight in the eye, seen blood pour out and splinters of skull go flying. We've lost Viljar, his parents thought, but they didn't say it out loud. They had Torje to think of.

At about two in the morning, Christin got through to one of the emergency numbers, and described Viljar's injuries.

'Your son is still on the island,' said the man at the other end.

'On the island?'

'Yes, they haven't brought the dead back over yet. I'm very sorry for your loss.'

Christin kept this to herself. It wasn't true until she had seen him herself. Some hours later, around seven, her phone rang. A voice asked a question.

'Has your son any distinguishing marks?'

'A scar. On his neck. A burn. From when he was little.'

'In that case he has been identified at Ullevål.'

'Identified?'

'That's all I can say.'

'Please tell me what you mean!'

'He's here. He's alive at the moment.'

They were asked to come right away. 'We can't say what the situation will be by the time you get here.'

'What do you mean?'

'I can't say any more. We want you here when we tell you more.'

They raced to the car. Torje was exhausted, and fell asleep on the back seat. His parents focused on the road. There's a sign here. There's a bend here. There's a junction here. They wound the windows up and down. Up and down. Up. And down. In an attempt to make themselves breathe.

They pulled up at the entrance to Ullevål hospital and ran in. They were taken to see Viljar in intensive care.

It was unreal. That was their child lying there. Their firstborn. The big brother. He lay deep within a white wrapping, with wires and tubes running into it. The information the hospital gave them was unambiguous: he is alive now, but you must be ready for anything.

The hours went by. In the afternoon the family was updated on the seventeen-year-old's condition.

'In all likelihood, he will survive the day.'

But the doctors could not say if Viljar would ever wake up.

And if he did, what sort of Viljar would he be?

*

On Utøya, the forensics teams had started their work. Recording and securing evidence. Everything was noted down on a pink form entitled *post mortem*.

One of the forensic technicians was Danijela Andersen, Håvard Gåsbakk's partner. She had not kept the news turned on because of their two little children at home, so knew nothing until Håvard called her that evening. She had never heard him sound so upset. 'It's insane! Sick. There are lots of them dead. They're children!'

Now she was taking over. Three teams divided the dead between them, working in pairs. Danijela and her colleague were to start with the ten who had been taken by boat to the mainland the evening before and were now laid out in the civil defence force's tent. Kripos had issued the teams with a hundred boxes of labels, number tags, plastic strips, tape, blood-sampling kits, black tarpaulins and body bags. The white body bags had zip fasteners and two carrying handles.

The weather had improved. It had brightened up and also turned warmer. They had to work quickly.

'Have you seen a dead body before?' the experienced Kripos colleague asked her before they started.

She nodded.

They removed the first white wool blanket.

A young boy. They photographed him and recorded his details on the pink form. Where the bullets had gone in and out, what injuries they had caused, abrasions, wounds. They laid him in body bag number 1.

Then a couple of boys in their underpants, who were given the numbers 2 and 3. Others were in sturdy wellingtons, waterproof jackets, woollen jerseys.

As she worked, Danijela always took care to remember that this was a human being who had been alive. She did up the girls' blouses if they had come open, pulled down a top if it had ridden up. From the moment she pulled aside the wool blanket to the moment she put them in the body bag, they were in her care. When she had finished, she stroked each one gently on the cheek. Finally, if necessary, she closed their eyes.

Halfway along the row she came to a boy with a lot of clothes on. Jeans, trainers, a windproof jacket, a jersey and a red and blue striped T-shirt. Or rather, no, it was white and blue striped, but now so soaked in blood that all the white parts had turned red.

Danijela rubbed a little of the dried blood off his face. He must have been a good-looking boy, she thought.

As he lay there on his back, his hands stuck up in the air. They were rather bent, and the same was true of his legs. He had stiffened in that position, draped over the rock.

She recorded everything. Filled in the form for the deceased. She patted his cheek. Closed his eyes. And took one last look at his handsome face before she pulled the zipper shut.

———

The interrogation room was on the sixth floor of the police headquarters. There was an experienced female interviewer waiting, while a team of detectives sat behind a glass wall. From there they could see and hear everything that went on in the room, while those in the interview room could only see themselves in the mirror glass.

Anders Behring Breivik had been locked in a cell at police headquarters at 04.49 that morning. Just before, he was asked whether he wanted a specific defence lawyer to act for him.

Breivik wanted Geir Lippestad. He was the lawyer from whom he had rented an office when he was running his firm, E-Commerce Group, with Kristian. They had shared a fridge and lunch room with the lawyer, who at that time was defending the neo-Nazi accused of murdering fifteen-year-old Benjamin Hermansen. Little had been heard of the lawyer since then.

Lippestad was still asleep when they rang.

'We have arrested an individual by the name of Anders Behring Breivik for the acts of terrorism. He wants you as his defence counsel.'

The name meant nothing to Lippestad. He was urged to think quickly about it, as the perpetrator had said there were three more terrorist cells and several more bombs in the city. The police wanted to interrogate the accused as soon as possible, but he refused to be interviewed without a defence lawyer.

By half past eight Lippestad was at the police headquarters. He shook hands with Breivik, and after a short conversation they entered the interrogation room together.

'So you're the one with the unfortunate task and honour of interviewing the biggest monster in Norwegian history since Quisling?' was Breivik's opening remark to his female interviewer.

The charge was read out to him. He was asked for his reaction to it. He said it was deficient, and he found it remarkable that it said nothing about his production of biological weapons and his intentions for their use.

He was informed that eight had been officially recorded dead in the government quarter and more than eighty on Utøya.

'Lots of them must have swum for it, then,' he said. And smiled.

In the time since the interview on Utøya he had finalised his list of demands. 'We are willing to grant an amnesty to all category A and B traitors if they dissolve Parliament and transfer authority to a conservative board of guardians, with me or other national leaders at its head,' he said. Once the demands on his first list were met, he would identify the remaining cells and thus save three hundred lives.

On his more limited list of demands he wanted the right to wear his Knights Templar uniform at his trial, which must be open and freely accessible to the media. He also had some demands regarding the conditions in which he would serve his sentence. 'You can't put Crusaders and Muslims together.' In the United States, prisoners were segregated to avoid conflicts, he said.

He was informed that a computer was on order for him. His demand to wear uniform for the committal proceedings and his trial was under consideration. They were also working on the matter of a printer; it was possible he would be able to connect to a machine elsewhere in the building.

'I hope that what I type isn't going to be deleted at the end of every day,' he said, and added that he also wanted access to Photoshop.

'That has been noted,' said the interviewer. 'The practical matters to do with the PC will be settled in due course.'

'No, I want this cleared up before I go on with the interrogation.'

'This cannot be a negotiating session,' said the interviewer. 'Your requests have been passed on.'

'In principle, all exchange of information is negotiation,' replied Breivik. 'And by the way, it would have been more appropriate for me to talk to someone with the authority to meet my demands. They are relatively modest, after all, but they are absolute!'

Twenty-four hours had passed since the bomb exploded. The government quarter was cordoned off. The armed forces had placed heavily armed soldiers at the Parliament, the Royal Palace and other sensitive buildings. Oslo was in a state of high alert. Now there were helicopters in the air. The police's top priority was to clarify whether there was any risk of further attacks.

'Are there any explosives around that have not yet been detonated?'

'In view of the fact that you are unwilling to open negotiations, you should save that question for later,' replied Breivik. 'It's not that I'm unwilling to explain, but I have to get something in return. If these modest demands are not met, I will do all I can to create complications, I will sabotage the trial, refuse legal representation and go sick.'

He showed them his plastered finger, which he feared would turn septic if it was not attended to soon.

The interviewer tried again.

'Is anyone else aware of your plans?'

'Yes, but I can't . . . This comes under the basic rules of the negotiation.'

The leader of the public prosecution came into the room to say that all the demands on the second list had been met. The police would arrange to collect his uniform, which he said was hanging in the wardrobe in his room.

Breivik turned to Lippestad and asked if he thought the police would keep their word.

'They have said it, so one can rely on that,' said the lawyer.

'Well in that case we can go on,' said Breivik, turning to the interviewer. 'You can draw up a list of your questions and give it to me. Then you have to limit yourselves to the questions on the list.'

'That's not how we work here; you can't have my questions in advance,' said the interviewer. 'Now, I hope you are going to play fair.'

He gave in, and started to explain. About the planning. About the Knights Templar. The bomb. Utøya. 'It would have saved time if you had read my manifesto. It's all in there.'

He asked for cigarettes. Marlboro Gold. 'I'll be more cooperative if you get me those.'

They gave him the cigarettes.

He asked if it was long until lunch. He said he would like pizza and cola.

These were brought. He ate with a good appetite.

After the meal break, the interviewer got straight to the point.

'I want to know what happened and why.'

'Are there Labour Party people observing this interview?' Breivik pointed to the mirror glass.

'The only people here are those directly involved in this interview,' he was told.

Breivik smiled. He smiled again when he was asked why he was smiling.

'It's a self-defence mechanism. People react differently, don't they?'

While the interview was in progress on the sixth floor of police headquarters, the police were searching the flat in Hoffsveien and Vålstua farm. The interrogator wanted to know if police lives were at risk in doing this.

Breivik shook his head. The only dangerous thing at Vålstua was a container of 99.5 per cent pure nicotine, he cautioned. Two drops could kill a person. They would have to wear thick gloves if they were opening it, and preferably a gas mask. It should be in a plastic bag on a shelf unit of chemicals, down at the bottom among a load of junk.

The plan had been to inject nicotine into the bullets, he said, so every shot would be lethal. But then he realised that would be against the Geneva Convention and abandoned the idea.

He drew a sketch map of the farm and marked where things were. That would make it easier for the police to find their way around.

'It sucks to take human life,' Breivik said suddenly. 'But it sucks even more not to act. Now that the Labour Party has betrayed its country and its people so categorically over many years, there's a price to pay for that kind of treachery, and they paid that price yesterday. We know that before every election the Progress Party gets torpedoed. The media dehumanises the conservatives. They've been doing that ever since the Second World War: continuous abuse of the cultural conservatives.'

The Knights Templar consisted of extremely gifted individuals, highly intelligent and highly potent, he explained. Those who had ordained themselves single-cell commanders were extremely powerful. The only problem with a single-cell structure was its limitation to the working capacity of one individual. 'I mean, if one person has to process five tonnes of fertiliser, you have no idea how much hard work that is.'

Then he asked for a break to go to the toilet.

The interview veered all day between Breivik's actual actions, his political universe and his wishes and whims. He could be complaining about the logistical problems that meant he did not have time to blow up the government quarter in the morning as planned, and thus also missed executing Gro Harlem Brundtland, only to say, 'I feel really good. I've never been mentally stronger than now. I had prepared myself for torture and so on, and I'm positively surprised that I haven't had to suffer it. I have no negative thoughts now, only positive ones.' In his cell, he had already planned how he could work out using simple objects such as a chair or a book, he said.

He was still a little high on chemical substances. The effect of the steroids on his body would not wear off for a couple of weeks. 'I'm biologically weak,' he explained. 'But I've compensated for that by working out.'

The interviewer produced a picture of Breivik in his full-length white protection suit with a hood, the one he had bought from the British professor of mathematics.

'Oh, have you seen the other photos too?' smiled Breivik.

'This is the photograph we want you to tell us about.'

'But the others are much more cooler! Well okay, it's Knights Templar Chemical Warfare and the photo shows the injection of biological weapons into the cartridge.'

'I'm not even wearing gloves! I should have been!' Breivik suddenly exclaimed. 'Have you seen my film yet?'

The interviewer had not.

'You ought to see it!'

He touched on his mother. 'Her life is over,' he said. 'Because if the media call me a monster her neighbours will too, and that means she can't go on living. But this task is much more important than me, much more important than her.'

It was late evening by now. He turned to Lippestad. 'You needn't sit and listen if you don't want to. If you, like, want to go home.'

'I shall stay until the end of the interrogation,' said the lawyer.

The question why was still to be answered.

'If you have that sort of pain in your heart, you know you have to inflict pain to stop the pain. But it felt absolutely awful. The first shot was the worst, directed at the biggest threat on the island . . . the one who was starting to get suspicious. If I'd had a choice, I would have skipped Utøya, it's too dirty, because even though it's extremely productive, as history is bound to show . . . it's still a hideous thing. It must be absolutely awful being a parent who's lost a child. But on the other hand, it was their responsibility to make sure their child didn't turn into an extreme Marxist working for multiculturalism. It's . . . '

He looked at the interrogator. 'It's a nightmare that I don't think you can understand until you've carried it out. And I hope you won't have to experience it because it was sheer hell. Taking another person's life. They were so scared and screaming in terror. It's possible they were begging for their lives. I don't remember. They may have said, "Please. Don't shoot." They just sat there and didn't do anything. They were paralysed, and then I executed them. One after another.'

Then he yawned. 'But listen, you people, I'm exhausted now. I hope this interview won't go on for much longer.'

But Never Naivety

Why on earth had they lain down just here?

The thought ran through Danijela's head.

It was early on Sunday morning; around eight o'clock. The island was quiet. No one was shouting orders, no one was screaming. The people there knew what they had to do and were focused on their work.

Danijela was on Lover's Path. There were ten blankets lying on the ground.

Under them were ten people. As a forensic technician Danijela was used to thinking like a detective. For what reason had the body ended up just here? Why was it lying like that? Had it been moved? How had death occurred?

They usually spent several hours examining a dead body; here they could allow themselves no more than half an hour. The dead were lying out in the open. The weather had turned warmer.

She was gathering evidence in a murder investigation, but the murderer had been caught and had admitted the murders. The case was pretty much solved.

In the course of Saturday they had examined around half of the dead and put them in the white body bags. Then the bodies were transported on the MS *Thorbjørn* back to the mainland, where black hearses were waiting to take them to the Institute of Forensics. It did not have enough cold storage, so they had hired refrigerated containers.

From where Danijela was now, on Lovers' Path, there was a clear view inland across the island, to the woods and the campsite. The path wound its way along the fence. Behind the wire netting the rocks dropped away sharply. On the wooded side of the path there was a clearing with a few pine trees dotted around it.

She crouched down beside the dead. That was her working position, kneeling over the bodies. She looked up, and then she understood. Squatting down here, you had the illusion of being hidden. A low rocky outcrop rose about half a metre above the path. If you lay down behind it, you might think you were hidden.

That was how it must have been, she thought. They believed they could not been seen.

She took off the first blanket.

Youngsters almost on top of each other, all together in a row along the narrow path. It pained her to see it.

First she took pictures of the whole group, then close-ups of each individual, from one side, then the other, from in front and from above.

She marked the location of the bodies with little flags in the ground. One flag at the top by the head, one at the bottom by the feet. Later on, GPS coordinates would be made of the site. Everything had to be done accurately. The next of kin would be able to know: it was here, precisely here, that we found your child.

She started from the right. First there was a boy a bit away from the rest, with several bullet wounds.

Then two almost tangled together. A tall, powerfully built boy had his arm round quite a small girl. Long dark hair protruded from her fluorescent yellow hood. The hair was wet. Her face was half covered. The forensic technician pulled the hood aside. All colour had drained from the face, the skin was shiny, smooth as ivory.

Danijela examined her wounds. One bullet had entered the back of her head and gone out through her forehead. Another shot had forced its way down through her throat and into her body, where it lay hidden.

Danijela carefully noted everything down. The girl wore jeans, stuffed into a pair of dark green wellies.

Danijela gently lifted away the arm of the tall boy holding the girl with the ivory skin. Whereas the others on the path were in jackets and warm tops, he was wearing a T-shirt and shorts. His hair was close-cropped, his face turned to the side. Like the girl, he had two wounds to the head. In his pocket he had a walkie-talkie. It was switched off.

'Mum, I've got to ring off now . . . ' Anders Kristiansen had told his mother that Friday afternoon. As a duty supervisor he had kept the two-way radio on. Messages were crackling in non-stop. '. . . because a policeman's just arrived to brief us. In fact I can see him coming over the hill. I'll have to go. Bye Mum!'

That was the last Anders's parents had heard from him. They had left Bardufoss early on Saturday morning, still knowing nothing about their son. Initially their elder son, Stian, was told that his brother was in Ringerike hospital, but it turned out not to be him after all. Stian was obliged to tell his parents they had been misinformed. He heard a scream down the phone line. Gerd could not stop howling. Calm, steady Gerd.

'My child!'

Gerd and Viggo could not face staying at the hotel with the other desperate, grief-stricken families at Sundvolden, so they stayed with Stian in Oslo. Some friends rang to comfort them, and said Anders was bound to be hiding somewhere. Perhaps he had swum to one of the little islands near by and was lying low there, not daring to come out.

'No, my boy wouldn't be lying low,' replied Gerd. 'It wouldn't be like him.'

A relation rang too. 'This is a sign from God!' said the devout Pietist. 'Anders had to die to make you open your eyes!' This member of the family said Gerd would have to find her way back to faith, the true faith. Losing her son was the sacrifice she had to make.

Gerd slammed the phone down.

It was Sunday, and time for church. The Kristiansen family had been invited to a remembrance service at the cathedral. They could not bring themselves to attend. Gerd did not want God mixed up in this.

The cathedral was full to the rafters. Outside there was a sea of flowers: roses, lilies, forget-me-nots. The city was in shock, the country in mourning.

Jens Stoltenberg was faced with the most difficult speech of his life. There in the cathedral, he struggled to hold back his tears.

'It feels like an eternity,' he said. 'These have been hours, days and nights filled with shock, despair, anger and tears. Today is a time for sorrow.'

As the leader of the country he could not just dwell on that sorrow, but also had to urge people to come together. 'In the midst of this tragedy I am proud to live in a land that has been able to stand upright at a critical time. I am impressed by all the dignity, consideration and determination I have encountered. We are a small country, but we are a proud people. We are still shaken by what has happened to us, but we will never relinquish our values. Our answer is more democracy, more openness and more humanity. But never naivety.'

That last line became the mantra – Norway's response to the tragedy. Overnight, Jens Stoltenberg went from being a Prime Minister from the Labour Party to being the leader of a nation.

Answering hate with love was the image of how Norway tackled that initial period. Stoltenberg's words tapped into people's feelings. He had been braced for the reaction to be one of hatred and revenge. But the opposite happened. People held hands and wept.

Viljar was in a coma, so Torje had to be the big brother.

Over the weekend, the doctors at Ullevål decided they would have to amputate Viljar's left arm. The main nerve had been shot to pieces. But they wanted to wait until he came round, if he came round.

When Torje heard this, he tucked his left arm up inside his sweater.

'I've got to find out what it's like, so I can teach him when he wakes up,' announced the fourteen-year-old. It was tricky to cut anything, impossible to do up his shoes, and thoroughly impractical all round.

'I've heard you can get a sort of one-handed tool that's a knife and fork combined,' said his father. 'We'll go out and buy one tomorrow.'

If Viljar was to wake at all, it was critical that it be soon. The longer he remained in a coma, the more serious the damage was likely to be.

Sunday night was the third night to pass without Viljar waking up. His parents took it in turns at his bedside, falling asleep with their heads on his blanket.

Sunday night, the man who had fired five shots into Viljar's body was secretly taken to the same hospital. The police wanted him X-rayed to make sure he did not have any kind of bomb trigger concealed inside his body.

Large numbers of detectives and analysts in the police and the intelligence services were combing through the manifesto and everything the perpetrator had left behind him in the way of papers, tools, chemicals and electronic trails. They were also looking for hidden codes and references in what he had written.

X-rays and scans did not detect any kind of detonator implanted in the body of the accused and he was sent back to the central detention unit just as the main police station was waking to a new morning. It was to prove a hectic day. Three intense days of interviews were over, and now the accused was to be officially charged. He wanted to be present in person and he wanted to wear uniform.

At the Law Courts, judge Kim Heger was preparing for the hearing. The police had sent him the accused's request to be in uniform for the proceedings.

Heger refused point-blank.

When the reply was communicated to Breivik, he complained that it was breach of promise. Nor had he been given pen and paper in his cell to enable him to prepare for the hearing, he objected.

'If you do not want to come to the committal hearing, your defence counsel will attend without you,' said the police.

'If my defence counsel does that, I shall appoint a new one, so the hearing will have to be postponed in any case.'

Then he changed his mind. He would attend the committal hearing after all, as long as he could have a printout of the manifesto. He wanted to read out a few pages of it to the judge.

'Since I'm not allowed to appear in uniform, I want to wear my red Lacoste jersey instead.'

This was permitted.

'And I want to shave.'

'We haven't got the facilities for that in the detention unit, but you can wash your face and clean your teeth.'

The crowd of reporters and curious onlookers began to grow in front of the Law Courts. The police judged there to be a high risk of an attempt on the life of the accused, and were out in force.

At about half past one, two armoured Mercedes SUVs drove up from the garage under the police headquarters. In one of them, the accused was sitting in the back seat, handcuffed and shackled. Some young people in the crowd at the courthouse had just attacked a grey Volvo on its way into the underground garage. They believed it to be transporting Breivik.

The two heavy black cars with uniformed motorcycle outriders in front and behind drove into the Vaterland Tunnel, which had been closed to all other traffic. Emerging from the tunnel, the cars swung across to the opposite carriageway, straight into the multi-storey car park known as the Ibsen House, and from there into the garage of the Law Courts.

The accused was accompanied into the lift, which took him to level eight, where the hearing was to be held. There were seven people sitting in room 828.

The accused looked around him in surprise as he entered. His handcuffs were attached to the shackles and he was finding it difficult to stand up properly.

'You may sit down,' said Kim Heger.

Breivik scanned the room.

'Where is everybody?'

'We are the only ones here,' replied the judge. 'This preliminary hearing is to be held behind closed doors.'

'Who decided that?' asked Breivik.

'It was my decision,' answered the seasoned judge, leaning forward to look at the accused over his spectacles.

'I bet it was the Labour Party's.'

'No, it was my decision, and this is how it is to be,' the judge said tersely. Breivik started to quibble, but was swiftly interrupted

'We must get on with the hearing,' said Heger. 'This is the way it is; we are the only ones here.' He began to read out the charges.

Anders Behring Breivik was formally charged under paragraph 147 of the Norwegian Penal Code, the so-called terror paragraph, which carries a maximum penalty of twenty-one years in prison, with the possibility of extension, if the convicted prisoner represents a danger to society.

The accused did not acknowledge his guilt, and demanded to be set free.

He expressed the wish to read something from his manifesto, and asked if he could read it in English, as that was his working language.

'No, the language of the law in Norway is Norwegian,' replied the judge.

Ignoring this, Breivik started to read out an extract from the manifesto, which the police had printed out for him as requested.

And what country can preserve its liberties, if its rulers are not warned from time to time, that this people preserve the spirit of resistance? he read, and went on: *The tree of liberty must be refreshed from time to time, with the blood of patriots and tyrants.*

Then he was told to stop. The judge was not prepared to listen.

A crowd of reporters was also gathering outside a country house at the foot of the Pyrenees in the south of France.

Gendarmes were guarding the gate. The couple living there had called the local police and asked for assistance.

On Saturday morning, the man in the house had turned on the computer to find out more about what had happened in Norway.

He had been working in the garden on Friday when his wife called out to him: 'We have to turn on the TV! Something has happened in Oslo – an explosion!'

The couple read about it on the web, watched the BBC, got worried.

'It must have something to do with Islamic fundamentalism,' Jens Breivik said to his wife. Terror had reached their peaceful home country. They sat in shock following the news, first from the government area and later from Utøya. Then they went to bed.

The next morning the seventy-six-year-old sat staring at the screen. The only thing he saw was a name written in bold letters: ANDERS BEHRING BREIVIK.

He understood nothing. There was only one Anders Behring Breivik in Norway. His son. What could he have to do with this?

He continued reading.

He read it all.

He was paralysed. He just sat there. He felt he was fainting. He blacked out.

It could not be possible.

That Monday, people came together. They felt the need to gather.

In the capital, over two hundred thousand people assembled on the square in front of the Town Hall, by the quayside. In Salangen there was a torchlit procession, in Bardu and on Nesodden. On that day, more than a million Norwegians took part in a gathering or in a procession, carrying roses.

On Utøya, all the dead had been recorded. It turned out that fifteen people had been counted twice. The new totals of those lost were sixty-nine killed on Utøya and eight in the government quarter. But few of them had as yet been identified.

In front of the Town Hall people stood with roses. The Crown Prince said *Tonight the streets are filled with love* and the crowd sang the national anthem *Yes, we love this country* as a canon, passing it between them. Then Nordahl Grieg's 'To Youth' – *Faced by your enemies, enter your time, battle is menacing, now make a stand.* The crowd filled the square, the quays, the whole Aker Brygge area and all the

streets around; it extended up past Parliament and as far as the
cathedral.

'We have been crushed, but we will not give up!'

The Prime Minister was on stage. People held their roses aloft.

'Evil can kill a human being, but never conquer a people!'

Hours later, when all the evening's briefings and meetings were over,
the Prime Minister walked quietly up Bygdøy Allé. He had walked
from his residence behind the Royal Palace and through the Frogner
district, and was now strolling down the middle of the avenue. The
air felt pure after the days of rain, everything had turned milder,
softer. He was with his State Secretary Hans Kristian Amundsen and
the Cabinet Office minister Karl Eirik Schjøtt Pedersen. Security
men were walking in front and behind them. Stoltenberg was humming a song from his youth. He searched for the words, and sang
them as they gradually came to him.

> I am quite drunk and walking down Bygdøy Allé
> And my only aim is to get home and sleep . . .

Amundsen joined in, trying to sound like the lead singer in the
Norwegian rock band deLillos.

> But before I do that! I have to see!
> The sun rising and people getting up
> Then I am safe, then I can sleep well . . .

Here, in these streets, the Prime Minister had grown up, here in
Frogner he had hung out in the same places as that lead singer, Lars
Lillo-Stenberg, in the 1980s. It was the time when they partied all
night in the large villas in the streets off the avenue, when late arrivals
at the after-party would turn up round the Stoltenberg family's breakfast table, when what was mine was yours and ours, when the hippie
era was still not quite over in Norway, when the yuppies hadn't taken
over yet, when life was simple and secure and these streets were his.

Little Oslo is a planet of its own

They were singing louder now.

All the streets are different lands
Every district a continent
And we zoom ahead, each and every one.

These same streets had also been home to Anders Behring Breivik, in the first years of his life. His fashionable Fritzners gate crossed the even more exclusive Gimle Terrasse, to which the three men were now on their way, making for number 3.

They had been invited to the home of Roger Ingebrigtsen, State Secretary at the Ministry of Defence. Two days earlier he had feared that his partner Lene had lost her only child – fourteen-year-old Ylva. Now her life was no longer in danger.

They took in the scent of July after rain. 'Like velvet,' said Stoltenberg. It was Norwegian summer at its best. Tomorrow was going to be a fine day. They took the steps up the little hill to where Gimle Terrasse lay.

Hans Kristian Amundsen had called in advance to say they were on their way. A little red-haired boy popped up at the entrance and asked: 'Are you coming to see Roger?'

Then he ran up the steps ahead of the security guards, ahead of the Prime Minister, to alert everyone inside.

The dining-room windows had been opened wide. Roger, himself from Troms, had gathered the families from his county, who had so suddenly been flung together in Oslo. At the long table sat Tone, Gunnar and Håvard, then Viggo and Gerd. Christin and Sveinn Are were sitting with Torje and Ylva's mother Lene.

There were four children missing.

They had no information about Simon or Anders. Viljar was in a coma, and Ylva had just come round from her operations.

Jens Stoltenberg went in. He wondered how this was going to go and he was afraid of saying the wrong thing.

'You came on foot?' asked their host.

'I like walking and it's about the only thing I *can* do. I haven't driven a car for six years so I've completely forgotten how to do that,' answered Stoltenberg.

They all laughed.

A gentle breeze blew in at the open windows. The street lights were starting to come on in the blue darkness out there, down there. The candles on the table flickered.

The Prime Minister went round greeting everyone, giving them hugs. They met him with warmth. It was good to be here, he thought, and the absurdity of that thought struck him. They talked. They laughed. They told tall tales, they talked about their children, oh so many lovely stories about their children, and they cried.

There was red wine. There was grilled asparagus. There was meat. There was a nice dessert. For many of them it was the first proper meal since Friday. Gunnar finally found his breath, somewhere deep down in his stomach.

Tone relaxed, and thought, this is odd – I'm enjoying the food. Being together like this gave them a sense of peace. Even Håvard thawed out. He did not say much, but he had emerged from his bubble. He followed the conversation, smiled sometimes, made an occasional comment. Then all at once, he got to his feet.

In his deep bass voice he started to sing.

> I've heard there was a secret chord
> That David played to please the Lord . . .

Håvard's voice trembled.

> It's a cold and it's a broken Hallelujah!
> Hallelujah. . .

Their loss had not yet hit them with full force. Death still seemed distant.

They knew it, but it was still not clear to them.

Their days would soon be heavy.

The next day, Jens Stoltenberg was dismayed when the emergency response unit started briefing him on its operation.

Stoltenberg knew Utøya and its environs like the back of his hand. He had rowed across, he had taken the MS *Thorbjørn*, he had swum and he had driven a motorboat in the strait. The Prime Minister took it for granted that the police had started out from the *Thorbjørn*'s jetty.

'From the golf course? Why?' he asked.

They had no good answer.

'That manoeuvre must have cost you a lot of time,' he said.

The Prime Minister grew even more concerned when he heard the account of the police boat getting water in its engine and stalling. The several changes of boat, the misunderstandings, the whole operation, he gradually came to realise, had been an odyssey of misadventure and terrible planning.

The coffin stood behind a pillar in the chapel of the hospital.

Six days after the massacre, Anders Kristiansen was identified. On the Thursday his parents were told that he had been found, and where the shots had entered his body.

They dreaded seeing him dead.

The last time they had been with him was when they drove him to the airport at Bardufoss in the middle of July. It was the summer holiday, and both parents were off work and wanted to come with him. When they saw him in the chapel, the pain was too great. It was impossible to take in. Gerd started talking as if he were still alive.

'Now, look how tall you are!' she said. Her son was 1.92 metres in height and he filled the whole coffin. 'You'll hit your head on the lid!' said his elder brother Stian through his tears.

They wanted to take him straight back home. But they were not allowed to; there were further examinations to be done. His parents wanted to wait for him. Stian persuaded them they ought to go on ahead to Bardu, and Anders would follow when he was ready.

'He saved up his money to travel and see the world, Mum. Let him make his last trip on his own. He's a big boy now.'

————

Lara could not believe it. She had to see for herself. The soul is always near the body, she thought, so if she was to meet Bano she had to do it now, while the body was still there.

They were in the chapel where the Kristiansens had been a little earlier.

'You go first, Lara,' her mother and father told her. They had come to a halt at the door.

She approached the open coffin step by step. Bano was wearing a long white gown. Her mouth was blue, and looked as if it was smiling. Her hair was tucked behind her ears. She had a sticking plaster on her forehead. Her hands were bluish and sort of shrunken. They were neatly folded on her chest.

The family had been told that one of the bullets had stopped just before it pierced her heart.

Lara stood and looked at her. It was Bano, but it was not Bano.

Suddenly she felt a force. Bano wants me to get through this! I have to, for Bano's sake.

Her big sister was right there, with her.

————

Thursday was also the day the Sæbø family had their time in the chapel.

Simon lay as if he were asleep. His hair was newly washed and was all soft and fluffy, like when he was little. It was a long time since Tone had touched his hair and felt what it was really like; he always put gel on it as soon as he came out of the shower. Now it was done exactly

the way he didn't want it. Tone tried to smooth the hair back the way
he liked it but she couldn't. It just flopped back.

'He definitely wouldn't have wanted his hair like that,' Tone said.

'I washed his hair with the same care, the same love as if he were
my own son,' said the woman who had followed them into the room.

Tone took hold of Simon's face and gave him a kiss, but immediately pulled back.

'He's all wet! Why is he wet?' she asked the woman.

'It's very cold in the refrigerated store, so it's a bit of condensation,
that's all,' she answered.

It was so final. Seeing him like that. They said the Lord's prayer.

Candles had been lit in the chapel and they burned calmly, lending a sense of something sacred. Tone had been dreading this. She had
thought someone would just pull out a drawer and show them their
son with a tag tied to his toe, like in films.

They stood there looking at his dear, white face, the skin turning
a little blue in places.

Gunnar had tears in his eyes. 'Imagine: he killed Simon without
even knowing who he was!'

———

That night, the sixth night, Viljar's mother Christin had a bad feeling.
Was Viljar about to give up? The doctors were afraid he might not survive another night. Infections were spreading round his body, so they
had to lower his temperature. He lay there utterly still. Pale, thin,
with a hole for an eye, surrounded by bleeping, humming machines.
He had still shown no sign of coming round.

'We don't know whether he will ever wake up again,' the doctors
said. But they asked them to carry on talking to him, touching him,
reading to him, talking about things that interested him, that made
him happy, that might make him want to wake up.

One of Viljar's friends, fellow AUF member Martin Ellingsen,
had come down from Tromsø. He was distraught. He had lost
Anders, Simon and possibly Viljar. Martin should have been on

Utøya himself, but he had such bad marks in German that his mother had packed him off on a language course at the Goethe Institute in Berlin. He was obliged to cancel his registration for the summer camp.

'Utøya's there every summer – come next year,' Anders Kristiansen told him. 'Go to Berlin instead.'

Now Martin was here, and he wanted to make Viljar understand that life is the coolest thing we have.

'Hi Viljar,' he started uncertainly, tailing off as he stood looking at his friend. Would Viljar ever wake up? Would he be able to talk? Would he be *Viljar?*'

'I've bought a crate of beer back home in Tromsø and we'll get stuck into that as soon as you're out of here,' said Martin. 'And Tuva says we can try our luck with all her friends.'

Martin gave a little sob. He kept his eyes fixed on Viljar's face as he talked. He was sitting on the edge of the bed. He said whatever came into his head, sharing gossip and quoting everything from rap lyrics to poetry.

'You can take the snowmobile out on Svalbard, Viljar! Or do you want to go to New York? *Hero at night, hero all the day, all the way to morning*, Viljar!'

But Viljar did not move.

Rays of light entered the room.

It was a lovely morning and it was going to be a fine day.

Viljar lay in his bed, pallid.

Then Martin started singing. Christin and Sveinn Are had gone quiet. Hope was ebbing away.

Martin sang, very quietly.

> If I could write in the heavens, yours is the name I would
> write!
> And if my life were a sailing ship, you would be my port.

Martin's voice cracked, but just as he was taking a breath to carry on a frail voice was heard from the bed.

. . . if I could bring down the clouds
and make a bed for you . . .
and this mountain were a piano . . .
then . . .

Viljar opened his one eye. He looked at them and smiled.

Part Two

Narcissus on Stage

The cell was in the basement of the Law Courts.

He sat on the bench waiting, with armed men standing guard outside.

They had picked him up from Ila prison early that morning, unlocked his cell door and brought him down to the prison garage. There they had asked him to get into a white van.

To the uninitiated, it looked like an ordinary van, not unlike the one he had hired the previous year and blown up outside the Tower Block in the government quarter.

In the van they fastened him to the seat with handcuffs and restraining belts. It was an armour-plated vehicle. He could not see out. With a number of police officers around him, he sat strapped for the half-hour that it took to reach Oslo. Upon arrival the driver steered the van straight down into the garage beneath the courthouse. From there they led him into the building and along several corridors, then locked him into the waiting cell in the basement, a security cell into which he was not allowed to take anything.

That was where he was sitting now, dressed in a dark suit with a freshly ironed shirt and copper-coloured tie.

His defence team had come down to greet him before they went back up to their room behind the main courtroom on the first floor.

Now he was alone. He was waiting for someone to come and fetch him. He was waiting for the curtain to go up.

The media ban had been lifted in the middle of December, so he knew in detail what the courtroom looked like, who the professional judges were, the lay judges, the prosecutors, the public advocates. He had prepared himself well and read everything that he could find on the case. He had taken a particular interest in the debate about whether he was sane and accountable for his actions.

For a long time, he found it entertaining. In fact, at first he did not take it entirely seriously and did not really relate to what the forensic psychiatrists had concluded. He was going to use the trial as a stage on which to perform, come what may. His operation had reached its third phase.

The clock in room 250 showed half past eight. Its face was grey, its hands of pure aluminium. The room was brand-new. But everything in it was muted, minimal, toned down.

The judges sat on a dais that was raised above floor level, though not by much. At their bench, made of knotless maple, were six high-backed black leather chairs. The two appointed judges would sit in the middle. Three lay judges and a reserve would be seated beside them. The appointed and lay judges would all vote on the final verdict.

Behind the chairs were low shelves of light wood that would soon be filled with thick ring binders containing the case documents. The judges would be able to turn round in their seats to find what they needed.

On the grey wall behind the judges hung the Norwegian coat of arms, a golden lion holding an axe on a red background. It was the sole element of colour in the room.

In front of the judges, at floor level, was a smaller desk with four chairs behind it. Places for the forensic psychiatrists. Their seats faced the public, not the defendant. It would be their faces that many would try to read in the coming weeks.

Most other issues were already clear. He had admitted to the actions, albeit not to any guilt, but that was a formality. If he were ruled to be of sound mind, he would get the most severe sentence the law could mete out to him, twenty-one years, with the possibility of extension if he presented a threat to society.

Or would he be held not accountable for his actions and be forced to undergo treatment instead?

Was he mad, or was he a political terrorist?

At an angle to the judges' bench, at floor level, was the prosecution bench and behind it places for the coordinating public advocates. The defendant was to sit facing the prosecution, between his defence team. Behind them was a bulletproof glass wall, and behind that were some seats for the public. Right behind the back row was the only window in the room, covered with bomb-proof foil. Pale grey blinds with a slight sparkle to them covered the frosted glass. They would remain closed for the duration of the case.

In the centre of the floor, between all the parties, stood a small desk with three sides and a chair. The table section could be raised or lowered. Those giving information or evidence could choose whether to sit or stand.

It was compact, everything felt close. The victims appearing as witnesses would be sitting only a few metres from the perpetrator, in the same seat where he himself would be cross-examined.

The room was divided in half lengthways. A low glass door, kept closed, separated the participants in the trial from the public, who were to sit in long rows running the length of the room. The Law Courts had tried to fit in as many seats as possible and the rows were so tightly packed that one could only edge along them. The sole access to most of the seats was via the central aisle. It would be impossible to leave the room unnoticed except during a break. The first row behind the partition was reserved for the courtroom artists and the commentators from the major media outlets. Less important media groups were in the second row. Then came next of kin, the bereaved, survivors and other people affected, their escorts and the public advocates. The support group for the victims' families and survivors had been allocated permanent seats, as had the leadership of the AUF. Other seat allocations would rotate throughout the trial. The two back rows were again for accredited press. Here there were electrical sockets and headset plugs for those requiring interpreters. From the interpreting booth, which had an unrestricted view of all the parties, there would be simultaneous translation into English, Kurdish or Georgian, depending on the media's needs and the nationalities of the victims and their relatives.

The room had never been used before. It did not have a single scratch.

In August the previous year, twenty days after the terrorist attacks, the man in the waiting cell had met the first pair of psychiatrists. There was one woman and one man: cool, buttoned-up Synne Sørheim and heavy, ruddy-cheeked Torgeir Husby.

Both of them had clearly indicated that they were uncomfortable about meeting him. They said they were not in a position, either emotionally or intellectually, to carry out the one-to-one interviews with him which would be the norm. They worried about potential hostage situations, they said, especially in the case of the female expert.

For the first eleven sessions he was in shackles and his left arm was fastened to an abdominal belt. He was placed in a corner with three conference tables between him and the two psychiatrists. There were two prison guards in the room throughout. Interviews twelve and thirteen were conducted in the visiting room. On those occasions he was locked into a cubicle behind a glass wall while the experts, one for each session, sat on the other side of the glass. The guards were then on the outside.

For the first meeting he put on his striped Lacoste jersey in muted, earthy colours, the one he had been wearing on the morning of his operation, when he took the getaway car to Hammersborg torg to park it and then walked through the government quarter under an umbrella in the drizzle.

The psychiatrists shook his hand. Then he was taken to his seat behind the three tables. In his right hand he had a piece of paper, which he put on the table in front of him. The first thing he said was that every forensic psychiatrist in the world probably envied them the task of assessing him.

This produced no particular response, so he went on. He had a list of seven questions, which they had to answer before he would cooperate.

'Why?' asked the psychiatrists.

'Well, I don't want to contribute to my own character assassination, do I?'

The experts were not prepared to answer any questions. These observations were to be done on their terms. The accused insisted he must know their view of the world before he could take part in the sessions. 'If either of you is on the ideological left, you're going to be biased,' he asserted.

Arguments were tossed back and forth. Breivik said they would no doubt try to gag him. 'The machinery of power is Marxist-orientated. After the war they sent Quisling's justice minister to the madhouse.' Breivik repeated that he had to find out what they stood for before he gave them any answers.

Finally the forensic psychiatrists conceded. They asked him to state his questions. He read from the piece of paper.

'The first is: What do you think about Knut Hamsun and the resignation of justice minister Sverre Risnæs after the Second World War? The second is: Do you think all national Darwinists are psychopaths?'

The psychiatrists asked him to explain the term 'national Darwinist'.

'A Darwinist who's a pragmatist. With a logical approach to political decisions. There are two approaches to a political problem: men are pragmatic, whereas women use their emotions to solve the problem. Darwinism views human beings from an animal perspective, sees things as if through the eyes of an animal and acts accordingly,' he said. 'One example is when America bombed Japan. They employed a pragmatic approach. Better to kill three hundred thousand but save millions. We consider that to be suicidal humanism.'

'Who are "we"?'

'We, the Knights Templar.'

The experts asked him to go on with his list of questions.

'Question number three is whether you think the American military command lacks empathy. Question number four: Explain the essential distinctions between pragmatism and sociopathy.'

'How do you interpret the word sociopathy?' asked the psychiatrists.

Breivik smiled. 'Isn't it the same as psychopathy, then?'

He said the subsequent questions would be more personal in nature.

'Question five: Are you nationalists or internationalists? Number six: Do you support multiculturalism? Number seven: Have either of you had any connection with Marxist organisations?'

'How will you judge whether we are telling the truth, if we answer your questions?' they asked.

He grinned. 'I already know. Thousands of hours as a salesman have taught me to predict with seventy per cent accuracy what the person I am talking to is thinking. So I know that neither of you is of Marxist orientation, but you are both politically correct and support multiculturalism. It's all I can expect.'

'Do you guess, or do you know what other people are thinking?'

'I know,' said Breivik. 'There's a big difference.'

He said he had studied a great deal of psychology and was able, for example, to tell the difference between people from the east and the west end of town by their clothes, make-up and watches.

At the end of the session he decided he would accept them. He looked at the experts and smiled.

'I think I've been lucky.'

In the first 'Status præsens' that they wrote, Sørheim and Husby drew a number of conclusions. 'The subject believes he knows what the people he is talking to are thinking. This phenomenon is judged to be founded in psychosis,' they wrote. 'He presents himself as unique and the focal point of everything that happens, believing that all psychiatrists in the world envied the experts their task. He compares his situation to the treatment of Nazi traitors after the war. Indicative of grandiose ideas,' they noted. 'The subject clearly has no clear perception of his own identity as he shifts between referring to himself in the singular and the plural,' they concluded. 'The subject uses words that he stresses he has invented himself, such as "national Darwinist", "suicidal Marxist" and "suicidal humanism". This phenomenon is judged to be one of neologism.' Such 'new words' could be part of a psychosis.

At the end of the thirteen sessions, the psychiatrists concluded that Anders Behring Breivik suffered from *paranoid schizophrenia*. They adopted the view that he was psychotic while carrying out the attacks, and that he was still psychotic when they were making their observations. He was therefore in criminal terms not responsible for his actions and should receive treatment rather than a sentence.

Breivik was permitted to read the report when it was submitted in November 2011. He said he thought they were trying to make a fool of him. They called his compendium 'banal, infantile and pathetically egocentric', motivated by his 'grandiose delusions about his own exceptional importance'. But they also described him as 'intelligent rather than the opposite'.

He had boasted of having an extremely strong psyche, stronger than that of anyone else he had ever known. Otherwise he would never have been able to carry out his attack on Utøya, he emphasised.

Then he started getting letters from supporters around Europe who felt he would serve their cause badly if he were deemed to be not accountable for his own actions. He suddenly understood what was at stake. He could be declared insane.

Then it would all fold.

The court could rob him of all honour. Judge him to be an idiot.

Just before Christmas he rang Geir Lippestad, who was basing his preparations on the conclusions of the psychiatric report. He asked the lawyer to come and see him right away.

He had sounded worked up on the phone, so on 23 December Lippestad assembled the whole defence team – four people – and went to see him at Ila prison. They listened to him through the glass

wall in the visiting room. Anders Behring Breivik asked them to
change strategy.

'I want to be found accountable for my actions,' he said.

The defendant was supported in this by those with the clearest
grounds for hating him. Several next of kin and bereaved family
members had been upset to hear that he might escape serving a
formal sentence. Mette Yvonne Larsen, one of the coordinators of the
public advocates' group, asked for another set of experts to be
appointed so that the court would have two reports to compare.
More and more of the public advocates began to press for a new
assessment to be carried out.

The prosecution did not want it. They had already started their
work based on the first report. Lippestad was against it. Breivik said
he'd had enough of shrinks. There was also the risk that a second
observation would produce the same result as the first, thought
Lippestad, making it even more difficult to advance the case in court
that Breivik was of sound mind, as he now wanted to affirm.

'It has never done a case any harm to shed some extra light on it,'
concluded Wenche Elizabeth Arntzen, the judge appointed by the
court to lead these negotiations. She requested that two new forensic psychiatrists be designated.

Norwegian forensic psychiatry circles are small, and many of the
higher-profile experts were ruled out because they had already
expressed their opinions in the media. But the court found Terje
Tørrissen and Agnar Aspaas, who met the criteria of neither being
close colleagues, nor having commented publicly on the case.

In addition to his conversations with the experts, Anders Behring
Breivik was now to be observed around the clock for four weeks.
Early each morning a team of a dozen nurses, psychologists and auxiliary psychiatric nurses were to come and spend the day with him,
talk to him, eat with him, play board games with him and then submit
written reports, which the new pair of experts would have to take
into account.

In mid-February 2012, two months before the trial was to begin, the first session with the new forensic psychiatrists took place. Breivik asked for the interview to be recorded, so Lippestad could listen to it afterwards.

Terje Tørrissen was a short man with a furrowed brow and flyaway hair. He greeted Breivik, who entered the room flanked by two prison officers.

'I want to inform you that we have not read the previous report,' said Tørrissen, speaking quietly in his lilting western Norwegian accent.

'Well I'm extremely impressed that you've been able to restrain yourselves,' smiled Breivik. 'I didn't think there was a psychiatrist left in the whole of Norway who hadn't made some comment, as it's very tempting in such an important case as this.'

Once Breivik had seen how he was being perceived in the media, he realised he had miscalculated the impact his trappings of chivalry would make. The uniforms, the martyr's gifts, the awards and decorations, the titles, even his language were ridiculed. He decided to tone down his rhetoric, referring to himself from then on as a foot soldier rather than a messiah.

'Just to put you fully in the picture,' he told Tørrissen, 'I have never behaved threateningly to anyone, apart from a window of three hours on the 22nd. I am polite and pleasant to everybody. The picture the media has constructed of me as a psychotic monster who eats babies for breakfast . . . '

He laughed. Tørrissen noted that the laugh was self-deprecating, reasonable and appropriate.

'. . . is pure rubbish and there's no need for you to be apprehensive about me. I look forward to our working together.'

Tørrissen asked him about his conduct during the open committal hearing ten days earlier, when Breivik had made a short speech. It provoked laughter from AUF members in the hall when he declared himself a knight of the indigenous Norwegian people. He called the murders defensive attacks, undertaken in self-defence, and demanded his immediate release. The laughter spread as he spoke, and after a minute had passed the judge halted him.

'If you know me, you'll realise that was just an act I put on,' explained Breivik. 'I am actually talking to a tiny group of people, a few thousand within Europe, though that number can grow. I know very well it's a description of reality that's wholly alien to most people. But it's a show ... I play my role. If I say I expect to be awarded the War Cross with Three Swords, I know I'm not going to be, of course. And when I say I expect to be released immediately, I know that isn't really going to happen either. I'm only following the path I've set out all along.'

'But why not just be yourself?'

'In a way I am myself, because I represent an entirely different picture of the world, which has been unknown since the Second World War. It exists in Japan and South Korea, but it's alien to a Marxist society.'

'What you call a Marxist society is really more of a social democratic society, isn't it?'

'I don't mind calling it a social democratic society. I can tell the two apart. But when I say cultural Marxist, that's to be provocative. In a way, it's a domination technique. They use such techniques on the left and they like calling other people obscurantists, so now we're using those tactics against the left. By the way, are you familiar with the seven questions I asked the previous experts?'

'No, but you can ask me them now.'

'When something big like 22 July happens in a country, it's impossible not to be emotionally affected. The psychiatry profession has no experience of politically motivated aggressors, and that's a major problem. You don't know how militant nationalists think, or how militant Islamists think, or for that matter how militant Marxists think. It's a separate world that I think very few psychiatrists have any knowledge of. You weren't taught about it at college, and I don't know if there's any additional professional training available either. Maybe you can tell me about that.'

Tørrissen could not. He replied that his mandate was to find out whether the subject was ill; that is to say, whether he was suffering from a severe mental illness or not.

Psychiatry's great weakness was that it had no response to religion or ideology, argued Breivik. 'If it had been up to your profession, all priests would no doubt have been shut up in lunatic asylums because they had had a calling from God!' he laughed, and described at some length how Islamists prayed five times a day to become fearless warriors, and how they got to have sex with seventy-two virgins in Paradise if they were killed. For his part, he had used Bushido meditation. He said that this involved manipulating your own mind to suppress fear, but also other feelings. 'That's the reason I seem de-emotionalised. I couldn't have survived otherwise.'

Nor should the psychiatrists underestimate the importance of what he had learnt from al-Qaida, he said. Islamic militants were his source of inspiration. He was like them. A politically motivated aggressor.

In contrast to the first two psychiatrists, Terje Tørrissen and Agnar Aspaas studied the language and opinions of websites on which Breivik had been active, such as Gates of Vienna and document.no.

'You can't isolate the ideological, even if you decide to leave it out of a report,' Breivik had stressed.

Just a couple of days before the trial, the new report was presented. This pair of psychiatrists concluded that Breivik suffered from *dissocial personality disorder* with *narcissistic traits*. He had a 'grandiose perception of his own importance' and saw himself as 'unique'. He had a vast appetite for 'praise, success and power' and was totally lacking in 'emotional empathy, remorse or affective expression' vis-à-vis those touched by the acts he had committed.

In legal terms, a narcissistic personality disorder means that a person is criminally responsible, because the disorder is not considered to be based in psychosis. Tørrissen and Aspaas concluded that Breivik was not psychotic either at the time of the acts of which he was accused, nor during the observation. He could therefore be held criminally liable.

These two reports were then pitched against each other as the case opened on the morning of Monday 16 April 2012.

*

For weeks the rain had deluged bare trees. Dirty grey snow had melted and run along the streets, leaving in its wake the detritus of winter, grass covered by the previous year's rotting leaves, and a season's dog mess. The city had still not had its spring cleaning.

The night-time frosts kept seeds and buds slumbering and daytime temperatures that crept a few degrees above zero were not enough to wake them. But in the course of the night, the cloud cover had broken. This Monday morning there were glimpses of colours that people had not seen for a long time. Wasn't that a little bud on the branch of the cherry tree? And that tulip on its way out of its sheath of leaves, would it be pink or yellow?

It was worse in nice weather, Gerd Kristiansen said. The grief was hardest to bear in the sunshine because Anders, *her Anders*, had so loved the sun.

Those who were to attend the first day of the trial had risen at dawn. Hours of queuing were anticipated to get through the security checks. Some white marquees with plastic windows, the sort you have at summer parties in case it rains, had been erected in front of the entrance to house mobile scanners.

There was barely an empty spot in front of the Law Courts; every square metre had been taken over by crush barriers or the press. Vans with antennae on their roofs were transmitting live pictures world-wide. The TV faces had momentous expressions.

The rays of the early morning sun created haloes round the journalists in the security queue; they glinted on the crush barriers and dazzled the police officers holding weapons loaded with live ammunition by the solid front door.

Beyond the first few metres of daylight, the building darkened. The staircase to the first floor wound its way round a glass lift. Black ropes divided the Law Courts into zones. The colour of your admission card indicated which zones you were allowed to be in. The blue ones were for those affected by the case: survivors, next of kin, the bereaved and public advocates. The black were the parties in the case; the green were healthcare workers. The press had red cards. All had to wear their laminated cards round their necks for the duration of the case.

The lanyards were black, apart from for those with red cards. They also had red lanyards which they were to keep visible, so they could easily be spotted if they strayed into the wrong place. On the cards were your name, your photo, your status and a bar code so the scanner would detect it if you tried to enter a restricted zone.

The whole first floor was set aside for the case. There were two large rooms with work stations for the press, one of them with simultaneous interpretation and an editing room for TV transmissions. There were waiting rooms for witnesses, rest areas and a big room where next of kin, the bereaved and the survivors would be left undisturbed. In the depths of the building was room 250, guarded by another team of police officers. Only a small band of people entered there.

The silver-grey hands were both pointing to the number nine.

The seats had filled up. Necks with black lanyards and necks with red lanyards created a striped effect in the rows. There were roughly equal numbers of each, about a hundred red, about a hundred black.

On the public side of the partition, selected photographers were standing ready to capture the entrance of the parties. The photographers were allowed to take pictures until the court was in session.

There were a number of wall-mounted cameras in the room; their lenses covered most angles. In the editing room, a TV producer from the Norwegian Broadcasting Company was seated in front of a bank of screens. She cut continuously and expertly from one shot to another: 'Camera 1, there, Camera 2, hold, over to Camera 6.' The pictures went direct to the live TV broadcast and to courtrooms all over the country.

Seventeen district courts were showing what the public in the courtroom could see. The regional courts had set up big screens and loudspeakers for the transmissions from Oslo.

In Nord-Troms District Court sat Tone and Gunnar Sæbø. Gerd and Viggo Kristiansen were there too. Now they would see him, hear him speak. The one who had taken their boys from them.

The Rashid family had fled the whole thing. For weeks the papers had been full of details of the coming trial. Mustafa, Bayan, Lara and Ali had just wanted to get away, so they were on a trip to Spain. They could not bring themselves to give the perpetrator the attention that following the trial would accord him.

The prosecution found their places. Then the public advocates, the defence. Police guards were already in position.

He is in the building, wrote a journalist from a news agency. The words flew out across the world: *Er ist in dem Gebäude. Il est dans le bâtiment.*

It was ten to nine.

The door of the waiting cell was opened. He stood up from the bench and was put in handcuffs. Court guards in pale blue shirts took him out and along the hallway.

The lift doors opened and he stepped inside with two guards. The lift was cramped. The three men were pressed close against each other.

The doors opened onto a white corridor. They stepped out, rounded a corner and turned into another corridor. The last stretch had been redecorated at the same time as room 250. The windows along the corridor were frosted. Their bolted frames were painted an industrial grey. The daylight barely penetrated from outside.

There was a court guard in front, then him, then another guard behind. He filled his lungs with air. He straightened up, pulled back his shoulders. The door to room 250 was opened. He went in.

Nobody there. He had entered a little corridor running along the side of the courtroom, a space where no one could see him. He followed the blue shirt barely ten more steps – then the hail of flashes, a cascade of clicking cameras. *He is in the room*, tapped the news reporters. Shining lenses were directed only at him.

They zoomed in on a pale face. He was less toned than before, a little jowlier.

He was unable to resist a smile. The moment he had been waiting for, preparing for, dreaming of. Now it was here. He pursed his lips to control the smile, nodded to his defence team and took his seat between them as he stole a glance at the audience. His eyes darted round the room; after all, this was not for him to look at them, but for them to look at him. Still, he just had to see, see them all, all those people looking at him.

His hands were cuffed in front of him and connected to a wide belt fastened round his hips. A broad-shouldered detention guard fumbled with a key to unlock the handcuffs. The accused gave an almost apologetic look to the audience as the man struggled to remove the cuffs. Once they were off, dangling from the hip belt, he clamped his right fist to his chest, thrust his arm out straight and then raised it in a salute. Long enough for the photographers to immortalise the moment, he held the clenched fist at head height. A gasp ran through the courtroom. It was five to nine.

He raises his arm in a right-wing extremist salute, wrote the news agencies. He pours himself a glass of water. Drinks. Looks at a pile of papers he has in front of him. Messages flashed out second by second from the journalists in the room.

The public prosecutors go over and shake hands with him!

Foreign journalists were bewildered to see this cordiality. Were they really shaking his hand?

The public advocates and the victims' defence lawyers shake his hand too!

In some countries they would have put him in a cage. They would have taken his suit and white shirt and cropped his hair. His gleaming silk tie would have been out of the question.

In a cage or not, there were many in the room who would willingly have seen him humiliated. And humiliation was what he himself feared most of all. Being reviled was nothing in comparison to being humiliated.

Having people uncover the cracks in him.

Tørrissen once asked him about vulnerability. 'Do you have a vulnerable side?' the psychiatrist had asked. 'Not being loved,' Breivik answered. 'That must be every person's greatest fear, not being loved.'

Now he hoped for one thing. That his mother would not appear in the witness box. She had been called to give evidence, but she had asked to be excused. She was his Achilles heel, he had told the psychiatrists. She was the only one who could disconcert him now, bring the whole thing down. That was why he had not agreed to any prison visits from her before the trial. Up to now, everything had gone as he wanted it. The eyes of the whole world were on him.

The public prosecutors and public advocates returned to their places after the handshakes. He sat down.

He sits down.

It was nine o'clock.

The judges come in.

The court rose; the two public prosecutors, the defence lawyers, the public advocates, the public, the press, everybody rose, except for one: the defendant.

He remains in his seat. He smiles.

That is to say, he tried to conceal a smile. He sat with his legs planted wide apart. Everyone could see that he was not in shackles beneath the desk. He shifted round in the comfortable chair, which had a good, broad back. He looked round, settled himself into the chair. His eyes scanned the rows of seats. Suddenly his lips curved into yet another smile. He had seen someone he knew. Kristian, his former friend and partner, was in the front row. What was he doing here?

Well, the tabloid *Verdens Gang* had invited him to use one of their places so he could tell their readers afterwards *what it was like to see his former friend again*. Both of them averted their eyes.

'The court is in session!'

There was a quick rap of the gavel on the bench. The head judge, Wenche Elizabeth Arntzen, made an authoritative figure. She was an experienced judge, around fifty years of age. She had short, greying hair, clear blue eyes and a thin mouth. At the neck of her robe was a hint of a lace blouse.

The accused wanted to set the agenda from the start, and spoke immediately.

'I do not recognise the Norwegian court or law because your mandate has come from parties that support multiculturalism.'

He cleared his throat. The judge looked straight at him and was about to say something when he continued.

'I am also aware that you are a friend of Gro Harlem Brundtland's sister.'

His voice was high-pitched.

The judge asked if that meant he wished to raise a concrete objection to her participation in the proceedings. The defence team shook their heads. Not as far as they knew.

No, he did not want that. He simply wanted to make a point.

Wenche Arntzen set out the procedural rules for the trial. She was rapid and concise. There was no time to lose here. She asked the accused to stand and confirm his full name and date of birth.

'Anders Behring Breivik, born 13th of February, 1979.'

He appeared meek now, and spoke in little more than a mumble.

When the judge came to his profession, she said, 'Well, you are not working.'

Breivik protested.

'I am a writer and I work from prison,' he said.

He was instructed to sit down.

Then the charges were to be read out by the female half of the prosecution duo, the blonde and elegant Inga Bejer Engh.

'Please go ahead,' said Arntzen.

Bejer Engh got to her feet. She appeared calm. In a clear voice she began to read out the charges: that he stood accused under the terrorism paragraph, §147a of the Norwegian Penal Code.

The Oslo public prosecution hereby judges that Anders Behring Breivik, in accordance with §39 or the Penal Code . . . should be transferred for mandatory psychiatric health care . . . for committing while in a psychotic state an act otherwise punishable by law.

In other words, the prosecution agreed with the first psychiatric report, which took the view that Breivik was sick and could be treated.

The charges continued. An act of terrorism, read Bejer Engh. An explosion. Loss of human life. Premeditated killings. Under severely aggravated circumstances.

The bomb detonated at 15.25:22 with violent explosive force and result-
ing pressure wave, intentionally putting a large number of people in the
buildings of the government quarter or at street level in direct mortal danger,
and caused massive material destruction . . . in the explosion he killed the fol-
lowing eight people . . .

The prosecutor read rhythmically, even expressively. All the syl-
lables were to be enunciated, all the names were to be heard. There
were no hesitations; she had practised these names. These names
meant something. These people had lived. They were the most
important people in this court case. They were the ones it was all
about.

He was at the entrance to the Tower Block, near the van, and died instantly
of massive injuries caused by the pressure wave and the impact of splin-
ters / objects.

She was at the entrance to the Tower Block, near the van, and died instantly
of massive injuries caused by the pressure wave and the impact of splin-
ters / objects.

There was only a pronoun to distinguish between the accounts of
the two lawyers' fates. They were there, precisely there, in the worst
place imaginable, when the bomb exploded. They were born in 1979
and 1977.

The public prosecutor took a sip of water. The glass beside her was
continually emptied and refilled. Apart from a stifled sob after some
of the names, the room was silent. Nobody cried openly. The
bereaved put their hands over their mouths so as not to make a noise.
They lowered their heads so as not to be seen.

The public prosecutor came to Utøya.

He was in front of the café building.

He was at the campsite.

He was in the small hall.

She was in the main hall.

She was on Lovers' Path.

He was in the wood east of the schoolhouse.

She was at Stoltenberget.

She was at Bolsjevika.

He was at the pumping station.
She was on the shoreline at the southern tip.
He was found at a depth of six metres.
He ran away and fell down a cliff.
All sixty-nine killed on Utøya were part of the charge.

In addition to the killings enumerated above, he attempted to kill a number of other people but was not successful in his intentions, said the prosecutor.

A reporter from a Swedish news agency murmured, almost to himself, on hearing for the first time where the bullets had entered: *The back of the head, they were shot in the back of the head.* The elderly man wrote it down in his report. At intervals of just a few seconds he sent new lines to his desk in Stockholm, where they corrected his typos, edited the text if it was too explicit, and swiftly sent it out to subscribers, TV stations and local papers all over Sweden. The man added a phrase after his first, *They were shot in the back of the head.* He tapped at his keys and sent some words of explanation to the subscribers – *as they fled. They were shot in the back of the head, as they fled.*

The accused did not look at Bejer Engh while she was reading; he kept his eyes down. But his defence lawyers had their eyes on her, listening. There was nothing else to prepare for that day. Now it was just their names and ages that were to sink in. Born in 1995, in 1993, in 1994, in 1993, in 1994, in 1993, 1996, 1992, 1997, 1996 . . .

Breivik had his head down. Sometimes he moved his lips, sucked them, fiddled with his pen, a special pen, soft, so he could not injure anyone with it; himself, for example.

Bejer Engh had moved on from the dead to the living.

It brought no relief. Amputations. Projectiles in the body. Injuries to internal organs. Damage to the optic nerve. Extensive tissue damage. Cerebral haemorrhage. Open fractured skull. Removal of the colon. Removal of a kidney. Projectile fragments in the chest wall. Skin transplant. Fractured eye socket. Permanent nerve damage. Shrapnel embedded in the face. Stomach, liver, left lung and heart damaged. Removal of fragments from the face. Arm amputated at the elbow. Amputation of arm and leg on the same side.

These were war injuries.

The events on Utøya generated a huge amount of fear in sections of the Norwegian population. The accused has committed extremely serious crimes on a scale not previously experienced in our country in modern times.

Bejer Engh had almost reached the end.

Breivik opted to continue looking down. He was later to call this considerate. *He didn't want to make this a worse day for the bereaved than it already was.*

At half past ten, the prosecutor finished and the accused was allowed to speak. He stood up and said: 'I admit the actions but I do not admit guilt, and I plead the principle of necessity.'

The court adjourned.

After the break, a thin-haired man took the stand. His movements were free and easy, he seemed self-assured. This was the other prosecutor, thirty-eight-year-old Svein Holden. He was to make the opening statement about the defendant's life, and his crimes.

While the accused had sat expressionless throughout the account of his killing of seventy-seven people, he now appeared to relax. He looked round the room while the public prosecutor was going through his life.

Months of police interrogations had produced several thousand closely written pages. What was true, what was untrue, what was significant, what was unimportant, ascertaining all this was the prosecution's task. Much of what Breivik had said had been followed up and checked, and the police had not found him to be telling overt lies.

But there were questions he answered evasively, such as those about the group to which he claimed to belong. The prosecution had concluded that the network Breivik maintained was set up in London in 2002, the Knights Templar, in which he said he was a commander, did not exist.

This was sheer fabrication.

Or was it fantasy? Delusion?

The question was, did Breivik believe it to exist?

Again, was this a madman or a political terrorist?

This was to be the central question throughout the ten weeks of the trial.

Holden argued for the former. He was of the opinion that a marked shift took place in Breivik's life in 2006. Breivik stopped paying his subscription to the Progress Party, he closed down the company selling fake diplomas, he lost a lot of money on shares and he moved back home to his mother. He started playing computer games at all hours.

On a big screen behind the public advocates, a picture came up of Breivik's room. This was how he had left it on 22 July, and how the police had found and sealed it later that day.

There was an open can of Red Bull on the desk. A safe on the floor. A printer. Post-it notes everywhere. Graffiti on the walls. An unmade bed.

The picture had been taken on a sunny day. Streaks of light found their way through the closed blind.

When he moved in here his life was unravelling, was the impression Holden gave. Was this when his delusions started to develop? At this time, Breivik was playing hardcore in *World of Warcraft* as Justiciar Andersnordic.

'Is it a violent game?' the judge interrupted.

'It depends how one defines violence,' replied Holden, and promised to come back to the question a little later.

It was after a year or two of gaming that he started to write his compendium, claimed Holden, that is to say, he authored little of it himself, but borrowed freely from what was available on blogs *out there*. Holden spoke at some length about the three books in the compendium, saying that he wanted to concentrate on the third, where Breivik himself was more present in what was written. This was the declaration of war, in which the reader is exhorted to join a civil war, and where notes on preparations and the instructions for making the bomb are included, Holden told the courtroom.

The relatives sat in silence, heads bowed, listening. The journalists tried to catch every word, some of them tweeting constantly. The moment Holden's words were out of his mouth, they were on the internet.

A heavily made-up CNN reporter in the first row sat listening with her headset carefully placed over her hair. A sultry, masculine musk spread from the back rows. It was the al-Jazeera reporter, who had just come back in after a live broadcast. Yes, the world was watching today.

Some of the AUF leadership were more engrossed in their mobile phones than in what the public prosecutor was saying. It was as if they did not really want to hear this, all this about the perpetrator and his life. For them, he did not exist as a person, insane or not, even with him sitting in front of them. It had been so abrupt, so acutely painful. Now they wanted to move on. They wanted to get away. Away from him. Nor did the AUF have any official attitude on the question of his soundness of mind; it was nothing to do with them, the constitutional state would have to deal with that. The crucial thing was that he must never come out. Messages were sent and received on their phones, all set to silent.

Holden started to speak about *acquisitions*. Weapons, equipment, chemicals for the bomb, fertiliser, uniform. The police had dressed a mannequin in the outfit the defendant had been wearing on 22 July, including the spurred boots caked in mud.

Breivik smiled when he saw a picture of the badge he had attached to the sleeve of his uniform. *Multiculti Traitor Hunting Permit*, it said. *Valid for category A B C only.*

Holden showed pictures of Vålstua farm on a bright summer's day; he showed pictures of the Electrolux blenders, the Chinese bags. The police had established that the bomb had been made exactly as Breivik described in the manifesto. They had carried out a test detonation of the same type of bomb, and Holden again showed pictures.

Breivik followed all this attentively. He was at a seminar about himself.

'He also made a film,' said Holden. 'The accused uploaded a movie trailer from the Window Movie Maker programme.' The film comprised ninety-nine images cut together.

Sacred tones filled room 250. An iconic black and white photograph appeared on the screen; the Red Army soldier planting the Soviet flag on the Reichstag in 1945. The birth of cultural Marxism, according to the film. Image after image showed post-war Europe being taken over by Marxists. The church-style music was interspersed with electronica. Then the soundtrack changed. The quarter-tones of Arabic music streamed from the courtroom loudspeakers and a man's voice sang a lament, *amanamananah*. There were pictures of veiled women, pregnant with grenades rather than babies; there were pictures of hordes of refugees on their way to Europe. Then came hope for change, marked by large, single-word captions: strength, honour, sacrifice and martyrdom. Medieval motifs and Knights Templar were accompanied by music from the computer game *Age of Conan*. The finale, entitled 'New Beginning', depicted the ideal society. The film concluded with a single sentence: Islam will again be banished from Europe.

Breivik's eyes had narrowed and were filled with tears. His mouth was drawn upwards towards his nose. His face flushed and he wept without shame, staring at the images as they faded out.

Until then, no one had seen him shed a single tear. Now he cried openly.

'Are you all right?' asked the female lawyer seated on his left, according to the lip-readers hired by *Verdens Gang*.

'Yes, fine,' replied Breivik. 'I just wasn't prepared for that.'

For the screening of his film. His. Film.

The court took a break.

In the hall outside, the journalists tried to find an explanation for his tears.

'He feels great, tender, warm love for himself. When he sees his own product he is terribly moved. That is how I interpret it,' said a psychologist to the media.

The tracks from *Age of Conan* were sung in old Norwegian by the singer Helene Bøksle. 'Picture it . . . you hear this song as you battle to wipe out one flank of the enemy. . . ' he had written in Book 3. 'That angelic voice singing to you from heaven . . . that voice is all you can hear as everything light turns dark and you enter the kingdom of heaven . . . that must really be the most fantastic way to die a glorious martyr's death.'

For a moment, he had been a knight again.

It was half past one when the prosecutor showed a picture of the island, 500 *metres long and 350 metres wide*, given to the AUF as a gift in 1950.

Breivik stifled a yawn.

Holden related the course of events from the time Breivik was transported over to the island on MS *Thorbjørn*. When the prosecutor reached what happened at the café building, he said he was going to play one of the emergency calls that was made from there.

Every time Breivik's lips curled into a smile, he doggedly attempted to moderate it. This time he hid the muscle movement by sucking his lower lip.

A dialling tone resounded from the loudspeaker system, into the room and into seventeen district courts.

A receiver was lifted, and a cool voice said, 'Police emergency line.'

'Hi, there's shooting on Utøya in Buskerud in the Tyrifjord,' said a girl in a broad accent. Her breathing was louder than her words. When she called she had just seen her boyfriend shot and killed. It was 17.26 and Breivik had been on the island for ten minutes. He had just entered the café building. The girl, whose name was Renate Tårnes, was hiding in a toilet.

The policeman asked if there were any more shots. Renate gasped for breath before she answered.

'Yes, it's going on the whole time. There's total panic. *He's in here.*'

The girl had lowered her voice to a whisper. She did not say anything more, just held up her phone so the operator could hear what she was hearing.

There was a sudden scream on the recording. Another. Several more. The courtroom was stock-still. Not a single movement. Not even the tapping of keys. You were there, outside it, yes, safe on a seat in the room, and yet you were there, caught up in the massacre. You heard the sound of Breivik's weapons. Initially, the shots were sporadic. They rang out singly, then a number in swift succession. Then more and more.

The recording lasted for three minutes. Holden played it all.

Three minutes. Fifty shots. Thirteen killed.

Many in the courtroom were crying.

Breivik looked down at a fingernail.

Before he glanced back up.

The Monologue

Day two. It was the day he had been preparing for.

Later, many others would set their mark on the case: the prose-cution, the witnesses, experts, the defence. But today, the floor was his alone.

He walked slowly to the witness box. In his hands he had a pile of papers. He laid them on the table in front of him and adjusted his cuf-flinks.

'You must restrict yourself to the truth in matters pertinent to your case,' the judge said severely.

'Dear judge Arntzen, I request that I be allowed to set out the framework of my defence, and I hope you will not interrupt me; I have a list of points—'

'You must lower the microphone a little for the transmission to the other courts to work properly.'

He was ready. This was the book launch.

'I stand here today as a representative of the Norwegian and European resistance movement. I speak on behalf of Norwegians who do not want our rights as an indigenous population to be taken away from us. The media and the prosecutors maintain that I carried out the attacks because I am a pathetic, malicious loser, that I have no integrity, am a notorious liar with no morals, am mentally ill and should therefore be forgotten by other cultural conservatives in Europe. They say I have dropped out of working life, that I am narcissistic, antisocial, am prey to bacteria phobia, have had an incestuous relationship with my mother; that I suffer from deprivation of a father, am a child murderer, a baby murderer, despite the fact that I killed no one under fourteen. That I am cowardly, homosexual, paedophile, necrophiliac, Zionist, racist, a psychopath and a Nazi. All these claims have been made. That I am mentally and physically retarded with an IQ of around eighty.'

He read rapidly. He had a great deal to get through. The meaning of the words was more important than how they were read. 'I am not surprised by these characterisations. I expected it. I knew the cultural elite would ridicule me. But this is bordering on farce.'

He glanced up and then looked down at his papers again.

'The answer is simple. I have carried out the most sophisticated and spectacular attack in Europe since the Second World War. I and my nationalist brothers and sisters represent all that they fear. They want to scare others off doing the same thing.'

The judges were watching him closely, listening attentively. How was he when let off the leash? Did he ramble? Was he consistent? This was the first time they had heard him speaking freely. How would he fill the half-hour allocated to him?

Norway and Europe were suffocated by total conformity, he told them. And what they knew as democracy was in reality a cultural Marxist dictatorship. This was familiar ground now.

'Nationalists and cultural conservatives were broken-backed after the fall of the Axis powers. Europe never had a McCarthy, so the Marxists infiltrated schools and the media. This also brought us feminism, gender quotas, the sexual revolution, a transformed church, deconstruction of social norms and a socialist, egalitarian ideal of society. Norway is suffering from cultural self-contempt as a result of multicultural ideology.'

The defendant proposed that there be a referendum asking the following question: Do you consider it undemocratic that the Norwegian people have never been asked about Norway becoming a multiethnic state? Do you consider it undemocratic that Norway takes in so many Africans and Asians that Norwegians risk becoming a minority in their own capital?

'Nationalist and culturally conservative parties are boycotted by the media. Our opinions are seen as inferior, we are second-class citizens and this is not a proper democracy! Look at the Swedish party Sverigedemokraterna and what is happening to them. In Norway, the media have conducted a systematic smear campaign against the Progress Party for twenty years and will go on doing so. Seventy per cent of British people see immigration as a major problem and think Great Britain has become a dysfunctional country. Seventy per cent are dissatisfied with multiculturalism.'

'Are you reading from your manifesto now?' asked the judge.

'No,' replied Breivik, and went on: 'How many people feel the same in Norway, do you think? More and more cultural conservatives are realising that the democratic struggle achieves nothing. Then it is just a short step to taking up arms. When peaceful revolution is made impossible, then violent revolution is the only option.'

He read in a monotone, without any sense of involvement. If he was animated inside, it did not show on the surface. It was like his time in the Progress Party. Even when he was on the podium, he had failed to inspire, failed to generate any enthusiastic applause. There was a bitter tone to his voice.

'People who call me wicked have misunderstood the difference between brutal and wicked. Brutality is not necessarily wicked. Brutality can have good intentions.'

People in the rows of seats sighed and shrugged. Some AUF members had started whispering together.

'If we can force them to change direction by executing seventy people, then that is a contribution to preventing the loss of our ethnic group, our Christianity, our culture. It will also help to prevent a civil war that could result in the death of hundreds of thousands of Norwegians. It is better to commit minor barbarity than major barbarity.'

He took a breath and embarked on a discourse about what he termed the Balkanisation of Norway and the witch hunt against cultural conservatives.

'Are the AUF and the Labour Party doing this because they are wicked, or because they are naive? And if they are only naive – shall we forgive them or punish them? The answer is that most AUF members have been indoctrinated and brainwashed. By their parents. By the school curriculum. By adults in the Labour Party. Still these were not innocent civilian children, but political activists. Many were in leadership positions. The AUF is very much like the Hitlerjugend. Utøya was a political indoctrination camp. It was—'

'I must ask you to moderate your words out of consideration for the survivors and the bereaved,' Arntzen said sharply.

'The certainty of my imprisonment does not frighten me. I was born in a prison, I have lived my whole life in a prison in which there is no freedom of expression, where opposition is not allowed and I am expected to applaud the destruction of my people. This prison is called Norway. It doesn't matter whether I am incarcerated in Skøyen or in Ila. It is just as pressing wherever you live, because in the end the whole country will be deconstructed into the multicultural hell we call Oslo.'

'Are you near the end, Breivik?' asked the judge. He had exceeded his limit of half an hour.

'I am on page six of thirteen.'

'You must start finishing off now,' said Arntzen.

'My whole defence hinges on being able to read the whole thing.' He took a sip of water and went on reading in a monotone. 'According to the Central Office of Statistics, immigrants will be in the majority in Oslo by 2040. And that does not take into account third-generation immigrants, adopted children, people who have no documents or who are here illegally. Forty-seven per cent of those born in the hospitals of Oslo are not ethnic Norwegians. The same is true of the majority of children starting school.'

The three male forensic psychiatrists sat looking at Breivik, while Synne Sørheim made copious notes on her laptop.

'European leftists assert that Muslims are peaceful and against violence. This is lies and propaganda.'

'Breivik, I must ask you to wind up,' Arntzen said urgently.

'It is not possible to abbreviate the framework of my defence,' he replied, adding, 'If I'm not allowed to set out the framework, there's no point my saying anything at all.'

The judge was determined to keep a tight rein from the start. She could not ease off on day two.

'There is a consensus between European elites and Muslims to implement the multicultural project in order to deconstruct Norwegian and European culture and thereby turn everything on its head. Good becomes evil and evil becomes good. In Oslo, aggressive cultures like Islam will increasingly predominate, spreading like cancer. Is this so hard to understand? Our ethnic group is the most precious and the most vulnerable, our Christianity and our freedom. Ultimately we will be left sitting there with our sushi and flatscreen TVs, but we will have lost the most precious—'

'Breivik!' said the judge. She pronounced his name abruptly, almost without vowels so it sounded like 'Brvk!'

'I have five pages left.'

'This goes far beyond what was requested yesterday,' said Arntzen, addressing Lippestad.

'I understand the court, but request that he be allowed to go on,' said Lippestad, but he also asked Breivik to cut down his text. He stressed that a limit of five days was set for his defence.

'This was originally twenty pages but I managed to compress it into thirteen. There's a lot of talk about these five days I've got. I never asked for five days, I only asked for an hour! That's this hour I've got now. It's critically important for me to explain all this,' exclaimed Breivik.

'Go on!' said Arntzen.

'Thank you!' said Breivik.

'Then we come to another European problem. Demands such as sharia law. Norway spends its oil money on social security benefits for immigrants. Saudi Arabia has spent one hundred billion dollars on

Islamic centres in Europe and financed fifteen hundred mosques and two thousand schools . . . '

Public advocate Mette Yvonne Larsen, responsible for liaison between the courtroom in Oslo and the district courts, broke in and said that victims and relatives of victims in the regional courtrooms had taken offence at the fact that Breivik was allowed to go on for so long.

'You have heard how the bereaved relatives are reacting. Will you show consideration for that?' asked the judge.

'I will,' replied the accused.

'Is it relevant to you?'

'It is relevant to show consideration.'

'In that case I ask you to do so and to conclude as quickly as possible.'

'I have three pages left,' said Breivik. 'If I'm not allowed to read to the end, I shall not account for myself to the court at all!'

Then prosecutor Svein Holden spoke. 'We consider it important that Breivik be allowed to continue.'

He went on.

'Oslo is a city in ruins. I grew up in the West End, but I see that the city authorities are buying apartments, public property, for Muslims, who create ghettos. Many Muslims despise Norwegian culture, feminism, the sexual revolution, decadence. It starts with demands for special dispensations and ends with demands for self-rule. Sitting Bull and Crazy Horse are heroes acclaimed by the indigenous people of the United States – they fought against General Custer. Were they wicked or heroic? American history books describe them as heroes, not terrorists. Meanwhile, nationalists are called terrorists. Isn't that hypocritical and highly racist?'

The judge regarded him intently.

'Norwegians are the indigenous people of Norway! Norway supports those who champion the indigenous peoples of Bolivia and Tibet, but not of our own country. We refuse to accept being colonised. I understand that my info is difficult to understand, because the propaganda tells you the opposite. But soon everybody will realise. Mark Twain said that in a time of change, a patriot is seen as a failure. Once he has been proved right, everyone wants to be with him, because then it costs nothing to be a patriot. This trial is about finding out the truth. The documentation and examples I have presented here are true. So how can what I have done be illegal?'

The psychiatrist Synne Sørheim was chewing gum as she typed her notes. The three men sharing the table with her all had their chins propped on folded hands, observing what happened in front of them.

Arntzen's fellow judges were leaning back, slightly sunken into the chairs with the tall black backs. Their eyes were fixed on the accused, while their faces were calm, revealing nothing. The corners of their mouths slowly sank into a resting position as Breivik's speech dragged on.

The accused drank from a glass of water.

'Have you finished, Breivik?' asked Arntzen.

'I've got one page to go.'

He set down the glass.

'Sarkozy, Merkel and Cameron have admitted that multicultural-ism has failed in Europe. It doesn't work. In Norway, the opposite is happening: we're going in for more mass immigration from Asia and Africa.'

He looked down at his papers and hesitated for a couple of sec-onds, then exclaimed, 'Well I'm censoring myself now, right, just so that's clear!

'We are the first drops of water heralding the coming storm! The purifying storm. Rivers of blood will run through the cities of Europe. My brothers and sisters will win. How can I be so sure? People are living with blinkers of prosperity. They are going to lose everything, their daily lives will be full of suffering and they will lose their identities, so now it is important for more patriots to shoulder responsibility, as I have done. Europe needs more heroes!'

His presentation had been polished in advance and his arguments built logically on each other, within his own universe, and he could not resist, as in the manifesto, repeating the best.

'Thomas Jefferson said the following: The tree of freedom must be watered from time to time. With the blood of patriots and tyrants . . . '

He cleared his throat.

'I'm almost at the end. The political elite in our country are so brazen that they expect us to applaud this deconstruction. And those who do not applaud are branded as evil racists and Nazis. This is the real madness – they are the ones who should be the subjects of psychiatric evaluation and be branded as sick, not me. It isn't rational to flood the country with Africans and Asians to the point where our own culture is lost. This is the real madness. This is the real evil.'

He drew breath.

'I acted on the principle of necessity on behalf of my people, my religion, my city and my country. I therefore demand to be acquitted of these charges. Those were the thirteen pages I had prepared.'

———

'What is your own relationship with Christianity?' asked the public advocate Siv Hallgren the following day. The lawyer, who had herself been a teenage mother, represented several of the bereaved relatives.

'Well, I'm a militant Christian and not particularly religious. But I'm a *bit* religious. We want a Christian cultural heritage, Christian religious instruction in schools and a Christian framework for Europe.'

'But what about you personally? Do you profess the Christian faith? Do you believe in the resurrection?'

'I'm a Christian, I believe in God. I'm a *bit* religious, but not *that* religious.'

'Have you read the Bible?'

'Of course. I used to, back when we were taught about Christianity in school. Before it was abolished by the Labour Party.'

Hallgren asked him to define Norwegian culture. The one he had killed for, in order to preserve it.

'You could . . . yes, you could say that the very heart of Norwegian culture is the Norwegian ethnic group.'

He hesitated for a moment, reflected and found the answer: 'Everything that's in Norway, from door handles to designs to beer labels to habits. It's all culture. Phrases, ways of addressing people. Absolutely everything is culture.'

Said Breivik.

The Heart of the Matter

At the centre of the court case there was a beating heart.

The dead.

The murders had almost been pushed into the background by the discussions of the perpetrator's psyche and ideas in the run-up to the trial. But it was the murders he was to be punished for, not the ideas.

Svein Holden and Inga Bejer Engh had been given responsibility for planning the trial the previous autumn. They were both young parents with a couple of children each and lived ordinary, privileged Norwegian lives. Holden went straight from leading a press conference about the first psychiatric report to the hospital for the birth of his second child.

The two public prosecutors spent a lot of time talking to the bereaved relatives and survivors as they planned the proceedings, fetched their children from nursery, prepared the trial, changed nappies, read interview transcripts, sang lullabies. Their meetings with other mothers and fathers only a few years older than them had a profound effect. Some were angry, others were weighed down by sorrow. Something was broken in all of them. The public prosecutors encountered both aggression and the story of my son. My daughter. Our child.

It was important both to retain the emotions and to keep them out of it. This was how the public prosecutors were reasoning as they asked themselves how best to set the parameters for the trial.

Svein Holden made a list:

Good contact with those affected.

Good procedures for the police.

Good overview of the trial.

Treat it like any other criminal case.

But it was not like any other criminal case. The scale was so large. Seventy-seven murders.

The Director of Public Prosecution had insisted that every single murder must be investigated. Time and place were to be established, when and how. Those who had lost their loved ones needed as much detail as possible; it was said to help in the healing process.

The police had learned from the response to the bombings in Madrid and London. In those trials, the cause and time of death were not established for each person, their individual fates were not treated as separate events by the court. They were simply referred to as victims of a terrorist attack.

The investigations must also be as thorough as possible so that they would stand up to potential conspiracy theories that might emerge in years to come.

Many wanted to make their mark on the trial. A campaign had started, pressing for all those who had been on Utøya and all those who had been in the government quarter to be named as victims in the charges. They had all been subjected to attempted murder, after all. In a standard trial, attempted murder would always be part of the charge.

The general rule was that if you were named in the charge, you also had to be called as a witness. It would exceed all time scales.

So where would they draw the line?

The two prosecutors were sitting in the office of the Director of Public Prosecution, counting. How many people were hit by projectiles in the government quarter? How many were hit by bullets on Utøya?

They ascertained the numbers and used that as the basis of who would be named in the charge. Those physically hit by metal or lead. In the government quarter there were nine, in addition to the eight who were killed. On Utøya there were thirty-three, on top of the sixty-nine killed.

The Director of Public Prosecutions made a few calculations; the timescale of the trial had already been established. It was to last ten weeks. Yes, it would work. They could all be called in as witnesses. There would be just enough time for that within the period they had at their disposal.

But how many had suffered direct harm in the terrorist attack?

With regard to the government quarter, they decided to write that 'an additional two hundred people were physically injured by the explosion'. That included cuts, fractures and hearing damage. As for Utøya, they wanted to focus on the trauma suffered by many of the youngsters as a result of seeing people they knew murdered, of losing their friends.

No one was to be forgotten, even if they were not named.

In a standard murder trial, pictures of the dead person are shown on a screen in the courtroom. These are both general shots showing where the victim was found and close-ups documenting the cause of death.

Svein Holden took the view that the same should happen in the 22 July case. 'That's what you do in a criminal case,' said Holden. 'You show pictures. Business as usual.' The pathologists agreed.

Bejer Engh was more sceptical. She was afraid it would be too violent. Again the public prosecutors sought the advice of the support group. The bereaved did not want any pictures at all. It would be too awful. In the government quarter some of the bodies were so badly damaged that only a few body parts remained. On Utøya, skulls were shattered, the victims smeared with blood and brains. The first set of pictures had been taken by the crime technicians on the path, in the woods, by the water's edge or on the floor in the café. Later, when the dead underwent autopsies, they were photographed once more, their bodies cleaned of blood so that the gunshot wounds were more evident. These were the two sets of pictures usually shown to a court.

The views of the next of kin persuaded Holden. The public prosecutors decided they would put the photographic evidence in folders,
which would only be given to members of the court.

Inger Bejer Engh wondered how she would cope with the pictures
herself. Should she just take a quick glance when she had to? Or
should she keep looking at them until she grew immune?

All the bodies of those shot and killed on Utøya had been X-rayed.
A three-dimensional picture was generated of each one. These pictures revealed where every bullet fragment had expanded in the
tissue. One could detect the bullet in a heart, splinters scattered
through a brain, metal that had sliced carotid arteries or entered
spines. One could track the path of every bullet, to find out which
of them was the lethal one.

The medical experts were preoccupied with showing the injuries
as clearly as possible and wanted to display the three-dimensional
images of the victims in court.

'We can't show their bodies on a screen!' objected Bejer Engh.

Everything that was shown in room 250 would be broadcast to
other courtrooms and there was no guarantee there would not be
someone there with an iPhone, taking pictures.

'What shall we do then, use drawings?' asked Holden.

In conversations with the pathologists, Holden came up with the
idea of a dummy they could point to. They would need a gender-
neutral dummy and a pointer.

All right. They would order a dummy.

But where was it to be positioned? On the floor? On a stand of
some kind? On a turntable? The dummy had to represent seventy-
seven different people. It was important that it be handled in a
dignified way.

And what should the dummy look like? What colour would its skin
be?

It could not be white. How would the parents of the non-white
victims react?

Nor could it be black; that would create the wrong impression too.

They reached a decision.

The dummy would be grey.

It was 8 May. The time was eleven a.m. The tables in the cafeteria, a short distance from room 250, were emptying because all who had been sitting there were heading back to the courtroom. In the recess the cafeteria had been taken over by a loud group of people. They sat a little closer to each other than the canteen users normally did, laughed rather more often and made more noise. They all had the same shade of hair, of skin, darker than most of those in the foyer area, and there were several generations of them together. They had ordered coffee and drunk water. They were family. They were going in for Bano.

They were Kurds, from Norway, Sweden and Iraq. Few of Bano's closest relations had been able to get visas for her funeral; their applications could not be processed in time. Bano was buried the day after she was identified. She was the first Muslim ever to be laid to rest on Nesodden. A female priest officiated in the church and an imam spoke at the burial.

The court case had been planned long in advance. Now her family were here for her.

Since the start of May, the court had been going through twelve autopsy reports a day. In addition to the submission of evidence about the injuries, every victim was remembered with a picture and a text chosen by the bereaved. It gave this first week in May a sense of ceremony. On this particular day, the court had reached Utøya victim number 31.

Places had been reserved for the relatives. An interpreter sat ready in the booth. Bayan tightly held the hand of Mustafa, who was sitting beside her.

The judge asked Gøran Dyvesveen, the forensic technician from Kripos, to speak slowly and clearly so the interpreter would not miss anything. He promised to do so. It was eleven minutes past eleven.

'Bano Rashid was on Lovers' Path. She died of gunshot wounds to the head,' said Dyvesveen. Three of the judges swung round to the shelves behind them to find the file with the picture of Bano. They could see her in several pictures in the file, lying on her side on the undulating path. They could see the general view of the murder victims lying close, close together, almost on top of each other. In one of the pictures, the ten were covered by woollen blankets. It made them look like a big lump on the path. It seemed they had come together for protection, there in their final moments.

Bano's uncle, Bayan's brother, was sitting on his sister's other side and had also gripped hold of her hand. Soon the whole row was holding hands. Sitting in front of the adults were Lara and Ali, among their cousins. They too were squeezing each other's hands.

On the wall of the courtroom was a screen, on which a picture of the path was shown – the scene of the killings, but without the victims. A red dot indicated where Bano had been found.

'The dot shows where her head was,' said the forensic technician.

Then his medical colleague Åshild Vege went over to the dummy, which was covered in a velvety kind of material. Grey velvet.

Vege went through the injuries inflicted on Bano. 'Bano died of gunshot wounds to the head. These caused instantaneous loss of consciousness and swift death.'

The same information was displayed on the screen on the wall. The eighteen-year-old's name and where the bullets had hit her.

Holden was a stickler for aesthetic impression in the courtroom. He wanted all the posters, all the graphs, everything that the forensic technicians, the expert witnesses and the pathologists brought with them to be linguistically correct and to be proofread one last time before they were shown. Holden insisted that everything be in the same black type in a font offering as little distraction as possible: Times New Roman.

Everything in court was to look neat and tidy.

The caption describing Bano's gunshot wounds was replaced by two pictures of her. Her parents had found it hard to decide which picture to send to the court when they were asked, so they sent two. One showed a smiling Bano in her *bunad* from Trysil. The other showed a smiling Bano in traditional Kurdish costume.

'Bano was born in the realm of *A Thousand and One Nights*,' began her public advocate. 'When Bano was seven, she fled the war in Iraq with her family. Everyone who knew her was sure she was really going to make something of her life . . . '

The lawyer's voice shook. Mette Yvonnne Larsen knew Bano well, had known her for many years, because her daughter was Bano's classmate and one of her closest friends. She read a short statement about the things that had engaged and enthused Bano and said she had been posthumously elected to the local council in Nesodden.

It was nineteen minutes past eleven. It had taken eight minutes.

The court moved on to Anders Kristiansen. Who was holding a protective arm round Bano when she died.

He was the next red dot on the path.

'Now we move to the steep slope down to the water. The cliff area. Five died there,' said Gøran Dyvesveen from Kripos, the day after pointing out Bano, Anders and the others who were killed on the path.

'All five were transported over to the mainland and were not in their place/site of death when the crime scene investigation started.'

He orientated them on the general map, which was enlarged on the wall-mounted screen. 'The steep slope lay just to the south of Lover's Path,' he said, pointing. 'This is where we saw the ten lying yesterday. This slope will be the focus of our attention now.'

The picture was taken from the water and illustrated just how steep it was. It was a drop of about thirteen metres. 'This is not a place where anyone would go down to the water as a matter of course,' said Dyvesveen. 'I would say it is so steep that you would not get back up again without assistance.'

A white circle on the picture showed a rock. The forensic technician explained that a boy was found lying there. The pathologist described the injuries. She always gave the victim's name and age first.

'Simon was three days short of his nineteenth birthday,' she said. She indicated on the dummy where the deadly bullet had hit him: entering his back and coming out through his chest. 'Simon died of the bullet wounds to his chest, which rapidly led to unconsciousness and death.'

Heavy breathing could be heard. Tone and Gunnar were finding it all totally unreal. Simon definitely wasn't here, in this place.

Public advocate Nadia Hall read the short eulogy. 'Social commitment and an interest in culture came early for Simon. He was the leader of his local youth council from the age of fifteen. He was the founder member of the AUF branch in Salangen and was due to go straight on from Utøya to a conference in Russia. He had been to Cambodia to make a film about water. His brutal murder before he reached nineteen is felt as a huge tragedy. The loss of Simon will leave many people poorer in the years to come. He leaves behind him a mum, a dad and a younger brother.'

Breivik spent most of the time looking down at his papers during the autopsy reports. He did the same that day.

He said nothing. He had no comment.

Once the court was adjourned for the day, Tone and Gunnar Sæbø went out with Anders Kristiansen's parents. The two sets of parents had been together for the last couple of days; they had finished in Oslo now and were going home to Troms.

On leaving the courthouse the four of them walked up towards the park round the Royal Palace. At the National Gallery, a policeman was blocking off the street. The parents stopped.

Then they saw it.

A motorcycle came at full speed, then a white van and finally a police car.

'Cobblestones! Are there any cobblestones here?' cried Viggo Kristiansen.

But there were no loose cobblestones.

The van sped past. The dads were left standing there.

'Oh, we would have thrown them hard!' said Gunnar Sæbø.

The two fathers looked at each other. Staring into the other's powerlessness.

'Why did we just sit there?' Viggo demanded fiercely. 'There in the courtroom. Why didn't we do anything? Why didn't we shout something? Why did we all behave so bloody nicely?'

They had even tried to stifle their sobs, there in the grey-painted room. They had not wanted to be noticed. Did not want to be any trouble.

Gunnar looked at Viggo.

'We were paralysed,' he answered. 'We are paralysed.'

The Will to Live

After a week of autopsy reports and eulogies for those murdered on Utøya, the schedule said: the aggrieved.

After the four-day break for Norwegian National Day, the court participants' faces looked tanned. The public in the courtroom dressed more lightly in the mid-May heat of Oslo. The bereaved families had gone home to their regions and were now following the trial from district courts all around the country.

There were no more words of remembrance to be read. Time had come for the testimonies of the survivors.

I lost my best friend.

I heard a loud, deep scream.

I'm not sure if I heard shots first, then screams, or screams first and then shots.

He begged: Please, please don't do it.

I thought it must be my turn next.

I had two rocks in my hands.

I put my tongue between my teeth to stop them making a noise.

The survivors were muted. They were grave. Many of them felt guilty. Survivor's guilt.

I was swimming just ahead of him. He dropped behind. Then I turned round and he wasn't there any more.

Or the girl who had removed a bullet from her thigh before she swam for it: *I was the delegation leader of my county, and I lost the three youngest.*

All the survivors were asked how they were now. There was no room for big words.

It's going fine. Kind of at half speed.

Or: *It'll be all right.*

Or: *It varies a lot, up and down, pretty hard going actually.*

Some of the young people Breivik had tried to kill asked for him to leave the room while they gave their evidence. But most of them wanted him there. Often, they did not deign to look at him. Whereas he was there in his seat, obliged to listen to them. No one cursed or spoke directly to him. The strongest expressions came from a girl who called him *blockhead* and *idiot*.

For many, it was a stage in working through their trauma to see him sitting there. The man who had opened fire on them would not be able to harm anyone again.

One boy had prepared himself for giving evidence more thoroughly than he had ever prepared for anything.

He was summoned to appear as a witness on 22 May.

It was Viljar.

After he started singing on that sixth night, he fell asleep again. He drifted in and out of consciousness, a state that gradually became more of a morphine-induced haze than a coma. He woke and slept, woke and dozed off again. His parents and the doctors still knew nothing about how his brain was faring, how badly damaged it had been by the shot through his eye that had smashed his skull. It was a good sign that he had remembered those lines of the song, said the doctors. But then he said no more after that, just went back to sleep again. The corners of his mouth would occasionally twitch when Martin said something funny, when his mother stroked his cheek and his father gave him a hug, or when Torje told him about the Norway Cup match he had played in. Only Viljar knew what was going on inside his head, and he lacked the strength to tell anyone.

The day he woke up and summoned enough energy to say something, he called out to his mother: 'Mum, I can't see at all well. Can you get my glasses for me?'

'Viljar, you've . . . lost an eye, you were shot in the eye, but the other eye—'

'It'll still be better with the glasses,' he insisted. These were his longest sentences since he was brought from Utøya.

'They're on the top shelf on the left just inside the living room in Roger's flat,' said Viljar.

And so they were. 'A really, really good sign,' the doctors said in relief.

Viljar was able to retell the tall stories Martin had recounted on that sixth night, the night the doctors said he came closest to death, when he grew colder and colder. Every heartbeat had been an exertion. His continuing pulse a succession of gifts. Viljar had been somewhere in among it all, the whole time; he remembered the cold and how much he had shivered. He recalled the hugs and the tears, and that he had wanted to respond, wanted to smile, wanted to open his eyes and laugh, but his body would not obey. It was too exhausted. And he had been so cold.

And then, when he woke up properly, he realised before they said it. So he said it himself.

'I know Anders would have been here now, and Simon, if . . . '

Viljar looked at Martin.

'They would at least have sent some kind of message, if they . . . '

Martin nodded. The tears flowed.

'. . . had been . . . They're dead, aren't they?'

Viljar had missed Anders's and Simon's funerals. They were held the week Viljar turned eighteen. Jens Stoltenberg attended Simon's funeral. At Anders's funeral, Lars Bremnes performed his song 'If I Could Write in the Heavens'.

Viljar stayed down in Oslo for a series of operations. It was only in October, three months after he had been shot, that they let him travel back to Svalbard.

He slept a lot. It was a real effort to regain his strength. He was a skinny teenager to start with, and had now lost twenty kilos. A red scar ran from the top of his head and down one side. His eye socket had been rebuilt. He had been fitted with a glass eye and a prosthetic hand.

Life was anguish and loss. Fear of death could paralyse him without warning. Often he felt like half a person. Not because of what had happened to him, but because he had lost his best friends. So many unlived dreams!

Over the winter he got the letter summoning him to give evidence at the trial.

He lay awake at night thinking about what he ought to say to make it right. He tested out phrases on his classmates the next day.

'You can shoot me as many times as you like! But you didn't get anywhere!' he tried. 'I'm damn well going to show this ABB that I can pull through all right!'

One evening Johannes Buø's family came round to see the Hanssens. Johannes, the fourteen-year-old judo enthusiast and Metallica fan, Torje's best friend, was killed in the woods by the schoolhouse. Johannes had lived on the island for the past few years with his parents and brother Elias, three years his junior. His father was the director of arts and culture on Svalbard. When Johannes's autopsy report was presented to the court at the beginning of May, the family went to Oslo to be there. Their places were behind the glass partition, so they found themselves staring at the back of the perpetrator's head. Elias suddenly moved from his seat to sit on his own at the far end of the front row. When the court rose for a break the freckled little boy with corkscrew curls got to his feet and went right up to the glass wall in the corner. There he stood waiting. He had noticed that when Breivik left his place among the defence lawyers and made his way out, he had to look in that direction. He would have to walk straight towards Elias. They would be separated only by the glass. Then, as Breivik approached, the little brother was going to fix him with the foulest look he could muster. And so he did.

In the Hanssens' living room, the Buø family did a sketch map of the courtroom for Viljar. 'He'll be sitting there,' they indicated. 'With his defence team. And you'll sit here.'

They drew a square in the middle of the room. The witness box. They put in the judges, the prosecution and the public.

'He'll be sitting two metres away from you, can you handle that?'

'The closer the better,' said Viljar.

He would have to rehearse what he was going to say if he wanted to get through this. He had to leave his feelings out of it or he would not be able to pull it off. That was why he was practising, so he did not find himself faced with anything that would throw him, anything he could not to tackle, anything that might make him break down. He would not afford ABB that satisfaction.

He was trembling as the plane landed in Oslo. But he was ready now. He must not let them down – this was for Anders, this was for Simon, it was for what they had believed in. As so often before, he wondered what they would have said now. What advice they would have given him. Anders on the content, Simon on the style. Once when he had got stuck, he started dialling Anders's number when he— Fuck! Anders is dead!

He had to do this alone. And he had to pull it off.

On 22 May, Viljar dressed in a black shirt and black trousers as befitted the gravity of the occasion. Over the shirt he wore a jacket in a dark blue. Around his right wrist he had a thin leather strap. He had stylish glasses with black frames. Nothing was left to chance when Viljar Robert Hanssen went to Oslo to give evidence.

He walked down the central aisle to the witness box with light steps. Breivik looked at him, as he always did when someone came in. Viljar caught his eye with a searing look, held it, focused, still held it.

'Hah,' thought Viljar. 'Empty. Just like Johannes's little brother said: "You won't find anything in his eyes."'

A gentle voice addressed him from the left. It was Inga Bejer Engh.

'Can you start by telling us what happened to you on Utøya?'

Yes, he could.

'I was at the campsite. My little brother was asleep in the tent. I went to the meeting in the main building to find out what had happened in Oslo. I remember talking to Simon Sæbø. I remember he said if this is something political, we aren't safe here either.'

He said they had gathered up everyone from Troms. Then they heard bangs. So they started running.

'We ran across Lovers' Path. My little brother and I made our way down a sort of slope, cliff-edge thing. The bangs were getting nearer, and in the end they were really, really close.'

The prosecution asked to see a map of the steep slope. Viljar did his best to point. 'Whether I was hit when I was jumping – here – or when I landed, I don't know, but I ended up down there and my brother was close by.'

At times while Viljar was giving evidence Breivik whispered little comments to one of the trainee lawyers in his defence team.

'Then I heard this crazy whistling sound in my right ear and I found myself by the edge of the water. I tried to get up several times, I was a bit sort of Bambi on the ice, you know, and I called out to my brother. But then I decided the best thing was just to lie down in the foetal position somewhere. I curled myself round a rock on the shoreline and stayed there. I was conscious the whole time. It was very strange being shot, it didn't hurt – it was just unpleasant. A new kind of pain. I lay there and started trying to get my bearings. I looked at my fingers and saw they were only hanging on by scraps of skin. I realised I couldn't see out of one eye and that something must be wrong there. I started running my hand over my head and eventually I came across something soft and then I touched my brain; I was feeling my own brain. It was a weird so I took my hand away pretty quick. I remember Simon Sæbø was lying there, but I didn't know then that he was dead. I remember I talked to him, said it would be all right and we'd get through it together.'

'Did you know him well?'

'Very well.'

'And you only found out later that he was dead?'

'Yes. I think I just didn't want to take it in . . . at the time. I remember it vividly, lying there, that . . . well, I've seen lots of bad American films about how important it is to keep breathing and stay awake. So I tried to go on talking, came out with lots of strange stuff. In the end I think I was burbling on about pirates or something.'

'Did anyone talk to you?'

'They shushed me. He must have come back again, I think, without me realising. So then they shushed me, like, "Please shut up!"'

'Your brother, what happened to him?'

'I lost track of him. The last thing I saw was him moving away from me. Like I was trying to get him to. I didn't see him again after that, and that was the worst bit for me. I tried to distract myself by thinking about things I enjoyed in everyday life. I thought about going back home to Svalbard, and driving the snowmobile and girls and other things that are really great. I thought about all sorts of things except where my little brother was. For me, dying wasn't an option and that was smart. Well, in a way I didn't realise how badly injured I was. I remember I started to feel freezing and get spasms. I was shaking like mad. I remember, though I don't know how long it lasted, that I passed out. I don't know when that happened but I think it must have been a little while before they came for us.'

From that point, Viljar could not remember anything until he was taken aboard a boat. 'The waves were knocking my back quite hard. There was a man beside me, asking, "What's your name? Where do you live?" to keep me awake. I remember asking if they'd seen a small, red-haired boy. And he said no.'

'Where did the bullets hit you?'

'I was hit in the thigh, just a slight graze. And then there's my fingers here, you can't miss that, I was shot in the hand, and then it was my shoulder, all this up here was pulverised. Then I was shot in the forearm, this little scar, and then I was shot in the head. If that makes five, then that's it.'

'And the shot in the head, how has it affected you since?'

'I lost this eye, but that's useful: it means I don't have to look over there.'

Viljar nodded towards the defendant, who was sitting to his right.

It took a second or two, as if Breivik needed a little time to appreciate what the boy in the witness box had said before starting to smile. The whole room smiled.

'But as for my brain and that . . . ' Viljar went on, 'I've still got my wits about me.'

There were chuckles in the courtroom. A few people laughed out loud. A sense of release. Breivik was still smiling.

'So we hear,' said Beijer Engh. 'And are things going to continue that way?'

Viljar had decided in advance what he was willing to share and what he was not. 'Reasonably terribly, decently badly,' he replied when asked how he was getting on at school. He could talk about phantom limb pain, operations on his head, the eye he could take in and out like a marble. But he wanted to keep what went on inside his mind to himself. The hell – he would not share that with ABB and the rest of Norway. He replied briefly to the prosecutor's questions about how things were for him now.

'Quite a challenge, all the anxiety and nerves,' he said. 'I only feel safe in a moving car. Anxiety and paranoia. I still seem to find things difficult. Not on Svalbard and maybe not in Tromsø, but I find it unpleasant being in Oslo. Being here now.'

He paused. 'I had to cancel my place at an AUF event because I got too scared to go. It's hard. Life has really changed,' he said, and told the court about everything he had had to relearn: holding a pen, tying his shoelaces. He who had been so active, played football, drove snowmobiles, went skiing, loved everything that was fast and exciting, now he could do none of that. He still had fragments of the bullet inside his head. They were too close to vital nerves to be removed. If these bits moved even a millimetre, it could be lethal. He had to avoid any risk of a blow to his head. For the rest of his life.

'I can't just wax my skis and set off any more . . . ' he said, and paused before he went on. 'We're all dependent on having self-confidence and feeling at ease. It does something to you when your whole face has changed and . . . '

At that, Breivik looked down.

Viljar had no more to say.

He had shared enough.

'I think you've finished, then,' said judge Arntzen.

'Fabulous,' said Viljar.

He stood up, spun on his heel and went. Out.

It was almost summer.

He had his life in front of him. He could walk, sit and stand. He had his wits about him. And many people to live for.

Psycho Seminar

'It's insulting!' cried Breivik. 'It's offensive!'

'Breivik, you get your chance to speak later!'

'It's ludicrous that I'm not allowed to comment here. This is being broadcast. It's insulting!' Breivik was bright red in the face.

'NRK must stop the broadcast!' ordered judge Wenche Arntzen.

The transmission faded out, away from Breivik's indignant face, to a picture of the main doors of the Law Courts, while the drama played out in courtroom 250.

The clash was about Breivik's life. For Breivik, it was about the right to a private life. For the court, it was about making the correct diagnosis.

Breivik had constructed his life story as a shining suit of armour. In the lustreless courtroom, within those matte grey walls, a pack of professionals had descended to try with a variety of tools to push, worm and force their way inside his defences.

It was Friday 8 June. The day before, the court had not sat.

Wenche Arntzen had been at her father's funeral. Supreme Court counsel Andreas Artzen had died two weeks earlier. The funeral was arranged for the first day the court was not in session.

The two professional judges in the 22 July trial came from the legal aristocracy. Wenche Arntzen's grandfather, Sven Arntzen, was Director General of Public Prosecution in 1945, and it was he who prepared the charges against Vidkun Quisling. John Lyng, grandfather of Arntzen's fellow judge Arne Lyng, was the public prosecutor in the legal purge of collaborators in 1945 and prosecutor in the case against the Nazi Henry Rinnan who, like Quisling, was condemned to death.

Lyng and Arntzen had with them the three lay judges, who had been selected at random from a list at the courthouse. A young, pregnant teacher of Colombian descent, a retired family counsellor in her seventies and a middle-aged consultant in the Department of Education. On the first day the court sat, there had been another lay person on the bench, but it emerged in the evening that just after the massacre he had posted on Facebook that 'The death penalty is the only just outcome of this case!!!!!!!!!!!' He was obliged to stand down, and the elderly family counsellor who was the reserve moved up to take his place.

These five judges were now observing Breivik's outburst.

He had sat there so quietly for eight weeks. Now he was completely freaking out.

The week before he had been quite satisfied. The defence had called witnesses who stressed that Breivik was not alone in his thinking. Historians, philosophers and researchers in the fields of religion, terrorism and right-wing extremism took the witness stand and set out where Breivik stood in an extremist, but not unknown, ideological landscape. Representatives of Stop the Islamisation of Norway and the Norwegian Defence League were also invited to present their political views.

The court heard from a variety of standpoints about a world in which Breivik's ideas were familiar. His thoughts were not bizarre distortions, but were in fact shared by many.

The defence had also wanted to call Breivik's ideological lodestar Fjordman, whose actual name turned out to be Peder Are Nestvold Jensen. Forced out from behind his Fjordman shield, a rather short man in his mid-thirties, with a rounded face and dark curls, appeared. He worked as a night watchman at a nursing home in Oslo and was an anti-jihadist blogger in his spare time. He refused to accept any responsibility for having inspired Breivik.

Breivik had made Jensen's ideas his own. The difference was that Breivik put this thinking into action.

Jensen did not want to give evidence and moved abroad, where the Norwegian police had no legal authority to compel him to come to court.

One other individual who did not attend was Wenche Behring Breivik. She had spent part of the autumn as an in-patient at a psychiatric clinic. When she asked to be excused taking the witness stand, the District Court gave its consent. She was considered 'unable' to appear as a witness.

Ulrik Fredrik Malt, professor of psychiatry, was an elderly gentleman who gave the impression of being used to holding forth. He was the first of a dozen experts who were to brief the court on psychiatric matters, to help it reach the correct verdict. Healthy or sick. Accountable or not. Sentence or treatment.

The grey-haired man took his place in the witness box and regarded the various parties. He spent the first hour on an introduction to the correct use of the handbooks on which the court would rely, before going on to the particular instance sitting a few metres away from him. 'The Commander. The messiah aspect,' he said. 'Life and death. I'm thinking of the executions. There's clearly something tending in the direction of notions of grandeur, but are they delusions of grandeur?'

No. Breivik had given in too easily. In the case of delusions, one became aggressive when ousted from one's elevated role. One was prepared to fight tooth and nail for the throne, whereas Breivik had simply toned down the significance of the Knights Templar and dropped the uniform as soon as someone told him it looked ridiculous.

Malt went on through the diagnosis chart.

'Let us look at dissocial personality disorder – cold indifference to the feelings of others. Marked, persistently irresponsible attitude to social norms and duties. Lack of ability to sustain lasting relationships. Low tolerance of frustration, low threshold for aggressive outbursts, including use of violence. Lack of ability to experience guilt or learn from punishment. Marked tendency to generate feelings of guilt in others or to rationalise conduct that has brought the patient into conflict with society.'

Many in the room had now mentally ticked off all the criteria. But – the criteria had to have been in place before 22 July if they were to count. 'I have not seen it said in any of the witness statements made by his friends that he was an ice-cold bastard. He did a little tagging, but so do a lot of people. He had some dubious accounts abroad, but those of us familiar with Oslo West circles know a fair amount of it goes on there. If that is a criterion, the number of people with the disorder will have to be adjusted radically upwards. Low threshold for outbursts of rage. No indication of that before 22 July. Lack of ability to experience guilt and learn from experience or punishment. It is possible there was a problem there.'

But it was not enough for Malt to be willing to make that his diagnosis. What about *dissocial personality disorder with narcissistic traits*, the diagnosis made by Tørrissen and Aspaas? 'If one looks at what he writes in the manifesto compiled in his bedroom, fantasies about power and money and ideal love are present. That he is unique and admires himself, yes, both of those. Unique rights, yes, we can say he feels he has those, because he definitely does not relate to the law. Lack of empathy, that certainly fits. It would be entirely natural to make a diagnosis of dissocial personality disorder with narcissistic traits. So far, so good, you may think. But it is not good. We now come to the question that we have to ask ourselves as a society, as human beings and as psychologists. What is it that these questions actually give us the answer to?'

An enormous question mark filled the whole screen on the wall.

Judge Arntzen interrupted to ask if it was time for a short break.

'That would be a pity,' exclaimed Malt. 'But we can leave that question mark there, because now we're coming to the really exciting part.'

Breivik was furious. 'He's got to stop!' he told Lippestad in the recess.

What enraged Breivik was that the testimony was being beamed directly to the TV viewers. Unlike the autopsy reports and witness statements from Utøya, this was going out live. And it was about his mind. People could switch on their sets, sit on their sofas and laugh at him. Yes, he would be allowed to defend himself at the end of each day. But whereas the psychiatrists' evidence would be broadcast, his responses would not. His comments would be filtered through cultural Marxist journalists and would never get out to people directly.

After the short break, Lippestad asked to speak and demanded that the witness be dismissed, because he had crossed the legal boundaries of personal privacy.

'The diagnoses he is presenting are, in parts, highly stigmatising.'

Malt was in the witness box, raring to continue. The whole thing degenerated into heated exchanges. The court retired to deliberate and reach a conclusion.

There was lively debate among those left sitting in the courtroom to await the outcome. Some of the public abandoned their seats in favour of the outdoor cafés around the Law Courts. The psychiatry seminar spilled out into the streets.

The trial had undergone a pronounced change of mood. While even the most seasoned crime reporters had been chastened as the courtroom mourned during the autopsy reports and the brutal witness accounts, the intellectual game of diagnosis loosened their tongues.

The same lively discussions were in full swing round canteen tables at work, between mouthfuls at top Oslo restaurants, among friends and colleagues, between couples. People on the bus started arguing about whether Breivik could be held accountable for his actions. Dinner-party guests were engrossed in the topic from their aperitifs through to the brandy and beyond. The case had turned the whole nation into amateur psychologists.

So many people in Norway had been affected by his actions, he had forced his way into their thoughts, and now they were wondering:

'What was wrong with Breivik?'

Their answers had a tendency to divide along party lines. People on the left were overrepresented among those who saw him as a right-wing extremist terrorist. He had tapped into contemporary trends, and these ideologies and ideologues had to be crushed by debate. In other words, he was of sound mind. The further to the right you looked, the more likely you were to find people who thought him insane. That he could not be taken seriously and was an irrelevance.

Insanity was also the view of those he most admired. The work of a madman. 'Is he crazy? Yes that's probably *exactly* what he is. Nuts. Clinically insane,' Fjordman wrote in a blog post. His conclusion was shared by several international anti-jihadists. Before 22 July, they had shared the same critique of Islam, the same world view. It had been so fine and pure. Now Breivik had sullied it with blood.

Breivik was overruled. Malt was permitted to go on. The enormous question mark came up on the screen again.

'It is one thing to set off a bomb. It is quite another to go ashore on an island and shoot young people and talk about it as if he had been picking cherries. Is there an illness that could account for what I would choose to call mechanical killing? And there is also a change in sexual behaviour, we know that.'

'Chairman. It's ridiculous for me not to be allowed to object here. This is being broadcast. It's offensive!' Breivik interrupted.

Arntzen asked him to be quiet.

'But my comments aren't being broadcast!'

'No, they are not.'

Malt had reached his conclusion.

'Autism, or Asperger's syndrome. Struggles to understand social signals. Has problems getting to grips with what others think and feel. What most people do to cope with this is to acquire expertise in social interaction. They become extremely polite, extremely proper and try to learn the rules of the game as best they can. But the point is that for them, empathy remains theoretical. They are incapable of sharing someone else's suffering. They can have friends. They can run businesses. It works fine, but when you want to have a close relationship with someone . . . And the two of you are meant to share feelings . . . They can't do it. And thus we come to the most important thing of all, and also the most painful . . . '

He paused for breath. 'The first time I saw Breivik enter this courtroom – and as psychiatrists we attach great weight to the first two or three milliseconds – it is important to note. I did not see a monster, I saw a deeply lonely man . . . Deeply lonely . . . Then quick as a flash he was inside his shell, making himself hard . . . But . . . At his core there is just a deeply lonely man. We have with us here not only a right-wing extremist bastard, but also a fellow human being who, regardless of what he has done to the rest of us, is suffering. We must try to put ourselves inside his brain, make his world comprehensible. His personality and extreme right-wing ideology are combined in an effort to get out of his own prison. He ends up ruining not only his own life but that of many others. We have with us here a fellow human being who will be left not only in his own prison but also in an actual prison. It is important for us to appreciate that this is something much more than a pure right-wing extremist. This is a tragedy for Norway and for us. I think it is also a tragedy for Breivik.'

The dissection was over. The cameras were turned off. It was Breivik's turn to speak.

'I would like to congratulate Malt for such an accomplished character assassination. Initially I was quite offended, but I gradually came to see it as quite comical.'

He had jotted various points on a sheet of paper. 'I never deviated from normal behaviour as a child,' he said. 'As for the assertion about loneliness: I have never been lonely. Not capable of friendship, that has in fact been disputed by my . . . er, that is, the people I was friends with before. Periods of depression: I have never been depressed. The claim that I have the right to decide who is to live and die: Che Guevara and Castro killed people in Cuba because people who call for revolution inevitably open up the possibility of people getting killed. It is claimed that I have never been in a long-term relationship. I have had two relationships of about six months' duration since 2002.

When you are working twelve to fourteen hours a day you have no time for a relationship. But I have been on dates during that period and I have had no problem making contact with women. The impression has been given that I hate women, but I love women. I hate feminism. Once I decided to carry out an armed operation I did not feel I would be justified in establishing a family, with a wife and children. Narcissism: as described here, half of Oslo West would fall into that category. It seems an idiotic diagnosis. Malt has been called in by the public advocates and it's important to be clear about their agenda of making me appear as crazy as possible, but not so much so that I am declared unaccountable for my actions. The judge in this case should dismiss all the psychiatric witnesses. This case is about political extremism and not psychiatry. Thank you.'

The next day, seven new witnesses were called, all of them psychiatrists and psychologists. The day after that, five more. Some had met him, others had not. Diagnoses flew this way and that.

Young psychologist Eirik Johannessen was among those who had spent most time with Breivik. He was employed by Ila prison and had held extensive conversations with the defendant about his ideology and his grand fantasies. As the trial proceeded, he was still having sessions with him, and had found no sign of psychosis. Breivik's ideas were an expression of extreme right-wing views, and the way in which he presented them could be accounted for by his inflated self-image, Johannessen concluded. He underlined that a succession of people had been observing Breivik weekly for ten months without detecting any psychotic traits.

The team at Ila ended up with a diagnosis of narcissistic personality disorder, just as Tørrissen and Aspaas had. Whereas Husby and Sørheim saw Breivik's references to his role in the Knights Templar as a sign of psychosis, Johannessen had a simpler interpretation: he is lying.

It was just something Breivik had made up. Something he well knew to be non-existent.

'Why do you think he tells these lies?' queried Inga Bejer Engh.

'He wants to recruit people to a network, but that's not easy if he's on his own. And then it helps to generate fear, and he wants his opponents to live in fear.'

'He lies in order to make us more frightened?' the prosecutor went on.

'And to make himself appear a more exciting person. Rather than a failure.'

When the word failure came up, Breivik produced a slip of paper and wrote something on it. He sat there uneasily, swinging his chair on to its back legs.

Johannessen cited a former friend of Breivik's who had told the court that Breivik always had great ambitions.

'Not achieving them, being a failure, was so hard to bear that it helped to push him towards extremism. His ideology became important to him as a way of saving himself.'

Johannessen saw Breivik's childhood and adolescence as a history of rejection. And when he decided to dedicate himself entirely to his ideology he found himself rejected even there, as in the case of his attempt to make contact with Fjordman.

Breivik took lots of notes as this witness was speaking. Every time the young psychologist intimated that he had lied or exaggerated his own importance, he lurched forward and made a note. Lippestad, sitting beside him, remained calm and chewed the arm of his glasses.

Johannessen drew attention to Breivik's ability to see himself from the outside, something a psychotic individual would not be able to do. 'At the end of a day in court, he might say, "Today I came across as a bit less accountable," and then we would see this same conclusion borne out by the commentators on TV in the evening.'

Johannessen left the witness box. Breivik had his chance to speak. He was incensed; he raised his head.

'It's completely wrong that Fjordman rejected me,' snarled Breivik. He had only contacted Fjordman to get his email address, and he had been given it.

'I have never been rejected by anyone in my whole life,' he concluded.

*

Finally, the two pairs of psychiatrists were invited to present their observations. The first duo had not changed so much as a comma of their original report. Nothing they had observed in court had changed their conclusion. Nor had they wished to receive the round-the-clock observations from the team that had followed Breivik for four weeks, which were ready just before the start of the trial. Sørheim and Husby had completed their report in November 2011, and they were standing by what they had written. Breivik was not accountable for his actions.

During the examination of the psychiatrists, judge Wenche Arntzen wondered how the two of them had reached their conclusion about all Breivik's delusions.

'His ideas about who should live and who should die, did you term them a delusion because they are so immoral?'

'Now I'm confused,' replied Synne Sørheim.

'Acts of terrorism can be ideologically justified, isn't that something a person can feel themselves called to, however absurd that may be?' asked Arntzen.

'I think we take a simpler starting point than the judge is able to do. Our approach is that he sat there alone in deadly earnest and devoted years to finding out who would have to die.'

In the psychiatry they represented, there was no category for moral deliberation.

The other pair of psychiatrists admitted they had been in doubt. All those days in court in which Breivik had not shown the slightest emotion had made Terje Tørrissen uncertain and he had asked to talk to him again. He went down to the basement and met him in the waiting cell. There he found him to be the same man he had got to know in the course of the observations, friendly, polite and adequate. In order to get through the trial he was playing a role, Tørrissen judged. In the supplementary statement that Aspaas and Tørrissen delivered during the trial, they described Breivik as a special case. His dulled state was a challenge to 'the prevailing classification systems and models of understanding, particularly in the matter of drawing the line between lack of reality and political fanaticism'. Under examination by Inga Bejer Engh, the pair withdrew their diagnosis of *dissocial per-sonality disorder*. All that remained were the *narcissistic traits*. They were thus left with the conclusion that he was accountable for his actions.

Once all the evidence had been heard, the prosecution had to reach a conclusion. Was he accountable for his actions or not? They were not sure he was not accountable, but they had serious doubts. It is an important principle of the rule of law that doubt should not be discounted. This had to apply, regardless of the crime. That was how they argued.

The prosecution's conclusion: not accountable for his actions.

On the final day of the trial, the aggrieved parties were to make impact statements, as is standard procedure in Norwegian courts. An employee in the government quarter grieved for lost colleagues; three mothers remembered their children and talked about how losing them had affected their whole family. The General Secretary of the AUF spoke about the loss to the political organisation; and finally, a girl who had lost her sister was to end the session.

The seventeen-year-old had been called by her public advocate the previous evening and asked if she could make the closing statement of the trial.

I can't do it, Lara thought.

She said, 'Yes, I can.'

On the busy morning ferry into the city, the ferry that Bano had loved, she sat looking out over the fjord, wondering what she was going to say.

How could she explain what losing Bano meant?

She was going to meet four friends at Check Mate, the café by the courthouse. The waiter lent her an order pad and a pen. She started writing, and then read it out. Her friends listened and made criti-cisms and suggestions. More of this, less of that. Only the best was good enough here. 'You've got to include where you all come from!' they said. 'Who you are, who Bano was!'

She wanted to opt out. She couldn't go through with it. She was freezing in her white crocheted top and her jeans felt too tight. But it was time to go. Her feet carried her past the security check, in through the heavy doors, up the winding staircase and into room 250.

Now she was on her way up the central aisle. Now she was going to face her sister's murderer.

She took her place in the witness box, afraid her voice would give way. Then she noticed a pair of eyes on her. The pregnant Colombian lay judge with the long dark curls was looking at her. She has kind eyes, thought Lara, and put down her piece of paper. She would say the most important things about Bano. What she had in her heart.

'Bano and I fled from Iraq in 1999. We fled from the civil war and Saddam Hussein. I had a real struggle with all the trauma and it took me a long time to feel safe here. I had nightmares that the police would come and get us. Bano helped me. There's two years between us, but we shared all our secrets. I remember her saying, "Even if you happen to lose friends, you'll never lose me."'

Her voice held. 'I had no idea then that she would be the one I lost first of all.'

Lara spoke of how she had done nothing but sleep in the time after Utøya. 'I dreamt that I was dead and she was the one alive. I mixed up what was real and what wasn't, and when I woke up I thought real life was the nightmare. It took me several months to understand what was what. It's made me feel guilty seeing how sad people are. It should have been me who died, then not so many people would have been sad.'

She managed to be entirely honest.

'When everyone was grieving, I just felt I was in the way. It wrecked my self-confidence. I was born as a little sister. I've never lived a life just as a big sister.'

There were ripples of movement along the rows of seats. It was the last day. It was over. But not for Lara.

'I had to learn to do things myself. I had to learn to start trusting other people. It's been a difficult time and I don't want to live like this. He didn't only take away my security, he took away the safest person in my life. The sorrow is as great as ever, the sense of loss is even greater, but there's something new.'

She paused.

'Hope. It wasn't there before. Bano didn't die for nothing. She died for a multicultural Norway. There's a huge empty hole and I'm heartbroken that she won't be at my wedding or see my children. But I'm proud of her, and I know she wants me to be happy.'

That was the way she ended. Bano was with her.

She turned towards her parents as she left the witness box. Their eyes were moist. Her father raised his hand and gave a little wave. So did her mother.

Lara felt warm all over. Their looks said: We are proud of you. We are so glad you are alive.

The Verdict

On 24 August 2012 the verdict was to be pronounced. The courtroom filled once more with the world press, who had lost interest after the first couple of weeks. There was pressure on seats again.

The accused was in place, his right-wing extremist salute was back, the prosecution came, the public advocates, the defence, the audience.

The judges entered and everyone stood up.

Wenche Arntzen remained standing to read the decision.

'Anders Behring Breivik, born 13 February 1979, is convicted of breaching §147a of the legal code, clause one letters a and b . . . to detention in custody . . . '

A smile spread across Breivik's face. Accountable for his actions!

He received the maximum penalty the law allowed: twenty-one years. But detention in custody meant that, as long as he represented a threat to society, the sentence could be extended by five years, another five years, another five years – until death claimed him.

Part Three

The Mountain

He slid down the cliff.
And threw himself behind a rock.
He slithered down the cliff.
And ran under the ledge.
He skidded down on soil and gravel.
And crept behind a boulder.
He leapt down in long strides.
He readied himself. Three jumps and he'd be down.
You know, Tone, our Simon's a fast runner and a good swimmer.
He had said on that Friday.
How many times had he slid down that cliff for Simon . . .
He slid in the night, he slid in the day, he slid in his dreams.
A hundred times. A thousand.
Over and over again he saw his son in front of him – jumping over
the log, not stopping halfway, but sliding on.
Run, Simon! Run!
Gunnar slid.
He slithered.
And then he stumbled.
Losing Simon was like falling into a black hole.

*

Masterbakk Lake lay tranquil. Occasional little rings spread across the surface; an Arctic char came up for air. Some ravens flew over the treetops.

It was late summer, two years after. Tone had gone to bed. Gunnar was sitting up.

He felt he had failed as a dad. Something had gone wrong in the upbringing of his son. He who had taught the boy about the dangers of nature: wolves, bears, avalanches. Storms, angry elks and deep water.

It had let him down when it really mattered.

Why did he wait so long to run? Why did he stay there, lifting people down, and not get away himself? He must have realised *he had to run now*!

They had brought the boys up to be considerate. Help others. Let others go first. Gunnar remembered when he had been the trainer of the boys' football team in Salangen. They had gone to compete in the Norway Cup, and Simon was angry because he did not get very long on the pitch, even though he was good. Gunnar impressed on him that they were all equal, the good players and the slightly less good. Everyone would play for exactly the same length of time, and if there was not enough match time for everybody, Simon would have to come off first. That was just the way it had to be.

Gunnar was back at his work in industrial and commercial develop-ment in Salangen. Sitting around idly did nothing to help. Tone was working three days a week with special needs children.

Håvard had got a place at a folk high school in Voss, on their sport and outdoor recreation programme.

But first he had gone to enrol for military service. When it came to filling in his personal details, he ground to a halt. Name, address, parents . . . siblings. . .

Siblings. Tick the box.

Should he tick the box?

Did he have a brother?

After Simon died, Håvard lost his foothold. The foundation was gone. The springboard on which the two boys had stood together gave way when one of them was gone. Initially Håvard was going to do it all. He took over the leadership of the Salangen AUF. He took over the homework-mentoring role for the refugees; he was going to be Håvard and Simon rolled into one. But it did not work. As the November darkness descended that first autumn, he broke down.

Every time he closed his eyes he saw Simon's face. Even so, he got cross when his mother shed tears and had no patience with his parents when they sat indoors, staring into space. He could not bear to live at home any more, and moved in with his girlfriend.

It was so painful. Too painful.

The big blue house in Heiaveien was too cramped now that there were only three of them. 'The House of Sorrows', Håvard called it.

Two thousand people attended Simon's funeral. As many people as there were inhabitants in town. Offices, shops and businesses all closed for the service. The Prime Minister had flown up, and spoke at the church.

All that summer, Simon had gone off to the churchyard in the mornings to his work as odd-job man. The very last thing he did before he went to Utøya was to cut the grass on top of what was to be his own grave. It was unbearable. Now it was his parents taking the steep path. Up the hill, round the curve in the road, and they were there.

Flowers, wreaths, hearts of roses, friends' letters, pictures, tears. Among all the tokens on his grave, there was a small handwritten note: *To Simon. My only Norwegian friend. Mehdi.*

Three days after Simon's funeral, Gunnar had a phone call from a friend.

'I've heard the Dahl cabin is being put up for sale.'

'Oh,' said Gunnar faintly.

A month later, his friend rang again.

'The cabin's on the market now. You can find it on the web. You and Tone have always wanted a cabin.'

It was rare to find plots of land for sale in the Masterbakk mountains. This was Sami territory, the realm of the reindeer. The mountain areas were the preserve of the reindeer herders, and every May the herds were there before they moved off east to other grazing. The few cabins on the fells above Salangen had been there for generations. New plots were never for sale.

But now there was the Dahl cabin, with its wonderful location, that nobody used. The family that owned it had moved south and no longer needed a cabin in the middle of Troms.

Nor did Tone and Gunnar. Their days were black. Their nights darker still.

The friend would not give up.

'Think of Masterbakk Lake when it's completely calm and the char are biting,' he said to Gunnar. 'Think of Lørken when the high slopes are yellow with cloudberries in August. Think of skiing down from Sagvasstind when the sun comes back in February. Think of the northern lights in the winter, when—'

'I know, I know,' said Gunnar. He lapsed into silence, and then added, 'I'll talk to Tone.'

A month later, the family friend rang again. 'The bidding has started.'

Okay then. Gunnar put in a bid too. But it wasn't worth thinking about; the bids were likely to go sky-high.

It wasn't the mountain peaks that drew them to it, or the fishing lakes. It was the prospect of getting away. Breaking free. Not free from the grief, for that had become a part of them, but perhaps the mountains could absorb a little of it.

The price rose. One last bid, they did not dare go any higher. Then the seller suddenly called a halt to the bidding.

Somebody, maybe a friend, had dropped a hint that Sæbø was among the bidders.

'Well, I think I've been offered more than enough for this cabin now,' said the seller. 'It goes to the most recent bidder.'

It was the Sæbø family.

The Dahl cabin had merged into its surroundings, and was in the process of being reclaimed by the natural world. The juniper bushes were encroaching on the walls. The mountain grass in the lee of the wind had become a resting place for the sheep. Bilberry scrub was growing up through the front steps. It had long been left uncared for, rot was spreading through the logs and the wood panelling had decayed.

Tone and Gunnar thought they would be able to patch it up, putty the windows, weatherproof the cracks. They could manage that.

'Let's raze this dump to the ground,' said their friend when he and Gunnar went up there one day to take a look. 'You two want a cabin for when the wind's blowing too, don't you? For when it's below zero? Let's build a new one. I'll take charge of the building work.'

That first 17 May without Simon, they were up there on the frozen crust of the snow.

The sky was clear, the wind had dropped; there was frost at nights and summer weather in the daytime. It was light around the clock.

They splashed petrol on the walls and the turf roof. Then they threw in matches. The old timber was alight in an instant. They stood watching the flames lick rapidly up the walls. Soon the roof was ablaze.

They were there with a few close friends. None of them could face being down in the town on National Day. The memories of the previous year were too raw. Tone did not feel up to seeing people. She had become withdrawn.

The snow was still piled high. Expanses of white all around them. Below the bonfire of the cabin, the water of Masterbakk Lake was still frozen, right between the twin peaks of Snørken and Lørken.

Oh, it was a beautiful place on this Earth!

But it was impossible not to think about the year before.

'Last year, Simon was on the podium . . . ' said Gunnar.

'Yes, and what a great speech he made!' someone said.

Tone forced out a smile.

'Imagine him telling that story about JFK,' said Gunnar.

They nodded. 'Yes, and to think of . . .'

One day Tone and Gunnar had come across the script Simon had prepared for his speech – the school president's 17 May speech.

Reading it was like listening to Simon's voice.

'They decided to name me J. F. Kennedy. He was a president like me, you know. But unfortunately he got shot in Dallas. I'm too much of an optimist to sit waiting for the same fate . . .'

It hurt so much.

It was the first 17 May, in the blackest of years, and here they were burning a cabin. Before long, all that was left were glowing embers in the snow.

The snow melted. Summer arrived.

'We just wondered if you needed any help,' said a couple with strong arms.

'Well, I was baking anyway,' said a neighbour, producing an apple pie from her bag.

'We've no particular plans for the summer, so if you need us, we've got time,' said some friends.

'I know someone who runs a sawmill, and these materials were going spare,' said a man.

'Perhaps you've got a use for this casserole?'

'They had a special offer on sausages, so I thought I might as well bring some along . . .'

'Do you need any help with the bricklaying? Seeing as I'm free.'

The Dahl cabin was a long way off the beaten track. At first you could only guess who those dots approaching from afar might be. As they got closer their heads would disappear behind the last hump in the hill, and all at once they were there. They were always carrying something. Some planks, a hammer, home-baked bread.

By the end of the summer the cabin was finished. All it lacked was a new sign over the door. A friend had had a sign made, with the name etched into it in swirly letters. He hung it below the ridge of the roof.

It was the most beautiful sign they had ever seen. The old Dahl cabin had gone; this hut was new and it needed a new name: Simonstua – Simon's Cottage.

Gunnar sat alone on the veranda. The sign hung behind him. Inside, Tone was fast asleep. Håvard was singing at a wedding.

The black hole still took up far too much space. They had to hold on tight so it would not swallow them up.

He was still sliding.

He slithered. He stumbled.

The sense of loss could drive him insane.

But they had started to see the starlit sky.

And the northern lights. And all the beauty around them.

Weaver's Heaven

'Are you in your weaver's heaven, Mum?'

It was as if she heard his voice. He always used to come dashing in, give her a hug and comment on the pattern in the warp before he charged off again. From the earliest of ages he had seen his mother weaving, her fingers knotting threads and one colour changing to another. He had admired how the threads made such lovely patterns.

Gerd Kristiansen was much in demand as a weaver in Bardu. Her tapestries hung on walls all around the village, served as bedspreads in Finnsnes and table runners in Salangen.

For her, weaving was like entering another world. She was able to collect her thoughts at the loom and find a breathing space after heavy shifts as an auxiliary nurse at Bardu care home.

One spring day her son had come into the room she had set aside as her weaving workshop. He stood there looking at her various pieces of work.

'Mum, can you weave one for me?'

'Oh, would you like one?' his mother answered happily. 'What colours do you want?'

'Blue, blue like the sky,' he replied.

She had spent a long time on it. She had mixed blue and white so his bedcover would turn out a real sky blue. When it was done, it was exactly as she had hoped. It was like lying in the grass on a fine summer's day looking up as wisps of cloud went by.

She had just finished it. Her son had run a hand over the soft blanket and thanked her, said how wonderful it was. Before he left.

That was two years ago.

In the first months she could not bring herself to touch the loom.

Now she was gradually starting again. But it was hard going, her fingers were stiff and slow and it wore her out.

Two years had passed, and life had only got worse.

The sense of loss, the emptiness, the lonely days. It was not true that grief faded. It grew. Because now it was final; he was never coming back.

Gerd was scared of meeting people, because it was embarrassing if she cried. It could come over her at any time, anywhere. She felt as though everyone around her thought things ought to be better by now. She could see it in people's eyes. Their looks said: You've got to move on.

Folk would ask her: 'Are you back at work now?'

As if that were any kind of measure. No she wasn't. Perhaps she could have coped, were it not for the fact that her job, too, meant dealing with life and death. At Bardu care home, old people were dying all the time. She could not take it. They were old and they died natural deaths, as was the way of things. But even so, they died. She could not take any more death.

The care home management had been flexible. She could come and go as she wanted, do shifts here and there if she felt up to it.

Her son was always crashing about in her head.

Viggo missed him constantly.

Their memories went in circles.

They buzzed round and round. They were there in their dreams. They were there in their sleepless nights.

Gerd called life 'existing minute by minute'. Every single minute felt like a battle. Time went on but life had stopped. Meanwhile, everyone else said they would have to build it up again. But how could they build up their life without their boy? As their elder son Stian put it when he was fed up with all the talk about Norway having won out over evil and hatred, 'I shall never win over anyone as long as I'm a little brother short.'

The roses, rainbows and democracy that were supposed to defeat the perpetrator only increased their sadness. It made them sick to hear party leaders say that Labour was the victim of the massacre. They were upset by AUF members' talk of 'reclaiming Utøya' before the murder victims had even been buried.

They could not forget AUF leader Eskil Pedersen's words on the first day of the trial: 'The pain is less now.'

Hadn't he talked to any of the bereaved, they wondered. Didn't he know anything about how the parents of his dead members were feeling? His *The pain is less now*, a bare nine months after the killings, made it impossible for them to listen to any of the other things he had to say.

The Kristiansen family felt bitter about a lot. First, the AUF. Anders had set up Bardu Workers' Youth League as a fifteen-year-old in 2008. He had been leader of the local branch for two years. When he became the head of the Youth County Council for Troms, the year after Simon and Viljar's attempted coup, he stepped down as leader of Bardu AUF and became the treasurer instead.

When Eskil Pedersen came to visit Bardu the year after Anders's death, the parents found out about it from the local paper. In *Troms Folkeblad* they saw the pictures of the AUF leader with new young members. No one had notified them. They had not had so much as a phone call to say that he wished to express his condolences to the parents of the late AUF treasurer in Bardu. No, Anders was dead, so he did not matter any more; that was how it felt to them.

The AUF had planned to mark the first anniversary of the massacre, 22 July 2012, on Utøya itself. The plans excluded the parents. They could come another day.

What? Were the parents not to be allowed to commemorate their sons and daughters a year on, in the place where their children had been killed?

No, because Utøya was the AUF's island.

Were there no grown-ups in the Labour Party? Were there no manners? No, the Labour Party just said it was the AUF's island and the young must be the ones to decide. In the end, the AUF gave in to pressure from the support group for the bereaved and they reached a compromise: the parents would be permitted to come at eight in the morning. But they had to make sure they were off the island before the surviving AUF members, those who had defeated the perpetrator, arrived. The last boat would be leaving the island at 11.45. After that, no parents were allowed to be there, because the young people were going to recreate *the Utøya feeling*.

'I would so much have liked to be there, to step into her world,' one father from Nordland county commented to the Norwegian Broadcasting Corporation. He had lost his sixteen-year-old daughter and wanted to 'step into the atmosphere, be there together with the AUF youngsters' to try to understand what it was about the summer camp that made his girl look forward to it all year. He simply wanted to be on the island along with the AUF crowd.

'I want to look for what was so important to my daughter here,' said a mother. 'Was it that little?'

Gerd and Viggo could not bring themselves to go to Utøya once they had seen the terms on which they would be allowed to attend. They did not feel welcome. Tone and Gunnar decided to go down anyway. Tone later said that the anniversary was the worst thing she had been through since Simon died. Making a hasty visit to the cliff, laying flowers by the rock and then hurrying off the island because the survivors were due to arrive, getting off the ferry at the *Thorbjørn*'s jetty and having to run the gauntlet of that merry throng of AUF members tripping over themselves to get aboard. Tone had had to duck her way through the crowd of young people. She felt they avoided meeting her eye. Maybe it was all part of being young, not dwelling on the dismal side of things. Being thoughtless.

At noon groups of AUF members were ferried over. Stoltenberg came, the Danish Prime Minister Helle Thorning-Schmidt came, the boss of the trade union confederation, Cabinet ministers, the left-wing Swedish singer Mikael Wiehe, the AUF leadership and lots of young people. They sat on the ground that sloped down to the open-air stage and listened to fine words about democracy and solidarity. The parents did not fit in there. There was a risk they might scream or shout, ruining the carefully choreographed event.

As part of the compromise deal the parents had been told they could return to the island after 5 p.m., because by then the AUF members would have gone off to the next item on their programme, the big memorial concert on the waterfront by the Town Hall. There was much excitement at the prospect that Bruce Springsteen was going to perform.

'Sometimes I wonder what my lad was caught up in,' said Gerd. 'Would he have turned out like that too?'

The first Christmas, the Kristiansen family had received a pre-printed Christmas card from the Prime Minister. From the AUF leader, not a word. Then Jens Stoltenberg telephoned them on their first New Year's Eve without Anders. On the second anniversary of the killings, the foreign minister Jonas Gahr Støre rang. He offered his condolences again the first time he passed through Troms after the massacre. Later they received a personal, hand-written letter from him, and a long letter from the vice-chair of the AUF, Åsmund Aukrust, who wrote of what Anders had meant to the youth organisation, how sad he was to lose him and how much he was missed.

The parents read those letters many times.

Grief is a solitary journey. Their great fear was that Anders would be forgotten.

It warmed their hearts when the Children's Ombudsman sent them a DVD of pictures and recordings of Anders taken at the National Youth Parliament at Eidsvoll, where he had been a delegate, and the County Council sent them recordings of the speeches Anders had made there. But the best thing of all was when Viljar visited. Then it was as if Anders was just about to step through the door.

What made them so bitter was the sense that nobody was taking any real responsibility for what had happened. At about the same time, a bus driver in the district stood accused of involuntary manslaughter because he had been *inattentive* for a moment, lost control of the vehicle and three people were killed. 'Is it that if you're far enough down the ladder, you get charged?' asked Viggo.

Questions went churning round in their heads.

Could one say that the police were *inattentive* on 22 July? Could one say that the authorities were *inattentive* beforehand? Could one say it was *irresponsible* that the crew of Norway's sole police helicopter were all on leave for the whole of July? Could one say that individual police officers had not followed the instructions for a 'shooting in progress' situation, indicating that direct intervention was required? Should anyone be charged with *negligence*?

Viggo could answer 'yes' to all those questions. He was angry when Stoltenberg said, *I take responsibility*. While not accepting the consequence of the errors by resigning. Events had exposed the fact that Norway had a police leadership which was paralysed in a crisis. The system had failed. Seventy-seven people had been killed. Was no one to be charged with anything?

Well yes, the perpetrator was under lock and key, and Viggo wished him all possible ill. He should have been sentenced to seventy-seven times twenty-one years in prison. But beyond that:

What responsibility did the AUF take for the children and young people on the island?

What security assessments had the AUF leadership made after the bomb in Oslo?

Were there evacuation plans?

Was there an emergency plan?

Was the MS *Thorbjørn* to be used in case of an evacuation of the island?

The AUF had not subsequently provided any answer to these questions. Viggo received no answers. The only thing he heard was that they were going to 'reclaim Utøya'.

A year after the killings, the AUF presented sketches, done by a firm of architects called Fantastic Norway. The pictures showed happy, computer-generated young people round the new buildings; a central clock tower; bright, attractive modern structures. Many of the bereaved felt the plans had been drawn up too soon. Their grief was still all-consuming. Is the building where my daughter died going to be torn down? Are young people going to take romantic walks round Lovers' Path where so many were slaughtered? Will they sunbathe on the rocks where youngsters bled to death?

Many of the bereaved protested about the plans that had been announced. The AUF leader responded: 'When it comes down to it, I think it has to be left to the AUF to decide this question.'

'Is that how an AUF leader should talk?' asked Viggo.

'Well, perhaps it is,' was Gerd's laconic reply. 'Perhaps the AUF has always been like that.'

They felt they had never properly understood what Anders was involved in. Who were these people? Former AUF leaders had gone on climbing, almost without exception. They had been lifted up into the machinery of power. They had been picked up as political advisers, state secretaries, been given jobs in the administration of government.

But for the organisation to be so ruthless towards those who were grieving, no, they had not imagined that. 'It's as if they want me to say: Hallelujah! My son was in the AUF,' sighed Gerd. 'The one thing I can say is that Norway didn't take care of Anders, and that the country isn't taking care of us now. Taking care of also means not forgetting.'

Viggo went out. He had something to do.

It was time to paint Anders's hut in the garden. It had been standing there untouched, just as Anders left it. His films were on the shelf. His jacket was hanging inside the door. Viggo had got hold of the right blue-green colour that Anders had once chosen.

His son had talked about painting the door, but he had never found time between all those meetings and trips back and forth to Tromsø. It needed a new coat now. Viggo had to keep at least something in order when everything else was falling apart around them. Grieving was heavy work.

Viggo could not get used to it, could not accept that Anders would never leap off the school bus again, that he would never again come walking up the path. That the school bus existed, the path existed, but Anders did not.

It was not only questions to the state apparatus, the police and the AUF that were churning round inside Viggo's head. He also had some questions for his son.

Why did you lie down on the path?

Why didn't you run?

What were you thinking, just before he fired?

Did it hurt?

He gave the hut one coat, the door two. He left the door open to dry.

'Think how pleased Anders would have been to see it looking so nice,' he said to Gerd when he came in.

They always went up to Anders's room when evening came. They always put his light on when it got dark.

When it was time for bed they looked in to say good night, sleep well and turned off the lights.

Gerd kept the room in order. That is to say, she did not tidy or move things, she just made sure it did not get too dusty. Stian liked wearing his younger brother's clothes when he was home on holiday. Some of Anders's friends had also picked out items of clothing, as reminders of him.

When Anders went to Utøya there was a brand-new suit hanging in his wardrobe. Gerd and Anders had gone shopping in Tromsø because the eighteen-year-old had wanted a proper suit. His first dark, grown-up suit. He wanted to see what they had at Moods of Norway. There, he tried on the finest suit he could find. Gerd had never seen him stand so tall and look so handsome.

'Get it,' she said.

'But it's expensive, Mum.'

'We'll split the bill,' said Gerd.

Then her eyes fell on a matching waistcoat. 'Try that,' she said.
It was a perfect fit. 'We'll take that too,' she said. 'I'm paying.'

They buried him in that suit. On the lapel they pinned three badges
that had been lying on his desk. *No to All Racism*, one of them said. *Red
and Proud*, said another. On the last, *AUF* shone white against red.

As he lay in his coffin in the white-painted chapel in Bardu, Gerd
spread the blue woven cover over him. Sky blue, blue as the sky. Just
as Anders had wanted it.

She could never weave with that colour again.

The Sentence

He had brought some of his clothes. But it wasn't like at home, where he had a wardrobe in his room.

Garments from his earlier life were kept in the storeroom with the other inmates' clothes. When he wanted to change, he had to ask.

Within a few months of starting his sentence he had had enough, and composed a letter of complaint to the Directorate of Correctional Service at Ila prison.

'Since it is usually quite chilly in the cell, I generally wear a thick sweater or jacket,' he wrote. 'I regularly have problems when asking for one. For some reason they often bring me one of my Lacoste jerseys, despite my having pointed out on several occasions that I do not want one of these as they are valuable and must be preserved from too much wear and tear. I have therefore ended up on various occasions having to freeze for one or two days until I can talk one of the warders into going down to the store to get one of the three proper sweaters.'

Anders Behring Breivik was detained in the high-security section; daily routines were strict. It annoyed him intensely. At home he had kept various creams and perfume bottles, whereas here he was not even permitted a tiny tube of moisturiser. Every morning he was given a little plastic cup with some of his day cream in it. Unfortunately the cream dried up and became unfit for use in the course of the day. This was grounds for complaint.

He was often given only enough butter for two or, at a pinch, three slices of bread, even though they knew that he ate four. 'This creates unnecessary annoyance because I either have to eat dry bread or be made to feel guilty for asking for more.' He described the warders' collection of the plastic cutlery and other items after meals as a form of low-intensity psychological terror. They came so quickly that he felt obliged to hurry his food and drink. And because he was not allowed a thermos flask in the cell, his coffee was cold when he got it, eighty per cent of the time.

In his complaint he alleged that he was considering reporting the prison to the police for breaches of the Norwegian constitution, human rights legislation and the Convention against Torture.

He was in solitary confinement, in a cell stripped of furniture, with white walls on which no decoration was allowed. The section was commonly known as the Basement. He complained about the lack of furnishing and the fact that he was 'denied the inspiration and mental energy which art on the walls' could provide. He also complained about the view: 'A nine-metre prison wall blocks out everything except the tops of the trees.' He complained that the windows were covered in a dark film that kept out some of the natural light. 'As a result I have to take vitamin pills to prevent vitamin D deficiency, among other things.'

Lighting was a general problem. The switch was outside the cell. It was frustrating to wait 'up to forty minutes' for them to turn up with his toothbrush and switch off the lights. The on–off switch for the TV was also outside the room. He had to tell them what he wanted to watch, and on which channel. The picture was poor and there was an annoying echo on the sound because the set was inside a secure box made of perspex and steel. As for radio, he was not pleased that he could only get P1 and P3 programmes and not the culture channel, P2. This was detrimental to his intellectual well-being.

He had three cells at his disposal. The first was a living cell with a bed, a place to eat and a cupboard. The second was a work cell with a typewriter firmly stuck to a table. The third was a workout cell with a treadmill. He was not satisfied with the running machine. He was not a long-distance runner, he had told the prison, but a body builder. Naturally, free weights were out of the question on security grounds, but already on his very first week in prison he had devised ways of toning his body with the help of his own body weight. Then he lost his motivation. Through the autumn of 2012 he lost his spark. 'A sense of resignation,' his lawyer called it.

He was working on a manuscript about the trial, with the title *The Breivik Diaries*. He was writing it in English. Norwegian readers did not interest him; it was the international book market that he wanted to reach.

But his working conditions were not the best. He could not move freely between the cells. He often had to wait when he asked to be transferred to the work cell. For a time, he did not want to go there at all. 'I feel that the price I have to pay for using this facility is too high, as I have to fight a daily battle to get access to the cell for a full working day.'

The worst part of being moved between cells was the strip searches. 'A strip search involves being ordered to take off all my clothes, which are then thoroughly checked, item by item,' he wrote. This was something he dreaded every day, he commented. It also annoyed him that he had to organise his papers again after every such search. He also had to remake his bed. The place was such a mess whenever they had been there.

If he did not use the work cell with the table-mounted typewriter, he was limited to pen and paper. He had been given a soft rubber pen and complained that he could not write more than ten to fifteen words a minute with it. The pen was not ergonomic and made his hand hurt.

There were various things about life in prison that he found painful. Among them the handcuffs he had to wear when he was moved between cells or taken out into the exercise yard. He claimed he had developed 'friction cuts' because 'the steel rim on the inside of the cuffs rubs the skin on my wrists painfully raw'. He noted that he had developed a sense of anxiety about handcuffs, perceiving them as 'a violation and mental burden'. There were several stresses and strains of that kind.

'The two cameras and the peephole in the door of the study cell contribute to a constant sense of tension and surveillance.' Checks through the hatch could come at inconvenient times, such as 'just at the moment one is using the toilet, which adds considerably to the sense of physical strain. It feels at times like a mental shock, especially if the hatch is slammed as well.' At nights he could be woken by a torch shining in through the hatch.

At times it was hard to concentrate when he was writing. Some of the other prisoners in solitary confinement turned up the volume of their music just to provoke him, he wrote. The sound of wardens yelling and fellow prisoners shouting also threw him out. 'I want peace and quiet. I want to be left undisturbed,' he wrote.

For a time, prison life had not been too bad. When the ban on letters and visits was lifted in December 2011, four months before the trial, there was a pile of correspondence waiting for him. Some of it was from like-minded people. He answered many of the letters, and what he wrote was then reproduced on various blogs. The police had kept their promise and had provided a PC, so he made a template for a letter of reply and could simply insert the name of the addressee and at times amend the introduction a little. Then all he had to do was ask for the letters to be printed out and then he could send them off by post. It was just as he had wanted it. His words were being disseminated. They were reproduced on blogs and floated round in cyberspace and got out to his supporters. His throne grew taller.

His only slight problem was a lack of stamps. He therefore urged all those writing to him to enclose stamps for return postage. His daily allowance of forty-one kroner did not go very far when stamps cost ten apiece.

One of his correspondents was someone calling himself Angus. That username put everything he received on the website *The Breivik Archive*.

In July 2012, a few weeks after the end of the trial, Breivik wrote to him: 'I shall sleep for a year now!' He wrote that he was very keen to establish contact with sympathisers on the internet, via blogs and on Facebook. He would be happy to write essays about the battle against cultural Marxism, multiculturalism and Islamisation.

'I sacrificed and forfeited my old family and friends on 22/7, so my correspondents will be the closest thing I have to a family. Don't be freaked out by that, because I can assure you I am corresponding with many brothers and sisters all round the world :-) I am now living in isolation and will very likely do so for many, many years. This is not problematic, as it was clearly my own choice. I am used to living ascetically, so it will not be difficult to carry on in the same way :-) In fact, it has given me a focused and balanced mind, not polluted by greed, desires and appetites – and one can work. If I tell myself this often enough, I'm bound to believe it in the end, haha!'

Prison inmate Anders Behring Breivik could, in short, communicate with anyone he wished. He could write anything apart from texts that could be seen as a direct incitement to criminal acts.

After the trial, Ila prison requested new guidelines about how to handle his correspondence. The answer came back that the existing rules were to be interpreted and applied more strictly. In the light of the act of terrorism committed by the prisoner, and what he had said at the trial about it still not being complete, all political statements to sympathisers were to be viewed as incitements to violence.

The tightened-up regime came into force in August 2012. Once the deadline for appealing the custody verdict passed in September, the PC was taken away from him. The detainee was no longer the responsibility of the police, but of the Directorate of Correctional Service. Only in special circumstances, and solely for educational purposes, were prisoners allowed to borrow a computer. The prison would not make an exception for Breivik.

This was a big loss to him. Without the PC he could no longer cut, paste and copy the letters he wrote. They had to be written one by one. In addition, they were now often stopped by the censor. His quality of life plummeted.

The conditions were degrading and unbearable, he wrote in his letter of complaint.

He was short of cash and wanted cigarettes, *snus* and his favourite sweets, liquorice logs. If he cleaned his three cells himself his daily allowance went up to fifty-nine kroner. He had done little cleaning in his life. At Hoffsveien his mother took care of it, and before that, when he lived on his own, his mother had come round to clean for him as well. At Vålstua farm, the grime had simply accumulated.

At Skien prison, where he had been held for a while, he had access to a mop. At Ila he was issued with a cloth.

'In other words, I am forced to scrub the three cells on my knees, which I find demeaning.'

———

While her son was serving his sentence at Ila, Wenche Behring Breivik went back and forth between Hoffsveien and the Radium Hospital. Some months after the terror attack, a tumour had started to grow inside her. It grew rapidly. She underwent an operation, and was given chemotherapy and drugs for the pain and the nausea.

As winter was coming to an end, she got a room on the second floor of the Radium Hospital. The cancer had spread to her vital organs.

On the glass door to the corridor where Wenche Behring Breivik's room was located, a sign informed visitors that no flowers or plants, fresh or dried, were to be taken on to the ward. External bacteria were to be kept out.

The walls of the corridors were greyish white. The doors were green, with black numbers stuck on them. A little sign hung on one of them, on a metal chain: Visitors are asked to report to the staff.

This was the room of the terrorist's mother.

The door to the room was wide. A bed could easily be wheeled in and out. But the room itself was narrow, with space beside the bed only for an armchair and a small table. The view had the same shade of grey every day, because the room was in a corner of the building where grey walls protruded. The room looked out over a roof a floor below, covered in grey shingle. If you rested your head on the pillow, you could see a little section of sky.

'I'm the unhappiest mother in Norway,' Wenche had told the police just after her son's arrest. 'My heart is all frozen up.'

Over the winter, her heart had thawed a little. She could not bring herself to think about the terrible thing that had happened. Nor to speak of it, nor to have it in her head. She wanted to remember what was good, what had been good.

One day in early March she decided to tell her story.

The ground outside the hospital was still white and hard as ice, trampled down after a winter in which new snow kept on falling. There hadn't been so much snow in the city for years, nor such treacherous pavements, nor such great skiing on the slopes above the hospital.

Wenche sat upright in bed in a pale blue hospital gown, her head held high. Her scalp was bare, with just a few downy bits of hair waving on top. Her blue eyes were fringed by eyelashes with black mascara, and there was a shimmer of grey-blue shadow on her eyelids. Her face was gaunt; her skin, with liver spots and patches of solar keratosis, was stretched thinly over sharp cheekbones. Her gaze was open and direct.

'I was so proud of . . . ' she began.

Her voice broke. She tried to pull herself together. 'I might start crying every so often, but it can't be helped . . . '

She went on from where her tears had interrupted her: '. . . proud of being the mother of . . . of Anders and Elisabeth . . . '

Her sobbing got the better of her, her shoulders shook. She struggled to be able to speak again. 'I, I . . . I did the best I could . . . '

She let her emotions have the upper hand for a few moments before getting a grip on herself and saying clearly:

'Oh, we thought we'd found happiness!'

There was a metallic note to her voice, something mechanical, something a little old-fashioned.

'Then it was Silkestrå. We bought a flat in 1982, moved in and started our homely happiness project. Which is the best thing that ever happened to me. Oh, I thought it was so nice. The children thought it was nice. We were looking forward to starting our new life. There'd be no more obstacles in our path. We could get busy on everything, things that needed doing, like decorating the flat, and I had my job as well, so they were grand times . . . '

Her phone played a little tune. She answered it.

'Yes, oh hello, Elisabeth. Yes, fine. Yes, really sick, I throw up every day. Much the same, pretty bad, yes. No, they haven't moved me yet, we shall have to see. Yes, they explain everything, but I lose the thread. You know, cancer patients have a tendency to be suspicious of what they're told. I don't really feel very good wherever I am, and I shall be going home soon now. All right, bye for now, Elisabeth.'

She went on with her story.

'Things weren't going well for Anders at the time. Dreadful. Lots of break-ups in his life. Of course he got overlooked in the midst of it all. When you're caught up in a conflict, you're blind to your children and other people. You don't see yourself clearly either. You can't.' She paused. 'And I felt guilty about being inadequate. I'm sure I did.'

'In what way were you inadequate?'

'I wasn't mature enough. I wasn't mature enough for the task.'

'What task?'

'Being a mother.'

She stopped, adjusted her back a little. 'This thing with Anders has something to do with my own childhood, I expect. The circumstances I grew up in were tough. I've never come across anyone who had a worse time. Very poor conditions. Really harsh conditions. I had to look after my mother. Most things were taboo. I don't know what I can say, without revealing too much. Everything was taboo. Sorry, I'm going to be sick now.'

'Shall I get a nurse?'

'Yes, please do.'

A young woman in a white uniform was fetched in from the

corridor and she called out to another nurse that the lady in 334 needed to throw up.

Afterwards Wenche sat in bed smiling; the queasiness had gone and she felt a bit stronger. She went on with her account. 'Well, we always come back to Silkestrå. All those cute little clothes and little presents in their bags when anyone had a birthday. That was how it was then. Lots of birthdays and school parties and nice things like that. And everyday life was much as it usually is, getting up early, school, home-work, children's programmes on TV, baking apple cake, just like ordinary people, nothing to find fault with.'

'It says in the report that Anders was passive when playing.'

'Well you have to consider. For one thing, they placed him up there at the centre, with strangers, in a strange setting, so it all goes wrong. I know very well it made him passive being up there. Anders was a self-conscious child. Reserved. And that psychiatrist who made his statement, the nasty one . . . they came round to the flat too, that psychiatrist or psychologist, to study us, judge us.'

They wanted to observe the bedtime routines in the family, Wenche remarked.

'And Anders was so neat and tidy, you know. He couldn't help the fact that he had an orderly mother.'

She took a breath. 'It wasn't his fault. I brought the boy up to be like me.' She gave a tired sigh. 'I'd said to Anders: we're going to start a new game here at home. You and I are going to get undressed, and we'll see who finishes first. I'll time us, starting now! So I timed us, and Anders won. And there was his neat little pile, with mine beside it, and that was wrong too. And when he got a real psychiatric . . . psychiatric . . . psychiatric, no. I can't find the word. Anyway, you have to get undressed first and then wash your hands, he was very keen on washing his hands, being clean, and then you put on your pyjamas, and then you have some supper and then clear up and so on, and then you wash your hands again. And they presented that as wrong, too.'

She shook her head.

'What did Anders like best when he was little?'

'He really liked to be praised when he'd been clever. When we played that undressing game in the evenings and he won, came first, he thought that was great. I could see how much he liked it. How they can say the opposite, that there was something wrong with the boy, I can't understand.'

'What did he play when he was at home?'

'We played Lego, we did. Playmobil. We played everything there was. Duplo, Taplo, Poplo, you name it,' she laughed.

'In the report from the Centre for Child Psychiatry it says that on the one hand you bound him to you, and the two of you slept close together in the same bed, while on the other you could suddenly reject him and say hateful things to him.'

'I still haven't finished,' she said, feeling for the thin plastic sick bag that lay close to hand.

'I'll go and get a nurse.'

'Well if it happens, it happens,' said Wenche.

Once the nausea had subsided, Wenche wanted to go on.

'There has to be room for . . . room for . . . what's it called again? There has to be room for – reconciliation, that's it. Time for reconciliation,' she said slowly, stressing every syllable. 'We can't change anything, after all. So let things rest. Try to understand instead. There's a lot still to find out.'

'For you too?'

'Yes, for me too.'

'Have you reconciled yourself to Anders's actions?'

'I reconciled myself a few months after it happened. I was convinced I'd be able to do it. Perhaps it's just that I'm a forgiving mother.'

'Have you forgiven him?'

'Yes, I have.'

'What do you think, was he sick or was it a political act?'

'It was a rational political act. No question. It was unexpected, but perhaps not that unexpected.'

'What do you mean?'

'I think we'll call it a day now. Better for us to follow up later.

Now, you go home and think it all through.' Right at the end, after all the goodbyes and wishes for better days, she said:

'Well, Anders is content now, anyway. At least that's what he told me.'

The nurse came in with painkillers. 'Oh, that's sweet of you,' said Wenche Behring Breivik to the young girl in white. 'Would you mind closing the window too? I'm freezing.'

The nurse closed the window, which had been on the latch, letting in the cold of the March day outside. Spring was taking its time. There was a hint of sleet in the air.

On the windowsill of room 334 there was a pink plastic orchid, still in its crisp cellophane packet. It was getting late. The scrap of sky that Wenche could see when she rested her head on the pillow was growing darker. From there she could see the tiny snowflakes, so light that they seemed to take forever to reach the ground.

───────

Wenche Behring Breivik died eight days later.

She passed away just before Easter. Her son sought permission to attend her funeral. His application was refused.

He had no contact with his father. Nor with his sister. None of his friends had written to him. Many of his closest friends said they had put him behind them. 'I'm through with Anders,' said one. And yet hardly a day passed without them thinking of him. Many of them were troubled by feelings of guilt. Should they have realised?

He had hardly anyone to correspond with any more. In the letters that he did receive, most of the words were blacked out. He replied to them with letters he knew would be censored. The correspondence petered out. The letters stopped coming. His prison cell had not become the writer's workshop he had planned. Some journalists asked for interviews. He visualised the queue of reporters eager to interview him, dreaming of being *the first*. But he did not want to meet any of them. If he gave an interview he imagined the queue evaporating, interest tailing off. He would no longer be in demand.

He did respond to one of the interview requests. The request arrived just after the trial He spent a long time thinking about whether to write back. Only a year later, in June 2013, did he decide to answer. The journalist had included a stamped addressed envelope. He located it among his other documents, where he had been keeping it for almost a year. He elected to start on a jovial note.

```
Dear Åsne! :-)
I have been following your career with
great interest since 2003. I both respect
and admire you for your mentality,
competence and intelligence, which afford
you opportunities that almost all women and
most men can only dream of ;-)
```

Flattery was the style he adopted. 'What's so unique about you is that you achieved so much at such a young age, and in addition to that are so beautiful! ;-)' he wrote.

Then he described the strategy he had employed throughout the trial. Double psychology, he called it. Calculated deception, to put it simply. A necessary evil to counter the propaganda and deceit of the other parties. And it was for this reason that the full truth about his operation had not come out. He wrote that ever since the trial he had wanted to be open about everything, but that he had been prevented from expressing himself since the stricter regime was implemented after the verdict.

```
I understand that among left-wing
journalists there is some prestige attached
to getting the opportunity to be the first
to really put the knife into the 'worst
ultra-nationalist terrorist in the European
world since WW2' and inflict the worst
```

damage, and there are undoubtedly many
'right-wing extremists' in Europe who would
have been retarded enough to contribute to
their own character assassination. In my
eyes, people like you are extremely
dangerous predators from whom I
instinctively want to keep my distance. I
know that someone like you will stab deep,
and if I were stupid enough to participate
you might even be able to stab deeper than
Husby/Sørheim and Lippestad. I have no wish
to contribute to this, either by meeting
you or by clarifying what remains
unclarified on any terms but my own. I
therefore do not want to have anything to
do with your work.

The letter changed tone.

I would like, however, to make you a
counter-offer. I have enough insight to
realise that 'The Breivik Diaries' will be
boycotted by the established publishing
houses, and therefore want to offer you the
chance of selling the book as a package
within your project, that is, that you top
and/or tail your book with a quick hack job
by me, with or without your name on the
book, and that you in addition get all the
income (the author's share). So you will
gain financially, while those you want to
impress will still congratulate you on a
great character assassination. I can live
with my story coming out in this form,
provided that the book is removed from the

```
boycott lists of at least some of the major
distributors.
To tie in with the book launch, provided
that it is successful, you will be given
the opportunity to conduct the first and
only interview that I shall give, and you
will also get the sales rights to this,
enabling you to write another crude
character assassination to 'wash your
hands' of any accusations that may by then
have been made that you are a useful idiot
etc.
With narcissistic and revolutionary wishes.
Anders Behring Breivik
```

That was how he signed off.

In a letter the following month, which he opened with the far cooler 'To Miss Seierstad,' he wrote that all criticism of him could actually be viewed as a bonus. It was so detached from reality as to give him a valuable advantage, which he wanted to exploit to the full against the propagandists. He was now waiting for the end of the ban on his freedom of speech and took the view that he should have the right to defend himself against all the propaganda now being pumped out. 'Because the "Character" who is being constructed and peddled by authors and journalists on the left is, after all, a very long way from the truth.'

No interview took place.

The inmate was annoyed at receiving the wrong letters. He only got letters from 'New Testament Christians and people who do not like me', he complained.

These were not the sorts of letters he wanted.

He wanted the other letters. The letters that must be piling up in the censor's office. The letters to the *Commander of the Norwegian anti-communist resistance movement*. The letters from the people who wanted a signed copy of his book. The letters to Andrew Berwick. The letters to Anders B. Those were the letters he wanted.

But they did not come.

He aimed to set up a prison alliance of militant nationalists with himself at its head. So far, he was the only member. But then, as the civil war spread, as people got swept along, inspired by his manifesto, he would be freed by his brothers.

In the meantime, while he was waiting, his Lacoste jersey was spared. It was safely put away in the prison's dark storeroom.

All he saw of the real world were the tops of the trees round the prison.

And its white walls.

Epilogue

It was only supposed to be an article for *Newsweek*.

'Get me anything you can on *that man!*' said *Newsweek* editor Tina Brown on the phone from New York. It was early on; the terrorist attack had only just hit us. The country was in shock. I was in shock.

I did not find out much about *that man* in the summer of 2011.

Having written about Norway's reaction to the attack instead, I put the country behind me, as always, and pursued my original plan for the autumn – covering the continuous uprisings around the Arab world. My next stop was Tripoli in Libya. While Norway was grieving, I went back to the Middle East.

Then the date was set for the trial. *Newsweek* asked me to write one more story when the court case against Anders Behring Breivik opened in April 2012. That was to be my second article about Norway. Until terror struck us, I had never written anything about my own country. It was uncharted territory. All my working life, I had been a foreign correspondent, starting off as a Moscow correspondent at twenty-three, straight from Russian studies at Oslo University. My home country was my refuge, not a place to write about. I came home from Tripoli just before the trial was due to start, got my accreditation and a seat in the courtroom, and found myself knocked sideways.

I was not prepared.

*

I sat in room 250 for the ten weeks of the trial. Within those walls we were drip-fed the details of the planning and execution of the act of terrorism, day by day. The testimonies were short, concise, tailored to the purposes of the trial. Sometimes they went deep, sometimes they broadened out. At times they supplemented each other and gave new perspectives while at others they stood alone. A witness could be in the box for ten or fifteen minutes, to be succeeded by another witness. These were drops of stories.

After the trial had finished, I realised I had to go deeper to find out what had really happened, and I started searching.

I found Simon, Anders and Viljar. I found Bano and Lara.

This is their story.

One of Us has come about thanks to all those who told me their stories. Some have chapters devoted to their childhood and youth while others appear as part of a background canvas of friends, neighbours, teachers, classmates, boy and girlfriends, colleagues, bosses and relations.

Parents and siblings have shared their family histories. Friends have spoken of comradeship.

We collaborated on a continuous basis. They all read their texts along the way. Still, I was met with great understanding that this is my book and my interpretation.

Some of the conversations went on for days and nights, others were short phone calls. We talked on the way down from a steep mountain, on long walks along the Bardu River, in bars in Tromsø or over Kurdish chicken stew in Nesodden.

I offer heartfelt thanks to those who shared the most. Bayan, Ali, Mustafa and Lara Rashid. Gerd, Viggo and Stian Kristiansen. Tone, Gunnar and Håvard Sæbø. And Viljar Hanssen and his family. They have told me about the worst thing of all: losing someone they loved.

Whether the stories are cut down to a few lines or cover several pages, it is the multitude of conversations that have made this book possible. Thank you all so much. I know what it cost you.

*

Most people are given their full name in the book, while some are referred to by their first names, like Marte and Maria. I felt it was right to use first names for the scene when the two childhood friends are holding hands, lying on the path. Their full names are Marte Fevang Smith and Maria Maagerø Johannesen. Marte was the only survivor of the eleven who were shot on Lovers' Path. The bullet did not cause any major injuries to her head, only to her balance nerve. She can't dance like she did before, while her best friend Maria died. What I have written about events on the path before and during the killing is based on what Marte remembers.

The first time I mention someone, I have usually put down their full name. Some people do not appear in the book until 'Friday' – the chapter about 22 July – and disappear from the account the moment they are killed. These were the most painful parts of the book to send to their families. I asked all the parents affected to read the sections about their children and choose for themselves whether they wanted their child to be part of the book. For me, it was important to describe for posterity exactly how that day was. In the end, no parent objected that I wrote about their child's moment of death. I am very grateful for that.

The surviving young people who contributed to the book were also sent their texts to read through and correct.

The other strand of this book is *that man*. A man many are reluctant to refer to by name. The perpetrator, the subject under observation, the accused, the defendant and finally: the sentenced prisoner. I do use his name. When writing about his childhood it was natural to use his first name; from 22 July onwards I use his surname or full name.

In journalism, it is important to go to the sources. This was the reason for my request for an interview with him. Its refusal obliged me to base my account on what others say about him. I talked to his friends, members of his family, classmates, colleagues and former political associates. I read what he himself had written: in the manifesto, on the internet and in letters. I also paid attention to what he had to say during the trial, and what he subsequently wrote in letters to the press and in official complaints.

Many of those close to him were unwilling to say anything. Some slammed down the phone. Others replied, 'I've put him behind me. I'm through with him.'

I was not through with him, and eventually I found people who would talk, most of them anonymously. Very few of his former friends and classmates are named in this book. It is as though having known him leaves one branded. Even so, a number of people made important contributions to my understanding of what Anders Behring Breivik was like in childhood, adolescence and adult life. In the chapter about his time as a tagger, those described are given their actual tagging names and will thus be recognised within their own circles. In the chapter on the Progress Party, no one demanded anonymity. I have given two business partners and two childhood friends new names.

I tried for a year to secure an interview with Wenche Behring Breivik but her answer, through her lawyer Ragnhild Torgersen, was always the same: No.

In March 2013, I called her lawyer again. She said she would talk to her client one more time. Torgersen rang back: 'Can you come to my office tomorrow?'

I was allowed to meet Wenche Behring Breivik on the condition that she and her lawyer be allowed to read through the interview afterwards. The agreement was that if Wenche Behring Breivik were incapable of reading through it herself – her cancer had entered its final phase – her lawyer would do it. This she did, and approved the use of the interview. Torgersen was also present during our conversation, and both of us recorded it. Parts of the interview appear in question-and-answer format; other parts are used to shed light on her son's childhood in the chapters about his early life.

Several times I also requested a meeting with Jens David Breivik, the perpetrator's father, but he would not be interviewed. I therefore had to restrict myself to what others told me about him. It was only when I sent him, in its entirety, what I had written about him that I

was able to enter into a dialogue with him, in which he corrected
items he felt were wrong and gave me new information about his son.

Reports from the Centre for Child and Adolescent Psychiatry
were an invaluable source of information about Anders Behring
Breivik's childhood. I also talked to the professionals who observed
him in that period. I judged this case to be so much in the public
interest that it justified using information from confidential reports.

In addition, reports from the expert psychiatrists associated with
the trial, Synne Sørheim and Torgeir Husby, Terje Tørrissen and Agnar
Aspaas, were extremely helpful. The accounts of what took place in
their meetings with Breivik are taken from their reports. Parts of
these reports have appeared in the media in printed form; I worked
from the uncensored versions.

I also made extensive use of the police interviews in the case. I had
tens of thousands of pages of interviews, witness statements and background documents to read through and select from. In some instances
I have used direct quotations from the interrogations. This applies to the
interrogations of the perpetrator on Utøya and at police headquarters
in Oslo, and to the interviews with his mother when she was brought
in on 22 July, both in the police car and later that same evening at the
police headquarters. The conversations between Anders and his mother
in the months leading up to his move to the farm, and later on in the
wake of 22 July, are reconstructed from what Wenche told investiga-
tors during the autumn of 2011. I have elected to make use of these
documents that are not publicly available because I consider it justified
by the vital importance of casting light on this terrorism case.

I have also used the police interviews of some witnesses who knew
Breivik. In these instances, I have given no names.

The couple with whom Anders Behring Breivik was placed on several occasions when he was two years old did not wish to contribute
to the book. The information I provide about them is taken exclu-
sively from their police interviews.

Other than that, I largely used the police interviews as background
information and to check the facts of Anders Behring Breivik's life.

*

In a number of places in the book, I refer to the perpetrator's thoughts or judgements. Readers might want to know: How does the author know this?

Everything is taken from what he himself said in police interviews, at the trial or to the psychiatrists.

I would like to give a few examples. In the chapter entitled 'Friday', I write in detail about Breivik's thoughts during the first killings. In that sequence, various sentences are lifted directly from the trial transcripts. Breivik described his feelings and thoughts both to the police in the days after the terror act and in court nine months later, as follows: 'I don't feel remotely like doing this' and 'Now or never. It's now or never.' These sentences are used as direct quotations. In some places his statements are turned into indirect speech: 'His body was fighting against it, his muscles were twitching. He felt he would never be able to go through with it. A hundred voices in his head were screaming: Don't do it, don't do it, don't do it!' It was Breivik who talked about his body and his muscles, and referred to the hundred voices screaming in his head. I have used his own words. That is how I have worked throughout the book. His thoughts set out here all derive from what he said in police or court documents.

My statement that it was easy for him to go on killing after the first assassinations is taken from what the gunman explicitly told the police and the court. He spoke at length about how difficult the first shot was and how easy it all felt once he broke through the barrier, an almost physical barrier. He said that initially it had felt unnatural to kill.

So the next question is this: Can we trust his account?

A journalist must constantly evaluate and bear in mind the degree of veracity in any statement. In Breivik's case, a number of his stories seem rather far-fetched. This applies particularly to his accounts of his childhood and youth, the positive gloss he puts on them and on his own popularity, and his claim to have been a king in hip-hop circles and a rising star in the Progress Party. My doubts about his portrayal of these sections of his life stem from finding a large number of accounts that contradict the idealised picture he attempts to convey. These testimonies largely agree with each other and they diverge markedly from his own version of events.

The other point at which he appears to be making things up is in his account of the Knights Templar organisation. The Norwegian police never found anything to verify his claims that the organisation existed or that he was a commander or leader of it. Nor could the prosecution discover that the organisation had any basis in fact.

These were the two subjects on which he declined to elaborate in court: his childhood and adolescence, and the Knights Templar. He said that the former was irrelevant and that his refusal to talk about the latter was to 'protect the identities of others in the network'.

The question of the Knights Templar was central to the discussion of whether Anders Behring Breivik was of sound mind. If the network did not exist, was it a delusion or a lie? The court's verdict affirmed the latter.

Regarding the day on Utøya, the terrorist explained in detail and on several different occasions what he did, the order in which he did it, and what he was thinking as he did it. He discussed this the same evening, on the island, and the next morning at the police station, and on a later site visit to the island, and to the psychiatrists and the court. He spoke in an easy, unforced way; he elaborated, made associations, thought over what he was not sure about and revised his account accordingly, and admitted that there were some things he could not remember. It did not appear to be difficult for him to repeat things, to respond to the same questions over and over again, as it can be when one has constructed a story. The police made a thorough check of his log claims and timings. Thus far they have found nothing in his Utøya account that does not tally with the statements of the young people who were there – in terms of the conversations he had, the words he shouted, or the concrete situations in which killings took place. The police have stated that in regard to his preparations and his implementation of his attack, they have not uncovered a single direct lie or misinformation.

However, there is some disagreement about when Breivik began the planning for his attack. The perpetrator claims it was back in

2002. Neither the police nor the prosecution think he started that early. My job is not to speculate, but to look for information. What we know from the police logs is exactly how long he spent on every website, and when. We know that he played hardcore computer games after moving back in with his mother in 2006 (for example, he played for seventeen hours one New Year's Eve). He gradually turned from the games to anti-jihadist and right-wing extremist websites. In the chapter 'Choose Yourself a World' I restricted myself to well-founded facts about how the game he was playing was constructed, and external elements such as what his room looked like and the fact that he tapped away at the computer keyboard. I went so far as to conclude that it was 'a good place to be', that 'the game drew him in and calmed him down' and that he lost interest in real life. I based the first of these statements on what he said, the second on comments from his friends and mother. I also based what I wrote on information from his fellow players, those who knew him as *Andersnordic*.

The police data provides an indication of what he was doing online at any particular time. It also indicates that the planning of the terror act came much later than he says, maybe as late as the winter of 2010, when he received the last rejection from the Progress Party and no response from his online anti-jihadist heroes. What we know is that he only started buying weapons and bullets in the spring of 2010. Later that year, he began to purchase ingredients for the bomb.

In researching his life, my first priority was to find the pieces and fit them together into the jigsaw puzzle of Anders Behring Breivik. There are still many pieces missing.

In August 2012, Norway's 22 July Commission presented its report. I relied on its account of the course of events during the terrorist attack. I used the commission's report to confirm the timing of events on that day. I also quoted from it for the telephone tip-off from Andreas Olsen and the conversations between Kripos and the operation manager on the question of issuing a nationwide alert, as well as Breivik's own calls from Utøya. In the report, these phone conversations are written down word for word.

I also referred to the report for the dates of Breivik's purchases of weapons, clothing, chemicals and fertiliser.

In mapping the course of events on 22 July I was helped by Kjetil Stormark's book *Da terroren rammet Norge* (When Terror Struck Norway). I also quoted private emails sent by Breivik that were included in Stormark's *Massemorderens private e-poster* (The Mass Murderer's Private Emails). Stormark also offered important advice during the writing process.

The scenes in which the lawyer Geir Lippestad is called by the police on 23 July and in which he meets Breivik on 23 December 2011 are taken from Lippestad's own book *Det vi kan stå for* (What We Can Stand By). The induction rituals of the order of Freemasons are taken from *Frimurernes hemmeligheter* (The Secrets of the Freemasons) by Roger Karsten Aase. The quotations from Carl I. Hagen are from Elisabeth Skarsbø Moen's *Profet i eget land – historien om Carl I. Hagen* (Prophet in His Own Country – the Story of Carl I. Hagen). The story of Monica Bøsei and Utøya is taken from *Utøya – en biografi* (Utøya: A Biography), written by Jo Stein Moen and Trond Giske.

Other books and magazines which provided useful background information but were not sources of direct quotes are listed in the bibliography at the back of this book.

The terrorist attack received wide and comprehensive coverage in the Norwegian press. Many of these articles proved valuable for my work. I also continually cross-checked with the trial reports of *VG* (*Verdens Gang*), NRK (the Norwegian Broadcasting Corporation) and the national news agency NTB. Details of the visit from Natascha were borrowed from *Dagbladet*, while particulars of Breivik's complaint to the Directorate of Correctional Service came from *VG*.

The log from which I quote in the chapters 'Poison' and 'The Chemist's Log' is taken from Breivik's manifesto. The dates have been correlated with the results of police investigations and appear to tally. The description of the bomb-making process has been studied by the police, who found it probable that he followed the procedure in his account.

The descriptions of the flat at 18 Hoffsveien were compiled on the basis of pictures and a visit to the premises in the summer of 2013. Descriptions of the areas behind the courtroom for the parties involved in the trial were made possible by a visit in October 2013.

The interviews with then Prime Minister Jens Stoltenberg were conducted on three occasions, the first straight after the terrorist attacks, in connection with the piece for *Newsweek*, the last the day after the second anniversary of the attacks, in July 2013.

Gro Harlem Brundtland gave an interview about her time as Prime Minister and the events of 22 July in February 2013.

This book has taken shape in close collaboration with my editors Cathrine Sandnes and Tuva Ørbeck Sørheim. Many thanks for all the suggestions, discussions and corrections. I could never have done it alone.

I have been ably assisted on the research side by Tore Marius Løiten, and as with all my previous books I want to thank my parents, Frøydis Guldahl and Dag Seierstad, who both know the rules for correct comma use and are my most critical readers.

One of Us is a book about belonging, a book about community. The three friends from Troms all belonged in definite places, geographically, politically and with their families. Bano belonged in both Kurdistan and Norway. Her greatest aspiration was to become 'one of us'. There were no short cuts.

This is also a book about looking for a way to belong and not finding it. The perpetrator ultimately decided to opt out of the community and strike at it in the most brutal of ways.

As I worked on the book, it came to me that this was also a story about contemporary Norway. It is a story about us.

To all of you who have told me drops or streams of stories, written to me or commented on my work: We made this book together.

Through the book, I want to give something back to the community from which it sprang. My royalties for this book in Norway are being donated in full to the 'En av oss' (One of Us) foundation. The foundation's statutes allow for the money to be distributed to a wide range of causes nationally and internationally, in the areas of development, education, sport, culture and the environment.

I have chosen to let those who contributed most to the book decide which causes will receive support.

I think that would be in the spirit of their children.

Åsne Seierstad
Oslo, 20 January 2014

Bibliography

Books

Aase, Roger Karsten: *Frimurernes hemmeligheter – fortalt fra innsiden*. Kagge Forlag, Oslo, 2009.

Arendt, Hannah: *Eichmann i Jerusalem – en rapport om ondskans banalitet*. Gyldendal Forlag, København, 1992 (Originally published as *Eichmann in Jerusalem: A Report on the Banality of Evil*, 1963.)

Borchgrevink, Aage Storm: *En norsk tragedie – Anders Behring Breivik og veiene til Utøya*. Gyldendal Forlag, Oslo, 2012. (Published in English as *A Norwegian Tragedy. Anders Behring Breivik and the Massacre on Utøya*. Translated by Guy Puzey. Polity, 2013.)

Breivik, Jens: *Min skyld? – En fars historie*. Juritzen Forlag, Oslo, 2014.

Bromark, Stian: *Selv om sola ikke skinner – et portrett av 22. juli*. Cappelen Damm, Oslo, 2012. (Published in English as *Massacre in Norway: The 2011 Terror Attack on Oslo and the Utøya Youth Camp*. Translated by Hon Khiam Leong. Potomac Books, 2014.)

Christensen, Marit: *Moren – historien om Wenche Behring Breivik*. Aschehoug Forlag, Oslo, 2013.

Cullen, Dave: *Colombine*. Hachette Book Group, New York City, 2009.

Fatland, Erika: *Året uten sommer*. Kagge Forlag, Oslo, 2012.

Griffin, Roger: *Terrorist's Creed: Fanatical Violence and the Human Need for Meaning*. Palgrave Macmillan, Basingstoke, 2012.

Høigård, Cecilie: *Gategallerier*. Pax Forlag. Oslo, 2007.

Holen, Øyvind: *HipHop-hoder – fra beat till bygde-rap*. Spartacus Forlag, Oslo, 2005.

Holen, Øyvind & Noguchi, Michael: *HIPHOP – Graffiti, Rap, Breaking og DJ-ing*. Cappelen Damm, Oslo, 2009.

Hverven, Tom Egil & Malling, Sverre: *Terrorens ansikt – skisser fra 22. Juli-rettsaken*. Flamme Forlag, Oslo, 2013.

Indregard, Sigve (ed.): *Motgift – akademisk respons på den nye høyreekstremismen*. Flamme Forlag/Forlaget Manifest, Oslo, 2012.

Jupskås, Anders Ravik: *Ekstreme Europa – ideologi, årsaker og konsekvenser*. Cappelen Damm, Oslo, 2012.

Juvet, Bjørn & Juvet, Aase Margrethe: *Med livet som innsats – historien om en redningsaksjon på Utøya*. Gyldendal Forlag, Oslo, 2012.

Kjelstadli, Knut (ed.): *Norsk innvandringshistorie. Bd. 1-3*. Pax Forlag, Oslo, 2003.

Koranen, oversettelse Einar Berg. Universitetsforlaget, Oslo, 1989. (The version used in this English translation is *The Qur'an*. Translated by Tarif Khaladi. Penguin Classics, 2008.)

Lahlum, Hans Olav: *Et kvart liv – Håvard Vederhus 1989–2011*. Cappelen Damm, Oslo, 2013.

Lippestad, Geir: *Det vi kan stå for*. Aschehoug Forlag, Oslo, 2013.

Moen, Elisabeth Skarsbø: *Profet i eget land – Historien om Carl I. Hagen*. Gyldendal Forlag, Oslo, 2006.

Moen, Jo Stein & Giske, Trond: *Utøya – en biografi*. Gyldendal Forlag, Oslo, 2012.

Moi, Toril: *Stemmer. Språk og oppmerksomhet*. Aschehoug Forlag, Oslo, 2013.

Østerud, Svein (ed): *22. juli – Forstå – forklare – forebygge*. Abstrakt Forlag, Oslo, 2012.

Østli, Kjetil Stensvik: *Rettferdighet er bare et ord – 22. Juli og rettsaken mot Anders Behring Breivik*. Cappelen Damm, Oslo, 2013.

Pracon, Adrian & Solheim, Erik Møller: *Hjertet mot steinen – en overlevendes beretning fra Utøya*. Cappelen Damm, Oslo, 2012.

Sætre, Simen: *Fjordman – ett portrett av en antiislamist*. Cappelen Damm, Oslo, 2012.

Schau, Kristopher: *Rettsnotater 22. Juli – rettsaken*. No Comprendo Press, 2012.

Sørensen, Øystein, Hagtvent, Bernt & Steine, Bjørn Arne (eds): *Høyreekstremisme – ideer og bevegelser i Europa*. Dreyer Forlag, Oslo, 2012.

Steen, Rune Berglund: *Svartebok over norsk asylpolitikk*. Forlaget Manifest, Oslo, 2012.

Stormark, Kjetil: *Da terroren rammet Norge*. Kagge Forlag, Oslo, 2011.

Stormark, Kjetil: *Massmorderens private e-poster*. Spartacus Forlag, Oslo, 2012.

Strømmen, Øyvind: *Det mørke nettet – Om høyreekstremisme, kontrajihadisme og terror i Europa*. Cappelen Damm, Oslo, 2012.

Viksveen, Thor: *Jens Stoltenberg – ett portrett*. Pax Forlag, Oslo, 2011.

Articles

Genocide in Iraq: the Anfal Campaign Against the Kurds. A Middle East Watch Report. *Human Rights Watch*, New York, 1993.

Knausgård, Karl Ove: Det monofone mennesket, *Samtiden* 3:2012.

Moi, Toril: Markedslogikk og kulturkritikk – Om Breivik og ubehaget i den postmoderne kulturen, *Samtiden* 3:2012.

Vanebo, Ove: Det etablerte Fremskrittspartiet, *Samtiden* 1:2013.

Other Sources

Breivik, Anders Behring: 2083. A European Declaration of Independence, 2011.

Erfaringsrapport, Domstolsarbeidet i 22. juli-saken, Oslo Tingrett, 2013.

Fylkesarkivet i Troms, rapporter og møtereferater, Ungdommens
    fylkesråd 2008-2011.

Rapport fra 22. Juli-kommisjonen, Norges offentlige utredninger,
    1012:14.

Sørheim, Synne & Husby, Torgeir: Rettspsykiatrisk erklæring till
    Oslo Tingrett, avgitt 29.11.2011.

Tørrissen, Terje & Aspaas, Agnar: Rettspsykiatrisk erklæring till Oslo
    Tingrett, avgitt 10.04.2011.

https://www.ssb.no/statistikkbanken/SelectVarVal/Define.asp?Mai
    nTable=InnUtNet&KortNavnWeb=innvutv&PLanguage=0&ch
    ecked=true

Quotations

165 H. L. Mencken.
'What is Political Correctness?' by William S. Lind. From Lind (ed.), *'Political Correctness': A Short History of an Ideology* (Alexandria: Free Congress Foundation, 2004). Lind's original quotation begins 'Most Americans look back at the 1950s as a good time.'

167 *The Qur'an*. Translated and with an introduction by Tarif Khaladi (London: Penguin Classics, 2008).

168 *Brave New World* by Aldous Huxley.
The Qur'an. Translated and with an introduction by Tarif Khaladi (London: Penguin Classics, 2008).

267 'Baby'. Written by Christine Flores, Ashanti S. Douglas, Christopher Bridges, Keith Edward Crouch, Terius Nash, Christopher A. Stewart and Justin Bieber. © Rze Music Publishing, Pookietoots Publishing, Songs Of Universal Inc., Havana Brown Publishing, Universal Music Corp., Ludacris Worldwide Publishing Inc., Baeza Music LLC, Bieber Time Publishing, 2082 Music Publishing, Human Rhythm Music. 'Childhood'. Written by Michael Jackson. © Mijac Music.

270 'Nothing Else Matters'. Written by Andrew Michael Saidenberg, James Alan Hetfield, Nathianiel Raubenheimer and Lars Ulrich. © Cloud 9 Holland Music Publishing, Creeping Death Music, World Of Andy Music, Universal Music Corp.

297 'Å Kunne æ Skrive' by Lars Bremnes. Translation by Sarah Death.

311 'Childhood'. Written by Michael Jackson. © Mijac Music.

353–4 *The Qur'an*. Translated and with an introduction by Tarif Khaladi (London: Penguin Classics, 2008).

404–5 'Vi Suser Avgårde'. Written by Lars Lillo Stenberg.

406 'Hallelujah'. Written by Leonard Cohen and Theresa Christina Calonge de Sa Mattos. © Bad Monk Publishing, Sony/ATV Songs LLC.

410 'Helt om Natten, Helt om Dagen'. Written by Lars Vaular. Translation by Sarah Death.
'Å Kunne æ Skrive'. Written by Lars Bremnes. Translation by Sarah Death.